Television's Top 100

Television's Top 100

The Most-Watched American Broadcasts, 1960–2010

WESLEY HYATT

McFarland & Company, Inc., Publishers
Jefferson, North Carolina, and London

LIBRARY OF CONGRESS ONLINE CATALOG DATA

Hyatt, Wesley.
Television's top 100 : the most-watched
American broadcasts, 1960–2010 / Wesley Hyatt.
p.   cm.
Includes bibliographical references and index.

ISBN 978-0-7864-4891-3
softcover : acid free paper ∞

1. Television programs — United States — Catalogs.
2. Television programs — United States — Chronology.   I. Title.
PN1992.3.U5H96 2012   2011046877

BRITISH LIBRARY CATALOGUING DATA ARE AVAILABLE

Front cover image © 2011 Shuttertsock

Manufactured in the United States of America

*McFarland & Company, Inc., Publishers
Box 611, Jefferson, North Carolina 28640
www.mcfarlandpub.com*

To Ronald Hyatt (1933–2007), a top father,
husband, friend, teacher, leader and human being.
You are much missed and warmly remembered.

Acknowledgments

In writing this book, I received considerable help from numerous people. Author Tim Brooks, along with Bill Gorman and Robert Seidman, who produce the excellent website TVbythe Numbers, were supportive from the beginning. During the course of writing, my friend Stu Shostak of Shokus Video in Chatsworth, California, offered his input and allowed me to quote from several interviews he has conducted. I also appreciate the continuing advice from another TV expert, Steve Beverly of Tennessee, who often joins me with Stu every three to four months on Shokus Internet Radio (www.sho kusradio.com) to discuss the industry.

I would also like to thank my boss, Patty Briguglio, and the rest of the staff at MMI Public Relations in Raleigh, North Carolina, for their interest in the book and suggestions they gave. I consider myself lucky to have such supportive colleagues.

A special thank you goes out to all of my family and friends who endured me having to tell them the last few months, "Sorry, I can't spend time with you right now — I'm working on the book." Chief among the souls who have nobly endured this response from me are John Bowser, Todd Day, Renee Duncan, Julie Ellis, Ed Emory, Kevin Grady, David Guinnup, Jimmy Lancaster, Bradford Taylor, and last but certainly not least my mother, Gayle Hyatt. I could not have completed this book without all of your kind understanding and consideration, and I sincerely hope you enjoy the final product.

Table of Contents

ACKNOWLEDGMENTS vi
PREFACE 1

Table of Contents

Preface

This book should not have been a reality.

That's not my opinion. That's what I heard from several experts who warned me how difficult it would be to find the needed information. Specifically, Tim Brooks, co-author of the go-to TV reference *The Complete Directory to Prime Time Network and Cable TV Shows 1946–Present*, and Bill Gorman and Robert Seidman, moderators of the everything-you-want-to-know-about-ratings website TVbythe Numbers, told me that the Nielsen ratings company is guarded about giving out information, and thus I'd probably have to find it out on my own. They were right.

And though this might be judged a foolhardy effort by some, I think it pays off in the end here. This is an eclectic list, reflecting the varied interests of viewers over the years, although admittedly with a bias to a time before endless cable and satellite options have divvied up the American TV audience and made it near impossible to attain these ratings.

What you have here, I will freely admit, is an educated guess based on many hours of research. I can guarantee you that the top 25 entries are correct, no question, but if you forced me to swear on a Bible that this is the definitive list of 100 different shows and movies that have the highest TV rankings, I would have to say no. I apologize for that, but hear me out first.

I have reviewed the weekly ratings in every issue of *Variety* from 1960 through 2000, along with cross-referencing listings in *The Los Angeles Times* and *The Washington Post* for clarification where necessary. Unfortunately, the listings were not always consistent, sometime just posting where a show finished without giving the actual rating. This is especially true for entry number 97, *Eight Is Enough*, where all I could determine after reviewing dozens of publications was that it finished that week with a rating somewhere between 32.7 and 34.2. To be safe, I've listed it on the low end, although it may belong anywhere up to 74, which naturally would bump down the series behind it a notch.

Also, in several entries information about a show's share numbers wasn't available, which could affect the order of the listings. Some entries scored the exact same rating and had to be separated by the share number.

This top 100 listing is a fluid document, which meant to give a better perspective of how popular certain TV programs were during their time, and tell the stories behind the shows.

About the Numbers

Entries present the program's **rating**, meaning the percentage of how many American homes with TV sets were tuned to watch the show at this time. The show's rating is followed by the **share** of the audience, meaning the percentage of how many sets that were actually turned on to watch television across America were viewing that program out of the options available. For example the *M*A*S*H* finale had a **Rating** of 60.2 and a **Share** of 77. Thus, more than six out of ten homes with TV sets in America in 1983 watched *M*A*S*H*, and more than three-fourths of them who had the set in use were *M*A*S*H* viewers as well. Where I have not been able to find the share number, I have listed it as "n/a" for not available.

This list is organized by ratings collected by the Nielsen rating company. You will notice that all but the last dozen or so listings had at least a third of all TV sets in America tuned to them based on their ratings. This proves they were all truly big events, and it is not surprising that the shares for each indicated they were viewed by at least half the people watching TV at the time, with one notable exception — see *Bonnie & Clyde* (78).

As the population grows, the number of viewers represented by a ratings point has changed to reflect the proportion of viewers accurately.

Setting the Criteria for Inclusion

To provide variety within the listings, I established the following rules:

1. As Nielsen provides its ratings to measure audience size for sponsors, only series with advertising are listed. Special events with huge audiences, often airing on all the networks, such as the assassination of President John F. Kennedy (at least 96.1 percent of all TV viewers in America watched some part of this coverage) and the Apollo 11 moon landing in July 1969 (93.9 percent of all TV viewers in America), did not have advertising and thus are excluded.

2. Nielsen changed its rating system in July 1960 to the one we currently use. This seems like a fair place to start this survey, for by 1960 87 percent of American households had a television, making it a pretty reasonable way to compare audiences once that saturation point was met versus just 23 percent when Nielsen issued its first seasonal ratings in 1951. The U.S. level of TV ownership has been at 98 percent since 1978. Thus, only the last 50 years (through October 2010) are calculated. See Appendix B for a listing of the highest-rated TV shows pre–1960.

3. Recurring popular specials such as the Super Bowl and the Academy Awards are listed once (under the highest scoring one). This also applies to specials starring individuals, which is why only one Bob Hope show made the list, or one Charlie Brown special, and so on.

4. Series are listed once under their highest rated episode. This includes special and final episodes during the original run. So, for example, *The Waltons' Thanksgiving Story* expanded TV-movie (which aired Nov. 15, 1973, and earned a 33.5 rating and 51 share) is excluded, because there is a regular episode of *The Waltons* that scored an even higher rating.

Now, some might believe that theatrical and/ or made-for-TV movies could be calculated as one category as well. I disagree — I consider each a unique work of art and thus worthy of inclusion. You may also quibble with me listing *Return to Mayberry* separately from *The Andy Griffith Show*, since the former was a TV-movie reunion of the latter's cast, but again, I consider them distinctly different shows. Whether you quibble with that or do not consider sports specials deserving of inclusion, or have any other objection, I understand your concern, but I believe there is enough variety to satisfy anybody's curiosity about what genres have performed best on TV.

Overview of the Entries

The list runs from the lowest ranking to highest ranking show.

Each entry includes the network of the program (limited to ABC, CBS and NBC), as well as day, date and air time of the entry. Shows are listed by the Eastern, Central and Pacific Time Zones. (Persons living in the Mountain Time Zone know too well that the times of network shows can vary greatly there. Mountain Time is included when a show aired live.) Next I have listed the competing network shows. For the few entries in the 1990s, I included shows on Fox as well, but not cable offerings, which would have overwhelmed the entry, and up until around the late 1980s cable's share of the TV audience was pretty low and inconsequential.

The cast and crew listings are limited to key personnel only. For actors, I have limited them to the top 15 performers each, except for *Seinfeld* (see 21) which highlights an excessive finale cast list. The actors are listed in the order they were presented on the show.

The rest of the entry includes my personal review of the show as well as extensive background, compiled from hundreds of sources (see the Bibliography for individual entries). Note: I include spoilers in my summaries.

For miniseries, summarizing only the highest-rated show was inadequate — like providing a description of just one book chapter — so I have included the entire storyline in condensed form.

I considered listing all the Emmy awards and

nominations for each show, but considering that the entry for *Cheers* would have 28 wins and more than three times as many nominations, including the Emmy summary for every show wasn't practical. Winners in the non-technical categories are listed.

I have viewed 80 percent of the shows, and in many cases re-viewed them, in order to get a better understanding of their appeal (or perplexing lack thereof, as the case may be). For the other 20 percent, I watched at least one episode of the series or series of specials if not the highest-rated show itself. There were four instances where I could not find a copy of the special to view from collectors or TV archives. It is sad but true — television history is still fleeting enough that some of its most-watched events ever are near impossible to find.

The happiest surprise for me during my research was to discover many interesting links between these entries. For example, "Born Free," the theme song to entry 73, was sung by three black men in drag in *The Longest Yard*, entry 86. Robin Williams made a joke about Leon Spinks in the *Mork & Mindy* episode (65) a few months after appearing as a guest on Spinks' fight with Muhammad Ali, which is entry 43. *A Case of*

Rape (87) referenced *Marcus Welby, M.D.* (40). It struck me as fascinating how interconnected these shows are, albeit unintentionally.

I thought about interviewing some former network programmers to find out why they thought these shows were so popular, but I realized that would be rather fruitless and unenlightening given some of the analysis I had seen in the past. Sometimes there is just no definitive explanation for a show's success. Take *The Bob Hope Christmas Special* at 7, for example. While Hope had been a strong TV draw for years, his recent movies had done poorly at the box office and apart from Neil Armstrong, the Christmas Special's guests, including Connie Stevens and Teresa Graves, were hardly A-list. Hope's support of the Vietnam War had drawn some criticism, and his formidable competition in 1970 included *Bewitched* on ABC and *The Jim Nabors Hour* on CBS, both top 25 shows at the time. Yet the special trumped them both and held the record as the highest-rated TV program ever for six years.

So although I will offer some theories about why these particular shows rated so well, I will leave it to the reader to draw conclusions.

THE HITS

100 — *Fatal Vision*

Nov. 19, 1984 (Part Two of two-part TV movie).
Rating: 32.7. **Share:** 49.

Aired on NBC Monday 9–11 P.M. Eastern and Pacific, 8–10 P.M. Central

Competition: *Monday Night Football* (Pittsburgh at New Orleans) on ABC, *Kate & Allie, Newhart*, and *Cagney & Lacey* on CBS

Cast: Karl Malden (Fred Kassab), Eva Marie Saint (Mildred Kassab), Barry Newman (Bernie Sagal), Gary Cole (Capt. Jeffrey MacDonald), Andy Griffith (Victor Worheide), Gary Grubbs (James Blackburn), Joel Polis (Brian Murtagh), Mitchell Ryan (Paul Stronbaugh), Wendy Schaal (Colette Kassab MacDonald), Scott Paulin (William Ivory), Barry Corbin (Franz Grebner), Albert Salmi (Judge Dupree). **Crew:** Daniel Wigutow, Mike Rosenfeld (executive producers), Richard L. O'Connor (producer), David Greene (director), John Gay (writer).

Synopsis. On Feb. 17, 1970, at 3:40 A.M. in Ft. Bragg, North Carolina, Capt. and physician Jeffrey MacDonald calls an operator and incoherently reports that his family had been attacked by four drug-crazed hippies. He survives, but his pregnant wife, Colette, and their two daughters die. Fred and Mildred Kassab, Colette's parents, support MacDonald, even when lead investigator William Ivory and his boss, Franz Grebner, suspect him of committing the murders. Bernie Sagal becomes MacDonald's lawyer against the government's case. The Army rules it has insufficient evidence to convict MacDonald.

When Fred sees a TV interview where his son-in-law's claims are inconsistent with what Fred and his wife witnessed, he reviews MacDonald's testimony and finds 123 questionable statements. A visit to the murder scene convinces Fred that his son-in-law is guilty. Brian Murtagh puts Fred in touch with U.S. Justice Department lawyer Victor Worheide to prosecute MacDonald, now living in Long Beach, California. Paul Stronbaugh of the FBI's chemistry and physics lab provides Fred with a graphic summary of how he believes the murders occurred, based on the four MacDonalds all having different blood types.

An Eastern District of North Carolina grand jury indicts MacDonald for trial without a motive in 1975. MacDonald appeals his case. Attorney James Blackburn, replacing the dead Worheide, convinces a Raleigh, North Carolina, jury that MacDonald is guilty. The U.S. Supreme Court rejects MacDonald's appeal, and he is sentenced to three consecutive life sentences in federal prison.

Backstory. When true-crime author Joe McGinniss was approached by Jeffrey MacDonald in 1979, the doctor intended for the writer to portray him as a man unfairly tarred and hounded by his in-laws on charges of murders he did not commit. But when *Fatal Vision*, the book by McGinniss, came out in 1983, the inability of MacDonald to explain contradictions in his version of events casted doubt on his innocence. *Fatal Vision* became a best seller and was an easy sell to NBC for broadcast the following year.

The TV-movie mostly hewed to the story the Kassabs told to McGinniss, who was portrayed in the TV-movie by Frank Dent. Fred Kassab married Mildred, a widow, and adopted her daughter, Colette, who wed Jeffrey MacDonald in 1963 with her parents' approval. "He was an all–American boy," Fred Kassab told Richard K. Rein in *People*. "He would charm the birds out of the trees."

MacDonald interned at Columbia-Presbyterian Medical Center in New York City before being commissioned in the Army Medical Corps and volunteering as a doctor for the Green Berets. MacDonald and his wife, Colette, and their two daughters, Kimberly and Kristen, relocated to the Ft. Bragg Army base.

All seemed fine until Feb. 17, 1970, when the Kassabs learned that their daughter and granddaughters had been beaten and stabbed to death. MacDonald claimed he had been knocked unconscious by four hippies, who then committed the murders and wrote the word "PIG" at the crime site. Investigators noted how the description sounded much like the Manson-Tate murders described in *Helter Skelter* (see 41) and surmised that MacDonald's description of the crime may have been inspired by an *Esquire* magazine article. They never found any people who matched MacDonald's description.

Even so, Fred and Mildred remained staunch defenders of their son-in-law and were glad when the Army dropped its case against him in October 1970. But then MacDonald barely talked to the Kassabs any more, and when he did, his statements were puzzling.

Odd explanations and conflicting comments by MacDonald led Fred to review the transcript of the Army's closed hearings and discover many discrepancies. For example, Jeff was stabbed 19 times, but most of his wounds were superficial, while the ones given to his wife and daughters went deeper. Fred wondered, why didn't the hippies kill MacDonald, or take any drugs from the medicine cabinet? For five years Fred and Mildred doggedly urged federal prosecutor to file murder charges against MacDonald.

"I have said that if the government wouldn't try Jeff, then I would kill the son of a bitch," Fred told *People*. "And I would do that, in a minute."

Following three appeals of his 1975 grand jury indictment, MacDonald went on trial in Raleigh in July 1979. He had a lot of financial support from Long Beach residents, including the police, because, as director of emergency room service at St. Mary's Medical Center, he was viewed as a model citizen. But a visit by the jurors to the still-intact crime scene, displays of bloody clothes, and MacDonald's detached demeanor combined to convince the jury he was guilty.

Prior to its initial airing, lawyers for MacDonald claimed the TV-movie was inaccurate and ignored new evidence about the case that could figure in a retrial. However, NBC's law department vice-president told *Variety* that airing the miniseries was "completely proper" and did not jeopardize MacDonald's chances for a fair retrial.

The show received largely favorable reviews due to its factual approach and high-quality production. "This four-hour drama is absorbing from beginning to end," Richard Zoglin commented in *Time* magazine. However, he added this caveat: "*Fatal Vision* is a dandy detective story, but it slyly skirts the real mystery: How could a man of such impeccable credentials, one so outwardly normal, be capable of these dark deeds?"

Indeed, the lack of a strong motive has been the one missing element of evidence. The book and TV-movie posit that MacDonald took amphetamines which led him into a rage after arguing with Colette that resulted in the deaths, but as the Army did not test the doctor for that after his arrest, there is no evidence to support that theory.

Part One of *Fatal Vision* aired Sunday, Nov. 18, 1984, with a 29.5/44. It averaged a 31.1/47 overall. Many think the second part did better primarily because *Monday Night Football* was then struggling in its first season without Howard Cosell as analyst.

At the Emmys, *Fatal Vision* scored five nominations, for Outstanding Drama/Comedy Special, Directing in a Limited Series or Special, Writing in a Limited Series or Special, Makeup, and Supporting Actor in a Limited Series or Special. It won in the latter category, earning Karl Malden his first statuette after four nominations for lead actor in a drama for *The Streets of San Francisco* in the 1970s. It also reteamed Malden with Eva Marie Saint, his costar from the 1954 film classic *On the Waterfront*.

The actor who benefited the most from the TV-movie was Andy Griffith. His portrayal of a slick if eccentric lawyer impressed Brandon Tartikoff, head of NBC Entertainment, and he suggested to programmer-turned-producer Fred Silverman that a similar character might work in a series. Silverman pursued that idea, and the result was *Matlock*, a lawyer drama which starred Griffith from 1986 to 1995.

Actor Albert Salmi played the judge in the 1979 trial. The project reunited him with Barry Newman, his co-star in the 1974–1976 NBC series *Petrocelli* where Newman played a lawyer, Salmi his assistant. Salmi, who suffered from severe depression and was struggling to find roles later in the 1980s, ended up killing his wife and then himself on April 22, 1990.

Meanwhile, MacDonald sued McGinniss for breach of contract and fraud, which resulted in an out-of-court settlement following a mistrial in 1987. He also appealed his case on several grounds, but kept losing in court. In 1995 Jerry Allen Potter and Fred Bost, authors of the book *Fatal Justice: Reinvestigating the MacDonald Murders*, defended MacDonald by saying that evidence supporting his charges had been suppressed by government prosecutors. As of this writing, MacDonald remains in prison and continues to appeal his case, maintaining that he is innocent.

99 — *Roots: The Next Generations*

Feb. 20, 1979 (Part 3 of 7-part miniseries). **Rating:** 32.7. **Share:** 50.

Aired on ABC Sunday 9–11 P.M. Eastern and Pacific, 8–10 P.M. Central

Competition: *White Lightning* (last hour of two-hour 1973 movie; repeat) and *The Paper Chase* on CBS, *The Eagle Has Landed* (last two hours of three-hour 1977 movie) on NBC

Cast: Georg Stanford Brown (Tom Harvey), Lynne Moody (Irene Harvey), Henry Fonda (Col. Frederick Warner), Olivia de Havilland (Mrs. Warner), Richard Thomas (Jim Warner), Marc Singer (Andy Warner), Bever-Leigh Banfield (Cynthia Palmer), Stan Shaw (Will Palmer), Irene Cara (Bertha Palmer), Dorian Harewood (Simon Haley), Ruby Dee (Queen Haley), James Earl Jones (Alex Haley), Al Freeman, Jr. (Malcolm X), Marlon Brando (George Lincoln Rockwell), Lynn Hamilton (Cousin Georgia). **Crew:** David L. Wolper (executive producer), Stan Margulies (producer), John Erman, Charles S. Dubin, Georg Stanford Brown, Lloyd Richards (directors), Ernest Kinoy, Sidney A. Glass, Thad Mumford, Daniel Wilcox, John McGreevey (writers).

Synopsis. In the late 1800s after moving to Henning, Tennessee, Tom and Irene Harvey discover that although slavery ended after the Civil War, racism did not. The Harveys' youngest daughter, Cynthia, marries mill worker Will Palmer, and they have a daughter named Bertha. She is the first member of her family to go to college, where she falls in love with Simon Haley. Simon goes to serve in the U.S. Army when World War I breaks out, then marries Bertha when he returns. Their children include a boy named Alex Haley.

As an adult, Haley pursues a writing career and encounters Malcolm X, who eventually entrusts him to write his autobiography. Haley then pursues his own family's history. Doggedly tracking leads, he travels to Africa and meets a griot (native storyteller) who confirms that Haley descended from a family dating back to the 1700s. With that news, Haley joyously cries, "You old African, Kunta Kinte! I've found you!" and the villagers welcome him as one of their own.

Backstory. When the last episode of the miniseries *Roots* (see 3) became the highest-rated TV show at the time, it was no surprise that ABC was more than willing to do a sequel. The success allowed executive producer David L. Wolper more latitude for the follow-up. It ran 14 hours, two hours longer than the first miniseries, and had an estimated budget of between $16 million to $20 million compared to $6 million for the original. Interestingly, the miniseries used only seven pages from *Roots* itself. Head writer Ernest Kinoy reviewed notes that Haley took while writing the book to craft outlines for each part's script, as well as some information from Haley's book *Search*.

The only actors to appear from the original were Georg Stanford Brown and Lynne Moody as Haley's great-great-grandparents, Tom and Irene Harvey. Brown also received the opportunity to direct an episode not featuring his character.

While the miniseries picked up when most of the original characters were dead, Wolper attempted to have two actors reappear. He wanted LeVar Burton to cameo as Kunta Kinte in a flashback, but Burton's agent wanted too much money so that idea was dropped. And Ben Vereen did not care to reprise playing Chicken George, so Avon Long assumed his role as a senior citizen in the first episode.

Wolper was luckier in that James Earl Jones, Henry Fonda and Olivia de Havilland told him they wanted to participate in the sequel. It was a rare TV role for de Havilland, and it marked the third time she and Fonda acted together as husband and wife, following the 1942 film *The Male Animal* and the 1962 Broadway play *A Gift of Time.*

Jones had met Haley years earlier, after reading *The Autobiography of Malcolm X.* "I got on a plane in the middle of a four-foot snowstorm, and somehow got up to Rome, New York, where Alex Haley lived," he recalled in *Roots: The Next Generations — The Legacy Continues* DVD feature. "No taxis, and I found my way from the airport to his house. I knocked on the door, I said, 'Mr. Haley, I just read your book,' and he said 'Come in!'" Jones also introduced Brown to Haley prior to *Roots.*

Another person contacting Wolper was Marlon Brando, who wanted to play a villain. Wolper accommodated that request and cast him as George Lincoln Rockwell, leader of the American Nazi Party, for an intense ten-minute scene in which Haley interviewed him for *Playboy* magazine.

As for the rest of the cast, a number of black actors who weren't in the original *Roots* appeared, including Ossie Davis as Simon's advisor Dad Jones, Paul Winfield as Dr. Horace Huguley and Beah Richards as the mature Cynthia Palmer. Kristoff St. John played Alex Haley at age eight, while Damon Evans portrayed the character from ages 17 to 25.

There was an effort to have black writers for the miniseries, as the original had none. Producer Stan Margulies asked Thad Mumford, who had written primarily for comedy and variety shows, to contribute. Mumford felt unnerved, not only because it was drama, but also because of the story's importance to black America, but he accepted the challenge. Teaming with partner Dan Wilcox and writing with him at night, Mumford co-wrote Part 5.

While working on the sequel, Wolper and Margulies created an hour-long documentary, *Roots: One Year Later*, to whet the appetites of viewers waiting for the sequel. It aired on ABC on Jan. 23, 1978, with Louis Gossett, Jr., as host, with disappointing numbers of 17.6/26.

One year later, *Roots: The Next Generations* ran on Feb. 18 through 23 and 25, 1979, against some pretty strong competition on NBC and CBS, including a repeat of *The Sound of Music* (see 76). Nevertheless, this episode finished fourth that week, behind *Mork & Mindy* (see 65) at #1, *Eight Is Enough* (see 97) at #2 and *Laverne & Shirley* (see 56) at #3.

The ratings for the rest of the miniseries were as follows: Part 1— 27.8/41, Part 2 — 29.5/41, Part 4 — 31.8/48, Part 5 — 31.8/48, Part 6 — 28.9/47 and Part 7 — 28.6/40. Its overall average was 30.2/45. Apart from the first installment, which aired in a different survey week, all the parts finished among the top 11 shows of the week. Still, some observers claimed because it did not dominate ratings like the original, it was a relative disappointment. Participants vigorously disputed that contention.

"I don't think anyone expected it to do what the first one did," said Brandon Stoddard, ABC's vice-president of dramatic programs and TV movies, in *The Los Angeles Times*. "That was a phenomenon, and something that was completely unique. I think this one did exactly as expected. Having a 45 share for the week is a major achievement — and at the same time to have the quality of drama we did is really extraordinary. We were really pleased with it."

"The other networks threw everything they had against us, and we won in every half-hour for the entire week," Margulies added in the same article.

It also survived some racist protests. In Huntsville, Alabama, 20 Ku Klux Klan members picketed the ABC affiliate showing the miniseries, while at the Nashville ABC station running it, someone burned a cross.

The Emmy voters awarded *Roots: The Next Generations* statuettes for limited series and supporting actor (for Brando, beating out cast mates Winfield and Al Freeman, Jr., in the category). Other nominations were for supporting actress (Ruby Dee), writing (Kinoy, for Part 1) and makeup.

ABC repeated the miniseries weekly from May 31 through July 12, 1981, but ratings were surprisingly poor, culminating in just 5.2/11 for the last show. The network allowed one more adaptation of the saga: *Roots: The Gift*, a Christmas tale involving Kunta Kinte, which ran on Dec. 11, 1988, and received an okay 15.4/24.

On Feb. 14, 16 and 18, 1993, CBS aired *Alex Haley's Queen*, based on the author's story about the early life of his paternal grandmother seen in *Roots: The Next Generations*, with Halle Barry as the title star. It was the #1 show of the week with average numbers of 23.9/37. It earned Emmy nominations for outstanding miniseries and supporting actress (Ann-Margret) and an Emmy win for hairstyling.

At the conclusion of *Roots: The Next Generations*, Haley appears on camera to deliver a coda. His words ring just as true more than 30 years after he first delivered them.

> All of my family members whom you have seen depicted in this television dramatization either were or are actually living human beings. We were deeply moved to see the book and film of *Roots* become perceived worldwide as synonymous with family. Before you get to the nations, the races, the creeds or any of the other circumstances we human beings like to regard as differences between ourselves, we are first many millions of families sharing this earth. After the miracle of life itself, our greatest human common denominator is families. I feel that's why *Roots* touched the universal human pulse.

98 — The 13th Annual Emmy Awards

May 16, 1961 (special). **Rating:** 32.7. **Share:** 64.
Aired on NBC Tuesday 10–11:30 P.M. Eastern and Pacific (tape delay for the latter), 9–10:30 P.M. Central

Competition: *Alcoa Presents: One Step Beyond* on ABC, *The Garry Moore Show* (repeat) on CBS

Cast: Dick Powell, Joey Bishop (hosts), the John Scott Trotter Orchestra. Presenters: Chet Huntley and David Brinkley (music for television and achievement in humor), Connie Stevens and Troy Donahue (drama writing and comedy writing), Elinor Donahue (children's programming), Audrey Meadows (supporting role in single program and supporting role in series), Harry Belafonte (drama directing and comedy directing), Art Carney (achievement in variety), Loretta Young (single performance actor in leading role and single performance actress in leading role), Carol Burnett (achievement in news). **Crew:** Bud Yorkin (executive producer), Bob Henry (director).

Synopsis. Under orchestral music, cameras survey stars in the audiences of the California and New York studios, including Emmy nominees Bob Hope, Garry Moore, Dinah Shore and Charles Bronson (none of whom won, unfortunately for them). Cut to Laraine Day, who shows the 24 Emmys to be dispensed tonight as well as families who used Crest, one of the show's sponsors. Hosts Dick Powell in Hollywood and Joey Bishop in Manhattan banter before introducing the Price Waterhouse representatives on both coasts. Viewers hear that they will see performers live and on film and videotape tonight. There was so much of the latter from the West Coast that Bishop at one point would grouse good-naturedly, "All the good stuff they gave to Hollywood!"

Between some sketches with current TV stars, most performers are on hand to accept their awards from the presenters. For six categories (documentary writing, engineering, art direction, cinematography, electronic camerawork and film editing), Powell revealed the winners, all of whom only had the chance to smile and nod with their awards briefly on camera. The longest applause was for the night's biggest winner — the *Hallmark Hall of Fame* presentation of "Macbeth," which won for Program of the Year, a Trustees Award for Hallmark Cards president Joyce C. Hall, lead actor (Maurice Evans), lead actress (Judith Anderson) and director (George Schaefer, who thanked Mr. Hall, Evans, Anderson and William Shakespeare, "not necessarily in that order").

Backstory. Contrary to contemporary belief, the Emmy Awards have not always been bloated affairs with weak, often unfunny introductions, sluggish pacing and little excitement. A case in point is this edition. It deftly mingled brief acceptance speeches (incredibly short ones by today's standards — few winners spoke more than three sentences and limited their thanks to only a handful of people) with sprightly skits to break up the presentation of awards. There was no clapping for nominees either, only winners, and few preambles to the reading of the nominees by the presenters either. Why can't today's Emmys be more like this?

A strong production is one element that this special had going for it, along with none-too-intimidating offerings on CBS and ABC the same night. But what probably pushed the audience to its highest level was the fact that exactly a week earlier, new FCC chairman Newton Minow addressed the National Association of Broadcasters meeting with all the network heads and publicly lambasted their work as having created "a vast wasteland," and asked, "Why is television so bad?"

With those colorful comments in mind, many people wanted to hear what the industry had to say in response on a show ostensibly celebrating the best TV has to offer. As it turned out, no one mentioned Minow or his words on the air. What viewers saw instead was the following:

• Amanda Blake, Lola Albright and Dorothy Provine singing a takeoff of Gilbert and Sullivan with "Three Little Single Girls Are We," in reference to their TV alter egos' unmarried status on *Gunsmoke* (see 24), *Peter Gunn* and *The Roaring Twenties*, respectively.

• Art Linkletter interviewing children about the medium as he did on his daytime series, with the usual amusing results. One tyke said his father lets him sip a little beer during commercials, while another said that in regard to advertisements, "I just sit there and suffer through them." A third kid told a nonplussed Linkletter that his favorite TV host was Bill Cullen, while yet another quipped that Emmy was "some stupid girl's name."

• The main family members of *The Many Loves of Dobie Gillis* appearing on film and receiving a ratings machine to record their TV watching. The men (including Dobie's beatnik pal Maynard G. Krebs) want to see wrestling, but mother Winnie insists they view cultural programming instead. Eventually all of them wind up looking through binoculars at the neighbor's TV showing wrestling.

• Yogi Bear and Huckleberry Hound also mock the ratings system in a cartoon.

• *Bonanza* (see 20) enacted in both British and Japanese versions by Lorne Greene and Dan Blocker. The latter rendition, *Bonanzai*, is politically incorrect by today's standards, using stereotyped Asian accents.

• Little Stanley Livingston appears to narrate a fairy tale about film editing using a clip from *My Three Sons*, with more errors cropping up every time until Livingston said the final take of them running backwards has become an art film in Sweden called *My Three Wild Strawberries*.

Actor Dennis Weaver was asked to do a spoof based on one of Shakespeare's great soliloquies referencing current TV series. He told Morrie Gelman and Gene Accas in *The Best in Television: 50 Years of Emmy* that, when approached with the idea, he responded, "I'm not really into making fun of *Hamlet*. I will do the parody if I'm able to approach it as though it were the real work." His deadpan recitation of lines like "TV or not TV — that is the question," and "Whether 'tis nobler to suffer the slugs and arrows of *Bonanza*, or switch to *Perry Mason*" was a hit with the audience and critics.

In another memorable moment, later shown in retrospective telecasts, Barbara Stanwyck, winner of lead actress in a series for the one-season *The Barbara Stanwyck Show*, accidentally tore her dress while heading down the aisle for the stage. She regained her composure and accepted the award, which she would win again in 1966 for *The Big Valley* and in 1983 for *The Thorn Birds* (see 14).

What really stands out from a current perspective, however, are the acceptance speeches. Many winners were warmly received, and they were succinct and heartfelt in their appreciation — or felt no need to say anything, as was the case with George Judd, Jr., the manager of the New York Philharmonic who turned up to accept for Leonard Bernstein winning for the best in music on television.

For example, when Rod Serling won for best writing in drama, he pointedly congratulated his fellow *Twilight Zone* contributors George Clayton Johnson, Charles Beaumont and Richard Matheson. Don Knotts, winner of supporting role in a series, took time thank "a very wonderful man, Andy Griffith" (see *The Andy Griffith Show* at 79). Sheldon Leonard claimed his statuette for best directing of a comedy (*The Danny Thomas Show*) by noting, "I'm proud to be part of this vigorous new medium." Even Joyce Hall thanked audiences "who were very understanding through our stumbling years" of the first few *Hallmark Hall of Fame* specials in the 1950s.

Sure, there were a few dead spots. The Academy of Television Arts and Sciences president Harry Ackerman gave a rather dry promotion of the organization's activities before delivering the Trustees Awards, and as happened before and would happen again, there were plenty of odd omissions, like the shows winning for best writing not being nominated as best series overall. In fact, apart from *Hallmark Hall of Fame*, the only production to win more than one Emmy this year was *The Twilight Zone*, for George Clemens' cinematography as well as Serling's writing, although it was not nominated for best drama series.

"This year's Emmy show was the smoothest in memory, perhaps even the best," wrote Henry Harding in *TV Guide*. "But it still wasn't an event to which members of the industry could point with unqualified pride." He noted how many of the winners were repeat honorees from earlier years and wondered why the most viewed and discussed TV event of the season — the presidential debates between Richard Nixon and eventual winner John F. Kennedy — had no nominations, even in the Program of the Year category, which went to the *Hallmark Hall of Fame* presentation of "Macbeth." Similar criticisms have been leveled against the Emmys ever since.

The Los Angeles–based Emmys held its first ceremony on January 25, 1949. Over the next few years it increased the categories to honor most major genres of television. The eligibility period varied too; by the time of this ceremony, it covered programs airing from April 1960 through April 1961. A restructuring in 1977 established the National Academy of Television Arts and Sciences as the group in charge of the nighttime entertainment honors. It now airs typically in August or September to honor programs from the previous season.

Despite some competing efforts, the Emmys have remained the leading award recognizing work in television. With TV viewership now in decline, it will be interesting to see how the Emmys will adapt.

97 — *Eight Is Enough*

Feb. 21, 1979 ("Best of Friends"). **Rating:** Between 32.7–34.2. **Share:** n/a.

Aired on ABC Wednesday 8–9 P.M. Eastern and Pacific, 7–8 P.M. Central

Competition: *The Amazing Spider-Man* (special) on CBS, *Supertrain* on NBC

Cast: Dick Van Patten (Tom Bradford), Betty Buckley (Abby Bradford), Grant Goodeve (David Bradford), Willie Aames (Tommy Bradford), Dianne Kay (Nancy Bradford), Connie Newton (Elizabeth Bradford), Lani O'Grady (Mary Bradford), Adam Rich (Nicholas Bradford), Susan Richardson (Susan Bradford), Laurie Walters (Joannie Bradford). **Guests:** Roseanne Arquette (Lori West), Joan Prather (Janet McArthur), Jeffrey Cotler (Irving J. Moore), Martin Azarow (Will Burdett), Tracey Gold (Tracey Kappleton), Missy Gold (Missy Kappleton). **Crew:** Lee Rich, Philip Capice (executive producers), Gary Adelson, Greg Strangis (producers), Gerald Mayer (director), Nick Thiel, David Braff (writers).

Synopsis. Thomas Bradford, a columnist for the *Sacramento Register* in California, is the patriarch of an octet of his offspring. His sons are David, the oldest with dark hair; Tommy, the middle boy with curly hair; and Nicholas, the adorable blond tyke. His daughters are Mary, the sensible, oldest girl with the flip perm; Joannie the breezy, fun-loving sister a year younger than Mary; Susan the redhead, a year behind Joannie; and Nancy the blonde and youngest girl. Their mother Joan died in 1977, but their father soon remarried Abby, who previously tutored Tommy.

In this episode, when Tommy learns that his friend Lori West is pregnant, he generously offers to serve as a surrogate father to her child and even marry her to help raise it. The family endorses Tommy's noble effort. Ultimately Lori is appreciative for Tommy's support but decides to handle motherhood without him. Meanwhile, oldest child David finds his live-in relationship with Janet McArthur crimped because his apartment is being sprayed for bugs. They are forced to reside at the Bradford household temporarily with all the attendant complications of trying to accommodate many people in a limited space. (Janet will become his wife in a few months.) Finally, youngest child Nicholas and his pal, Irving J. Moore, learn that their lemonade stand is not immune to competition from the Kappleton twins.

Backstory. Based on the memoirs of newspaper columnist Thomas W. Braden (published in 1975), *Eight Is Enough* was developed for television by William Blinn after he contributed to the writing of the miniseries *Roots* (see 3). The highest-rated episode of *Eight Is Enough* appeared in the same week as that miniseries' sequel, *Roots: The Next Generations* (see 99) — and it outperformed the latter.

Blinn sold the series to ABC with hopes of having an unknown actor star in it, but network programming head Fred Silverman favored installing Dick Van Patten in the lead. That turned out to be one of the easiest casting decisions for the series, which ran into several unexpected bumps by the time it came on the air on March 15, 1977, as a midseason replacement for the concluding *Rich Man, Poor Man — Book II* on Tuesday nights from 9 to 10 P.M. Eastern and Central.

The biggest problem involved the original actor playing David, Mark Hamill. Signed to appear in the initial batch of six episodes ordered, he was not happy with the assignment, having just finished the lead in the upcoming blockbuster movie *Star Wars* and expecting more film work as

a result. After shooting the pilot, Hamill had a car crash in December 1976 that required major reconstructive plastic surgery. His immediate replacement was Grant Goodeve.

The bad luck continued backstage when Diana Hyland, playing Tom's wife Joan, died less than two weeks after the premiere of *Eight Is Enough* due to complications from cancer. The producers decided against recasting that character as well, so they created the new character of Sandra Sue "Abby" Abbott to eventually fall in love with Tom and become his new spouse. She was a youthful companion for Tom; in fact, actress Betty Buckley was six months younger in real life than Laurie Walters, who played one of her TV daughters.

To help Abby remember the birth order in the family, Nicholas told her in one episode of a memorable mnemonic phrase employed to keep everyone straight, from oldest first: "Dumb Martians Just Sit Nervously Eating Tender Noodles." It was that kind of cute comic interplay along with modest complications that made *Eight Is Enough* the pre-eminent contemporary family comedy drama of its time. Finishing its abbreviated first season at #23, it returned to the ABC lineup following a summer break as the leadoff series on the network's Wednesday night schedule, where it stayed most of the rest of its run.

In its new slot, *Eight Is Enough* constantly beat its competition on NBC and CBS and finished the next three seasons just shy of the top 10: #12 in 1977–1978, #11 in 1978–1979 and #12 in 1979–1980. About the only major figure who disliked it in public was Thomas W. Braden, the man whose clan served as the model for the Bradfords. He probably was too close to the source to enjoy the changes in the way his family was portrayed.

"The enormous popularity of *Eight Is Enough* was, I suspect, connected to a feeling of comfort people experienced in watching the exploits — often harebrained exploits — of this big, loving and goofy family," Van Patten wrote in his autobiography. "The Bradfords were not wrapped up in war, economic crisis or the battle over America's culture that had preoccupied the country for so long. For many people, the Bradfords represented a reaffirmation of family life in a world that had long seemed consumed with other things."

As for why this rather humdrum episode of *Eight Is Enough* placed a surprisingly strong #2 on the same week ABC aired *Roots: The Next Generations*, part of the reason may be due to viewers trying to avoid the debut of *Supertrain*, NBC's overhyped yet underdeveloped comedy-adventure (it was never exactly one or the other) that was meant to be another *Love Boat* but turned out to be a costly disaster that represented Silverman's flailing leadership as head programmer at NBC (he moved there from ABC in 1978). He was fired from the post in 1981 following three consecutive seasons with the network remaining in third place.

However, Silverman did install a more popular audience attraction opposite *Eight Is Enough* starting April 18, 1979. *Real People*, one of the first series to spotlight interesting members of the public as its stars, came close to beating *Eight Is Enough* in the 1979-1980 season, finishing just a few tenths of a ratings point behind it at #14 overall. The next season *Real People* was decisively triumphing over *Eight Is Enough*, coming in at #12 that season, while the former winner dropped out of the top 30. Combined with rising costs for production thanks in part to an expanding cast (the regular cast now included Susan's husband, baseball player Merle "The Pearl" Stockwell, Tommy's pal Ernie Fields and Abby's nephew Jeremy Andretti, who lived with the family), ABC decided the fifth season was enough. The series went into reruns Saturday nights at 8 P.M. Eastern and Pacific and the final episode aired on Aug. 29, 1981. The series appeared in reruns on local TV stations a year later.

The Academy of Television Arts and Sciences displayed little love for *Eight Is Enough* during its run, nominating the series just twice, both in 1978, for film editing and for single performance by a supporting actor in a comedy or drama series. The latter was for Will Geer as a man who stole the Bradfords' Christmas presents but was caught in the act by Nicholas, who mistakenly thought he was Santa.

Eight Is Enough returned in two TV-movie revivals on NBC. *Eight Is Enough: A Family Reunion* aired on Oct. 18, 1987, and had the original Bradford bunch pop up except for Buckley as Abby — she was replaced by Mary Frann. Buckley also did not show up for *An Eight Is Enough Wedding*, seen on Oct. 15, 1989; Sandy Faison played the character as David married for a second time.

There was a touch of sadness behind these get-togethers and the years thereafter. As Van Patten noted in his autobiography, fully half of the actors who played his TV children — Adam Rich, Lani O'Grady, Willie Aames and Susan Richardson — later acknowledged they were addicted to drugs in some form during or after the series aired. Richardson said she took them in order to lose weight after her pregnancy. While she, Rich and

Aames overcame their dependencies, O'Grady never did. She died of drug intoxication on Sept. 25, 2001, just one week before what would have been her 47th birthday.

Eight Is Enough was little noticed thereafter until the 2008 political campaign season, where Democratic candidate Barack Obama invoked the phrase to rally people against Republicans remaining in charge of the White House. However, the increased use of the slogan did not encourage an official release of any of its episodes on DVD, nor did a live reunion of the cast (minus Richardson and Rich) on *The Today Show* on March 1, 2010 (Buckley made it this time).

---

96 — *Fish*

Jan. 3, 1978 ("Mike's Career"). **Rating:** 32.8. **Share:** 47.

Aired on ABC Tuesday 8:30–9 P.M. Eastern and Pacific, 7:30–8 P.M. Central

Competition: *The Fitzpatricks* (last show; last half-hour of 60-minute episode) on CBS, *NBC Reports: Medicine in America* (second half-hour of three-hour documentary) on NBC

Cast: Abe Vigoda (Phil Fish), Florence Stanley (Bernice), Barry Gordon (Charlie Harrison), John Cassisi (Victor Kreutzer), Denise Miller (Jilly Papalardo), Lenny Bari (Mike), Todd Bridges (Loomis), Sarah Natoli (Diana Pulaski). **Guest:** Dorothy Green (Mrs. Wilson). **Crew:** Danny Arnold (executive producer), Gary Shimokawa (director), Norman Barasch, Roy Kammerman (producers-writers).

Synopsis. A detective with Manhattan's 12th Precinct until his retirement, Phil Fish becomes a foster parent along with his patient wife, Bernice, at their somewhat shabby suburban home, despite both being old enough to be grandparents. They take in five abandoned and troubled youngsters from the children's center: tubby and energetic Victor, pretty Jilly, John Travolta–like Mike, adorable Loomis and wisecracking Diana. Loomis was the youngest in the bunch, as well as the only black child in the otherwise Caucasian household, while Mike looked too old to need to be living under adult supervision.

Supervising and advising the Fishes in their capacity as substitute father and mother was Charlie Harrison, a nebbish whose squishy pleas for tolerance regarding the kids often got on Phil's nerves. So did the kids, with Phil often having to talk Loomis out of locking himself in the basement, among other challenges.

In this episode, Mike finds a fan willing to finance his bid for a singing career. He is disturbed to find out that Mrs. Green, a wealthy, middle-aged divorcee, actually has more interest in his body than his voice. Will Mike compromise himself with her to achieve his ambitions, or will he spurn her advances, even though it means he will be stuck living with the Fishes, four other delinquents and no foreseeable business prospects? If you do not know the answer, you obviously have not been watching television lately.

Backstory. One of the very few shining lights for ABC during its dismal 1974-1975 season was a midseason situation comedy set in a New York City police squad room. Debuting Jan. 23, 1975, *Barney Miller* started slowly but built up a following that made it a top 20 hit two years later. Many cited the supporting character of Det. Phil Fish as part of its appeal. With droopy eyes and a laconic delivery, he appeared barely conscious and comfortable just sitting and talking in the station, much less chasing crooks. The distinctive portrayal earned Abe Vigoda back-to-back Emmy nominations as supporting actor in a comedy in 1976 and 1977, breaking into a category shut out for ABC since Michael Constantine of *Room 222* competed for the statuette in 1971. It got Vigoda noticed by executives as well.

"What happened in *Barney Miller* was Abe Vigoda, no one had ever seen a character with that particular rhythm before, and I think ABC fell in love with that rhythm," director Gary Shimokawa told Shu Shostak in 2007. He later added, "They found his character to be very popular, so they came to [executive producer Danny Arnold] to spin it off. I don't believe that would've been Danny's first choice."

Arnold's concoction for Vigoda, *Fish*, debuted on Saturday, Feb. 5, 1977, replacing *Wonder Woman*. Its cast included Florence Stanley, who had appeared as noble Bernice a few times previously on *Barney Miller*, as had Todd Bridges, but as a different juvenile criminal character. "I want you to be on a TV show," Arnold told Bridges after being impressed with the latter's work, and he held true to his word with him here.

"Being on *Fish* was great," Bridges recalled in his autobiography *Killing Willis*. "I loved acting, and I was thrilled to go to the set every day." It established him as a teen idol, and the exposure led to his best-known role as Willis on the hit sitcom *Diff'rent Strokes* from 1978 to 1986.

Unfortunately for *Fish*, the cast was about the only exciting element of the series. Everything else seemed off, including the lead character. Here Fish was more irritable and loud than on the previous show, though Vigoda kept his character's deadpan sarcastic delivery intact.

Arnold and his creative team were out of their element writing for children, who rarely seemed to escape the clichés of being troublemakers who wound up proving they had hearts of gold by the end of each episode. In fact, the writing overall was subpar from what had been allowed on *Barney Miller*. Consider this typical lifeless repartee from one episode: "I couldn't find Victor anywhere," says Charlie. "Look in your subconscious under 'P,' for panic," responds Fish.

Even the laughter was faked, although that was not the original intent. "*Fish* became a problem because Abe, he wanted to do the show in front of an audience," Shimokawa recalled. "And Danny [Arnold] didn't want to do the show in front of an audience. But Abe gave him so much grief that Danny just said, 'Well, forget it. We'll do it front of an audience.'"

That situation led to Shimokawa joining the series as director because his predecessor, Jeremiah Morris, was unaccustomed to overseeing a show taped before a studio audience. Shimokawa did eight episodes, including this one, but ironically the series wound up having no audience because of the difficulties of shooting so many scenes with five young actors often on stage at the same time. Because they were mostly minors, scenes with the children were taped first out of sequence for the final show. "But after we let go of the kids, the adult scenes would take for-friggin'-ever," Shimokawa said. "We were there [until] three, four in the morning."

Shimokawa also found that the leading man's delivery was not as sharp as it had been on *Barney Miller*. "Abe really thought he was the funniest guy on the planet, and sometimes he thought that whatever came out of his mouth would be funny, and it wasn't," he said. Emmy voters must have shared the same sentiment, as Vigoda no longer appeared in the nominations after 1977.

With these drawbacks, it is amazing that *Fish* did actually win an Emmy award, for art direction or scenic design for a comedy series for an episode in its first season. But it was virtually the only highlight for the spin-off.

The first 13 episodes of *Fish* did not do particularly well in the ratings, scoring an 18.1 average to finish at #49 for the 1976-1977 season, but ABC renewed it. To boost its appeal, the network reran it following *Barney Miller* Thursdays nights in the summer of 1977 before returning it to Saturdays on Aug. 13, but ratings remained low, and it went off there on Nov. 5, 1977, before returning with this show.

Why ABC pre-empted *Laverne & Shirley* (see 56) one week to run this episode instead remains a mystery, although one can presume that network officials thought the exposure behind the hot lead-in, *Happy Days* (see 64), would result in people following *Fish* to its new time slot on Thursdays. (This sort of special pre-emption of a hit to promote a new or struggling series was novel for the time but later became an occasional practice despite its dubious long-term success. For an example of another situation like this, see *You Again?* at 63.) The network turned out to be wrong.

It was obvious that its popularity here stemmed solely from following *Happy Days*, as the ratings for *Fish* fell precipitously when it followed the hit *Welcome Back, Kotter* on Thursdays. It finished the 1977-1978 season at #43 with an 18.5 average. After 35 episodes, *Fish* last aired on June 8, 1978.

According to Bridges, the reason the series ended was not due to its so-so ratings but its star. "When the second season of *Fish* came to an end, Abe Vigoda demanded more money to do a third season," Bridges wrote. The producers refused, and that was the end of *Fish*— and Fish the character, as he did not return to *Barney Miller* even though that series remained on the air through 1982.

Vigoda never had another regular series role. He spent the next few decades with sporadic acting jobs while denying rumors he was dead (his phlegmatic Fish probably lent credence to such gossip).

On Feb. 7, 2010, Vigoda and Betty White appeared in a Snickers commercial during Super Bowl XLIV (see 4), a spot that ranked on audience surveys as a favorite of viewers during the highly rated game. But while that advertisement led to a revival of interest in White, including a Facebook campaign on the Internet that successfully resulted in White hosting *Saturday Night Live*, it did not translate into similar excitement for a revival of Vigoda, or *Fish*, for that matter.

Fish finally became available on DVD in October 2011, when the first season appeared as an extra in Shout Factory's box set of the Barney Miller series. This was surpising, given that there was little demand for a show that probably excited ABC programmers more than anyone else when it was first created.

95 — The Andy Williams Christmas Show

Dec. 14, 1971 (special). **Rating:** 32.8. **Share:** 47. Aired on NBC Tuesday 9–10 P.M. Eastern and Pacific, 8–9 P.M. Central

Competition: *ABC Movie of the Week* (*The Trackers*; last hour of 90-minute show) on ABC, *Hawaii Five-O* (last half-hour of 60-minute show) and *Cannon* (first half-hour of 60-minute show) on CBS

Cast: Andy Williams, the Lennon Sisters (Dianne, Peggy, Kathy and Janet), the Osmonds (Alan, Wayne, Merrill, Jay and Donny), Claudine Longet. **Crew:** Andy Williams (executive producer), Alan Handley (producer-director), Marty Farrell, Milt Rosen (writers).

Synopsis. It's the holiday season at the household of Andy Williams, which means that he and his wife Claudine Longet and their children, Noelle, Christian and Bobby will be joined by Andy's sister Janie; his brothers Don, Dick and Bob; and his parents to celebrate the occasion, along with two singing groups. Andy kicks off the entertainment by singing his recent hit "Where Do I Begin" (see 17 — *Love Story*) in five different languages. He joins the Lennon Sisters to sing "Close to You" *a capella*, followed by some seasonal tunes. Then Andy's brothers accompany him and the Lennon Sisters with "Thank You Very Much" from the movie musical *Scrooge*, followed by Andy's 1963 Christmas favorite "Holiday Season."

After Longet sang, there was a sketch where the family appeared as puppets enacting a French fable, apparently in honor of Longet's Parisian roots. Later, Andy sang yet another movie song, "Bless the Beasts and Children" from the film of the same name. (It was nominated for an Oscar for Best Song a few months after this special ran, just as "Thank You Very Much" had been earlier in 1971.) During this number, Andy's son Bobby fed birds on camera in keeping with the tune's theme. Andy resurrects another song he first recorded in 1963, "Song and a Christmas Tree," interpolated with "The Twelve Days of Christmas." He closes the show with a ballad he had not released on record, "If We Only Had Love."

Backstory. Certain stars have for whatever reason been more connected to Christmas than others, and Andy Williams is one of them. This dates back to the 1963 release of the million-selling *Andy Williams Christmas Album*, which coincided with his long-running TV series. He introduced the standard "It's the Most Wonderful Time of the Year" and other tunes there, and today more radio stations play those songs than any other of the dozens of top 40 hits Williams had from 1956 through 1973.

In an interview for the "Holiday Moments" episode of *TV Land's Top 10* (telecast on Dec. 11, 2005), Williams said he enjoyed being associated with the season on his specials and in taping them. "The shows are always beautifully done," he said. "The music is beautiful. The scenery is great. People, I think, want to celebrate Christmas, want to see a great Christmas show."

Part of its appeal was nostalgic, as it reminded him growing up in Iowa in the 1930s before he and his brothers — yes, the Don, Dick and Bob seen in the special — went to Hollywood in the hopes of making it as a singing quartet. They found some work but not as much as they had anticipated. Williams split with his three brothers in 1953 to pursue a solo career. After the breakup, the other Williams brothers only performed professionally with Andy during the latter's Christmas specials.

Andy was able to secure a steady job as the in-house singer on *The Tonight Show Starring Steve Allen* from 1954 through 1957, and towards the end of his stint there he finally had some hit records with songs like "Butterfly." He became a big enough name to host three consecutive summer shows from 1957 through 1959, then only appeared in specials thereafter until NBC allowed him regular TV exposure with *The Andy Williams Show* debuting on Sept. 11, 1962. The series was always loved more by the industry than the public at large, as it won three Emmys as Outstanding Variety Series without ever finishing in the top 30 for any of the five seasons it ran. (It ended on May 7, 1967.)

One of Williams' discoveries was the Osmonds, who were originally four brothers in a singing quartet just like Andy once was. He added them as regulars midway during the first season, and they became Andy's virtual TV family, with Donny and Marie joining them later. Members of the Osmonds would appear in seven straight Andy Williams Christmas specials.

Marie Osmond loved appearing with Andy, but she was uncomfortable with her body image. "We had taped an Andy Williams Christmas special ... when we all wore holiday attire, complete with fake fur hats and scarves and winter parkas," she recalled in her 2009 autobiography. "Nothing makes a girl feel more like a formless blob than a parka!" Osmond later added that she overheard one producer talk to another in the hallway during the taping and say, "How do we get the fat sister out of the camera shot?"

Even though the Osmonds were finally a hit music act with "One Bad Apple" in 1971, they had little to do with this special other than show up. The special itself came after Williams had spent two years doing occasional NBC specials, including Christmas ones of course, before trying another variety series on Sept. 20, 1969, but it too failed to catch on and aired its last show on July 17, 1971.

It had to have been a sweet triumph for him to return to the network five months later with the biggest hit special of December 1971, especially given its tough competition. *The ABC Movie of the Week* and *Hawaii Five-O* both were regular top 15 hits in the 1971-1972 season. Maybe viewers just wanted a break from the drama and enjoy carols from Andy and crew as a relief during the Yuletide season, because this guest lineup hardly screams blockbuster television, especially given how the Lennon Sisters bombed with their own ABC series with Jimmy Durante from Sept. 26, 1969 through July 4, 1970. Also, they and Claudine Longet rarely received airplay on popular radio stations.

The Andy Williams Christmas Show finished in second place for the week behind *All in the Family* (see 25). It replaced parts of two hour-long bombs introduced in September 1971 that ended in midseason, the last half of the crime drama *Sarge* and the first half of the variety series *The Funny Side*.

Despite this massive success, there was no Christmas special for Williams in 1972. However he came back to celebrate Noel on NBC on Dec. 13, 1973, and Dec. 11, 1974. He kept those specials intimate, with only his immediate family as regulars. Unfortunately, Andy's private life became messy after the airing of the last one. In 1975, Williams divorced Longet, with the male half claiming that the reason was that he spent too much time touring and recording songs. ("In danger of becoming a workaholic, I was so obsessed with building my career that everything, including my family, suffered as a result," Williams said in his autobiography *Moon River and Me*.) In the wake of the breakup, Longet dated skier Vladimir "Spider" Sabich until he was found dead from a shooting on March 21, 1976. Longet was charged with causing his death, but she insisted that the gun discharged accidentally, and Williams publicly supported his ex-wife. A jury agreed with that position and acquitted her in 1977, but her musical career never recovered.

The publicity about Williams standing by his wife while a cloud of suspicion hung over her may have hurt his syndicated musical series, which lasted only one season (1976–1977). He also had his last stint as host of the Grammy Awards in 1977. Thereafter, Williams was hard to find on television any time, not just Christmas.

The drought was broken with the appearance of *Andy Williams' Early New England Christmas* special on CBS on Dec. 7, 1982. Three years later, NBC ran *Andy Williams and the NBC Kids Search for Santa* on Dec. 20, 1985, where he appeared with the juvenile stars of various NBC series, including most of the children from *The Cosby Show* (see 22). It was a rather contrived affair, but NBC nonetheless repeated it on Dec. 7, 1986. Then there were no more network offers for Christmas shows for Andy. He had to settle to do them as stage shows in Branson, Missouri, during much of the 1990s, even after the release of *The New Andy Williams Christmas Album* in 1994.

On Dec. 17, 1997, the singer good-naturedly appeared on Comedy Central's *The Daily Show* in taped bits that claimed he was doing a Christmas special for them. In 2001 there was a retrospective special, *Happy Holidays: The Best of the Andy Williams Christmas Specials*, which has occasionally rerun on public television stations. While his biggest hit TV special is hard to find, it is reassuring to know that his recordings remain widely available and probably will continue to entertain future generations of Americans who love the spirit of the season.

---

94 — *The Flip Wilson Show*

Nov. 4, 1971 (Episode 2.8). **Rating:** 32.8. **Share:** 51.

Aired on NBC Thursdays 8–9 P.M. Eastern and Pacific, 7–8 P.M. Central

Competition: *Bearcats!* on CBS, *Alias Smith and Jones* on ABC

Cast: Flip Wilson, The George Wyle Orchestra. **Guests:** The Jackson 5 (Michael Jackson, Tito Jackson, Jermaine Jackson, Jackie Jackson, Marlon Jackson), Lily Tomlin, David Reuben, (Bob) Hudson and (Rod) Landry. **Crew:** Monte Kay (executive producer), Bob Henry (producer), Tim Kiley (director), Flip Wilson, Hal Goodman, Herbert Baker, Larry Klein, Bob Weiskopf, Bob Schiller (writers).

Synopsis. Flip introduces his audience to "Ralph the Invisible Wonder Dog," who performs tricks that no one can see. The first sketch has Lily visiting Flip, a grocer, to purchase goods she cannot remember, causing Flip to enact commercials featuring the brands. It ends with Lily knowing the name of her last item because it does no advertising. The Jackson 5 sing a medley of their #1 hits "I Want You Back," "ABC" and "The Love You Save." Next, Hudson and Landry perform a travel agency routine.

Lily Tomlin does the monologue that won her a spot on *Rowan and Martin's Laugh-In* (see 53) about being a "rubber freak" ("One afternoon I simply went berserk at a Playtex girdle factory"). The Jackson 5 returns and Flip threatens to beat lead singer Michael Jackson if he doesn't get into the group to make it the Jackson 6. Flip winds up consigned backstage by the group as they perform their current hit, "Never Can Say Goodbye," with the camera focused on Michael most of the tune.

After a Hudson-Landry man-on-the-street segment, the final sketch has Tomlin as Hortense Barncastle, hostess of *Chapter Chatter*, a book discussion TV series with sex expert Dr. David Reuben. Hortense unsuccessfully makes passes at Reuben until Geraldine Jones (Flip) arrives and grills Reuben, telling him, "I didn't have to read your book. I've *lived* your book!" The show ends with Flip bringing his guests on stage and thanking them, including bumping his hips with all of the Jackson 5 members.

Backstory. In the early 1970s, the most popular variety series starred a black comedian who received his own series just five years after making his national TV debut. *The Flip Wilson Show* was an unlikely yet very likable hit, a series that proved to be the last NBC variety series to make the top 10. Ironically, the bright, urbane, hip comedy program would be knocked off the air by competition from its polar opposite, a stark, prosaic drama set in the 1930s — *The Waltons* (see 69).

The Flip Wilson Show debuted as NBC's Thursday night leadoff series on Sept. 17, 1970, following well-received guest visits by Wilson on some sitcoms and many talk and variety series such as *The Carol Burnett Show*. On the latter he portrayed Geraldine Jones, a sassy, loose-limbed, liberated lass who would become his best-known and most loved character on his own variety series. Unlike other comedians who did drag and let their audiences know clearly that they were really a man in a dress, Wilson wholeheartedly adopted the attitude of a sleek sister and portrayed Geraldine perfectly.

Wilson had the chance to do either a sitcom or variety series for NBC. He and his management felt his range would be better showcased in the latter. They were fortunate in connecting Wilson with Bob Henry as his producer. Wilson was simpatico with Henry, a man who previously produced similar low-key NBC stars such as Dinah Shore and Andy Williams. Neither man was too fond of the Hollywood celebrity scene, and both preferred to take thing easy, making them a perfect match in temperament for creating Wilson's weekly series. (By the end of the run, Wilson was co-producer of the show with Henry.)

Henry loved the way Wilson took material given to him and rewrote it to fit his needs, although the producer would intercede whenever he felt Wilson's approach was not correct for the script. It was not unusual for a lot of ideas to be rejected the first day of writing before approving one to use in that week's program.

Herbert "Herbie" Baker, the head writer, often worked out his ideas for each show with Henry based on the guest star in mind. "Like, Lily Tomlin signs up with computer dating. Flip wants a date. They find they are right for each other but the computer says no...." Henry told William A. Fry in *Life Studies of Comedy Writers: Creating Humor.* "Many times Herbie and the writers all work on the phone at night, when they will cook up an idea between them, a great idea. They'll work out the outline, Herbie will call me, and I'll OK the idea or not." Their material almost always was family-friendly; there were no reports about censorship controversy for this series. In fact, children were a big part of the audience, latching onto Wilson's catchphrases such as "The devil made me do it!" and "What you see is what you get!"

The other writers included Bob Schiller and Bob Weiskopf, who enjoyed working with Wilson almost as much as they claimed to have hated working on *The Red Skelton Hour* (see 68). They, along Wilson and Hal Goodman, won Emmys for their writing in 1971, the same year *The Flip Wilson Show* won for best variety series. The show and the writers would be nominated for Emmys again in 1972 and 1973, as would the show's directing in 1971, 1972 and 1973, but there were no more wins.

This program had the same top rating as Flip's Jan. 14, 1971 show with Roberta Flack, Steve Lawrence and Zero Mostel. However, this one is a better representation of a typical *Flip Wilson Show.* Tomlin and the Jackson 5 were recurring guests, while the appearance of Hudson and Landry reflected Wilson's desire to feature up-and-coming talent, even if that duo never did

much nationally besides having close to a top 40 hit with their comedy record "Ajax Liquor Store" in 1971. It was that record's humor that led Wilson to invite them on his show.

As for Dr. David Reuben, if any comedian could get laughs out of the author appearing to promote his hit book *Everything You Always Wanted to Know About Sex (But Were Afraid to Ask)* without turning the comedy raunchy, it would be Wilson. He succeeded mightily. The show is quite enjoyable except for the Hudson and Landry sketches, which proved they were not in the league of Tomlin, Wilson and the Jackson 5.

The Flip Wilson Show reigned as NBC's highest-rated series from 1970 to 1972, finishing #2 both seasons, the first behind *Marcus Welby, M.D.* (see 40) and the second behind *All in the Family* (see 25). It slipped to #12 in its third year when CBS's *The Waltons* started gaining ratings in the middle of the 1972-1973 season to come close to tying it. By the following season it was no contest. *The Waltons* regularly defeated *The Flip Wilson Show,* and now the former series was #2 while Wilson finished at #48. His last show ran on June 27, 1974.

Reruns of *The Flip Wilson Show* did not appear until 1980, when the show was cut to half an hour to emulate the success *The Carol Burnett Show* had in that format starting in 1977. Unfortunately the somewhat awkwardly edited repeats were not a success.

Wilson's TV career appeared to be adrift the rest of the 1970s, with infrequent appearances that appeared to grow more trivial every year. It even seemed somewhat jinxed. One prestigious possibility, of hosting a live Broadway show on NBC's *The Big Event* in February 1977, fell apart when the musical revue in question, a revival of *Hellzapoppin* starring Jerry Lewis, closed before opening. Yet Wilson said such debacles left him relatively unfazed.

Explaining his circumstances to Tom Joyner on the syndicated *Ebony/Jet Celebrity Showcase* in 1983, Wilson noted, "It was one of the most successful shows in the history of television. So that allowed me likewise to be one of the most successful parents in the history of television too." When *The Flip Wilson Show* went off, his sons were 13 and 11 and his daughters were nine and seven, and Wilson wanted to fulfill his obligations to his family to raise them right, unlike the harsh conditions he had endured as a child. (He was raised mostly in foster homes after he and his 17 brothers and sisters had been abandoned by their parents.) Wilson also told Joyner that the smooth-talking Rev. LeRoy of the Church of What's Happening Now was his favorite character on the show, although he admitted that everybody loved Geraldine the best.

In 1998, TV Land added the 1980 repeats of *The Flip Wilson Show* to its lineup. Wilson discussed the series fondly in several interviews, even though he had liver cancer that would claim his life before the end of the year. The reruns were again not a success, but they have appeared in DVD since that time.

If you are curious about watching this episode in full, it is available for viewing at the Paley Center for Media in Beverly Hills, California. It is worth viewing to give you a fair idea of how this unassuming man was once the nation's comedy sensation.

93 — *Peter Pan*

Dec. 8, 1960 (special). **Rating:** 32.8. **Share:** n/a.
Aired on NBC Thursday 7:30–9:30 P.M. Eastern and Pacific, 6:30–8:30 P.M. Central
Competition: *Guestward Ho!, The Donna Reed Show, The Real McCoys* and *My Three Sons* on ABC, *The Witness, Dick Powell's Zane Grey Theater* and *Angel* on CBS
Cast: Mary Martin (Peter Pan), Cyril Ritchard (Captain Hook/Mr. Darling), Maureen Bailey (Wendy Darling/Jane), Margalo Gillmore (Mrs. Darling), Sondra Lee (Tiger Lily), Jacqueline Mayre (Liza), Joe E. Marks (Smee), Norman Shelly (Nana/Crocodile), Joey Trent (John Darling), Kent Fletcher (Michael Darling), Lynn Fontanne (narrator). **Crew:** Richard Halliday (executive producer), Sumner Locke Elliott (writer), Vincent J. Donehue (director).

Synopsis. In London, after Mr. and Mrs. Darling put their children to bed, Tinkerbell, a fairy, surveys the kids' bedroom to help her pal, Peter Pan, find his missing shadow. Peter awakens Wendy Darling and tells her he is from Never-Never Land. Peter spreads fairy dust on Wendy and her brothers John and Michael, to allow them to fly to his island. They arrive and meet six Lost Boys who are trying to avoid Tiger Lily and her fellow Indians as well as Captain Hook, his henchman Smee, and the rest of his crew. The captain has a vendetta against Peter Pan because the latter once fed Hook's right hand to a crocodile who is determined to eat the rest of Hook. The crocodile also swallowed a clock, so when Hook hears ticking in the sea, he knows the beast is near.

Hook ties up Tiger Lily but Peter saves her. She returns the favor, and the Indians and the Lost Boys strike up an alliance. Wendy and Peter grow fond of each other. When Hook abducts Wendy, Peter and the Indians set out to save her. Hook is chased off the boat by the crocodile and the gang returns to Never-Never Land, where Liza the maid has arrived to take the Darlings home. Wendy brings the Lost Boys back with her and convinces her parents to adopt them while Peter leaves. Years later, Peter visits a grown Wendy and bonds with her daughter Jane.

Backstory. After Jerome Robbins choreographed Mary Martin in the acclaimed TV special *Ford 50th Anniversary Show* (June 15, 1953), Martin enlisted him to direct and choreograph a new stage version of *Peter Pan* starring her that was being created. Robbins adapted parts of four previous versions plus the original script presented by Sir James M. Barrie in London in 1904. It was a calculated risk, given that the 1953 cartoon movie version by Walt Disney Productions was a big hit that had several memorable tunes of its own such as "You Can Fly."

After many alterations were made, *Peter Pan* tried out in San Francisco. Mary and her husband, Richard Halliday, hired composer Moose Charlap and lyricist Carolyn Leigh to write four songs to augment the show after hearing Frank Sinatra sing the duo's composition "Young at Heart" on the radio. Charlap and Leigh created "I'm Flying," "I've Got to Crow," "I Won't Grow Up" and "Tender Shepherd." But the play opened to dismal reviews, and some of Martin's friends recommended she abandon it to prevent a disaster.

Instead, the principals decided that what was wrong was that *Peter Pan* was not a full-blown musical. To that end, Robbins, who did not feel comfortable with Charlap and Leigh, enlisted his friends, composer Jule Styne and lyricists Betty Comden and Adolph Green, to supplement the score with their own works. Their tunes included "Never-Never Land," "Distant Melody," "Ugg-a-Wugg," "Wendy," "Mysterious Lady" and "Captain Hook's Waltz."

With these additions plus a deliciously campy portrayal of Hook by Cyril Ritchard, this version finally took flight. After a tryout in Los Angeles, *Peter Pan* opened on Broadway on Oct. 20, 1954, to rapturous reviews. It ran 152 performances through Feb. 26, 1955, before taking a break to rehearse it as a live TV show to air on March 7, 1955 — the first time ever that the original cast of a stage musical performed the entire show on TV.

This occurred because Martin wanted *Peter Pan* to be seen by the widest audience of children available, and as luck would have it, NBC began a monthly series on Oct. 18, 1954, called *Producers' Showcase* that presented Broadway plays. For a half-million dollars, NBC bought the rights to air it. Due to time constraints for commercials, the show had to cut out 17 minutes of material (mostly second choruses of songs), but when it debuted, it had the largest TV audience up to that point for an entertainment show and gave NBC its first ratings victory against its CBS competition *I Love Lucy*.

Peter Pan was named Program of the Year at the Emmy Awards, with Martin named best actress in a single performance. Emmy nominations went to Ritchard for best supporting actor and Robbins for choreography. (Martin and Ritchard won Tony Awards for their Broadway performances.) The show was such a success on TV that it was recreated live again on *Producers' Showcase* on Jan. 9, 1956, with Martin and Ritchard back in costume. The network stored all the original sets in hopes of producing a third go-round, although that would not take place for a few years at the two leads pursued other roles.

Then NBC made an offer too good to refuse: They could videotape the musical so that Martin and Ritchard would not have to repeat their roles ever again. The network also came to Martin with an early evening time slot sold to a sponsor and studio space in Brooklyn to tape the production, and all that won her over. She also agreed to a deal that when the show was repeated, she would receive 50 percent of her original fee.

So in 1960, Martin rehearsed and taped *Peter Pan* for four weeks between her performances on Broadway of *The Sound of Music* (see 76) at NBC's color studios in Brooklyn. This setup forced her to get an apartment in that borough during that period to handle her rigorous schedule. She rehearsed from 11 A.M. through 6 P.M. during her *Sound of Music* non-matinee days of Mondays, Tuesdays, Thursdays and Fridays. Her husband served as executive producer.

As for Ritchard, NBC wanted him to return so much that they bought out his contract for a play in Australia to have him rejoin the project. Jerome Robbins' original choreography and staging from the Broadway show was retained, as was the music and plot. The latter included a memorable moment when Peter Pan speaks to home viewers directly and implores them to clap to save the life of Tinkerbell when the fairy drinks poison that Captain Hook planned for Peter to consume.

John Lesko conducted the orchestra for the 1960 show. The main supporting cast remained the same as in 1955 and 1956 except for the roles of Wendy, John and Michael, who naturally had to be recast as the original actors were now too old.

The show finished second for the week behind *Gunsmoke* (see 24). It pre-empted the regularly scheduled *Outlaws*, *Bat Masterson* and *Bachelor Father* that night. There were no Emmy nominations for it this time, apparently because voters thought they had honored it enough during the mid–1950s.

NBC repeated the musical on Feb. 9, 1963, and March 2, 1973, each time to large audiences. That recurring appearance was a mixed blessing to one of its participants. "Frankly, I'm tired of being associated with Tiger Lily," Sondra Lee confessed in *Sing Out Louise!* by Dennis McGovern and Deborah Grace Winer. "But the attention to that production is unwavering, unflagging. People still recognize me and stop me on the street. I finally changed my hair from blonde to red."

On Dec. 12, 1976, NBC unveiled a remake of *Peter Pan* with Mia Farrow in the lead and Danny Kaye as Hook. This *Hallmark Hall of Fame* presentation was telecast as part of *The Big Event* (the name NBC gave its series of Sunday night specials; for its highest-rated offering, see *Gone With the Wind* at 6). It received only so-so numbers of 18.0/27 and scored poorly with the critics, even though it somehow received an Emmy nomination for Best Children's Special. It has seldom been seen since, whereas the reputation of the Mary Martin *Peter Pan* remained strong enough to spur its release on home video by the 1980s.

Despite Martin's popularity via *Peter Pan*, the actress had only a limited association with TV until her death in 1990, with her most in-depth involvement being as co-host of *Over Easy*, a public television series geared for senior citizens, from 1981 until its cancellation in 1983. By that time, her success with *Peter Pan* on TV had become overshadowed by a bigger one featuring her son, actor Larry Hagman, as its star. For details on his triumph, see *Dallas* at 2.

92 — *Brian's Song*

Nov. 30, 1971 (*ABC Movie of the Week*). **Rating:** 32.9. **Share:** 48.

Aired on ABC Tuesday 8:30–10 P.M. Eastern and Pacific, 7:30–9 P.M. Central

Competition: *Hawaii Five-O* and *Cannon* (first half-hour) on CBS, *The Funny Side* and *Nichols* (first half-hour) on NBC

Cast: James Caan (Brian Piccolo), Billy Dee Williams (Gale Sayers), Jack Warden (Coach George Halas), Shelly Fabares (Joy Piccolo), Judy Pace (Linda Sayers), Bernie Casey (J.C. Caroline), David Huddleston (Ed McCaskey), the Chicago Bears players and crew (Themselves). **Crew:** Paul Junger Witt (producer), Buzz Kulik (director), William Blinn (writer).

Synopsis. In 1965, Gale Sayers wins a spot on the Chicago Bears football team and learns that in the interest of integration, he is to be the first black to room with a Caucasian, Brian Piccolo, another rookie pro fullback. In their first season together, Gale excels and wins the attention and the awards, while Brian becomes a good friend. When Gale twists his leg during a game, Brian sets up rehab equipment at Sayers' home and works out with him to get his buddy back into shape quickly. Brian says he wants to beat him for his spot on the team fair and square, so that everyone knows he deserves the position.

After Gale successfully recuperates, he notices that Brian is losing a little weight and coughing hard during a game. Bears coach George Halas feels that Brian is not giving 100 percent any more and tells Brian to see a doctor. Halas tells Gale that Brian has cancer and will undergo an operation to remove part of his right lung. A tearful Gale tells the rest of the team about Brian's condition and suggests that they sign the game ball and deliver it to him in the hospital. The operation did not catch all the tumor, and the cancer spreads. Gale tells Brian he loves him and hugs his wife Linda and Brian's wife Judy before Brian passes away at age 26.

Backstory. To many critics and TV fans, *Brian's Song* was the first TV-movie that gave the genre legitimacy as an art form. Although there had been nearly 200 feature-length (90-minute or longer, counting commercials) films created for the medium by the time this aired, they were regarded largely as inferior to theatrical releases, with many of them serving as either pilots for potential series or weak remakes of evergreen entertainment offerings. Indeed, there were relatively few Emmy nominations for them through 1971, and none had claimed the statuette in the Outstanding Single Program — Drama or Comedy category, as *Hallmark Hall of Fame* specials earned them instead.

This belief changed in the wake of *Brian's Song.* The moving production won five Emmys out of 11 nominations, including Single Program — Drama or Comedy, Supporting Actor (Jack Warden), Writing Achievement in Drama, Cinematography and Film Editing. It might have claimed one more had the leads, James Caan and Billy Dee Williams, not competed against each other for Outstanding Actor. If that was not enough, writer William Blinn received a Peabody Award for Outstanding Achievement in Entertainment (another first for a TV-movie), and the telemovie became the first to be released later in movie theaters. Clearly plenty of people were impressed by this song.

The story grew out of talks between Gale Sayers and Al Silverman, then the editor of *Sport* magazine. Silverman thought there were the makings of a book in the friendship Sayers had with Brian Piccolo and their life stories.

Both men were distinguished athletes. Prior to joining the Bears, Piccolo led the nation in rushing and scoring his senior year at Wake Forest University in Winston-Salem, North Carolina, while Sayers set several records at Kansas University in Lawrence. Drafted #1 to go to the Kansas City Chiefs, Sayers instead went with the Bears due to his desire to work under coach George Halas. Coincidentally, Piccolo came to Chicago at the same time as a free agent. The two men had met previously at the College All-Star game before going pro.

The resulting book, *I Am Third* by Sayers with Silverman, came out in 1971. Later, the script for the telefilm adaptation was approved by Sayers and by Piccolo's widow Joy. Louis Gossett, Jr., was originally slated to play Sayers in the film. Sayers was concerned when he noticed that Williams (Gossett's replacement) was rangier than him in size, and he ran slower than Caan in real life. But careful camera angles and editing concealed the latter fact.

As for Caan, he had played football at Michigan State in the 1960s, but he never saw much action on the team before turning his focus to acting. He turned down the role three times because it came after he filmed *The Godfather* (see 27), which was expected to be a big hit that would lead him to a major career in features; his managers thought being on a TV-movie had a stigma attached to it.

The first day of filming centered on Brian and Gale meeting. Joy Piccolo was on the set and started crying because Caan's mannerisms reminded her of her late husband. Meanwhile, Williams found that he and Sayers shared an introspective quality, and the two became friends.

The movie used some archive footage of the Bears in action. The main actors appeared in scenes filmed at Notre Dame Stadium when the Bears took on Cleveland, with Judy Pace and Shelly Fabares in the stands and Caan, Williams and Jack Warden on the sidelines in costume. The training camp sequences were filmed at St. Joseph's College at Rensselaer, Indiana, while the interiors were shot in Los Angeles. The Sayers' home may have appeared familiar to astute TV viewers: It was the set used for *Bewitched* with only slight alterations, as both that series and this TV-movie were productions of Screen Gems.

The emotional scenes presented challenges to all involved, but they carried them off without a hitch. Everyone was in peak form. Williams' locker room speech to the team about Brian's deteriorating condition remains a tearjerker, particularly knowing that several Bears players who knew Piccolo participated in recreating that event.

The show finished second in the weekly ratings behind *All in the Family* (see 25). After it aired, Screen Gems took out an ad in the Dec. 22, 1971, issue of *Variety* with 27 citations heaping praise on the production. One was a comment from sportscaster Howard Cosell on his ABC radio show: "[It] makes you proud to be a member of the human race."

The impact of *Brian's Song* extended to the music charts. Michel LeGrand's instrumental theme made the *Billboard* top 60 listings in 1972. Unbelievably, his memorable score lost the Emmy to John Williams' now-forgotten compositions for "Jane Eyre," a *Bell System Family Theatre* special. It did better at the Grammys, winning for Best Instrumental Composition.

Besides LeGrand, Caan and Williams, other Emmy nominations were for directing, film sound editing and film sound mixing. It was the highest-rated TV-movie shown on the *ABC Movie of the Week* since that series began on Sept. 23, 1969 — but it was topped less than two months later by *The Night Stalker* (see 84). Nonetheless, its large number of viewers helped the series to finish the 1971-1972 season with its highest ratings average at #5. The series' popularity dropped dramatically after that, and the *ABC Movie of the Week* was cancelled in 1975.

On Nov. 21, 1972, ABC reran *Brian's Song* on the *ABC Movie of the Week* to incredibly strong numbers of 30.4/48, making it the highest-rated TV-movie on the network during the 1972-1973 season. Three more times thereafter, ABC repeated the film, on Nov. 14, 1973 (23.1/35), Nov. 9, 1974 (14.7/25) and May 14, 1976 (14.1/27).

On Dec. 2, 2001, ABC presented a remake with Sean Maher as Piccolo and Mekhi Phifer as Sayers. Although more realistic in depicting the ravages of cancer on Brian's body, this effort largely lacked the emotional resonance of its predecessor. Although its ratings were okay (9.1/14), there were no Emmy nominations, and it did not become a favorite repeat. Seven years later, the 2008 Emmy awards included the original movie's scene of Gale visiting Brian in the hospital as one of the top 10 classic moments in dramatic television for viewers to choose as their favorite.

Piccolo's legacy remains in place with the Chicago Bears, who named an annual player courage award after him, and at his alma mater Wake Forest University, which established a cancer fund drive to work on research and treatment for the disease. Sayers retired at the end of the 1971 football season due to injuries, and he was inducted into the Pro Football Hall of Fame in 1977. He has since devoted much of his time to the support of philanthropic activities.

91—*Dallas Cowboys Cheerleaders*

January 14, 1979 (*ABC Sunday Night Movie*). **Rating:** 33.8. **Share:** 51.

Aired on ABC Sunday 9–11 P.M. Eastern and Pacific, 8–10 P.M. Central

Competition: *Kaz* (last show in this time slot) and *Dallas* on CBS; *Centennial* (second of two hours) and *Weekend* on NBC

Cast: Jane Seymour (Laura Cole), Laraine Stephens (Susan Mitchell), Bert Convy (Lyman Spencer), Bucky Dent (Kyle Jessop), Dallas Cowboys Cheerleaders (Themselves), Pamela Susan Shoop (Betty Denton), Ellen Bry (Joanne Vail), Jenifer Shaw (Kim Everly), Katherine Baumann (Ginny O'Neil), Lauren Tewes (Jessie Mathews). **Crew:** Robert Hamner (co-executive producer-writer), James T. Aubrey (co-executive producer), Bruce Bilson (producer-director).

Synopsis. Magazine editor Lyman Spencer notices how TV cameras train themselves more on the Dallas Cowboy Cheerleaders during football games than the players, and how many men fantasize about them. To boost sales, he decides that a profile of them will be the cover story on his monthly publication. He enlists reporter Laura Cole, who just happens to be an ex-flame of his, to go undercover, win a spot on the cheerleading squad and do an exposé that will make the next issue a hot seller. Cole puts aside her dislike of Spencer and plunges into her assignment.

During the tryouts, Cole learns that there are plenty of shenanigans which can provide some juicy reading, despite the efforts of stern Susan Mitchell to keep the women in line. For example, Joanne Vail thinks she is too good for the likes of Kyle Jessop, whose best days as a football player are behind him but nevertheless hopes to mount a comeback with the Cowboys. And poor, sweet Jessie Matthews is trying to avoid a man who wants to force her to pose naked in pictures by using his knowledge about skeletons in her closet.

The more Cole learns about the plights of those involved, the less she wants to reveal their heartaches to the world. She decides to put Spencer in his place and let him know what a great organization the Dallas Cowboy Cheerleaders are — after she makes it to the final roster, of course.

Backstory. It was not enough in early 1979 that the city of Dallas had its own hit soap opera on TV named after it (see 2). It also had to become part of the title of one of the mindless features made for the medium, designed to show off scantily clad women bouncing in outfits that emphasized their breasts and buttocks. It was more of a tease than a TV-movie, yet it turned out to be the most popular of its genre to air in the 1978-1979 season, to the dismay of anyone with taste.

Actually, the Dallas Cowboys Cheerleaders themselves created plenty of consternation on their own when they debuted in stadiums in 1972 as the first professional squad on the NFL sidelines. With lower necklines and tied tops that exposed an ample amount of cleavage and navels, and tighter shorts that emphasized every curve in the legs, they looked like they belonged in sexy movies, particularly when they gyrated to the tunes. The fact that they appeared mere feet away from Tom Landry, perhaps the most strait-laced and taciturn of all pro football coaches, created an even more mind-boggling juxtaposition.

It was publicity-seeking Dallas general manager Tex Schramm who made the change with the cheerleaders and not Landry. In 1975, Schramm's secretary Suzanne Mitchell expanded her duties by becoming the cheerleading squad's manager and agent. She promoted them as half wholesome and half suggestive. "Sports has always had a very clean, almost Puritanical aspect about it, but at the same time, sex is a very important part of our lives. What we've done is combine the two," she told Bruce Newman in *Sports Illustrated*.

TV crews began spending an inordinate amount of time capturing the cheerleaders in action. An indignant woman wrote to newspaper advice columnist Ann Landers complaining about the "sexier and more naked cheerleaders" on display, and Landers was in agreement with her, saying that this development was a sign of the "last gasps of a dying civilization."

All the controversy did was stir up more interest in the squad every year. In 1976 there were 250 applicants for 37 spots on the team. Two years later, that pool more than quadrupled to 1,053 hopefuls trying out. That sort of popularity naturally led to all the other NFL teams copycatting the Dallas model, with the Baltimore Colts being so obvious in following the originals that they wore almost identical outfits. "Everyone's trying to out–Dallas Dallas," Atlanta Falcons assistant general manager Curt Mosher grumbled to Newman, but his franchise followed suit as well.

What is most amazing about this trend is that at the time, the Dallas Cowboys Cheerleaders earned only $14.12 per game per person, had to clean their own uniforms and were out of the squad if they missed two practices. This situation naturally created a huge economic disparity between them and the rich players they encouraged fans to support, but there was no one really stepping in to suggest that the cheerleaders unionize and improve their lot.

It was natural in the sex-obsessed world of television in the late 1970s that the cheerleaders would also appear outside their football games. The first major exposure occurred on Sept. 4, 1978, when ABC aired *The 36 Most Beautiful Girls in Texas*, an hour-long special seen before *Monday Night Football* in the Eastern and Central time zones and after the game in most other markets. Hosted by Hal Linden, the rather perplexing lineup of guests included Billy Crystal (who did his Howard Cosell impersonation), Melinda Naud (star of ABC's ill-fated *Operation Petticoat* sitcom), Charles Nelson Reilly and Joey Travolta, John's virtually forgotten brother.

Four months later, *Dallas Cowboys Cheerleaders* sashayed onto ABC's movie lineup and scored a victory so huge it helped *The ABC Sunday Night Movie* finish at #15 for the 1978-1979 season. Bert Convy managed to snag a "special guest star" designation, while Bucky Dent was credited for a "special appearance," even though the latter was hardly an actor, or a football player, for that matter. (For the uninitiated, he was a major league baseball shortstop from 1973 to 1984, winning the 1978 MVP award for his efforts in the World Series. Why he was cast for this apart from his name value is hard to say.)

Helping the movie's ratings was the fact that the real Dallas Cowboys defeated the Los Angeles Rams 28–0 for the NFC conference championship a week earlier and scored an impressive 39.1/56 for CBS. Alas, Dallas would lose to Pittsburgh in a great Super Bowl match-up the following week on NBC, 35–31, which as of this writing is the fifth highest-rated Super Bowl ever with a 47.1/74 (see Appendix A for more details).

While its ratings were impressive, it actually finished third in the weekly standings, behind the highest rating ever for *Mork & Mindy* (see 65) and then *Laverne & Shirley* (see 56) at number two. Still, the fact such froth—and even that may be too heavy a word to describe *Dallas Cowboys Cheerleaders*—had such a huge turnout was seen as a discouraging sign of the times about the quality of late 1970s TV programming. It would take nearly five years until another TV-movie scored higher ratings than *Dallas Cowboys Cheerleaders* (see 8—*The Day After*). A sarcastic, jaded ABC executive commenting about its success understandably did not want to have the following quote attributed to him in *TV Guide*, even though it was quite telling: "My faith in human nature has been restored."

There were no Emmy nominations for *Dallas Cowboys Cheerleaders* (big surprise, eh?), but its enormous popularity guaranteed there would be a follow-up. The sequel, *Dallas Cowboys Cheerleaders II*, debuted nearly a year to the date on ABC Jan. 13, 1980, with Laraine Stephens being the only cast member from the original to return. This time she monitored the squad as they faced the rigors of performing both at the Super Bowl and on a USO tour. The executive producers remained the same (Robert Hamner and James T. Aubrey—the same Aubrey who had been thrown out of the CBS presidency in 1965 after a controversial tenure that included reports he favored having sexy women on the network's series), but Michael O'Herlihy was director and Stephen Kandel was writer. Most of the cast were little-known actors with the exception of John Davidson in the lead.

For whatever reason, be it overexposure or people's memories of the sheer awfulness of the first movie, *Dallas Cowboys Cheerleaders II* was a disappointment, racking up respectable but not blockbuster numbers of 20.5/32. And when ABC reran the original *Dallas Cowboys Cheerleaders* on Aug. 22, 1980, it garnered a rather weak 11.2/22. There would be no *Dallas Cowboys Cheerleaders III* or TV series.

While the squad continues going strong on the sidelines at football games, the TV-movies they inspired have not as of this writing been released for home viewing. Unless you like hackneyed dialogue and plotting, poor acting and low production values broken up by seductive dance moves, that's probably for the best.

90—*Return to Mayberry*

April 13, 1986 (*NBC Sunday Night Movie* TV-movie).
Rating: 33.0. **Share:** 49.
Aired on NBC Sunday 9–11 P.M. Eastern and Pacific, 8–10 P.M. Central

Competition: *The Man with the Golden Gun* (repeat of 1974 movie) on ABC, *Dream West* (part one of four-part miniseries) on CBS

Cast: Andy Griffith (Andy Taylor), Ron Howard (Opie Taylor), Don Knotts (Barney Fife), Jim Nabors (Gomer Pyle), Aneta Corsaut (Helen Crump Taylor), Jack Dodson (Howard Sprague), George Lindsey (Goober Pyle), Betty Lynn (Thelma Lou), Howard Morris (Ernest T. Bass), Maggie Peterson-Mancuso (Charlene Darling), Denver Pyle (Briscoe Darling), Hal Smith (Otis Campbell), Richard Lineback (Wally Butler). **Crew:** Andy Griffith, Dean Hargrove, Richard O. Linke, Robin S. Clark (executive producer), Bob Sweeney (director), Harvey Bullock, Everett Greenbaum (writers).

Synopsis. Andy Taylor quits his job in Cleveland and heads to Mayberry but car trouble forces him to stop at a gas station run by his old pals, Goober and Gomer Pyle. He is officially back in town to see his son, Opie, and Opie's wife Eunice as they are about to have a child, but his real intention is to run for sheriff again. The trouble is that his friend and former deputy, Barney Fife, wants to do the same. Opie edits the local newspaper, where Andy's buddy Howard Sprague works part time, and former drunk Otis is now an ice cream man. Meanwhile, Wally Butler, a conniving motel and restaurant owner, enlists prankster Ernest T. Bass in a plot to create "the Mayberry Monster" at Myers Lake to encourage tourism.

Andy runs into Barney's old flame Thelma Lou and encourages her to meet Barney again, and the two rekindle their romance. But Barney is envious of how people still call Andy sheriff, and he goes overboard warning people about the Myers Lake "sea monster." Andy knows he needs to take charge, particularly now that his wife, Helen, has arrived to say she is ready to move back to Mayberry. Bass confesses, and Andy hatches a successful plan to expose Wally and have Barney take the credit. Barney tells the town to write in Andy's name for sheriff and then weds Thelma Lou.

Backstory. *The Andy Griffith Show* (1960–1968), this reunion telemovie and two other spin-offs all made this top 100 listing. For *The Andy Griffith Show*, see 79; the spin-offs are *Gomer Pyle, U.S.M.C.* (see 55) and *Mayberry R.F.D.* (see 50). Clearly America loved the fictional town of Mayberry, North Carolina, particularly from the 1960s through the 1980s.

Although reunions of TV casts stretch back all the way to 1967 with *The Danny Thomas Show*, the nostalgia trend did not go into full gear until 1985, with the regulars on *Perry Mason, I Dream of Jeannie* and *Peyton Place* re-teamed for new TV-movies. However, that activity was not the reason behind putting together the principals for *The Andy Griffith Show* again.

The idea behind the reunion occurred to Griffith when he, Don Knotts and Ron Howard appeared as presenters at the 1983 Emmy Awards. "I was surprised at the amount of audience laughter," Griffith recalled to Jane Hall in *People* magazine. The favorable reception from the audience made an impression on him and, eating dinner after the ceremony with the other men, he proposed reviving their characters one more time. Both men responded enthusiastically, even though they were busy with projects that would preclude them from participating immediately. Knotts was a regular on *Three's Company* (see 37), while Howard was preparing to direct the 1984 feature film *Splash*.

Everyone's schedules finally allowed them to film a new TV-movie over 19 days in early 1986. (It helped that executive producer Dean Hargrove was producing Griffith's current series *Matlock*, and was able to coordinate filming between the two projects.) Because the original sets had been demolished following the cancellation of *Mayberry R.F.D.* in 1971, the town's exteriors were recreated at Los Olivos, a three-block-long community in California with a population of 350.

At least one star of the movie admitted he was worried about trying to recapture the magic of a series that was still in reruns in more than 70 markets across America after going off nearly 20 years earlier. "I was tossing and turning because I was nervous about this," Howard told *Time* magazine. "I'm so relieved that the feelings are good."

Griffith was more sanguine, telling the same publication, "It's like we finished the old show on Friday and started this one on Monday." He was pleased when Howard asked his advice on how to play one scene.

Howard and Griffith looked the most visibly different from their 1960s selves in the special, with Griffith now having gray hair and Howard not only tall and grown up but also sporting a mustache. On the other hand, there was George Lindsey, who was a regular on *Hee Haw* at the time of the filming, wearing pretty much his same outfit from *Andy Griffith Show* days as he did on *Hee Haw*. "They're going to have to bury me in my Goober hat," Lindsey told Jane Hall in *People*.

There were reports that Gomer (Jim Nabors) would be shown singing in the choir, but if filmed, those scenes were cut. Instead, Nabors shared most of his scenes with Lindsey, and they both seemed somewhat wasted here.

Return to Mayberry is a rather variable TV-movie, with some great moments and others that should have been dropped from consideration. The chief error is the Mayberry monster plot; Goober, Gomer and even Barney appear denser than they already are when they see a dummy dragon head stick out of the water and a couple of oversized prints in the ground. It is overextended, probably to help with the movie's running time, and features a cardboard villain with Wally Butler, who is devious but not intimidating. The best episodes of *The Andy Griffith Show* had Barney facing an opponent who was mentally and/or physically imposing to him until Andy rescued him; here, Andy is just stopping a self-centered jerk who is never a credible threat. He is considered so pathetic that even Andy refuses to arrest him, telling him instead to redeem himself. Huh?

Another botched scene was a visit to Aunt Bee's grave, which had a poorly done imitation voiceover that should have been deleted. Bee's portrayer, Frances Bavier, was still alive during the filming, but she did not want to end her retirement living in Siler City, North Carolina. And speaking of Siler City, the idea that this real town of less than 10,000 people would have its own TV station to cover a story on Barney is more amusing than some of the script's intentional jokes. I also could have done without revisiting the Darlings, a family of yokels in the backwoods (including the musical group the Dillards) seen in a few early 1960s shows; they seem more in line with the stereotyped comical Southerners in *The Beverly Hillbillies* (see 12) than *The Andy Griffith Show*.

On the plus side, the show retains the original's deliberate, laidback pace, particularly in the comic byplay between Griffith and Knotts. It was wise not to trot out Otis doing his drunk routine and locking himself in the jail as protection — that just would have been pathetic and stretched credulity, and besides, Hal Smith looked adorable driving an ice cream truck. And it corrected one of the original series' few injustices among fans by finally marrying Barney and Thelma Lou.

Howard is as friendly as ever as Opie, and the decision to have his character leave town with his wife and kid to enjoy a better-paying job in New York is an encouraging development that there is indeed life outside Mayberry. Finally, one quote Griffith provided as Taylor when toasting Barney and Thelma Lou's marriage was pithy and appropriate in terms of the show's bond with its audience: "There's something about Mayberry and Mayberry folk — it never leaves you. No matter where life takes you, you always carry in your heart memories of old times and old friends."

Against an often-repeated James Bond film on ABC and a new CBS miniseries that few cared to follow, *Return to Mayberry* finished #2 for the week behind *The Cosby Show* (see 22). NBC repeated it on Aug. 25, 1987, with so-so results (12.8/22).

CBS ran two more get-togethers after this one. The first was *The Andy Griffith Show Reunion* (Feb. 10, 1993), which was mostly a series of interviews from the regulars and celebrity fans of the show. A decade later, *The Andy Griffith Show: Back to Mayberry* (Nov. 11, 2003) had Griffith, Howard, Knotts and Nabors reminiscing on a set replicating the old courthouse, with clips from the original series' first four seasons only (the ones with Knotts, which Griffith thought were the best) and short appearances on film by guests like Howard Morris. It finished #1 for the week, proving that people still love Mayberry.

If you are one of those people, by the way, visit Mt. Airy, North Carolina, near the Virginia border at the foothills of the mountains. It's Griffith's hometown that inspired the show, and they celebrate that fact heartily.

89 — *60 Minutes*

Jan. 20, 1980. **Rating:** 33.0. **Share:** 50.
Aired on CBS Sunday 8–9 P.M. Eastern and 7–8 P.M. Central (approximately), 7–8 P.M. Pacific
Hosts: Mike Wallace, Harry Reasoner, Dan Rather.

Crew: Don Hewitt (executive producer), Nancy Lea, Richard Clark, Philip Scheffler (producers).

Synopsis. After the traditional ticking of a stopwatch is interrupted by previews of the night's stories, and then a pause for commercials, the following segments aired on this edition of TV's most watched newsmagazine:

• "Bette Davis" is a profile of the legendary actress, with Mike Wallace interviewing the subject as well as her daughter, Barbara Davis "B.D." Hyman, her adopted son, Michael Merrill, and her fellow thespian and co-star in many films at Warner Bros. studios in the 1930s, Joan Blondell, who died less than a month before this aired. As always, Davis is frank. This piece won an Emmy.

• "The Thunderbirds" is the name of the U.S. Air Force precision flying team. Harry Reasoner not only interviews pilots Maj. John Kazier and Capt. R.D. Evans, he even gets to ride with them in formation in the air, accompanied with cinematography and musical accompaniment worthy of a film playing a theater. The series repeated this story after four members of the team died in a training exercise in Nevada on Jan. 18, 1982.

• "PDAP" stands for the Palmer Drug Abuse Program in Houston, which gained national attention in 1979 when Carol Burnett's daughter, Carrie Hamilton, went into treatment for her addiction at the facility when she was just 15. Dan Rather discusses the program with PDAP founder Bob Meehan.

Backstory. What a kick it is to report that television's longest-running and best newsmagazine was also the highest-rated show ever to follow a Super Bowl. It was a vindication of a show most people had written off when it debuted on Sept. 24, 1968, when it finished consistently far behind *Marcus Welby, M.D.* (see 40) in its first years. But when it moved to Sundays from 6–7 P.M. in January 1972, following the end of the football season, it gradually built momentum; exposure at the Sunday 9:30–10:30 P.M. slot during the summers of 1974 and 1975 was very beneficial to it.

By the summer of 1975, industry observers were surprised to note that *60 Minutes* had finished as the third-most popular series during that season, scoring ratings never associated with a network news series. In December 1975 CBS moved it to 7 P.M. and kept it on year round, and in 1976, the series won a prestigious Peabody Award "as a program which clearly indicates there is a large and important audience for serious broadcast journalism." Though its overall rating that season of #52 was not spectacular, it was higher than any other news program had ever received, and it zoomed up to #18 in the following season (1976-1977). It has remained in the top 30 ever since. Imre Horvath, a *60 Minutes* producer until he left CBS in 1980, told Irv Broughton in *Producers on Producing* that having good interviews is essential to effective segments on the series.

60 Minutes has been a very effective post–Super Bowl show. CBS first ran it after Super Bowl V in 1972, when it received a solid 20.3 rating and 36 share. The network ran *The New Perry Mason* two years later, which bombed with a 12.7/20, then tried the Phoenix Golf Open (16.5/31) in 1976 and *All in the Family* (30.4/47) in 1978 before *60 Minutes* its 1980 record-setting appearance. In 1982 the program slipped a little but still finished strong with a 26.2/36, but CBS didn't air it after the Super Bowl again until 1992, when it earned a 16.8/30. It has not followed the Super Bowl since, but continues to draw large audiences on Sunday nights for CBS.

Beginning in 1979 with *Brothers and Sisters* on NBC, the networks have alternated launching new shows or specials after the Super Bowl, usually with poor results for the former. Besides *Brothers and Sisters*, *MacGruder & Loud* (ABC, 1985), *Grand Slam* (CBS, 1990) and *Davis Rules* (ABC, 1991) all bombed, which led the networks to try airing special episodes of regular series including the lowest performer to date, *Alias* in 2003 (10.6 rating, 20 share), which ABC unwisely delayed starting until after 11 P.M. Eastern time.

88 — *Ben Casey*

Jan. 21, 1963 ("A Cardinal Act of Mercy," second of two parts). **Rating:** 33.0. **Share:** n/a.

Aired on ABC Monday 10–11 P.M. Eastern and Pacific, 9–10 P.M. Central

Competition: *The New Loretta Young Show* and *Stump the Stars* on CBS; *David Brinkley's Journal* on NBC

Cast: Vincent Edwards (Dr. Ben Casey), Sam Jaffe (Dr. David Zorba), Bettye Ackerman (Dr. Maggie Graham), Henry Landers (Dr. Ted Hoffman), Jeanne Bates (Nurse Wills). **Guests:** Kim Stanley (Faith Parsons), Gary Crosby (Harold Spencer), Glenda Farrell (Martha Morrison), Timmy Everett (Willy Morrison). **Crew:** James Moser (executive producer), Matthew Rapf (producer), Sydney Pollack (director), Norman Katkov (writer).

Synopsis. Once again, as it tends to happen every week, chief resident neurosurgeon Ben Casey in-

volves himself intimately with a patient at County General Hospital. This time it is lawyer Faith Parsons, a heroin addict who undergoes surgery for a spinal tumor. She makes a noticeably poor impression on some members of the staff with her bossy nature. While Dr. Casey placates Parsons by conceding to all her demands for morphine while recuperating, his mentor, Dr. David Zorba, realizes that she is craving pain medication more than what is required during recovery and orders her supply cut off.

But Parsons is clever and tricks Willy Morrison, the son of fellow hospital patient Martha Morrison, into getting her the drugs she needs. Casey decides the best method of treatment is to make Parsons quit cold turkey. During his time with Parsons, Casey learns about her father's demanding, perfectionist tendencies, and he surmises that the pressure of that situation might have resulted in her drug use. While the recovery is harrowing, Parsons survives and leaves County General to reenter society. The show ends on a cautionary note as Casey and Zorba discuss the fact that only one percent of all addicts are fully cured.

Backstory. This two-part episode of ABC's only top 10 hit series in the 1962-1963 season marked the first filmed TV role for its acclaimed lead guest star Kim Stanley, a much-admired stage actress. (Check out a tribute to her work by her colleagues that appeared in the 2004 documentary movie *Broadway: The Golden Age*, available on DVD.) Stanley needed the extra money the work would provide her. The part might have appealed to her because it struck close to home: In real life Stanley was an alcoholic with a domineering dad.

But Stanley had a phobia of performing before cameras. Director Sydney Pollack told Jon Krampner in *Female Brando: The Legend of Kim Stanley* that, to expedite things, "I shot three cameras, sometimes four, at the same time, so I could combine the close-up, medium shot, master shot, over-the-shoulder shot, whatever, so she wouldn't have to match anything." All that left Pollack to do was edit film from each camera for the final product. Apart from Stanley suffering from laryngitis that put her in bed for two working days, there were no major difficulties in shooting the episode, and the result won praise from many quarters.

At the 1963 Emmys the series claimed its only two statuettes (out of 13 nominations total during its run) for this episode, for Stanley for lead and Glenda Farrell for support. Pollack and writer Norman Katkov received nominations for this episode, along with the series' editing team for their overall work that season. Despite previous nods for contention in such categories as best drama, actor (Vince Edwards) and supporting actor (Sam Jaffe) in 1962, *Ben Casey* would spend the rest of its life shut out from Emmy competition.

The Emmy wins capped the best season ever for *Ben Casey*, which became ABC's first top 10 hit to air on Monday nights when it finished at #7 for 1962–1963 — and it remained the only series with that status until movies and *Rich Man, Poor Man* both cracked the list in 1976. Indeed, *Ben Casey* was like a beacon of light for ABC in 1962–1963, as its next highest-rated series that season was *Wagon Train* (see 48) all the way down at #25. It was the worst overall performance by the network in five years. The fact that *Ben Casey*'s lead-in was the weakly rated *Stoney Burke* makes its popularity even more impressive.

While it was not a big draw when it began on Oct. 2, 1961 (CBS had its long-running game show *I've Got a Secret* against its last half-hour in its first year), *Ben Casey* exploded in its second season against weaker competition. Soon, CBS had to deal with the irritating fact that that many viewers of *The Andy Griffith Show* (see 79) were turning the channel after it ended to check out a show featuring what was known as the "surly surgeon."

Edwards beat more than 100 contenders for the lead role. His smoldering dark looks were credited for making this medical series a hit, but in truth all aspects of the production were very professional, and it definitely was never as melodramatic as its NBC medical drama counterpart of the time, *Dr. Kildare*. That series reached its season peak in 1961–1962 at #9. Interestingly, it began and ended its run in the same years as *Ben Casey*.

The series even had an impact on the music charts. Pianist Valjean had a top 30 instrumental hit with "Theme from *Ben Casey*" in 1962. This was followed a few months later by a parody record by Dickie Goodman, "Ben Crazy," which mocked the series' opening lines said by Dr. Zorba (with chalk drawings of symbols for each word), "Man — Woman — Birth — Death — Infinity" by punctuating each word by chuckles after it, along with its other conventions like its dramatic background music. That record fell just short of the top 40. Edwards himself attempted to achieve chart success by releasing some vocal records at the same time, but he wound up only in the bottom third of the Hot 100 with a couple of releases.

The public's enthusiasm for this series eventually dwindled. Seeing that *Ben Casey* was its only top 10 hit in 1962–1963 (actually its only top 20 hit), ABC unwisely decided to relocate it in the fall of 1963 to run opposite the #1 show on TV, *The Beverly Hillbillies* (see 12). The program's ratings sank. ABC tried to resuscitate it by re-installing it at its old Monday slot in the fall of 1964, but its numbers never recovered.

Jaffe left the series at the end of the 1964–1965 season, complaining he had nothing to do any more, but his wife in real life, Bettye Ackerman, remained with it. Replacing him in the role of the experienced physician advising Casey was Franchot Tone as Dr. Daniel Niles Freeland. Stories became serialized in an effort to emulate the success of the hot new nighttime soap opera *Peyton Place*, but audiences stayed low, advertisers bailed out and some stations stopped carrying it.

ABC aired its last episode of *Ben Casey* on March 21, 1966, canning it before summer reruns even though it was airing repeats of the show daily at 1 P.M. Eastern at the same time, and replaced it with *The Avengers*. The daily repeats ended a year later, with the series unable to beat *As the World Turns* on CBS airing against its last half-hour. ABC tried another nighttime medical series three years later, and it was an even bigger hit: *Marcus Welby, M.D.* (see 40).

Edwards, who had directed 12 episodes of *Ben Casey*, continued to pursue that profession as well as act and even tried to continue his singing career, but he never found the same level of success he had here. In 1988 he filmed *The Return of Ben Casey*, a syndicated TV movie that served as a pilot, but since the original black-and-white series had been little seen in the color-dominated TV world since the 1970s, it attracted only a small audience and did not become a series. (*Ben Casey* had been under consideration to return to TV earlier in 1973 as an NBC daytime soap opera, but the network nixed the revival.) Eight years later Edwards died of cancer at age 67.

As for Stanley, her fear of film remained, and she did less than ten movie and TV acting roles in the wake of her Emmy win here. She remained a much-respected actress nonetheless, getting Oscar nominations for best actress for *Seance on a Wet Afternoon* (1964) and supporting actress for *Frances* (1982). After she won another Emmy for playing Big Mama in the 1984 Showtime remake of *Cat on a Hot Tin Roof*, she retired from acting. She died in 2001 at age 76.

Ben Casey remains legally unavailable for home

viewing as of this writing. It is a sad way to treat one of the best hospital dramas ever to air on the medium.

87 — Friends and Nabors

Oct. 12, 1966 (special). **Rating:** 33.0. **Share:** n/a. Aired on CBS Wednesday 9–10 P.M. Eastern and Pacific, 8–9 P.M. Central

Competition: *The Man Who Never Was* and *Peyton Place* on ABC, *Bob Hope Chrysler Theater* on NBC

Cast: Jim Nabors, Andy Griffith, Tennessee Ernie Ford, Shirley Jones, Marilyn Horne, the Nick Castle Dancers, the Alan Copeland Orchestra. **Crew:** Richard O. Linke, Saul Ilson, Ernest Chambers (producers), Saul Ilson, Ernest Chambers (writers), Stan Harris (director).

Synopsis. With American Motors as his sponsor, Jim Nabors appears in his first starring network TV special alongside some very big supporting guests. There is Andy Griffith, his former co-star, who performs a comic variation on Giuseppe Verdi's opera *La Traviata*. Later, a star from that musical genre, Marilyn Horne, sings "Libiamo libiamo" from that opera along with Nabors. The other primary sketch featured Griffith and Tennessee Ernie Ford as hillbillies suddenly without a TV set (Ernie shot the tube when he confused the NBC peacock for a real chicken).

Nabors' big solo was "If My Friends Could See Me Now" from the Broadway musical *Sweet Charity*. Shirley Jones' featured number was "I Have Dreamed" from another theatrical show, *The King and I*. Horne offered "Crude sorte, amor tiranno" from Rossini's *L'Italiana in Algeri*. Beside his previously mentioned duet with Horne, Nabors teamed with Jones to sing "In Their Shoes," which included a Shirley Temple takeoff by Jones. The special's top medley was performed by Nabors and Ford. The two men sang a collection of parts of railroad-themed tunes, including "Down in the Valley," "Wabash Cannonball," "The Rock Island Line," "Drill, Ye Terriers, Drill," "Gandy Dancers' Ball," "John Henry" and "Casey Jones." After Nabors said good night to his millions of viewers, most of them turned off the set or changed channels rather than view *The Danny Kaye Show* following this special.

Backstory. If anyone doubts how popular Jim Nabors was in 1966, consider this fact: Not only did he have the #2 show in America with *Gomer Pyle, U.S.M.C.* (see 55), he also had the third most popular special of the year. Only a special with Bob Hope (see 7) and the second showing of *A Charlie Brown Christmas* (see 61) outranked this show.

Pre-empting the top 10 hits *Green Acres* and *Gomer Pyle, U.S.M.C.*, *Friends and Nabors* was the first step on television to show the world that Nabors could do more than play America's favorite rube in the military. Nabors had employed his resonant baritone vocals on TV a few times before outside of *Gomer Pyle, U.S.M.C.* (and in a couple of episodes of that series, as a matter of fact), but none of those venues allowed him to showcase that talent as well as his acting the way this special did. This was meant to establish him as a personality, not just a comic actor.

Nabors' manager and *Friends and Nabors* executive producer, Richard O. Linke, told William Price Fox, Jr., in that week's *TV Guide* cover story, "I've got another Al Jolson on my hands. You see how I got him dropping down on one knee when he's doing 'Swanee.' He hasn't got that voice throb yet, but it's coming." Linke added that he saw Nabors doing one more year of *Gomer Pyle, U.S.M.C.* before pursuing roles on Broadway and movies. However, he conceded that breaking the image of his hit character would require considerable effort. As he put it, "Going from a warm puppy to a leading man is no easy job."

Variety reviewer "Mor." somewhat condescendingly commented, "Although *Friends [and Nabors]* must have been an unalloyed treat for the sticks viewers, it was not the best vehicle for springing Nabors out of Gomer Pyle role in a more general category of homespun host and entertainer. The show was clearly dominated by the nonpareil C&W [country and western] comedic expertise of guests Tennessee Ernie Ford and Andy Griffith, and Nabors came off looking like his video Marine in soup and fish costume."

Friends and Nabors finished #1 for the week and sparked an unexpected string of hit albums. The LP *Jim Nabors Sings Love Me with All Your Heart* was in record stores when the special aired; it immediately hit the album charts and stayed there more than a year, eventually being certified gold for amassing more than a half million sales. It consisted mostly of covers (remakes of the original songs) and had no singles that made *Billboard*'s Hot 100. He even covered "Swanee" on it, which must have made his manager happy.

Nabors went on to have 12 more albums make the charts over the next six years despite little airplay and no hit singles from them. Two of them were gold-certified, the debut LP *Jim Nabors'*

Christmas Album (1967) and *The Lord's Prayer and Other Sacred Songs* (1968). His chart performance was so strong that Nabors finished in the top 500 of a 2001 ranking of album artists of the last 50 years, ahead of more familiar musical acts such as Jan and Dean, Jim Croce, the Everly Brothers and even Doris Day.

Given this demand for him on vinyl, as well as a desire to escape from Gomer, Nabors starred for CBS in a one-hour sequel to his original special called *Girl Friends and Nabors*. It aired on Thursday, Oct. 24, 1968, at 8 P.M. Eastern and Pacific as a replacement for *Hawaii Five-O* and, as its title implied, it featured only female guest stars: Carol Burnett, Vikki Carr, Mary Costa and Debbie Reynolds. The only crew member from the original special to return was Linke as executive producer. It did well, but was not a ratings blockbuster like the original.

Nabors announced during the 1968-1969 season of *Gomer Pyle, U.S.M.C.* that he would stop doing the incredibly popular series after five years on the air. (In four of those five years it was one of TV's top three series, including 1968-1969.) CBS executives could not convince him to change his mind, even though they did not want to lose a hit. "Jim didn't want do another year," *Gomer Pyle* regular Ronnie Schell recalled in a 2007 interview with Stu Shostak. "He wanted to sing."

The network agreed to do a variety series starring Nabors (in the slot where *Girl Friends and Nabors* ran) the following fall. Nabors insisted that Schell and *Gomer Pyle* co-star Frank Sutton work as regulars on his new series. Schell had played Corp. Duke Slater and Sutton was Pyle's sergeant, Vince Carter, on *Gomer Pyle*. Schell, a comedian before he was an actor, had no problem segueing into the looser nature of the sketches, but Sutton had a less improvisational background, so it took him some time to get accustomed to the new format.

The Jim Nabors Hour debuted Sept. 25, 1969, and though it was no *Gomer Pyle, U.S.M.C.*, it did end its first season a very respectable #12 and forced the cancellation of its NBC competition, the previously successful western *Daniel Boone*. Unfortunately for Nabors, his series had viewers who were predominantly older, poorer and urban than average, all of which were anathema to CBS in 1971 when it decided to purge its schedule of cornpone series like *The Beverly Hillbillies* (see 12) and *Mayberry R.F.D.* (see 50). Even though was a strong second against its white-hot competition *The Flip Wilson Show* (see 94) and completed its second season at a decent #29, CBS cancelled it, with its last program airing May 20, 1971. "There were tears," Schell said of the final taping.

That cancellation seemed to stop all the momentum Nabors had built within the entertainment industry. His singing was out of style with record buyers within a year. In fact, on the May 16, 1983, NBC special *Motown 25*, there were hoots and hollers from the studio audience when Nabors' soulless, over-enunciated take on Stevie Wonder's hit "You Are the Sunshine of My Life" was played.

Linke's hopes of his client making Broadway came to naught, while Nabors' few movie roles were supporting ones in bombs like *Stroker Ace* (1983). His best TV exposure was being the traditional opening guest for every season of *The Carol Burnett Show* through 1978. The few times he worked on a series as a regular, they were one-season misfires: the Saturday morning sitcom *The Lost Saucer* (1975-1976), in which he hated playing an alien, and his 1978 variety effort *The Jim Nabors Show*, which earned him his only Emmy nomination (he lost to Phil Donahue).

Nabors at least has this consolation: Only Elvis Presley, Bing Crosby, Andy Griffith, John Wayne, Carol Burnett, Danny Thomas and Bob Hope had variety specials that rated higher than this one.

---

86 — *A Case of Rape*

Feb. 20, 1974 (TV-movie). **Rating:** 33.1. **Share:** 49.

Aired on NBC Wednesday 9–11 P.M. Eastern and Pacific, 8–10 P.M. Central

Competition: *Cannon* and *Kojak* on CBS, *The Hellstrom Chronicles* (last hour of 90-minute 1971 theatrical film) and *Doc Elliot* on ABC

Cast: Elizabeth Montgomery (Ellen Harrod), Ronny Cox (David Harrod), William Daniels (Leonard Alexander), Cliff Potts (Larry Retzliff), Rosemary Murphy (Muriel Dyer), Patricia Smith (Marge Bracken), Ken Swofford (Det. Riley), Jonathan Lippe (Det. Parker), Alex Hentelhoff (Dr. Goldstone). **Crew:** David Levinson (executive producer), Louis Randolph (producer), Boris Sagal (director), Robert E. Thompson (writer, from a story by Louis Randolph).

Synopsis. Ellen Harrod has a loving relationship with her husband, David. While he is away on business, Ellen attends an adult school program with her friend Marge Bracken, who introduces Ellen to Larry Retzliff. Larry takes the women home, then knocks on Ellen's door, saying he needs to call for help due to car trouble. He proceeds to rape Ellen. Afraid and conflicted in the aftermath, Ellen fails to report the attack to police, but does visit a free clinic where Dr. Goldstone tests her for VD. When her husband comes home, she lacks the nerve to discuss the incident with him. Larry rapes her again in a parking garage, prompting Ellen to report this molestation.

The police treat Ellen dispassionately and callously, questioning her possible motives for claiming rape. Adding to her woes, David is incapable of having sex with her. Her lawyer, Leonard Alexander, tells her that not reporting the first rape makes it harder to convict Larry. The latter's lawyer, Judith Dyer, portrays him favorably and paints Ellen as a promiscuous woman by grilling Ellen about her premarital sex life and other topics. That discussion, along with Larry's lies claiming he had consensual sex with Ellen, leads to his acquittal. The ending narration reveals that Ellen divorced David (whose support for her wavered in the trial), while Larry pled guilty to leaving the scene of another rape and received up to five years in the state penitentiary.

Backstory. Amid a montage of women of all shapes and colors, William Daniels narrates this chilling opening to *A Case of Rape*: "It's estimated that every 12 minutes, a rape occurs somewhere in this country. Fewer than one-fourth of all rapes are reported to the police. There's no typical victim of rape. She may be any age, any race, any background, single, married, divorced. The incidence of rape is rising faster than any other crime of violence." The film then focuses on Elizabeth Montgomery's character as Daniels adds, "This woman is about to become a statistic. She's going to be raped."

A Case of Rape was not the first TV-movie to deal with the subject, but it was without a doubt the pioneer in tackling the violence of the crime and the poor treatment its victims received at the time. This was miles ahead of how pop culture and most of the rest of society then regarded the crime, viewing it more in terms of sexuality and even jesting about it. For example, in the 1973 movie *A Touch of Class*, which was nominated for an Oscar for Best Picture, feminist Glenda Jackson quipped to George Segal, "My one chance to get raped, and you can't get your bloody trousers off."

Filming on the TV-movie began in October 1973. According to *The Los Angeles Times*, the script was based on incidents from the files of the district attorney's office of a large city. Screenwriter Robert E. Thompson previously earned an Oscar nomination for co-writing *They Shoot Horses, Don't They?* (1969).

There was some discussion by NBC officials whether to have Ellen attacked a second time. Elizabeth Montgomery felt that the second attack was integral to the story. Worried that they would lose the popular actress (who ended her eight-year run on the ABC sitcom *Bewitched* in 1972), the scene was retained.

The well-constructed script pulled no punches in depicting the degradations Ellen endured in reporting the rape. The police call for her in the waiting room by asking who is the rape victim. The photographer documenting her bruises acts like a lecher in having her pose for the pictures. She is told several times that the charge of rape is a terrible allegation to make. Det. Riley is especially aggressive in his treatment with Ellen, although he claims to do so to make sure of the veracity of her tale. He questions whether she brought on Larry's treatment of her. "Some women enjoy the idea of rape, of force," he says. He also cautions her against taking Larry to court because of the publicity from it and tells her bluntly, "Even if you win, you lose."

Then there is Leonard Alexander, Ellen's lawyer, who discusses her rape in the open, in a crowded elevator car, which he said he did to prepare her for what she would hear from Judith Dyer when the latter interrogates her on the stand. Ellen wonders just how committed Alexander is when she sees him having a friendly conversation with Dyer while the jury deliberates her case. Ellen gets little support from family and friends.

Tom Selleck (without his trademark mustache) has a bit part as Stan, whose newlywed wife argues with him at a party also attended by Ellen and David (home from his business trip). The other guests tell the Harrods that Stan and his spouse are planning to divorce over cheating allegations, but they are amused and joke that who cares which one did the cheating. David says that he thought the way Stan's wife moved her body encouraged men to have sex with her anyway, a statement which enrages Ellen.

To top it off, it is revealed that Larry had been in police lineups three times before Ellen's case, all on charges of rape and assault, but none of his accusers identified him. That fact, Alexander warns her, cannot be used in court. The jury believes Larry over Ellen, as does her husband to a certain extent. But Ellen grows stronger despite the abuse her character takes in public. "What I said in there about not being guilty, I meant it," she tells David outside the courtroom with him during deliberations. "And nobody is going to shame me into believing otherwise — not even you."

After the verdict, Larry makes his way to Ellen, offers his hand to her and says, "No hard feelings." She responds, "If you ever come near me again, I'll kill you." Given Montgomery's intense delivery and perfect performance, you believe Ellen really would do that if given the chance.

A Case of Rape finished #1 for the week and helped NBC win the weekly survey period as well. This was particularly impressive given how the competing *Cannon* and *Kojak* on CBS routinely beat the NBC Wednesday night movies during the 1973-1974 season.

A Case of Rape won unanimous raves from the critics and received three Emmy nominations, although surprisingly best writing was not one of them — but the script for CBS's movie *Cry Rape!* was. Airing Nov. 27, 1973, *Cry Rape!* concentrated on the husband's revenge for this act. It too had high ratings (27.6/43).

For *A Case of Rape*, Emmy nominations went to Boris Sagal's direction, Richard Bracken's editing and Montgomery's performance. Not one of the three would ever win the statuette despite the trio's 17 nominations. Also-ran Montgomery had stiff competition that year: The winner was Cicely Tyson in the acclaimed *The Autobiography of Miss Jane Pittman*, while the other contenders included Cloris Leachman for *The Migrants*, Carol Burnett for *6 RMS RIV VU* and, in her TV dramatic debut, Katharine Hepburn in *The Glass Menagerie*.

This was Montgomery's seventh Emmy loss, following a guest role on *The Untouchables* in 1961 and five failed consecutive bids on *Bewitched* from 1966 through 1970. She would have two more Emmy nominations, for starring in *The Legend of Lizzie Borden* (1975), another high-rated TV-movie, and the miniseries *The Awakening Land* (1979).

But Montgomery did not need an Emmy to validate herself as a great actress. As a result, she remained constantly in demand for TV-movies until her death on May 18, 1995. Like Ellen Harrod in *A Case of Rape*, Montgomery was a survivor.

85 — *The Longest Yard*

Sept. 25, 1977 (first aired theatrically in 1974). **Rating:** 33.1. **Share:** 53.

Aired on ABC Sunday 9–11:30 P.M. Eastern and Pacific, 8–10:30 P.M. Central

Competition: *That's Entertainment Part 2* (second two hours of three-hour 1976 movie debut) on CBS, *Kill Me If You Can* (TV movie) on NBC

Cast: Burt Reynolds (Terry Crewe), Eddie Albert (Warden Hazen), Ed Lauter (Captain Knauer), Michael Conrad (Nate Scarboro), Jim Hampton (James "Caretaker" Sparrow), Harry Caesar (Granville), John Steadman (Pop), Charles Tyner (Unger), Mike Henry (Rassmeusen), Jim Nicholson (Ice Man), Bernadette Peters (Warden's Secretary). **Crew:** Albert S. Ruddy (producer–story writer), Robert Aldrich (director), Tracy Keenan Wynn (screenwriter).

Synopsis. Terry Crewe, a quarterback who left the NFL in a point-shaving scandal, goes to Florida's Citrus State Prison for stealing his girl's car and driving it into the bay in Palm Beach County. Warden Hazen wants him to coach Hazen's semi-pro team of guards, but Terry refuses, despite efforts by Capt. Knauer and Rassmeusen to break him. Hazen then forces Terry to play quarterback for a team of his fellow inmates against Hazen's guards' team, or else he will extend his sentence.

Slowly, the toughest inmates join Terry, helped by his coach, fellow ex-player Scarboro, and his assistant, Caretaker. The latter gets game film of the guards' team by making Terry have sex with the warden's secretary, then dies from an electrocution caused by Unger, who finks on Terry's team to the guards. The inmates are down only two points at halftime. Hazen then tells Terry that Unger will name Terry as an accessory to Caretaker's murder unless Terry lets the guards win by 21 points. Terry obeys and leaves the field for an ostensible injury after allowing three touchdowns in the third period. His teammates ostracize him.

When the guards take cheap shots at the inmates, Terry rejoins and rallies his team. Despite Granville being hospitalized along with Scarboro, who wanted to play again, Terry scores a touchdown as time runs out to win the game. He gives the ball to a dazed Hazen.

Backstory. A friend of producer Albert Ruddy was one of the richest women in America. She married a good-looking football player who was the first draft pick of the Los Angeles Rams. The next season, he was useless, suffering from a torn knee and torn tendon, plus other ailments. After that, Ruddy ran into the player and his wife at a fancy men's store in the Los Angeles neighborhood of Westwood. "And he's in front of a three-way mirror, trying on a tweed jacket, and the salesman has two other tweed jackets," Ruddy recounted in *Doing Time on The Longest Yard*, a documentary in the movie's 2005 DVD release. "And he says to her, 'Well, should I take the blue, the green or the brown?' She says, 'Take all three, because when I kick you out, you'll need them.'"

The incident sparked Ruddy's imagination, and he wondered what would have happened if the player beat her up, went to jail and had one last chance at redemption. It took five years for his concept to be produced. He enlisted screenwriter Tracy Keenan Wynn to flesh out the story. The final script was finished on Sept. 6, 1973. Drafted as director of the project was the experienced Robert Aldrich.

Ruddy had only one actor in mind to play what the script described as an 11-year former MVP who left the game eight years earlier. He approached Burt Reynolds about the role when the latter was filming *The Man Who Loved Cat Dancing* (1973) in Utah. Even though Ruddy did not have a script, Reynolds loved the plot description Ruddy provided to him. Reynolds had played football at Florida State University and a knee injury had derailed his pursuit of that career, so the role resonated with him.

Reynolds recommended that his buddy Jim Hampton play Unger, but Hampton wanted the role of Caretaker instead. Reynolds also recommended Bernadette Peters for her part. For Reynolds' nemesis, Aldrich sought Eddie Albert, with whom he worked in the 1956 film *Attack!* Aldrich also wanted to incorporate some other name actors like Ernest Borgnine and Richard Jaeckel in the cast, but did not have the budget to afford them.

Ruddy decided that using a real-life prison would work best for the film. He, Aldrich and Reynolds toured Oklahoma State Prison and thought it was perfect, but unfortunately an inmate riot burned it to the ground after they returned to Los Angeles. They went to see Georgia's Gov. Jimmy Carter (later president of the United States) about using the maximum security George State Prison in Reidsville. Carter, eager to have tax money from a film company to benefit his state's coffers, had no qualms about letting the cast and crew film there. When meeting with the trio, Carter joked with Reynolds that he would replace the actor in case he was held hostage by inmates.

Actually, Reynolds really was concerned about how the convicts would react to him, so he sent them movies where he played a "badass" (as he put it in his autobiography *My Life*) and they liked what they saw of him. Ruddy did his part by compensating nearly 1,000 prisoners for their participation, and some real prisoners were incorporated in the filming.

The Longest Yard also employed in its cast some actual football players, including the just-retired Hall of Fame linebacker Ray Nitschke of the Green Bay Packers, who intimated Reynolds during filming. "He hit you so hard your body went into shock," Reynolds recalled in *My Life*. Nitschke warned the other players he would kill them if they hurt Reynolds, because that was his job to do it to the actor. Somehow Reynolds survived him, as well as many other tough tackles.

The final 45 minutes of the film included some plays not rehearsed but called by Reynolds, to keep it spontaneous. That included a pass Reynolds made to Ernie Wheelwright, an actual player with the Atlanta Falcons, who went downfield before being stopped at the one-yard line, making it a perfect setup for the final rush to score by Reynolds.

According to both Reynolds and Ruddy, on the set, Aldrich often wanted to be like Woody Hayes, the cantankerous Ohio State University football coach. Reynolds was shocked when Aldrich told Albert, sitting in the stands under the hot sun, that he was not allowed to leave the location for any reason, but Albert shrugged it off as just the tough way Aldrich treated cast members and said it did not bother him.

As for Albert's character in the movie, Ruddy laughed off as inaccurate the claims of some critics that the warden represented President Richard Nixon in the latter's play for power and intimidation even though he was weak himself.

Although the story was set in Florida, all of the location filming occurred in Georgia. For example, the opening car chase was filmed in Savannah, doubling for Palm Beach, Florida.

When it was released, *The Longest Yard* became one of the biggest box office hits of 1974, yet it earned only one Oscar nomination, for film editing. (It was the fourth and final nomination for no wins in that category for Michael Luciano.) Members of the Academy of Motion Picture Arts and Sciences apparently had an animus against Aldrich, who was never nominated for Best Director despite a career that spanned nearly 30 years with 32 films and included his services as president of the Directors Guild of America.

The biggest challenge to adapting the movie for television was not the sex scene between Peters and Reynolds or the somewhat violent football game plays, but the numerous instances of foul language, starting right at the beginning when

Anitra Ford spouted several curse words while playing Reynolds' girlfriend. There was a considerable amount of looping (replacing dirty words via voiceovers) in order to clean up the film for broadcast. Helping make this film a TV success was the fact that it aired when Reynolds was having his biggest hit in movie theaters with *Smokey and the Bandit.*

The Longest Yard performed very well in reruns on ABC, first on Jan. 21, 1979 (24.6/39), followed by Jan. 6, 1980 (22.1/30), Sept. 7, 1980 (19.9/33) and finally May 15, 1981 (11.5/21). It was remade in 2005 with Reynolds in the role of Pop and Adam Sandler assuming the lead role, and unofficially redone in a 2001 British film called *Mean Machine*, this time with soccer as the sport.

---

84 — *The Night Stalker*

Jan. 11, 1972 (*ABC Movie of the Week*). **Rating:** 33.2. **Share:** 48.

Aired on ABC Tuesday 8:30–10 P.M. Eastern and Pacific, 7:30–9 P.M. Central

Competition: *Hawaii Five-O* and *Cannon* (first half-hour) on CBS, *NBC News Special* ("Suffer the Little Children") and *Nichols* (first half-hour) on NBC

Cast: Darren McGavin (Carl Kolchak), Carol Lynley (Gail Foster), Simon Oakland (Tony Vincenzo), Ralph Meeker (Bernie Jenks), Claude Akins (Sheriff Warren Butcher), Charles McGraw (Captain Edward Masterson), Kent Smith (D.A. Tom Paine), Barry Atwater (Janos Skorzeny), Larry Linville (Dr. Robert Makurji), Jordan Rhodes (Dr. O'Brien). **Crew:** Dan Curtis (producer), John Llewellyn Moxey (director), Richard Matheson (writer, from an unpublished story by Jeff Rice).

Synopsis. In Las Vegas, a string of murders occur, beginning with a saloon worker. Carl Kolchak, jaded reporter for *The Daily News*, asks Dr. O'Brien and then his girlfriend, Gail Foster, about the death. Gail says the victim knew karate yet was assaulted fatally. The second death baffles Kolchak and Sheriff Butcher, as the corpse is found lying in a wide expanse of sand with no footprints around it. Like the first woman, she lost a lot of blood. A third body plus the theft of plasma from a local hospital prompts the sheriff, the D.A., Las Vegas Police Capt. Masterson and FBI agent Bernie Jenks to hear a report from Dr. Makurji, the coroner. He confirms there was human saliva found in bite marks of the victim, prompting Kolchak to speculate that the murderer is a vampire.

Against the wishes of the officials and his cranky boss, managing editor Tony Vincenzo, Kolchak investigates more and learns that the suspect, Janos Skorzeny, is a sexagenarian Rumanian immigrant whom bullets cannot stop. Kolchak finds the house where the vampire lives and discovers a victim tied to the bed. Skorzeny arrives and Kolchak holds him at bay with a cross until he drops it. Jenks saves Kolchak, who stops Skorzeny by pounding a stake in his heart. But the D.A. forces Kolchak to leave town by threatening to charge him with murder. Carl tries in vain to explain the cover-up afterward to anyone who will listen.

Backstory. "I have never come across a better story than *The Night Stalker*," proclaimed producer Dan Curtis on the 2004 DVD release of the TV-movie. Considering he had been active in television since the spooky daytime soap opera *Dark Shadows* in 1966 and 17 years later produced one of TV's highest-rated miniseries, *The Winds of War* (see 23), this is high praise indeed.

Curtis had directed two feature films based on *Dark Shadows* by 1971, the year that the series ended. Barry Diller, then ABC's vice-president for feature films, told him the network wanted him to direct a horror TV-movie. Curtis had no interest until Diller let it slip that the screenplay was written by Richard Matheson, considered one of the genre's finest authors, and the favorite writer of Curtis to boot.

Matheson based his script on *The Kolchak Papers*, an unpublished book written in 1970 by Jeff Rice. Rice was a reporter for the *Las Vegas Sun* newspaper from 1966 to 1968 before moving to Los Angeles. He combined his experiences there (including an itinerant reporter pal named Alan Jarlson acting as partial inspiration for Kolchak and his blustering boss serving as the basis for Tony Vincenzo) with his love of horror films to create what he termed "Dracula meets *The Front Page*."

Rice submitted his novel to an agent in November 1970. Unbeknownst to him, that agent represented Matheson as well, and for a tidy sum he had the author adapt the manuscript, which was not copyrighted, for an ABC movie of the week. Rice did not hold the agent's double-dealing against Matheson, who he said preserved 75 percent of the original story. Rice retained the rights to do any sequels along with work as the movie's location consultant when filming was underway in Las Vegas. With that settled, Matheson submitted his final draft of what was originally titled *The Kolchak Tapes* on Aug. 15, 1971.

Curtis first told Diller he did not want to direct the film, so the executive allowed him to just produce it. Still cautious, Curtis said he wanted to see the script before committing to the project. "I loved it," he said.

But Curtis earlier had submitted what Matheson thought was a low bid to adapt one of his books into a movie, and Matheson was livid about the situation. So when Curtis met with Matheson, the author was cold at first. Yet when Matheson read the script notes from Curtis that indicated to him that the producer-to-be did have great ideas for the picture, his opposition softened. The two became friends.

To direct, Curtis picked John Llewellyn Moxey, who he met in England and drafted to direct the videotaped ABC special *The Strange Case of Dr. Jekyll and Mr. Hyde* (1967) when it was to star Jason Robards, Jr. The project unraveled and Jack Palance took Robards' place while Moxey lost his job to Charles Jarrott. Moxey came over to America to start working in Hollywood; he was established there by the time Curtis tabbed him for *The Night Stalker.*

Darren McGavin was Curtis' first pick for Kolchak. McGavin came up with Kolchak's memorable outfit that looked out of place in 1972, much less in blistering hot Las Vegas: a porkpie hat, a seersucker suit, shirt and tie. He felt that since the character was said to have been fired in New York years earlier, he should dress the same way he had when he left Manhattan in the early 1960s.

In late August 1971, the cast and crew filmed the movie in 12 days on a budget of $450,000, with exteriors shot on the Las Vegas Strip before returning to Los Angeles for interiors.

"When we finished *The Night Stalker*, nobody knew what we had," Curtis said. "It was a little horror movie. Nobody was getting excited about it." The only inkling was an industry screening that prompted such positive reactions that Diller turned to Curtis and said, "We should've released this as a feature!"

The Night Stalker finished third for the week it ran, behind *All in the Family* (see 25) and *Marcus Welby, M.D.* (see 40). It's easy to see why it was so popular. It's alternately fanciful, realistic (the location filming was a smart idea to add believability), amusing and scary, and it works beautifully, with the conspiracy element at the end being even more credible today following national scandals that have to come to light since 1972.

However, the autopsy of the first victim may provoke some laughs among viewers of a certain age. The supervising doctor is played by Larry Linville, later the comic, somewhat incompetent Dr. Frank Burns on *M*A*S*H* (see 1). Rice auditioned to play the role, but Curtis decided to give Linville the part.

The film's numbers prompted ABC to order a sequel. *The Night Strangler* finished 14th in the ratings when it debuted on Jan. 16, 1973, so ABC wanted another TV-movie. But McGavin did not like the script, which Matheson co-wrote, so ABC settled for rerunning *The Night Stalker* a year later on Jan. 16, 1974. Ratings were pretty solid (22.0/33), so executives suggested that McGavin try playing the character in a series. McGavin agreed only if he could be executive producer, having fallen out with Curtis during the production of *The Night Strangler* when Curtis also served as director.

But the idea of hard-bitten reporter Kolchak encountering a different supernatural force every week was hard to swallow. *Kolchak: The Night Stalker* finished 74th for the one season it ran (Sept. 13, 1974–Aug. 30, 1975). Even so, like a vampire, it had an amazing afterlife. CBS repeated the show on its Friday late night schedule from May through December 1979 (with a summer break), the summer of 1981, and once again for six months in 1987 and 1988. During the time of the last run, Janos Skorzeny was the name of a character played by Chuck Connors on *Werewolf*, a 1987-1988 adventure series on Fox. Clearly the concept had some die-hard (pardon the pun) adherents; they just were not as plentiful as the audience that showed up for the original movie.

On the film's DVD, Curtis mourned the loss of such movies as *The Night Stalker* on network TV. "In those days, we had fun.... They didn't have to be an event. They just had to be entertaining, fun, good, scary, dramatic, whatever," he said. He sounded almost as cynical as Kolchak — but he was right.

83 — *The Ten Commandments*

Feb. 18, 1973 (*ABC Movie Special*; first appeared theatrically in 1956). **Rating:** 33.2. **Share:** 54.

Aired on ABC Sunday 8 P.M.–Monday 12:30 A.M. Eastern and Pacific, 7–11:30 P.M. Central

Competition: *M*A*S*H*, *Mannix* and *Barnaby Jones* on CBS, *Disney* (last half-hour of 60-minute show) and *Hec Ramsey* on NBC

Cast: Charlton Heston (Moses), Yul Brynner (Rameses), Anne Baxter (Nefertiri), Edward G. Robinson (Dathan), Yvonne De Carlo (Sephora), Debra Paget (Lilia), John Derek (Joshua), Sir Cedric Hardwicke (Sethi), Nina Foch (Princess Bithiah), Martha Scott (Yochabel), Judith Anderson (Memnet), Vincent Price (Baka), John Carradine (Aaron). **Crew:** Cecil B. DeMille (producer-director), Aeneas MacKenzie, Jesse L. Lasky, Jr., Jack Gariss, Fredric M. Frank (writers).

Synopsis. An edict to kill the first-born males in Jewish families in ancient Egypt prompts Yochabel to put her infant in a basket on the Nile River for safety. Princess Bithiah rescues the child and names him Moses. The pharaoh, Sethi, adopts Moses along with his natural-born son, Rameses. Moses learns of his heritage, reunites with Yochabel and his brother Aaron, and joins the oppressed Levites by working among the slaves. When he kills Baka, Sethi's master builder, for whipping Joshua, he is banished, as Dathan reveals that Moses is actually a Hebrew.

Exiled in the desert, Moses meets and weds Sephora, then talks to God (represented by a burning bush) and learns that his destiny is to lead his people out of Egypt. He warns Rameses, now the pharaoh, and his wife, Nefretiri, who lusts for Moses, that plagues will follow if the Jews are not freed, culminating in the angel of death claiming the life of first-borns, including Rameses' son.

The pharaoh releases the 8,000 Jews, joined by wily Dathan, who weds Lilia. Dathan complains about Moses, even after he parts the Red Sea for the Jews to cross and closes it on Rameses' men, causing the latter to drown. Moses receives the Ten Commandments from God on Mount Sinai and uses the tablets to destroy the Golden Calf some Israelites worshiped, causing an earthquake that swallows nonbelievers including Dathan. After more years of wandering, Moses transfers leadership of his people to Joshua.

Backstory. "The Greatest Event in Motion Picture History," as it so modestly claimed in its tagline when originally released, *The Ten Commandments* fills that bill to some viewers. And thanks in part to its repeated annual airings on ABC during Passover since the late 1970s, it is the picture that comes to mind first among most Americans when the term "Biblical epic" is mentioned.

However, a sizable number of people, including many critics, find it hokey and campy. This opinion has little to do with the technical aspects; indeed, the special effects were top-of-the-line for their time, with the spectacular opening and closing of the Red Sea alone costing $1 million in 1955 dollars and taking months to film. They received the only Oscar win for the picture out of seven nominations (the others were for picture, film editing, sound recording, cinematography, art direction-set decoration and costume design).

The derision has more to do with its occasionally florid dialogue delivered by several actors appearing over-the-top or miscast. In 1989, Billy Crystal memorably parodied Yul Brynner and Edward G. Robinson's delivery in the movie on the Academy Awards (see 13).

Unintentional laughter was not the goal behind making the movie, of course. It came to producer-director Cecil B. DeMille following the huge triumph of his 1952 film *The Greatest Show on Earth*, which despite being that year's top money earner has never performed particularly well on TV. DeMille next wanted to redo his 1923 silent hit *The Ten Commandments*, which used the Biblical story of Moses receiving the tablets as a backdrop for a modern tale showing the consequences of a man breaking God's law. "For more than 20 years, and increasingly in the years since World War II, people had been writing to me from all over the world, urging that I make *The Ten Commandments* again," DeMille wrote in his autobiography. After some consideration, he decided it would be better to focus just on the story of Moses for his planned epic. He did allow several crewmen from the silent movie to work on the new version; DeMille was known for his devotion to those who impressed him with their work.

With a 308-page script calling for more than 70 speaking parts, the film would be a major undertaking. That attracted many actors, and scared off others. Despite DeMille's decades of being a top moviemaker, some actors such as Cornel Wilde and Jane Darwell turned down roles. Several of the actors who did appear were not the original choices. For example:

• William Boyd was DeMille's pick for Moses, but the actor had become so famous on TV as Hopalong Cassidy that he felt that children who saw the movie would be confused by him playing a different part. DeMille's assistant producer Henry Wilcoxon remembered that Charlton Heston, who had starred in *The Greatest Show on Earth*, had a face that resembled Michelangelo's marble statue of Moses, and he drew the hair of the statue onto a picture of Heston to convince DeMille the actor was the right choice.

• Originally William Holden was to play Rameses. But when DeMille went to see Yul Brynner star in *The King and I* on Broadway, he was so taken by the dynamic portrayal that he offered the star the role during intermission.

• Audrey Hepburn was slated to be Nefretiri. However, because Anne Baxter had a better figure for the sheer costumes, she was in and Hepburn was out.

• Jack Palance was to be Dathan (a mixture of many Israelites mentioned in the Bible), but his agent rejected the offer. DeMille replaced him with Edward G. Robinson, who was a blacklisting victim in the 1950s. Although strongly anti–Communist, DeMille felt that Robinson was unfairly targeted as a Red sympathizer and gave the actor his first major film role of the decade. It revived his career.

Nine makeups were designed for Heston to use as Moses aged over the years. Part of the movie was shot in Egypt. The outdoor scenes used 8,000 extras and 5,000 head of livestock, all shuttled to the desert location in trucks and buses.

DeMille helped Heston craft his character. "He kept me insulated from the casual, jokey camaraderie of a movie company," Heston wrote in his autobiography *In the Arena*. "Once I was in the makeup and wearing the Levite robe, I kept pretty much apart." Heston was allowed a personal connection by having his newborn son play the baby Moses.

Doing the film on location in Egypt involved a number of challenges. There was a political revolution for nearly two months, but DeMille had cordial relations with new president Mohammed Naguib and thus received permission to film amid the pyramids and many locations mentioned in the Bible, usually with Heston and some extras. In November 1954 DeMille suffered a heart attack on the set but, taking his medication and following strict orders from his doctor, he completed work in Egypt. The rest of the shooting took place in Hollywood and employed many outfits and props used in the 1954 movie *The Egyptian*.

Shooting the film lasted nearly a year and ended on Aug. 13, 1955, the day after DeMille's 74th birthday. The production cost $13.2 million, a stupendous amount for the time. When *The Ten Commandments* opened on Nov. 8, 1956, it earned back its costs and much more, becoming one of the highest grossing movies of all time adjusted for inflation. Paramount re-released it to theatres in 1966 and 1972 to more earnings before selling it to ABC.

The movie's TV debut finished second in the ratings for the week behind *All in the Family* (see 25). Its best repeat ratings were the following year,

when it chalked up a 30.8/48 for the second of a two-part showing on Feb. 13, 1974, and on March 25, 1979, when it came in with a 27.4/48. By that time *The Ten Commandments* had become a staple of Passover-Easter night programming on ABC, where it has remained ever since. A break in 1999 prompted many complaints.

The movie also disappeared briefly when there was an ABC miniseries remake that aired on April 10 and 11, 2006, with Dougray Scott starring as Moses. Critics dismissed it, and ratings were unimpressive — 4.6/11 for the first night and 3.9/10 for the second. That version already has been forgotten by most viewers. The 1956 version remains the greatest to many fans.

82 — *How the West Was Won*

Feb. 6, 1977 (*ABC Sunday Night Movie*, Part 1 of 3). **Rating:** 33.2. **Share:** 51.

Aired on ABC Sunday 9–11 P.M. Eastern and Pacific, 8–10 P.M. Central

Competition: *Switch* and *Delvecchio* on CBS, *Tail Gunner Joe* (last two hours of three-hour TV movie) on NBC

Cast: James Arness (Zeb Macahan), Eva Marie Saint (Kate Macahan), Bruce Boxleitner (Luke Macahan), Kathryn Holcomb (Laura Macahan), William Kirby Cullen (Josh Macahan), Vicki Schreck (Jessie Macahan), Anthony Zerbe (Capt. Martin Grey). **Crew:** John Mantley (executive producer), Jeffrey Hayden (producer), Burt Kennedy, Daniel Mann (directors), Ron Bishop (writer).

Synopsis. Zeb Macahan leads the family of his sister-in-law Kate on a trek toward Oregon in the early 1860s so that her sons, Luke and Josh, can avoid participating in the Civil War. Capt. Martin Gray is hell-bent on capturing Luke for deserting the Union Army, so much so that he becomes a bounty hunter. Luke actually was forced to join the army when he went looking for his missing dad and was drafted against his will, but that does not matter to Gray.

When Luke is shot and provided refuge by the Simonites, a band of religious followers, he falls in love with Erica Hanks. She follows him when he finally leaves her group.

As the other Macahans attempt to find peace in the middle of an Indian tribal war, Luke attempts to rejoin them peacefully (he refuses to kill another human unless it is the only option left).

Backstory. The saga of the Macahans began as a TV-movie in 1976, emerged as a miniseries in 1977, and became a TV series in 1978. It was a very rough offshoot of *How the West Was Won,* a movie that came out in 1962.

The 1962 epic had no Macahans, but it did tell the story of a family named Prescott moving from the East to California in the mid–1800s, and that apparently was enough to inspire a scaled-down TV version. The popular and Oscar-nominated film made its TV debut on ABC with an impressive 26.0/46 on Oct. 24, 1971. ABC reran it to strong numbers first as a two-part entry on Jan. 21 and Jan. 22, 1973 (22.0/34 and 21.0/31, respectively), and then on one night on Jan. 5, 1975, getting a 22.4/34. What led to a transfer to TV was the fact that actor James Arness and executive producer John Mantley were unemployed following the 1975 cancellation of *Gunsmoke* (see 24), and both wanted to do another western. Likewise, MGM Studios needed a hit TV production, so they decided to adapt the storyline from *How the West Was Won* because they owned that property.

The result was *The Macahans,* which aired on ABC on Jan. 19, 1976. It included all of the actors who portrayed the characters in this follow-up, although the character names were different for Bruce Boxleitner (Seth Macahan vs. Luke) and William Kirby Cullen (Jeb Macahan instead of Josh). It also included Richard Kiley as Timothy Macahan (Zeb's brother, who was reported missing in the sequel), Frank Ferguson as Grandpa Macahan and Ann Doran as Grandma Macahan. Airing against *All in the Family* (see 25), the TV-movie performed well enough that ABC allowed it to be followed up with a miniseries. This was the first of three parts broadcast a year later.

"I was particularly pleased with my performance in *How the West Was Won* because I got to play a character who was the complete opposite of Matt Dillon," Arness wrote in his autobiography. "Jeb Macahan was sort of a wild man, unlike the steady lawman I'd played for 20 years on *Gunsmoke.* Macahan tested my skills, and the plaudits I received for my acting in the miniseries brought me great satisfaction."

The ratings stayed strong through Part 2, airing Feb. 7, 1977 (31.8/49), and Part 3, airing on Feb. 14, 1977 (32.4/50). The miniseries finished with average numbers of 32.5/50, truly astounding. It led to ABC installing it at as a one-hour series on Feb. 12, 1978 on Sundays at 8 P.M., but it did not outperform *Rhoda* and *On Our Own* on CBS. When ABC tried it as a weekly two-hour series

Monday nights following the football season, results were disastrous. It went off the network on April 23, 1979.

There were two Emmy nominations for the miniseries, for Saint as Lead Actress in a Limited Series (she lost to Patty Duke Astin for *Captains and the Kings*) and Special Musical Material, for theme writer Jerrold Immel (there was no award given in the category; the Academy of Television Arts and Sciences could and did allow for no wins). When it became a series, it notched an Emmy nomination for makeup and a win for Ricardo Montalban for single performance by a supporting actor in a comedy or drama series.

In 1982 the miniseries was edited into hour-long segments and added to the series episodes to create a total of 42 shows that were sold to local stations for airing once a week beginning in September 1983. It was retitled *The Macahans* (yes, the original TV-movie title) for these showings. As of this writing, none of any versions of *How the West Was Won* are available on DVD.

81— The Cotton Bowl

Jan. 1, 1972 (35th edition). **Rating:** 33.3. **Share:** n/a.

Aired on CBS 1:45–4:30 P.M. Eastern, 12:45–3:30 P.M. Central, 11:45 A.M.–2:30 P.M. Mountain and 10:45 A.M.–1:30 P.M. Pacific

Competition: Sugar Bowl (Oklahoma vs. Auburn, began an hour earlier) on ABC, Rose Bowl preview on NBC

Hosts: Lindsey Nelson (play-by-play announcer), Tom Brookshier (color commentator). **Crew:** Not known.

Synopsis. The Penn State Nittany Lions (10–1) took on the Texas Longhorns (8–2) in the latter's fourth straight Cotton Bowl appearance. Texas was favored despite more losses because the Penn State loss came from a 31–11 drubbing from highly regarded Tennessee in the season closer, breaking a 15-game winning streak for the Nittany Lions and making some feel the latter was overrated. The game proved otherwise.

With rain falling during much of the game, Texas scored first on a field goal kicked by Steve Valek, followed by the same from by Penn State's Alberto Vitiello. Valek added another three-pointer to make it 6–3 Texas at the half. But Texas did a poor job of handling the ball, fumbling it five times, and on three of those occasions (including the first field goal), Penn State took advantage and scored. The Nittany Lions racked up 17 points in the third quarter, first by a one-yard touchdown by Penn State running back Lydell Mitchell, who had scored a record 29 touchdowns that season. Then Penn State quarterback John Hufnagel executed a 27-yard pass to Scott Skarzynski, who ran 38 more yards to score the second touchdown, followed by a 37-yard field goal by Vitiello after the Nittany Lions recovered a Texas fumble.

In the fourth quarter, Vitiello added one more field goal and Hufnagel did a four-yard run into the end zone to add ten more points for Penn State. The final score was 30–6.

Backstory. The Cotton Bowl has been an established post-season championship football game for Division I universities since Jan. 1, 1937. It was created a decade after the start of the Rose Bowl (see 67), and two years after the launch of a pair of other New Year's Day NCAA football championships, the Orange Bowl in Miami, Florida, and the Sugar Bowl in New Orleans, Louisiana. Four years after it began, the game hosted whoever was the winner of the Southwest Conference against another non-conference opponent.

With Red Grange by his side, Lindsey Nelson covered the Cotton Bowl on NBC through 1957. The next year, CBS got the broadcasting rights and used a different set of play-by-play announcers and color commentators, including Nelson again in 1963 and 1968. Finally, Nelson became the regular play-by-play announcer for the game on CBS for 16 consecutive years (1970 to 1985), with Tom Brookshier joining him in the booth from 1970 to 1974. Nelson's continuous service calling the bowl was a record at the time, and when he did his final one, bowl officials gave him a sports jacket and the CBS crew gave him a watch.

Nelson believed that the explosive popularity for the Cotton Bowl in the 1970s emerged from a 1970 game between the undefeated Longhorns vs. the similarly unstoppable Notre Dame Fighting Irish; Texas won 21–17. The two teams met again the following year, and this time Texas was on the losing end, as Notre Dame triumphed 24–11. "It was the start of a stretch during which the aggregate ratings of the Cotton Bowl exceeded those of the Rose Bowl, and it set the Cotton Bowl up as one of the truly great events of the country and the showcase collegiate sports event for the CBS network," Nelson wrote in his autobiography.

This 1972 game marked the ascension of Penn State as a major college football team under the leadership of Coach Joe Paterno. It was the third straight bowl victory for the Lions (their first one

in the Cotton Bowl under his leadership), and the game produced the second-widest margin of victory in Cotton Bowl history since 1945.

The display by the offense was very impressive. Lydell Mitchell ran for 146 yards and was named outstanding player of the game. But the defensive efforts deserve saluting as well. The Nittany Lions broke down the Longhorns' wishbone offense and prevented Texas from scoring a touchdown for the first time in 80 games, going all the back to October 1964.

"Everybody did a great job," said Penn State defensive captain Charlie Zapiec. "I never even dreamed we could hold them to no touchdowns. I thought they'd score at least two. When they drove on us the first time and didn't score, that gave us a lot of confidence. They were a lot less awesome after that."

New Year's Day 1972 was apparently the day for big blowout wins throughout college football. Beside what happened to the Longhorns, Nebraska routed Alabama 38–6 in the Orange Bowl, and Oklahoma smashed Auburn 40–22 in the Sugar Bowl. The only close match-up was Stanford upsetting Michigan 13–12 in the Rose Bowl. On TV it was no contest, as the Cotton Bowl prevailed over everything else that year by a wide margin.

CBS held the TV rights for the Cotton Bowl through 1992. NBC broadcast the classic for three years after that, then CBS resumed its coverage for three years starting in 1996. But since 1998, the Cotton Bowl has assumed the role of a "lesser" post-season game (it was not included as part of the Bowl Championship Series restructuring that year). While the competitors may not be the marquee names in college football sports for that season, the Cotton Bowl has remained a television attraction on Fox every New Year's Day since 1999.

80 — Summer Olympics

Sept. 4, 1972 (Games of the XX Olympiad). **Rating:** 33.3. **Share:** 55.

Aired on ABC Monday 8–10:30 P.M. Eastern, 7–10:30 P.M. Central

Competition: *Gunsmoke, Here's Lucy, The Doris Day Show* and *Cade's County* (all four were repeats) on CBS; *Monday Night Baseball* on NBC

Hosts: Jim McKay, Chris Schenkel. **Crew:** Roone Arledge (executive producer).

Synopsis. Teams from 121 nations compete in Munich, West Germany, with plenty of emerging stars — Olga Korbut in gymnastics, Mark Spitz in swimming — as well as controversies, such as the U.S. men's basketball team saying it was robbed of a gold medal by unfair officiating and refusing to accept the silver medal. There was a battle between the United States and the Soviet Union over medal tallies as well, with the latter edging ahead in total medals counts (99 gold, silver and bronze metals won as compared to 94 for America). It all made for increased interest in the games thanks to clever packaging by ABC Sports.

As audiences peaked on Labor Day, Sept. 4, 1972, tragedy struck overnight. Eight Palestinian terrorists entered the Olympic village and captured nine Israeli athletes. They demanded the release of 234 Palestinian prisoners or else they would kill their hostages. The games continued until protests from Israel halted them temporarily. Finally Jim McKay told the audience, "Our worst fears were realized tonight — they're all gone."

Backstory. This edition of the Summer Olympics showed the world that ABC was a leader in sports. Almost every time it played highlights of the games, it won in the ratings, with more than half the TV sets in use on average tuned to its coverage. It might have set a record if it was not for the Munich massacre.

The shootout at the military airport nearly 18 hours after the incident began, with the Arab militants being able to kill the hostages, put a horrible black eye on the festivities, making many complain about the lax security at the games and how the German authorities badly mishandled and underestimated the situation. The games, which started Aug. 26, continued to be played until Sept. 10.

ABC Sports director Roone Arledge made the call to Leonard Goldenson as soon as he heard of the standoff and told him he wanted to go live with the satellite feed over the entire network until it was resolved. "You've got it," Goldenson told him. Arledge wrote in his autobiography, "I figured the Germans would have the situation quickly under control." He discovered to his horror that they did not, and they even rejected an offer from the Israelis to send in a trained rescue crew. An early report that all the hostages had been freed turned out to be wrong.

At the Emmys, producer Arledge and the videotape editors won awards. McKay and Keith Jackson were nominated for individual achievement in sports programming. For their coverage of the Munich massacre, Arledge and McKay both had the unusual distinction of winning for their news coverage.

79 — The Andy Griffith Show

Jan. 29, 1968 ("Barney Hosts a Summit Meeting"). **Rating:** 33.4. **Share:** n/a. Aired on CBS Monday 9–9:30 P.M. Eastern and Pacific, 8–8:30 P.M. Central

Competition: *Luther* (middle half-hour of 90-minute drama special) on ABC, *The Danny Thomas Hour* (first half-hour) on NBC

Cast: Andy Griffith (Sheriff Andy Taylor), Frances Bavier (Aunt Bee), Ronny Howard (Opie Taylor), George Lindsey (Goober Pyle). **Guests:** Don Knotts (Barney Fife), Paul Fix (Mr. McCabe), Richard X. Slattery (Capt. Dewhurst), Michael Higgins (Mr. Clifford), Alan Oppenheimer (Mr. Ruskin), Ben Astar (Mr. Vasilievich). **Crew:** Sheldon Leonard (executive producer), Bob Ross (producer), Lee Philips (director), Aaron Ruben (writer).

Synopsis. Barney Fife, working with the state police in Raleigh, North Carolina, endeavors to impress Capt. Dewhurst by finding him a safe and secure mansion in his (Barney's) old community of Mayberry to host a top-secret conference between Russian and American officials. He assures them the use of Mr. McCabe's place, but the crotchety coot is just as cranky toward Barney as when the policeman was a child and refuses to let his home be used. Meanwhile, the leaders are driving toward Mayberry expecting a regal facility. With the possibility of losing his job before him, Barney pleads with his former boss, Sheriff Andy Taylor, to make room at his home for the dignitaries. Andy reluctantly complies.

While not totally thrilled with the setting, the diplomats agree to give it a shot, but interruptions by Andy's son Opie and friend Goober (who asks for a picture of the men) hinder the talks. The tide changes at night when the restless men raid the icebox and Andy's Aunt Bea fixes them her famous downhome cooking. This setting loosens their spirits and the men reach some agreements. Barney and Andy, returning to the home in the morning, see the men depart in a jovial mood. Barney and Andy talk on the latter's porch before Barney heads back to the capital city and Andy remains to keep peace in Mayberry.

Backstory. A series that has provided joy and warmth for generations of Americans since 1960 was born out of its star's professional displeasure. In 1959, Andy Griffith regretted the fact that his Broadway musical *Destry Rides Again*, where he played the lead character, struggled to find audiences during its run of just over one year, in which time he and the cast often had to perform in matinees during holidays. Sick of the stage work, he did not want to return to nightclubs, where he had broken into show business doing comic monologues, and his movie career had flopped with a few bombs like *Onionhead* (1958). "So I told Abe Lastfogel, then head of William Morris [talent agency], that I would like to try TV," Griffith wrote in the foreword to Sheldon Leonard's autobiography *And the Show Goes On.* "It seemed like the only thing left."

Leonard, then the producer of the hit sitcom *The Danny Thomas Show*, met Griffith and the actor's manager, Richard Linke, after a performance of *Destry Rides Again* to discuss the concept Leonard concocted with writer Artie Stander. The series would have Griffith play Andy Taylor, a sheriff, justice of the peace and editor of the local newspaper who lived in the small Southern town of Mayberry as a widower with a son. To introduce the character (and avoid shooting a pilot), Griffith would make a guest appearance on *The Danny Thomas Show* to arrest the titular character for speeding through his town.

Though the presentation drew from Griffith's background of living in the town of Mt. Airy, North Carolina, the actor was not totally sold on the idea, but he went ahead and filmed the episode, which was well-received when it aired on Feb. 15, 1960. Selling it as a series to General Foods, the sponsor of *The Danny Thomas Show*, was no problem.

Other cast members included Don Knotts, who had just moved to California to follow *The Steve Allen Show* only to see it get canceled. Knotts had a part in the 1955 Broadway play *No Time for Sergeants* that starred Griffith, and the two became friends there. "I saw Andy's pilot on *The Danny Thomas Show* and noticed he didn't have a deputy," Knotts recalled to Richard Kelly in the book *The Andy Griffith Show*. "I learned Andy was on vacation in North Carolina, so I called him and said, 'It would be neat if you had a deputy.' He said, 'Yeah, that's a good idea. Why don't you talk to Sheldon Leonard?'" The addition of Deputy Barney Fife, whose false bravado masked a tendency towards being jittery, changed the show's dynamic so that Griffith played a much wiser sheriff than in the pilot — and only a sheriff, not other jobs — to compensate for Barney's ineptness.

Rounding out the original cast was Ron Howard (then billed as Ronny) as Taylor's six-year-old son Opie and Frances Bavier as Andy's plump live-in housekeeper and relative, Aunt Bee Taylor. The show debuted on CBS Oct. 3, 1960, following *The Danny Thomas Show*, and proved to be even more popular than its lead-in, finishing #4 for the season while *The Danny Thomas Show* ended at #12.

When the series began, Sheriff Taylor had a girlfriend, pharmacist Ellie Walker, but she vanished at the end of the first season. While Griffith claimed the writers did not know how to work in such a headstrong character, her portrayer, Elinor Donahue, later told Eddie Lucas in *Close-ups: Conversations with Our TV Favorites* that she requested to be freed from her three-year contract with the series due to emotional and physical exhaustion (she was dealing with what later would be diagnosed as anorexia). It would be three years before Andy had another regular girlfriend, Helen Crump, played by Aneta Corsaut.

Griffith drew on his North Carolina background to make Mayberry resemble Mt. Airy, Andy's birthplace, and he went over the scripts to make sure they sounded authentic to the region. There were also a few other characters added before 1965; for details on some, see *Gomer Pyle, U.S.M.C.* at 55.

In 1965 Knotts left the series for an unusual reason. Griffith had been telling him he planned to end *The Andy Griffith Show* after five years ever since Knotts joined him, so the latter looked for other work and secured a deal to star in pictures for Universal. At the last minute, Griffith decided to stay with his program, but Knotts already was committed to his Universal contract. However, he did consent to make a few guest appearances thereafter, including this episode.

When Knotts returned to *The Andy Griffith Show* for "Barney Hosts a Summit Meeting," the series was now #1, and his fifth guest visit was highly anticipated by loyal viewers. The weak dramatic competition aided the turnout as well. It is a typically pleasant outing that brings more smiles than laughs, but there's nothing wrong with that. Despite its continuing success, Griffith planned to leave the more-popular-than-ever series to pursue other offers. Its final episode on CBS nighttime ran on Sept. 16, 1968.

When its reruns were up for sale to local TV stations in 1970, CBS Films boasted to prospective buyers that it had been first in its time period throughout its nighttime and daytime runs. (It was the first series since *I Love Lucy* to finish in the top 10 every season in its nighttime stretch, and it ran in daytime from 1964 to 1970.) Those outlets who thought it would perform just as well on their lineup almost always found success, even in urban markets outside the South where it really prospered.

The Andy Griffith Show earned three nominations without a win as best comedy series in 1961, 1962 and 1967. Knotts racked up an impressive five wins as a supporting actor in 1961, 1962, 1963, 1966 and 1967 (the last two being guest shots), and the one time Bavier was nominated for supporting actress, in 1967, she won as well.

Griffith has reprised Sheriff Taylor in selected circumstances since 1968. These include an appearance on the series' successful spin-off *Mayberry R.F.D.* (see 50); a guest shot on *Saturday Night Live* in 1982 when Ron Howard was the host and parodied the series; and appearances in the 1986 reunion movie *Return to Mayberry* (see 90) and in a 2008 campaign ad for presidential candidate Barack Obama.

78 — *Bonnie and Clyde*

Sept. 20, 1973 (*CBS Thursday Night Movies*; first released theatrically in 1967). **Rating:** 33.4. **Share:** 38.

Aired on CBS Thursday 9–11:15 P.M. Eastern and Pacific, 8–10:15 P.M. Central

Competition: Billie Jean King vs. Bobby Riggs (sports special) and *The Streets of San Francisco* on ABC, *Ironside* and *NBC Follies* on NBC

Cast: Warren Beatty (Clyde Barrow), Faye Dunaway (Bonnie Parker), Gene Hackman (Buck Barrow), Estelle Parsons (Blanche Barrow), Michael J. Pollard (C.W. Moss), Denver Pyle (Capt. Frank Hamer), Dub Taylor (Ivan Moss), Evans Evans (Velma Davis), Gene Wilder (Eugene Grizzard). **Crew:** Warren Beatty (producer), Arthur Penn (director), David Newman, Robert Benton (writers).

Synopsis. Restless, half-naked waitress Bonnie Parker espies Clyde Barrow trying to steal her mother's car. She becomes fascinated with him, even when learning that he is nothing more than a bank robber, and joins him in stealing money in Texas and other states. Bonnie's only regret is that Clyde is impotent with her.

Mechanic C.W. Moss becomes their driver, and Clyde's older brother Buck and his high-strung wife Blanche join the gang as well. The quintet not only steals the car of a young couple, Velma and Eugene, but also have them ride along. When Eugene tells them he is an undertaker, the mention of a profession associated with death upsets Bonnie, and she tells Clyde to get them out of the car, which he does.

A foreboding tone emerges as Bonnie visits her mom and the latter tells her to keep running or she will die. In a shootout, Buck is mortally wounded and Blanche is apprehended. C.W. takes injured Bonnie and Clyde to the home of his dad, Ivan. Texas Ranger Frank Hamer gets a confession from Blanche that directs him to the gang. While Bonnie and Clyde consummate their love, the police are hot on their trail. Using Ivan as a lure, Hamer and other officers ambush Bonnie and Clyde and pump a hail of bullets into the duo's lifeless bodies.

Backstory. Robert Benton and David Newman were *Esquire* magazine editors who loved movies. They read a book on John Dillinger (1963's *The Dillinger Days*) and were inspired to do a film based on a footnote they read about other famous criminals of the early 1930s.

"We decided to try and write an American New Wave movie about Bonnie Parker and Clyde Barrow," Benton said in *Backstory 4: Interviews with Screenwriters of the 1970s and 1980s.* They wrote an outline and then an 80-page treatment one summer, becoming fascinated by the facts of how the duo basked in the celebrity of their notoriety.

The screenplay caught the eye of Warren Beatty, whose paramour at the time, actress Leslie Caron, encouraged him to pursue the movie despite concerns it would be overshadowed by another crime drama planned for release in 1967, *In Cold Blood.* Convinced by Caron that it would be a hit, Beatty signed on to produce the project, the first time he assumed that role. However, he curtly told Caron that she could not play Bonnie, as her French accent and age (she was five years his senior) would work against her believability on screen.

Benton and Newman tried to have Francois Truffaut direct the movie. He did not, but did spend several days with Benton and Newman reviewing their treatment and suggested they watch the 1949 film *Gun Crazy* as an example of a stylish gangster script. After Truffaut's rejection, Benton and Newman suggested that Beatty enlist another French New Wave director, Jean-Luc Godard. But Beatty ruled out Godard when the latter wanted to shoot during the Texas winter.

Beatty favored Arthur Penn, who directed him in *Mickey One* (1965). Penn was reluctant, as he was not interested in directing a gangster film, and he had just endured a disastrous experience directing a major bomb, *The Chase* (1966). But he liked working with Beatty, and he took the assignment when the actor assured Penn he would receive the right to a final cut on the film.

Penn expressed a few concerns about the script, chiefly about depicting a sexual liaison between Bonnie, Clyde and C.W. Moss. The latter was a composite character of five gang members employed by Bonnie and Clyde over the years. Benton and Newman found indications that this happened with the couple with several henchman, and that Clyde was bisexual if not homosexual. Penn thought the proposed scenes would overwhelm the movie, and Beatty agreed, as he preferred to play Clyde as someone whose impotency was cured by Bonnie.

The director also had screenwriter Bob Towne contribute to the script. He put the Eugene and Velma scene ahead of Bonnie meeting her mother and foreshadowed the fatalistic end for the duo in both.

But the slow-motion ending of the duo's killing was the director's idea, which he called "spastic, yet balletic" in *Arthur Penn's Bonnie and Clyde*. The point he was making was that those living with violence eventually come to an end with it, and the deaths are often painful and messy. (In real life, Bonnie and Clyde were shot multiple times, though not in the circumstances depicted in the film.)

After rejecting Caron for Bonnie, Beatty pursued his previous girlfriend, Natalie Wood, to co-star with him. Wood rejected the role, while Caron ended her relationship with Beatty soon thereafter. Tuesday Weld was pregnant and did not want to go to Texas for the location filming. Penn had seen footage of Faye Dunaway's first picture *The Happening* (1967) and was impressed, so he tested her and took her to Beatty for final approval.

Many people in Texas shared their memories of the duo with the film cast and crew during the production. Still, the filmmakers stressed they were not making a documentary and altered some incidents for dramatic effect, a fact lost by some of its severest critics.

Bonnie and Clyde was a film first for several people. It was the movie debut for Gene Wilder, who took a one-week absence from performing in the Broadway play *Luv* to join the company in Texas. Beatty and Penn both told him they had seen his stage work and thought he was right for the part, although Penn said he had never imagined the role to be a funny one.

For another Broadway transplant, Charles Strouse, this was his first film score. He got into a fight with Beatty during the recording of the background music that was so intense that Penn had to pry them apart, but they later made peace.

Jack Warner, head of Warner Brothers, disliked the final motion picture and had it released in only a few cities in August 1967. Sharing his opinion was *New York Times* critic Bosley Crowther, who dismissed the movie as buffoonery that celebrated violence. But the critical tide began to turn when Penelope Gilliatt of *The New Yorker* gave the first favorable review. Pauline Kael went even further in the same publication, writing a 9,000-word essay praising it as one of *the* greatest cinematic triumphs.

Momentum for *Bonnie and Clyde* built up by late 1967. It even inspired a top 10 hit in 1968, "The Ballad of Bonnie and Clyde" by Georgie Fame. "Foggy Mountain Breakdown" by Flatt & Scruggs became a top 60 entry on the pop charts that same year thanks in part to its inclusion in the movie. The movie scored ten Oscar nominations. Two of them were wins (for supporting actress Parsons and for the cinematography), and the rest were for best picture, actor, actress, supporting actors (Gene Hackman and Michael J. Pollard), director, screenplay written directly for the screen, and costume design.

Many saw its appeal as addressing contemporary concerns even though it was set more than 30 years earlier. The themes of *Bonnie and Clyde* include the importance of fame as part of the gangsters' appeal, class distinctions (they robbed from the banks that foreclosed on needy people) and even the generation gap. Ivan, C.W.'s father, hates his son more for his tattoo than his crimes. (C.W.: "I don't see what's so bad about it." Ivan: "You wouldn't!") That disgust leads Ivan to set up Bonnie and Clyde to be killed.

When CBS ran *Bonnie and Clyde* to open the 1973–1974 season of its Thursday night movie series, it appropriately followed *The Waltons* (see 69), which had a similar Depression backdrop but certainly not the same style. CBS edited three minutes out of the movie, including a good chunk of the finale, rendering the bloody finish rather tame.

As well as *Bonnie and Clyde* performed, finishing #1 for the week, it might have done even better if it had not run against the Billie Jean King–Bobby Riggs "battle of the sexes" tennis match on ABC, which finished third for the week with a 28.1 rating. (Coming in second was *All in the Family*— see 25.) Of course, CBS slotted it there to blunt the game's rating, so network leaders were happy nonetheless.

CBS reran *Bonnie and Clyde* on Sept. 27, 1974, with a solid 22.3/39. Since then, it has become a fixture on most "greatest movie of all time" lists. For a movie planned to emulate the French New Wave, it instead set its own style and profoundly influenced American cinema for years to come.

77 — *The Dean Martin Show*

Jan. 15, 1970. **Rating:** 33.5. **Share:** n/a.
Aired on NBC Thursday 10–11 P.M. Eastern and Pacific, 9–10 P.M. Central
Competition: *It Takes a Thief* (last episode in this time slot) on ABC, *Escape from Fort Bravo* (second hour of two-hour movie released in 1953; rerun) on CBS
Cast: Dean Martin, The Golddiggers, Ken Lane, Les Brown and His Band. **Guests:** Sammy Davis, Jr., Andy Griffith, Paul Lynde, Glen Ash. **Crew:** Greg Garrison (executive producer), Bill Colleran (director), Paul Keyes, Arnie Kogen, Rod Parker, Ed. Weinberger (writers).

Synopsis. Following the usual lush playing of Dean Martin's theme song "Everybody Loves Somebody" (a #1 hit in 1964), the host appears in this week's installment that features two big-name guests appearing on the series for the first time — Sammy Davis, Jr., and Andy Griffith — and one familiar face, Paul Lynde, who had been on the show several times this season as comic support. (Glen Ash, a comedian-singer, was an Andy Griffith protégé who acted opposite him a year later in the short-lived *The New Andy Griffith Show*.) Amid Dean's customary humorous ad-libs, there are two primary comedy segments. Griffith contributes a monologue dealing with "the birds and the bees," while Lynde plays a cocktail lounge pianist trying to be heard among loud, obnoxious customers.

The many musical numbers include Davis' version of "Wichita Lineman" and Griffith singing "Lydia the Tattooed Lady." Davis joins Martin for an extended medley that includes two of Sammy's hits, "What Kind of Fool Am I?" and "I've Gotta Be Me," along with "Sam's Song," "I Can't Give You Anything But Love," "Pennies from Heaven," "Stay Away from My Door," "Back in Your Own Backyard" and "Birth of the Blues." On his own, Dean croons "Open Up the Door and Let the Good Times In" (which cracked the top 60 on the *Billboard* pop chart in 1967 when Martin released it as a single) and "I Don't Know Why."

Backstory. "You know, I've signed the NBC contract for 34 millions. God! I am not worth it. What do I do? I do an hour; and out of that hour, I sing maybe ten songs. The rest, I talk. And I make fun of my wife, of my children, of my mother-in-law, of myself, of my drinkin'."

Those words to journalist Oriana Fallaci in *Look* magazine in 1967 were about the most elaborate statements Dean Martin ever made in describing his hit series that ran for nine years. While not a perfect summation of the show, it does accurately reflect how its star viewed it. That nonchalance, both on and off air, appealed to many viewers but bothered others, who regarded it more as indifference. Yet it's the image that helped him shake off his previous reputation of just being straight man to Jerry Lewis from 1946 through 1956, and it made *The Dean Martin Show* NBC's first variety series to crack the top 10 regularly since *The Perry Como Show* in 1956 and 1957.

NBC's desire for Martin to host his own series sprang from his several well-received appearances as a guest star in specials as well as a guest host on ABC's *The Hollywood Palace*, as well as his return to the music charts with the popularity of "Everybody Loves Somebody." Martin preferred to work in the more leisurely hours of nightclubs and theatrical movies, so he made what he thought were ridiculous demands that NBC would reject — a large salary, total ownership of the series for repeats, a schedule where he only would tape it on Sundays with virtually no rehearsal, and even the right not to sing if he did not feel like it. To his shock, NBC was so eager to have him that they conceded to all of his requests. It debuted on Sept. 16, 1965. The ratings the first season were nothing spectacular, although they did outshine the competing *The Long, Hot Summer* on ABC and improve upon Dean's weak lead-in, the sitcom *Mona McCluskey*. By the second season Dean's series made the top 15, one of only three NBC series there (*Bonanza* was #1 and *The Virginian* was #10).

In 1967 NBC nearly lost Johnny Carson as host of *The Tonight Show* thanks to the network's poor treatment of the star. They knew they needed to do better in order to retain talent, so they offered Dean that $34 million contract that lasted three years. It paid off well for both parties, as Dean's series regularly won its time period in 1967-1968 and 1968-1969, finishing at #8 for each season. It still usually beat its ABC and CBS competition in the 1969-1970 season, even though the ratings dropped a little to end it at #14.

This episode scored so highly during that

season probably for two reasons. One was "Location, location, location"—it aired right after the very popular *Bob Hope Christmas Special* (see 7), and a sizable percentage of the millions of Americans who watched that show stuck around for this one. The other was its two guests. Andy Griffith remained a very popular TV star in 1970, and many people knew that Martin had spent years on and off the stage in Las Vegas hanging with fellow "Rat Pack" member Sammy Davis, Jr., and wanted to see if their chemistry remained the same.

According to music director Lee Hale in *Backstage at The Dean Martin Show*, which he co-wrote with Richard D. Neely, the medley of songs he created for Davis and Martin came across flat during the taping until the star took a pratfall to throw Sammy off guard. The trick worked, Davis cracked up and the medley finished much looser than when it started.

Unfortunately, it was around this time that Martin was splitting up with his wife Jeanne after two decades of marriage, which shocked everybody. The press identified his girlfriend as Gail Renshaw, a 22-year-old Miss World–USA when Martin first met her in Las Vegas in October 1969. "You want to know about my marriage plans— well, I can tell you that I don't have the girl yet," Martin told a *Photoplay* reporter. "It's as simple as that. Gail's a great gal, but I'm not about to rush into anything. Anyway, as I say, neither of us has made any decisions."

As news of Martin's personal life appeared in the press, he agreed to record new lines to replace jokes he had made about his wife on some episodes before they aired, to deflect criticism of being insensitive. But Dean's image as a family man in real life was ruined, and his ratings started to slide. "*The Dean Martin Show* would never be the same," concluded Hale. (Hale insisted that Dean covered for another celebrity who really was involved with Renshaw, by the way. He did not specify who the person was, but his clues unmistakably indicated Bob Hope.)

The Dean Martin Show ended the 1969-1970 season with one Emmy nomination, for Variety or Musical Series. It lost, just as it had in 1967, 1968, 1969 and later in 1972. Its last Emmy nominations were for guest appearances by Foster Brooks and Ruth Buzzi in 1974.

By the end of the 1971-1972 season, *The Dean Martin Show* was failing to crack the top 30. NBC kept faith in the series and moved it from its Thursdays at 10–11 P.M. Eastern and Pacific slot in September 1973 to Friday nights at the same time,

renaming it *The Dean Martin Comedy Hour*. But it was far behind movies on CBS, and NBC decided its borderline finish of #38 for the season was not good enough for renewal. The series ended on May 24, 1974.

Martin showed up in NBC specials the rest of the decade, sometimes for Christmas shows but mostly as host of celebrity roasts honoring notable names with insults and jokes. On May 11, 1979, NBC aired a two-hour special, *The Best of Dean*, that included clips of his series without any new Martin footage in it. That same year, MCA attempted to sell 100 edited half-hours of the series to local stations as *The Best of Dean Martin*, but there was not enough interest shown to make it a success. (However, 26 selected hour-long shows did appear on a few stations by 1980.)

Yet Martin's legacy remained strong, even if he rarely turned up on TV from the 1980s until his death in 1995. On the *NBC 75th Anniversary Special* on May 5, 2002, several clips celebrated the performer, with Bob Newhart appearing in person to recount how often he guested on the program. Along with a revival of appreciation of the Rat Pack era via the 2001 remake of *Ocean's Eleven* (Martin had appeared in the 1960 original), a new round of popularity led to production of a 29-volume *Best of the Dean Martin Show* DVD collection in 2003.

There were fights over the legal rights to selling the old episodes for a time, with NBC claiming it had ownership, but they eventually were cleared and it can be purchased currently at www.dean variety.com. Unfortunately, as of this writing, the series' highest-rated show remains unavailable.

---

76 — *The Sound of Music*

Feb. 29, 1976 (movie special; first released theatrically in 1965). **Rating:** 33.6. **Share:** 49.

Aired on ABC Sunday 7–10:25 P.M. Eastern and Pacific, 6–9:25 P.M. Central

Competition: *60 Minutes, Sonny and Cher, Kojak* (repeat) and *Bronk* (first half-hour) on CBS, *Disney, Ellery Queen* and *Columbo* on NBC

Cast: Julie Andrews (Maria), Christopher Plummer (Capt. Von Trapp), Eleanor Parker (Baroness Schraeder), Richard Haydn (Max Detweiler), Peggy Wood (Mother Abbess), Charmian Carr (Liesl), Heather Menzies (Louisa), Nicholas Hammond (Friedrich), Duane Chase (Kurt), Angela Cartwright (Brigitta), Debbie Turner (Marta), Kym Karath (Gretl). **Crew:** Robert Wise (producer-director), Ernest Lehman (writer).

Synopsis. Sister Maria prefers to spend time in the hills of Austria rather than attend to her duties as a nun. Noting her behavior, Mother Abbess sends her to the home of widowed Capt. Von Trapp, who needs a governess to take care of his troublesome seven children (Leisl, Louisa, Friedrich, Kurt, Brigitta, Marta and Gretl). She wins them over through her love of music, and they bond with her as much as they dislike their father's new girlfriend, the icy Baroness Schraeder. While family friend Max Detweiler thinks the Von Trapp children have the talent needed to make them a hit musical group, the baroness feels threatened and thus falsely congratulates Maria for luring a romance out of Capt. Von Trapp. A distraught Maria, feeling that she is tearing the family apart, discreetly leaves the home.

Back at the abbey, Maria confesses to Mother Abbess that she is uncertain how she feels about the captain. She is urged to return and discover if he really loves her. The children greet her happily but inform Maria that their father plans to wed the baroness. A dejected Maria plans to leave until Capt. Von Trapp admits he has fallen in love with her and wants to marry her. After the wedding, the Nazis overtake Austria and plan to force the Captain to join them. The family sings at a public concert, then makes a daring escape with the help of the nuns before crossing the border to freedom.

Backstory. Hundreds of texts have attempted to analyze exactly why *The Sound of Music* is so overwhelmingly popular with most audiences, today as well as when it first premiered. Here is my humble take on it, leaving aside the melodious tunes, and in the movie the superb direction, editing and location cinematography: The story focuses on a young woman trying to find her place in the world, and a father attempting to reconnect with his children. These are two very powerful themes that resonate with nearly everyone, and when you combine that with the other elements, the result is intoxicating to all but the most cynical of viewers.

Producer-director Robert Wise and writer Ernest Lehman make this adaptation of the long-running Broadway hit (1,443 performances from 1959 to 1963) feel more like a movie than just a filmed musical. The two men had the same approach on *West Side Story* in 1961, but it is even more impressive here given the location shooting in Austria. Few movies begin as memorably: a sweeping shot through the clouds down to Julie Andrews twirling on a hilltop as she trills out the title tune.

"I spent weeks in Salzburg before starting *The Sound of Music*," Lehman told John Brady in *The Craft of the Screenwriter*. "The picture would have been totally different if I had never gone to Salzburg. I got many ideas for the screenplay just from seeing locales and thinking of ways of working them into the movie."

There was also some manipulation of the order of songs from the Broadway version, whose book was written by Howard Lindsay and Russel Crouse. (Lindsay and Crouse based it on Maria Trapp's book *The Story of the Trapp Family Singers*.) Lehman thought it was wrong to have the Mother Abbess sing "My Favorite Things," and that it would work better when Maria is trying to pacify the children. In the stage production, Maria wins the children over with "The Lonely Goatherd," which Lehman transformed into a show with the Bil Baird Puppets supposedly being manipulated by Maria and the children for the enjoyment of Max, the baroness and Capt. Von Trapp.

A few songs were removed ("No Way to Stop It," "An Ordinary Couple" and "How Can Love Survive?"), which seems at first glance like blasphemy to do to the final musical created by Richard Rodgers and Oscar Hammerstein II (the latter died in 1960). For the film, Rodgers created "Something Good" as a replacement for "An Ordinary Couple" when Maria and the captain profess their mutual love, plus "I Have Confidence," a solo for Andrews. Dropping the other two songs meant that the baroness and Max could be played in the movie by non-singers.

Lehman was hired to work on the film in 1962 while the musical still was on Broadway. 20th Century–Fox had bought the property under the condition that their film could not be released before Jan. 1, 1965, in order to avoid undercutting its potential run on stage, and Fox wanted to make sure it had the potential hit ready to go into movies after that date. Originally director William Wyler was hired, but he proved to be more interested in making the Nazis more important in the storyline, so he was out after Lehman sent his first draft for his approval. When Wise saw a copy of Lehman's script, he eagerly joined the project.

Wise lived up to his surname by reviewing Lehman's suggestion to use Julie Andrews as Maria and agreeing to it immediately once he saw unreleased footage of her from *Mary Poppins*, her big 1964 hit movie. To many people, Andrews was simply perfect for the role, able to handle all the high and low notes in its score plus the comic and romantic elements of the part. She set the tone for a pleasant shoot that nonetheless went five weeks over its schedule. But when the movie previewed on Feb. 1, 1965, in Minneapolis and received a standing ovation at its intermission, Fox knew it had a hit, though maybe not how big a hit. Premiering in theatres March 2, 1965, it was still running in many of them a year later.

The movie won five Oscars out of ten nominations, for Best Picture, Directing, Film Editing, Music (which was actually given to Irwin Kostal for scoring it) and Sound. The other nominations were for Best Actress (Andrews), Supporting Actress (Peggy Wood), Art Direction-Set Direction, Cinematography and Costume Design. There was no nomination for Lehman, but he felt the movie's enormous success validated his work just as well as an Oscar would. (Adjusted for inflation, *The Sound of Music* is one of the top 10 money-making pictures of all time.)

Although both the original cast and soundtrack albums were multimillion sellers (they stayed on *Billboard*'s LP chart for nearly five years, including stops at the #1 position), and the songs from them are considered standards sung by a multitude of different artists, it is surprising that no versions of them ever cracked the top 40 on the singles chart. The closest anyone came was Herb Alpert and The Tijuana Brass with their instrumental version of "My Favorite Things," which made #45 in 1969.

In late 1974, following a successful theatrical re-release, 20th Century–Fox TV president William Self peddled one showing of the movie for sale to all three networks as part of a package of pictures from the studio. ABC purchased the deal for $15 million. It became the second-highest rated movie of the 1975-1976 season behind *Jeremiah Johnson* (see 42).

NBC signed a 20-year exclusive deal for *The Sound of Music* in 1978, and put its first showing in a tough time slot, opposite the last night of *Roots: The Next Generation* (see 99) on Feb. 25, 1979, where it performed very respectably with a 21.6/30. More controversial was its decision to edit nearly a half-hour out of the film to fit a 3½-hour time slot with commercials, cutting some songs in the process. By the 1990s the televised film had hosts such as Billy Bush and even an audience participation spot.

When the NBC contract ended, the Fox network ran it in 2001. Then ABC gained control of the movie the following year and slated it for Christmas showings (rather appropriate, given how "My Favorite Things" by Barbra Streisand and the Supremes, among other artists, became a

standard part of most popular radio station's Christmas playlist). By then, the movie was a hit in theatres in a sing-a-long version where audiences follow the lyrics on screen. Some of the more dedicated (or deranged) fans dress up as Maria, a nun or a Nazi for these events. The NBC sitcom *Will & Grace* memorably parodied such gatherings in its Jan. 5, 2006, "Von Trapped" episode.

On Oct. 28, 2010, the cast reunited one more time on *The Oprah Winfrey Show* to celebrate the movie's 45th anniversary DVD release. To many people, it is simply the best movie musical ever.

---

75 — *Elvis: Aloha from Hawaii*

April 4, 1973 (special). **Rating:** 33.8. **Share:** 51.
Aired on NBC Wednesday 8:30–10 P.M. Eastern and Pacific, 7:30–9 P.M. Central
Competition: *The Farmer's Daughter* (movie special; network TV debut of 1997 film) on ABC; *The Sonny and Cher Comedy Hour* (repeat; last half-hour) and *Medical Center* on CBS
Cast: Elvis Presley, J.D. Sumner and the Stamps Quartet, The Sweet Inspirations, Kathy Westmoreland, Charlie Hodge, James Burton (lead guitarist), John Wilkerson (rhythm guitarist), Ronnie Tutt (drums), Jerry Schiff (bassist), Glen Hardin (pianist), The Joe Guercio Orchestra. **Crew:** Elvis Presley and RCA Record Tours (executive producers), Marty Pasetta (producer and director), Joe Guercio (musical director).

Synopsis. Crowds wait outside the Honolulu International Center Arena as "Also Sprach Zarathusra" accompanies them. They enter, then Elvis Presley arrives at the height of the dubbed theme and takes a guitar to strum as he, the band and backup singers launch into "See See Rider." Next is his 1972 hit "Burning Love," sped up. Viewers see some shots split into four uneven parts — let's call it a "quad screen."

Elvis says hi, receives the first of several leis from a woman in the audience, and states, "We're going to try to do all the songs you wanna hear." He then sings the Beatles' "Something" and Frankie Laine's "You Gave Me a Mountain," both of which he had never released on record. A "quad screen" follows with outdoor island scenes mixed with Elvis vocalizing "Early Morning Rain."

Elvis shows his swagger during "Steamroller Blues" and "My Way." "Love Me," "Johnny B. Goode," "It's Over," "Blue Suede Shoes," "I'm So

Lonesome I Could Cry," "I Can't Stop Loving You" and "Hound Dog" follow.

"Blue Hawaii" is in "quad screen," then comes "Suspicious Minds," band introductions, "I'll Remember You," "Hawaiian Wedding Song," "Long Tall Sally," "Whole Lotta Shakin' Goin' On," "Ku-u-i-po," "American Trilogy," "A Big Hunk of Love" and finally "Can't Help Falling in Love." The "Big E" leaves the stage as the show's soundtrack LP is plugged.

Backstory. No serious survey of 20th century pop culture is complete without discussing Elvis Presley. "The King of Rock and Roll" impacted music (where he notched 20 #1 hit singles and nine #1 albums from 1956 to 1973, among many other achievements), movies (he was voted among the top 10 box office stars from 1961 through 1966, even though most of his films were not consider great entertainment) and television. Following his generally high-rated appearances on *Stage Show, The Milton Berle Show, The Steve Allen Show* and *The Ed Sullivan Show* in 1956 and 1957, and a guest appearance on a Frank Sinatra special in 1960, Elvis was off TV until his "comeback" special, *Singer Presents Elvis Presley*, ran on NBC on Dec. 3, 1968. It scored a hefty 32.0 rating and was #1 for the week it aired. Then he took another sabbatical from the medium for five years, chiefly to appear in Las Vegas, before returning with this, his biggest TV exposure ever.

Elvis's longtime manager (and some would argue exploiter) "Col." Tom Parker announced on July 8, 1972, that with technological improvements to broadcast events as they actually happen via satellite now in place, a special Elvis concert would take place in Hawaii to allow the singer's fans worldwide the chance to seem him live all at one time. (Elvis never appeared in concert overseas despite his popularity in most countries, and many suspect it was because Parker was not a legal citizen of America and therefore could not join his client on tour without encountering visa problems.) He planned it for the fall, but MGM objected, as the movie studio had the documentary *Elvis on Tour* coming out in theaters at that time; Parker pushed back the concert date. Parker was credited as one of the "Production Coordinators for All-Star Show."

Elvis: Aloha from Hawaii was broadcast live via satellite to many countries on Jan. 14, 1973. However, that same date was when Super Bowl VII was played, and since NBC was carrying that popular event (it earned a 42.7 rating), the Elvis show had to be delayed for broadcast in America. That suited producer-director Marty Pasetta fine, as it

gave him time to edit the concert. He convinced Presley to record five songs on stage after the concert ended to be included in the final videotaped show on NBC.

The concert benefited the cause named after a Hawaiian native, the Kuiokalalaini Lee Cancer Fund, on the urging of Eddie Sherman, a columnist with the *Honolulu Advertiser* newspaper. Lee wrote the island hit "I'll Remember You," which Elvis sang on the show in honor of the musician who wrote it (Lee had died in 1966). Elvis prompted cheers from the audience when he told them the goal of raising $25,000 for the fund had been surpassed by $50,000 (very impressive in 1973 dollars).

Elvis looked pretty good throughout the show, coming out wearing a white suit with spangles that form an eagle emblem and sporting a big ring on his left hand. He looks trim amid his sideburns and black hair. He has good rapport with the audience, telling them "My Way" is one of his favorites while tossing some sash scarves to them. He plays with his lei, and they love every second of it.

The special replaced the *NBC Wednesday Mystery Movie* and provided NBC with a rare win that season in the time slot, as *The Sonny and Cher Comedy Hour* and *Medical Center* on CBS and the *ABC Movie of the Week* regularly trounced it. (Even so, the network retained the *NBC Wednesday Mystery Movie* for a second season in 1973-1974, but ratings remained poor and it went off soon thereafter.) In bizarre counterprogramming, ABC ran *The Farmer's Daughter*, the network debut of a black-and-white film that had won Loretta Young an unexpected Oscar for best actress 25 years earlier. The results were anemic numbers (10.3/16); only one other movie on network TV scored lower ratings during the 1972-1973 season. It marked the last time a black-and-white movie made before 1960 made its network TV debut in prime time. NBC repeated the Elvis special as a replacement for the *NBC Wednesday Mystery Movie* again on Nov. 14, 1973 (16.4/25).

The special's success helped propel the album *Aloha from Hawaii Via Satellite* to #1 on the *Billboard* chart within a month, knocking the powerhouse *Dark Side of the Moon* by Pink Floyd out of the top. The album included six tunes Presley recorded in 1972 in Madison Square Garden to make it a double LP. "Steamroller Blues" was released as a single from *Aloha from Hawaii Via Satellite* and peaked at #17.

This album would be the last chart topper for Elvis, and only one other Presley single would surpass the performance of "Steamroller Blues":

"Promised Land" barely cracked the top 15 in late 1974. It was a dubious sign that by 1976, the most-heard Presley vocal on top 40 radio came from Memphis deejay Rick Dees doing a mock impersonation of Elvis offering thanks at the end of the million-selling novelty record "Disco Duck."

Even so, "The Pelvis" remained an A-list name in high demand. He made news when he refused to let any clips of this special or others appear on *NBC: The First Fifty Years* on Nov. 21, 1976. Presley was the only celebrity who opted out of that celebration. The decision probably came from Parker, who as the years went by made sure Elvis appeared only in ways that would provide Parker with maximum financial benefit.

Parker did agree to another videotaped Elvis concert, to run in 1977. Unfortunately, years of prescription drug abuse took their toll and caused heart failure that resulted in Presley's death on Aug. 16, 1977, at age 42. Less than two months later, *Elvis in Concert* aired posthumously on CBS Oct. 3, and scored an impressive 33.2 rating. In one of his last public appearances, Elvis looked puffy in the face and body.

Portrayals of the King on TV since his death have ranged from reverential to ridiculous. The former included a 1979 TV-movie with Kurt Russell (see 6 — *Gone with the Wind*) and a 1990 series with Michael St. Gerard, both titled *Elvis*, and the NBC tribute special *Elvis Remembered: Nashville to Hollywood* on Feb. 8, 1980 (12.7/20). *Elvis Meets Nixon*, a 1997 TV-movie made for cable, portrays Presley and President Richard M. Nixon as fools when they met in 1970 to fight drug abuse. Elvis impersonators have appeared on talk shows (*Late Night with David Letterman*) and sitcoms (*The Golden Girls*, with Quentin Tarentino as one of the *faux* Presleys). Reports even surfaced that people were seeing him alive in the late 1980s, and some witnesses became guests on *The Oprah Winfrey Show*.

Three decades after his death, Elvis remains larger than life on a screen barely able to contain his legacy. The King has become the Legend.

74 — AFC Division Championship Game

Jan. 2, 1982 (San Diego Chargers vs. Miami Dolphins). **Rating:** 33.9. **Share:** 52.

Aired on NBC Saturday 5–9 P.M. Eastern, 4–8 P.M. Central, 3–7 P.M. Mountain, 2–6 P.M. Pacific

Competition: *Annie and the Franklins* (variety special) on CBS; *Open All Night* and *Making a Living* on ABC (ABC and CBS shows seen head-to-head against game only in Eastern and Central time zones)

Cast: Don Criqui (play-by-play announcer), John Brodie (color commentator), Bryant Gumbel (host-anchor).

Synopsis. Miami was a three-point favorite coming into this playoff game, which was expected to be a close battle. It lived up to that and more, although it did not appear that way for the home team in the first quarter, as the Dolphins fell behind 24–0. San Diego's first score came from a field goal by Rolf Benirschke, followed by three touchdowns led by quarterback Dan Fouts. But in the second quarter, Miami replaced David Woodley at quarterback with Don Strock, who rallied the team to score 17 points while the Dolphins defense prevented San Diego from adding to its tally. The score was 24–17 at halftime.

In the third quarter both sides scored, ending the period tied at 31–31. Each team scored a touchdown in the fourth quarter, but with four seconds left in the game, Dolphins kicker Uwe von Schamann had a potential game-winning, 43-yard field goal attempt blocked by Chargers tight end Kellen Winslow. The game headed into overtime, and to the frustration of home fans at the Orange Bowl Stadium, von Schamann had another kick blocked at the 11:27 mark. Benirschke, who could have ended up being blamed for losing the game by missing a 27-yard attempt in overtime, redeemed himself by kicking a 29-yard field goal 13 minutes and 52 seconds into the extra period. The 41–38 final in favor of the Chargers remains the highest-scoring NFL playoff game as of this writing.

Backstory. There are professional football contests, and then there are ones like this, which has been nicknamed the "Epic Game." There were 11 team records set in this game, including Fouts throwing 33 of 53 passes for 433 yards, an unprecedented offensive production in a league play-off. Indeed, most of the records involved offense, including most total yards by two teams (1,036) and most passing yards by two teams (836).

Another record (13 receptions for a total of 166 yards) was set by tight end Kellen Winslow. In addition to blocking Miami's field goal attempt win in regulation, he scored a touchdown. And he accomplished it all while suffering from dehydration, severe cramps, a pinched nerve in his shoulder and a gash in his lips that needed three stitches.

It was quite a display of football at its finest, and I cannot imagine there were too many people in the Eastern and Central time zones upset because this contest extended so long that it preempted the *Barbara Mandrell and the Mandrell Sisters* variety series that opened NBC's Saturday night lineup in 1982.

Coming into this game, the San Diego Chargers were 10–6 and the Miami Dolphins were 11–4–1. The Dolphins' loss here marked their fourth consecutive failure to win the playoff game since 1974. The game finished #2 in the week's ratings (behind a Jan. 3 NFL divisional playoff game that scored a 35.7/53).

The two key offensive players for the Chargers in this game later had careers in network broadcasting. Fouts became an analyst for ABC's NCAA football games starting in 1997. Two years later, the network drafted him to serve as part of the new team for *Monday Night Football*, with Fouts supplying color along with comedian Dennis Miller, while Al Michaels handled the play-by-play.

When ABC decided in 2002 that the combination was not working as well as hoped amid flat ratings and mixed reviews, and the network had the chance to add admired analyst John Madden to its Monday night lineup, Fouts was demoted back to NCAA football coverage. ABC figured that even though it traditionally had used three announcers on *Monday Night Football*, Madden was a fine enough analyst that he only needed Michaels to help him.

Benirschke served as host of the daytime version of the NBC game show *Wheel of Fortune* starting on Jan. 9, 1989, replacing Pat Sajak when the latter started an ill-fated late night talk show on CBS (Sajak stayed with the syndicated version of the show, where he remains as of this writing). But the performance of the kicker there was found to be lacking; with ratings dropping, he was dismissed from the series on June 30, 1989.

The jubilation over the Chargers' win turned out to be short-lived: They lost the AFC conference championship 27–7 to the Cincinnati Bengals on Jan. 10, 1982. It was bitterly cold (nine below zero) and Fouts could not hold the ball well in conditions that he was not used to facing in balmy San Diego. As of this writing, the Chargers have yet to appear in a Super Bowl.

73 — *Born Free*

Feb. 22, 1970 (first released theatrically in 1966). **Rating:** 34.2. **Share:** 53.

Aired on CBS Sunday 7–9 P.M. Eastern and Pacific, 6–8 P.M. Central

Competition: *Land of the Giants* and *The F.B.I.* on ABC, *Wild Kingdom*, *Disney* (rerun of "Big Red") and *Pogo* (cartoon special) on NBC

Cast: Virginia McKenna (Joy Adamson), Bill Travers (George Adamson), Geoffrey Keen (John Kendall), Peter Lukoye (Nuru), Omar Chambati (Makkede), Bill Godden (Sam), Robert Young (James), Bryan Epsom (Baker), Geoffrey Best (Mr. Watson), Robert Cheetham (Ken), Surya Patel (Doctor). **Host:** Dick Van Dyke. **Crew:** Sam Jaffe, Paul Radin (producers), James Hill (director), Gerald L.C. Copley (writer; a pseudonym for Lester Cole).

Synopsis. George Adamson, senior game warden in the northern province of Kenya, kills a man-eating lion and its mate and takes their three cubs to his wife, Joy. She names the smallest one Elsa, after a schoolmate who was petite but also bright and brave. Joy mothers Elsa, who accompanies her when George is away. When the lions are big enough to be dangerous, they are taken to the Rotterdam Zoo — all but Elsa, to whom Joy is attached.

Joy and George go to the coast to resolve the problem of a goat-eating lion, as well as cure George of his malaria. When they return, Elsa plays with elephants, causing a stampede in the village. John Kendall, George's boss, insists that Elsa be sent to a zoo. "I can't let her be caged the rest of her life," Joy protests. She asks for three months to train Elsa to survive in the wild.

After fruitless efforts at a reserve 340 miles away, John gives them an extension to try Elsa at a location only 35 miles from where she was born. She finally goes out in the bush and kills game, and is left there. John and George later return to Nairobi for a week, and they find Elsa and her three cubs on their last day. "We saw her many times again, born free and living free," Joy says. "But to us, she was always the same — our friend, Elsa."

Backstory. Based on the 1960 nonfiction book by Joy Adamson, *Born Free* is a wonderful family film, filled with gorgeous scenery as it thoughtfully meditates on the rights of animals and the way humans interact with them. Joy knows that she must let go of her maternal feelings for the lion yet refuses to let imprisonment become Elsa's fate. "She was born free and she has the right to live free," Joy says.

Born Free did reasonably well when it was initially distributed, but there was little reason to expect it to be a blockbuster when it was telecast. But it was, thanks to careful strategy and publicity by CBS as part of what programming head Mike Dann dubbed Operation 100 — a plan to overtake NBC in the 1969-1970 season.

CBS had held the title of TV's annual No. 1 network since the 1956-1957 season, when it beat out NBC for the first time since the networks had been competing against each other in radio in the late 1920s. It was a source of pride for Dann to keep that record during his tenure in the 1960s. But he made poor choices for five new series in the fall 1969 schedule — all but one, *Medical Center*, lasted no more than two years — and by midseason NBC led in the ratings by a considerable margin. Dann realized he had to make radical changes if CBS were to retain its title, so he cancelled a few shows, relocated others and installed specials and events designed to grab eyeballs.

"But no program epitomized our promotional success more than *Born Free*," Dann wrote in his memoirs. "It was Fred Silverman's idea to run *Born Free* on a Sunday evening because, he argued, it was a kids' show, and if we put in the right time slot, the whole family would watch it." So Dann pre-empted *Lassie*, *To Rome with Love* (one of his loser 1969 newcomers) and *The Ed Sullivan Show* to run the movie there. To increase turnout, the beloved Dick Van Dyke served as host for the special event.

"And in the four or five days leading up to the show, we promoted *Born Free* in three or four separate trailers," Dann wrote. "During the commercial break in weekday soap operas, we played clips of the movie's drama and heartbreak for the housewives, in the evening we played clips of the hunting scenes and the action for the fathers, and on the Saturday morning before the show we played clips of the cute lion cubs in between the kids' cartoon shows."

The appeals to the different demographics worked, and *Born Free* became CBS's highest-rated movie up to that time except for the 1964 and 1965 repeats of *The Wizard of Oz* (see 52). But though it finished a strong #1 for the week and gave a ratings boost that helped CBS eclipse NBC in the ratings for the 1969-1970 season, *Born Free* could not save Dann ultimately. CBS owner Bill Paley was convinced by others in the organization that Dann had lost his magic touch by having to resort to the gimmicky Operation 100 approach, and Dann resigned. Silverman assumed his role later in 1970.

As for *Born Free* the movie, its stars Bill Travers and Virginia McKenna were husband and wife in real life. They both worked closely for nearly a

year with 19 wild and half-tamed lions and lionesses in depicting Elsa's progression from a cub to a chaser. The duo learned how to sit, talk and sleep with lions, as well as how to feed them and play with them. "It was essential that we show no fear," McKenna told *Look* magazine. "Lions have no mercy for the frightened."

"No lion is a safe lion," added Travers, who nevertheless appeared comfortable in caressing the animals used in the picture.

The producers, director and technician filmed the scenes while protected behind a heavy wire. "I may have been the director, but the lions told us all what to do," quipped James Hill. George Adamson served as chief technical advisor on the film.

Born Free was photographed entirely on location in the Republic of Kenya with the cooperation of the Kenya Game Department and the Kenya National Parks. The filmmakers also thanked help from Haile Selassie of Ethiopia and the Game Department of Uganda.

The movie's writer, Lester Cole, was one of the "Hollywood Ten" who refused to testify before Congress in 1947 about suspected Communists in the entertainment industry. A co-founder of the Screen Writers Guild in 1933, he lived in London in the 1960s after being blacklisted from work on films in the United States and wrote under the pseudonym Gerald L.C. Copley for this movie. He later returned to America to teach screenwriting at the University of California at Berkeley before dying in 1985.

The majestic title tune (music by John Barry, lyrics by Don Black) was a staple on easy listening radio stations by the time of its TV debut, thanks to a top 10 hit instrumental version by Roger Williams in 1966; it won the Oscar for Best Song. Matt Munro sang the tune in the movie; a vocal version by the Hesitations also made the American top 40 in 1966. Barry claimed an Academy Award for Best Score too.

To capitalize on the film's success, CBS aired an hour-long documentary sequel called *Lions Are Free* on March 31, 1970, at 7:30 P.M. It reran the feature film to good ratings on March 14, 1971 (23.4/38) and so-so numbers on Nov. 21, 1971 (18.0/27). When ABC repeated the film on Aug. 15, 1975, it fared very poorly (7.4/17) and ranked as one of the 10 lowest-rated movies on TV that year.

A movie sequel, *Living Free* (1972), had few links to the original and did poorly at the box office. It debuted on NBC Nov. 27, 1976, with an unimpressive 14.4/27. That network also tried *Born Free* as a series, but it only ran from Sept. 9 through Dec. 12, 1974, opposite CBS's *Gunsmoke* (see 24).

If you find any of the story of *Born Free* too cute and precious, look for the 1970s *Carol Burnett Show* spoof where Carol played Joy and Harvey Korman played George as they attempted to force out to the wilderness Elsa, played by Tim Conway in a lion suit. It is hysterical.

---

72 — Sanford and Son

Dec. 27, 1974 ("Once a Thief"). **Rating:** 34.3. **Share:** n/a.

Aired on NBC Fridays 8–8:30 P.M. Eastern and Pacific, 7–7:30 P.M. Central

Competition: *Kung Fu* (repeat) on ABC; *Planet of the Apes* (last episode) on CBS

Cast: Demond Wilson (Lamont Sanford), Whitman Mayo (Grady Wilson), LaWanda Page (Aunt Esther Anderson), Hal Williams (Officer "Smitty" Smith), Howard Platt (Officer "Happy" Hopkins). **Guests:** Ron Glass (Herman Edwards), Don Rickles (Voice of Fight Announcer). **Crew:** Bud Yorkin (executive producer), Bernie Orenstein, Saul Turtletaub (producers), Herbert Kenwith (director), Winston Moss (writer).

Synopsis. When Lamont's friend Herman is released from jail, Lamont invites him to stay at his home. Suspicious housesitter Grady hides his radio in the freezer when he learns that Herman spent years behind bars for stealing a hi-fi set. The radio is very important to Grady, as he has a bet on a boxing match that will air the next day.

Aunt Esther visits Lamont and Grady and says she needs help at the hardware store she operates with her husband. The two men convince her to take Herman without revealing his past, but Esther learns the truth and fires Herman. That night, Grady attempts to listen to the fight without defrosting his radio first, and it explodes. Herman fetches a portable radio so the men can hear the contest. When Officers Smitty and Happy appear, Grady pretends to tune in the dead radio on the boxing match for the cops, as he thinks Herman stole the good radio. His ruse is revealed when Lamont returns and tells the truth. Herman insists he bought the radio, and the police accept his explanation.

The following day, Esther offers Herman his job back after learning it was Lamont and not Herman who lied about the latter's background.

Grady discovers another truth — Herman did buy the radio, but only put a down payment on it, and Grady owes the balance.

Backstory. In the summer of 1974, the man who played the most ornery junkman on television, Redd Foxx, seemed to channel his character's ire to the powers that be over his hit sitcom *Sanford and Son.* He had a list of demands he wanted addressed by NBC, including a private dressing room with a window and a rehearsal hall with a mirror. The network refused to capitulate, and new producers Bernie Orenstein and Saul Turtletaub made some *Sanford and Son* episodes featuring the son but not the father.

Playing that son was Demond Wilson, who did his best to remain neutral in the controversy. Actually, Wilson seemed to thrive somewhat in being in the dark during the early part of his career. For example, when he went to audition for the touring company of the Broadway hit *The Boys in the Band*, he had no idea that his character and all the others on stage were gay.

Wilson eventually made his way to Hollywood. While doing a guest shot on *Mission: Impossible* in 1971, he received a call from his agent to audition for a guest shot as a burglar on *All in the Family* (see 25). He won over the series' executive producer, Norman Lear, and unknowingly earned a regular role on another program.

With his partner Bud York, Lear was creating an American adaptation of the British sitcom *Steptoe and Son*, which failed to sell when they tried it with Caucasian leads. York and Lear then considered using black actors. They first approached Cleavon Little to play the younger lead, but Little was unable to do it. However, he did suggest they use Foxx as the father, as he had played a junkman in the 1970 film *Cotton Comes to Harlem.*

Foxx had made his name on "dirty" comedy records for about a decade before he began receiving national TV exposure in the mid–1960s. As a colorful man with a quip, he was in demand in the mid to late 1960s as a frequent guest on everything from *The Mike Douglas Show* to *The Hollywood Squares.* York and Lear took him along with Wilson as stars of their adaptation. Wilson frequently played the straight man to Foxx as Fred, who always seemed to have a scheme that he thought would benefit him but usually end up causing Lamont grief in the process.

Installed a midseason replacement for the crime drama *The D.A., Sanford and Son* debuted on Jan. 14, 1972, to lead off NBC's Friday night lineup. It became a top 10 fixture almost immediately and ended the 1971-1972 season at #6. *Sanford and Son* was the highest-rated new series of the season, and the highest-rated NBC sitcom since *Hazel* made #4 in the 1961-1962 season. *Sanford and Son* went on to surpass *Hazel* by finishing at #2 in 1972-1973 and #3 in 1973-1974. And then came the Foxx–NBC standoff.

With Foxx gone at the start of taping the series' fourth season, the producers decided to bump Whitman Mayo's character Grady Wilson up to lead. Grady was someone whose brain did not always fire on all cylinders, so he often unwittingly helped Fred with his schemes. In Season 4, Grady became the caretaker of Fred's house and garage while Fred was said to be visiting his family in St. Louis. With Grady's new role, the dynamics of the show shifted during those episodes. "There was a strange edge with Redd left," Wilson acknowledged to J.R. Young in *TV Guide*. "In fact, to be perfectly honest, everybody panicked. People screamed. Tempers flared."

Eventually, however, everyone calmed down and got on with the business of doing a show. But the Foxx-less episodes display just how flimsy the series was without him. Grady is a weak lead (a fact that was forgotten when NBC unwisely gave him his own spin-off, *Grady*, from Dec. 4, 1975 through March 4, 1976), the lines are not snappy and the plot plods despite the efforts of the cast. Missing from the show was Lamont's frequently seen buddy Rollo Larson, played by Nathaniel Taylor, but the most glaring absence was the usual exchange of putdowns between Fred and Esther, the towering, Bible-quoting sister of his late wife.

What made this episode a hit was that the other options on CBS and ABC were so pathetic that they virtually encouraged viewers to settle for this. I cannot imagine too many people who watched thought it was great entertainment. "I haven't been too happy with the scripts, but it's getting better," Wilson tellingly noted a few episodes after taping "Once a Thief." "It was hard to write around Redd, and hard with producers who haven't done black shows before."

NBC eventually agreed to Foxx's requests and he returned to *Sanford and Son*. The series ended the season at #2.

Sanford and Son remained NBC's top-rated sitcom and series at #2 in the 1975-1976 season. It slipped considerably to #27 in 1976-1977, even though there were several new characters introduced, including Aunt Esther's husband Woody (played by Raymond Allen), who was mentioned in "Once a Thief." Still, it looked to be a lock to return for a seventh season when ABC programming head Fred Silverman convinced Foxx to do a variety series for the network, which bombed in 1977, and Wilson refused to return to it. The circumstances forced *Sanford and Son* to end on Sept. 2, 1977.

Two weeks later in the same Friday 8–8:30 P.M. Eastern and Pacific slot, *The Sanford Arms* debuted on NBC with the supporting cast retained. Fred and Lamont supposedly left town and their old place became a hotel, an implausible development. It went off after five weeks. Foxx attempted to revive his character in a 1980 NBC series called *Sanford* (Lamont was nowhere to be found), but that lasted barely more than a year.

Foxx, who made people laugh faking a heart attack on *Sanford and Son* by clutching his chest and saying, "I'm coming, Elizabeth!" in reference to his late wife, passed away from one himself while rehearsing his new series *The Royal Family* in 1991. *Sanford and Son* still remains popular in reruns on several stations 40 years later.

71—*Here's Lucy*

Sept. 14, 1970 ("Lucy Meets the Burtons"). **Rating:** 34.3. **Share:** 52.

Aired on CBS Monday 8:30–9 P.M. Eastern and Pacific, 7:30–8 P.M. Central

Competition: *The Family Jewels* (first half-hour of two-hour movie released theatrically in 1967) on ABC, *Rowan and Martin's Laugh-In* (last half-hour) on NBC

Cast: Lucille Ball (Lucy Carter), Gale Gordon (Harrison Otis "Uncle Harry" Carter). **Guests:** Richard Burton, Elizabeth Taylor, Army Archerd, James Bacon, Marilyn Beck, Joan Crosby, Joyce Haber, Dick Kleiner, Morton Moss, Robert Rose, Vernon Scott, Cecil Smith (Themselves), Cliff Norton (Sam the plumber), Vanda Barra (Vanda), Brook Williams (Mr. Williams). **Crew:** Gary Morton (executive producer), Cleo Smith (producer), Jerry Paris (director), Bob Carroll, Jr., Madelyn Davis (writers).

Synopsis. During her lunch break, Lucy Carter and her pal Vanda wait outside the hotel where Richard Burton and Elizabeth Taylor are staying to get a glimpse of the glamorous couple. While Taylor is out shopping, Burton is in his room asking Mr. Williams, the hotel manager, to suggest a way to sneak out of the building (he wants to get Liz's diamond ring fixed). He sees an opportunity by switching clothes with Sam the plumber. Burton nearly escapes until Lucy grabs him to handle a leak at her office. As she fails to recognize him and the crowd swells, Burton goes back with Lucy to Harry Carter's Unique Employment Agency.

At the office, Lucy still thinks Burton is a plumber and forces him to repair her faucet. Harry arrives and clears a path for Burton to leave while a stunned Lucy awkwardly chats with the star. When Burton inadvertently leaves behind the ring in Sam's coveralls, Lucy tries it on, only to get it stuck on her finger. An upset Burton takes Lucy back to his hotel room, where Taylor screams about the news, particularly because she and Burton have a press party that night. But Lucy comes up with a plan.

That evening, the Burtons greet reporters Cecil Smith, Joyce Haber, James Bacon and Vernon Scott and show Elizabeth's ring to them as Lucy stands behind a curtain and sticks her left arm out through Taylor's gown. Lucy's gesticulations test the Burtons' patience, but in the end they forgive her.

Backstory. "Lucy Meets the Burtons" was a turning point for *Here's Lucy*. The third sitcom starring Lucille Ball debuted on Sept. 23, 1968, to mediocre to poor reviews, with many finding it passé and unoriginal compared to its competition on NBC, *Rowan and Martin's Laugh-In* (see 53). While it finished #9 in the 1968-1969 season and #6 in the 1969-1970 season, some CBS executives privately believed that Ball and her program were tired, as upscale, wealthier and younger audiences were not flocking to it. They planned to cancel it at the end of the 1970-1971 season.

Then Ball had a chance encounter with the world's most famous married couple at the time, with the latter saying they loved her series and wanted to be on it. With little time to spare, Lucy and her husband Gary Morton (her show's executive producer) contacted her best writers, Bob Carroll, Jr., and Madelyn Davis (formerly Madelyn Martin), to do the script. It was so solid that it earned one of the only two Emmy nominations for *Here's Lucy* (the other was for Gale Gordon as supporting actor, also for the 1970-1971 season).

The script's original opening scene had Lucy telling her boss Harry (her late husband's brother) that she was taking a coffee break at work, but it was dropped prior to filming due to the length of the episode. Lucy's take-charge attitude on the set peeved both director Jerry Paris and Burton himself; the latter criticized her bitterly in his private diaries, which were released posthumously.

Despite the disagreements, the episode generates hearty laughter and works beautifully. The enter-

tainment reporters and columnists who played themselves did a believable job, and Brook Williams is particularly amusing in his scene with Burton. At the end of the episode, there was a curtain call with Lucy introducing the cast and telling the audience, "Thank you, ladies and gentlemen, for one of the most wonderful nights I've ever had in my whole career."

Thanks to "Lucy Meets the Burtons," *Here's Lucy* finished the 1970-1971 season at #3, ahead of *Laugh-In*. But eventually the weak storylines doomed it. As it moved a half-hour later to start at 9 P.M. Eastern and Pacific for the 1971-1972 season, where it faced *Monday Night Football* directly during the fall months in the Eastern and Central time zones, it fell to #10. It declined to #15 in 1972-1973, the first time ever Ball did not finish in the top 10 for a season. By the time it went off on Sept. 2, 1974, the series ended at #29, and CBS canned it in part because Ball refused to modernize it. "She only knew how to do her show," said Stu Shostak, Lucy's personal film archivist. "She thought everybody still saw her as Lucy Ricardo. Television changed, but she didn't. She played for the studio audience and not the audience at home."

Shostak added that *Here's Lucy* lasted so long basically out of viewers' habits: "People were used to seeing her on Monday nights." Ball seemed to resent the growth of adult comedy on TV during the early 1970s. Shostak claimed Lucy refused to let CBS put *All in the Family* (see 25) on the same night as *Here's Lucy* because she was offended by its content. Ironically, *Maude*, a spinoff of *All in the Family*, assumed the Monday time slot previously held by *Here's Lucy* in September 1974.

Ball rarely acted following the cancellation of *Here's Lucy*, but she did host plenty of specials. On one, *CBS Salutes Lucy — The First 25 Years* (Nov. 28, 1976), Burton actually said a few words in favor of his former co-star. Calling the episode a study on one's ego, he noted, "Never has mine been so charmingly deflated as it was when Lucille Ball had a go of it."

The popularity of that special, as well as "Disco Lucy," a dance version of the *I Love Lucy* theme that came close to cracking the top 20 in early 1977, apparently encouraged CBS to install *Here's Lucy* as the opening show in its midmorning daily lineup on May 2, 1977, ahead of *The Price Is Right*. But *Here's Lucy* fared so poorly against NBC reruns of *Sanford and Son* that it was pulled six months later.

"After *Here's Lucy*, they were actually going to take a year off with specials and then return,"

Shostak said. But CBS was no longer interested in a series with Ball. In 1980, a desperate Fred Silverman offered her a possible series deal as part of a special. However, *Lucy Moves to NBC* received disappointing numbers when it aired on Feb. 8 (16.7/26), so that idea was scratched. A year later, Viacom, the distributor of *Here's Lucy*, finally sold its repeats to local TV stations. It bombed, and by the time Ball died in 1989, it virtually had been forgotten. A few DVD releases started appearing 15 years later, but none have been big sellers.

Even with its failings, *Here's Lucy* stands as a testament to Lucille Ball's enduring drawing power. Having three series, each running six years, with all but two of the seasons in the top 10, is an unmatched record.

70— Christmas with the Bing Crosbys

Dec. 10, 1972 (special, as part of a series of presentations by *The Bell System Family Theatre*). **Rating:** 34.4. **Share:** 50.

Aired on NBC Sunday 8–9 P.M. Eastern and Pacific, 7–8 P.M. Central

Competition: *The F.B.I.* on ABC, *M*A*S*H* and *The Sandy Duncan Show* on CBS

Cast: Bing Crosby, Kathryn Crosby, Nathaniel Crosby, Mary Crosby, Harry Crosby, Sally Struthers, David Hartman, Edward Villela, the Nick Perito Orchestra. **Crew:** Bob Finkel (executive producer), Marty Pasetta (director), Buz Kohan, Bill Angelos (writers).

Synopsis. With the title holiday just two weeks away, Bing Crosby, one of the top crooners of the 20th century, joins his wife, Kathryn, and their daughter and two sons to celebrate the occasion by singing "Home for the Holidays." Following it is an abbreviated rendition of Charles Dickens' *A Christmas Carol* where David Hartman plays Scrooge while Bing appears as the ghosts of Christmases past, present and future. Sally Struthers stars in the next segment as a woman struggling to put on a pageant in an elementary school with uncooperative students. She and Hartman then enact a musical adaptation of O. Henry's classic short story "The Gift of the Magi," where they play a poor couple who wind up buying each other an extravagant present that cannot be used because of what they sold to afford the item.

Kathryn and her three children contribute the tune "When You're Living with Santa Claus" to the festivities. Bing reappears in the next scene, but only as a narrator. Dancer Edward Villella offers his interpretation of the Anatole Frances' "The Juggler of Notre Dame." Then Bing rejoins his family to sing carols, ending with the hit that has been associated with him since he first sang it for the 1942 movie *Holiday Inn*: "White Christmas" by Irving Berlin.

Backstory. It's hard to believe that Bing Crosby, an entertainer associated in many people's minds with Christmas even today, did only 12 consecutive years of specials for the season on TV before his death in 1977, with the last one airing posthumously. Then again, the medium became popular when Crosby decided to cut back on his workload after flourishing in virtually every facet of show business for the first half of the 20th century, particularly the 1930s and 1940s. He had much success during that period on the music charts (over 280 charted entries from 1931–49, with 36 of them hitting #1, including of course the biggest selling single of all time, "White Christmas"), the movies (an Oscar for Best Actor for 1944's *Going My Way*, plus several years as one of the ten most popular actors), and radio, where he had a long-running hit nighttime series from 1936 until 1954. For the latter, he began taping his shows in advance in 1946 so he could spend more time playing golf, his favorite activity. By the '70s he had such a leisurely approach to work viewers should be grateful that they saw him on TV as much as they did.

Born Harry Lillis Crosby in 1903, Bing (his nickname came from a favorite comic strip, *The Bingville Bugle*) turned up occasionally on his own TV specials and variety shows in the 1950s, including *The Ed Sullivan Show* (see 11). He made cameo appearances on *I Married Joan* in 1953 (as a new neighbor who resembled you know who) and *The Phil Silvers Show* in 1957 (as himself, being conned by Sgt. Bilko to make a stop at the base during a cross-country tour). He also performed in "High Tor" on *Ford Star Jubilee* in 1956 opposite Julie Andrews. Crosby also established his own television production company. Its biggest successes were *Ben Casey* (see 88) and *Hogan's Heroes* (CBS, 1965–1971). Crosby appeared on neither of them.

Always in demand, Crosby did not perform his first TV Christmas show until Dec. 24, 1962, with guests Mary Martin and Andre Previn. *The Bing Crosby Christmas Show* was the first color special on ABC, which had wooed Crosby from NBC radio in 1946 with the promise of letting him tape his shows if the ratings stayed strong. The network definitely wanted him as a regular TV attraction, but he resisted until he agreed to star in a sitcom called — what else? — *The Bing Crosby Show*, debuting Sept. 14, 1964. But audiences preferred watching Andy Williams (see 95) on NBC, so the program lasted just one season, with its final airing on June 14, 1965.

Thereafter, Crosby showed up frequently as a guest host on ABC's variety series *The Hollywood Palace* until its 1970 cancellation. In 1966 Crosby had his first Christmas show with his children on *The Hollywood Palace*, or rather only his children (Harry, Mary and Nathaniel) with his second wife, Kathryn, whom he married in 1957. He did not include his grown-up sons from his first marriage to Dixie Lee, who died in 1952. Of those boys from the first marriage — Gary, Dennis, Phillip and Lindsay Crosby — only Gary pursued a show business career like his dad. He shocked the industry when he published the tell-all book *Going My Own Way* (1983), portraying his father as a callous child abuser. Other Crosby children decried it as being a false picture of their father that Gary created to get publicity. In any event, he never became a star like his dad.

Getting back to the Christmas shows, Bing, Kathryn, Harry, Mary and Nathaniel enchanted viewers so much that the quintet returned every Yuletide season on *The Hollywood Palace* the next three years, followed by individual holiday specials with guest stars. The first was *Bing Crosby's Christmas Show* on NBC Dec. 16, 1970, the second *Bing Crosby and the Sounds of Christmas* on Dec. 14, 1971. Both specials performed fine, although not nearly as well as those by his occasional movie co-star Bob Hope (see 7).

Then came *Christmas with the Bing Crosbys*; why it became a sensation is open to speculation. True, it did have as one of its guest stars Sally Struthers, a regular on TV's #1 series at the time, *All in the Family* (see 25), but other specials and TV shows had her and other *All in the Family* cast members of the sitcom as guests and did not soar into the ratings stratosphere. It may well have been a combination of the lagging competition (*M*A*S*H* was a ratings loser in 1972 — see 1 for more details — and *The F.B.I.* would be cancelled the following season), and just a desire by many to enjoy a Sunday night before Christmas with a man who sang the carols clearly and passionately.

The holiday follow-up to this special was *Bing Crosby's Sun Valley Christmas Show*, which aired

Dec. 9, 1973, and scored the second-highest ratings for a Crosby special with a 32.3. The next year, NBC decided not to produce a new show but reran *Christmas with the Bing Crosbys* instead on Dec. 15, 1974. By that time, Crosby had appeared on several TV commercials for Minute Maid orange juice (Crosby had a financial stake in the company).

Bing moved to CBS the following year for *The Bing Crosby Christmas Show* on Dec. 3, 1975. The next year's Yuletide installment was another repeat, this time of *Bing Crosby and His Friends*, a special first seen on NBC on Feb. 27, 1972, that already had been rerun on CBS on Oct. 9, 1974. Its reappearance seemed to indicate that Crosby was getting ready to retire altogether.

Ten months later, on Oct. 14, 1977, Crosby died of a heart attack while playing his favorite sport, golf, in Madrid, Spain. As luck would have it, his death occurred after he had taped his last special. CBS ran *Bing Crosby's Merrie Olde Christmas* on Nov. 30, 1977, and it earned an impressive 30.8/44.

On Dec. 6, 1978, CBS presented *Bing Crosby: The Christmas Years*, which notched a 20.2/30. Exactly one year later, NBC presented another retrospective, *A Bing Crosby Christmas ... Like the Ones We Used to Know*, which scored a 15.9/24. The first posthumous special featured Kathryn Crosby as host, while the second employed Gene Kelly. The 1979 special was repeated on Dec. 14, 1981 (14.8/22) and released on DVD in 1998.

Following Bing's death, his wife, Harry and Nathaniel by and large removed themselves from show business. On the other hand, Mary Crosby decided to continue to pursue an entertainment career, but not as a singer (look at any Crosby Christmas special and you will see that it focused on Bing during the carols). She decided to become a serious actress, and though it took a few years to establish herself, she managed to one-up her father in the ratings in a massive way when it hit. For more information, see 2 —*Dallas*.

69 — *The Waltons*

Feb. 7, 1974 ("The Fulfillment"). **Rating:** 34.5. **Share:** n/a.

Aired on CBS Thursday 8–9 P.M. Eastern and Pacific, 7–8 P.M. Central

Competition: *Chopper One* on ABC, *The Flip Wilson Show* on NBC

Cast: Richard Thomas (John-Boy Walton), Ralph Waite (John Walton), Miss Michael Learned (Olivia

Walton), Ellen Corby (Esther "Grandma" Walton), Will Geer (Zeb "Grandpa" Walton), Judy Norton (Mary Ellen Walton), Jon Walmsley (Jason Walton), Mary Elizabeth McDonough (Erin Walton), Eric Scott (Ben Walton), David W. Harper (Jim-Bob Walton), Kami Cotler (Elizabeth Walton), Earl Hamner (Narrator). **Guests:** Victor French (Curtis Norton), Ivy Jones (Ann Norton), Tiger Williams (Stevie). **Crew:** Earl Hamner (creator–executive story consultant), Lee Rich (executive producer), Robert L. Jacks (producer), Nick Webster (director), Michael Russnow, Tony Kayden (writers).

Synopsis. John and Olivia Walton invite Stevie from the Jefferson County orphanage to stay with their family in their Virginia mountain home in the 1930s. Other residents are John's mother and father, and John and Olivia's children John-Boy, Jason, Mary Ellen, Erin, Ben, Jim-Bob and Elizabeth. Stevie is remote due to his history of trusting people and then being disappointed by them. John-Boy visits blacksmith Curtis Norton and notices discomfort between Curtis and his moody wife Ann. Back at the Waltons, Stevie misbehaves during dinner, so John tells him while he is at his house, he will have to follow his rules. The next day, Olivia drops by to talk to Ann, and she confesses that she is infertile and distressed about it.

Stevie avoids the other children and informs Olivia that he does not want to play any of their "damn games." Olivia responds by threatening to punish Stevie for his profanity. Stevie then accidentally knocks over Grandma Walton's peeled apples and runs away until he is picked up by Curtis. John-Boy is at the Norton home when they arrive, and Curtis returns the child when he learns his real story.

When Ann learns that Stevie is an orphan, she thinks the Waltons are plotting to place him with her family. She wants her own baby, but she recognizes before he returns to the orphanage that she and Curtis should have Stevie in their lives. They go to adopt Stevie.

Backstory. Television's most successful family drama — unless you consider sudsy complications on soaps like *Dallas* (see 2) to be drama — is *The Waltons*, and a more unlikely hit is harder to find. Chances are if you told someone in 1972 that a series in the Depression starring a mostly unknown cast would emerge the eventual champ over its competition *The Flip Wilson Show* (see 94) on NBC and *The Mod Squad* on ABC, both in the top 25 at the time, they would have scoffed. Actually, the saga of making *The Waltons* into a series seems pretty illogical, looking back on it.

A native of the Virginia mountains, writer Earl Hamner had carved out a successful career creating scripts for television when Delmer Daves decided to write and direct his adaptation of Hamner's 1960 autobiographical novel *Spencer's Mountain*. The resulting movie, released in 1963, disappointed Hamner, as Daves changed his narrative considerably, even relocating the story to Wyoming.

Hamner decided to rectify that portrayal with another autobiographical story, this time a script designed to be a TV-movie called *The Homecoming*. In writer Irv Broughton's *Producers on Producing*, Hamner recalled writing that script: "My father had only been dead about a year, and it was very painful because it reminded me so much of him and the type of man he was." Each family member in the story corresponded with one of Hamner's brothers or sisters, with John-Boy, the oldest son, representing Hamner himself. All the actors cast as the children and Grandma in *The Homecoming* would assume the same roles in *The Waltons*. For various reasons Patricia Neal (Olivia), Andrew Duggan (John) and Edgar Bergen (Grandpa) did not reprise their parts in the series.

Director Fielder Cook needed a narrator for *The Homecoming* and wanted an actor to sound as authentic as Hamner. None of those auditioned captured what was needed, so Cook enlisted Hamner to handle the job. Hamner performed the same duties on the series, and he kept his native accent intact.

The TV-movie was a hit, finishing with a 25.3/39 when it debuted on CBS on Dec. 19, 1971. (*Spencer's Mountain* had aired on CBS four years earlier on Oct. 13, 1967, and performed even better with a 27.2/49.) Emmy nominations went to Cook and Hamner for their work. In the wake of that success, Hamner pitched the idea of a weekly series, even though CBS programming head Fred Silverman expressed concerns about whether there were enough stories to write about a family set in rural Virginia 40 years earlier.

Hamner told Broughton that the changes in converting *The Homecoming* to the series were not that great, apart from filming the series in the mountains in California (the TV-movie's exteriors were filmed in Jackson Hole, Wyoming). In the series Hamner compressed time and events that happened in his or his family's own life to serve as the basis for some stories.

Even with the popularity of *The Homecoming*, most viewers stuck with NBC and ABC rather than watch *The Waltons* when it debuted Sept. 14, 1972. But CBS owner Bill Paley stood behind the series, and the press did as well. Eventually audiences came to watch it in droves by the end of the season, when it finished #19 and caused *The Mod Squad* to lose so many viewers that ABC canceled it. The turnaround culminated with a TV-movie special, *The Waltons' Easter Story*, which earned a stunning 29.4/48 when shown on April 19, 1973.

With that success in mind, CBS called for another special TV-movie the next season. *The Waltons' Thanksgiving Story* aired on Nov. 15, 1973, and compiled even better numbers of 33.5/51. *The Homecoming* did nearly as well when rerun on *The CBS Friday Night Movie* on Dec. 7, 1973 (28.7/49). Clearly there was a big demand for *The Waltons* in 1973-1974, and it peaked with that season's 20th episode.

Unfortunately, "The Fulfillment" reflects the belief of what some critics termed the series' tendency to be cornball rather than honest. It is too calculated in its setup and obvious that the Nortons will adopt Stevie. Even worse, a sequence where Jason asserts that as the second oldest child he should get to stay up late with John-Boy and the other adults fails to connect as either good drama or comedy.

Still, the emphasis on establishing an authentic atmosphere in the production, direction and acting compensates for the rather wobbly script. There is also the retrospective charm in knowing that guest star Victor French would be a regular from 1974–1977 and 1982-1983 on TV's other successful period family drama, *Little House on the Prairie*.

This episode finished second in the ratings this week; #1 was the other top CBS series, *All in the Family* (see 25). That would be the same order both series finished for the 1973-1974 season. *The Waltons* remained in the top 10 the following season, and the top 20 through the 1977-1978 season. Against the imposing competition of ABC's *Mork & Mindy* (see 65) in 1978 and 1979, it slipped somewhat but still ended a respectably strong second in its period. It finally ended after eight years on Aug. 20, 1981, spending all the time at the leadoff series for CBS's Thursday night lineup.

The Waltons earned two of its 12 Emmy awards this season, for writing (where winner Joanna Lee and nominee John McGreevey both competed for the award) and lead actress (Michael Learned). Other major nominations for the series in 1973-1974 were in the drama series, lead actor (Richard Thomas), supporting actor (Will Geer), supporting actress (Ellen Corby) and director (Philip Leacock) categories. It finished its run with a total of 37 Emmy nominations.

The Waltons continued in six TV-movie reunions, with the first three—*A Wedding on Walton's Mountain, Mother's Day on Walton's Mountain* and *A Day for Thanks on Walton's Mountain*—airing on NBC in 1982. The final trio appeared on CBS: *A Walton Thanksgiving Reunion* (1993), *A Walton Wedding* (1995) and *A Walton Easter* (1997). Hamner wisely saw to it that as his actors aged in the series and TV-movie follow-ups, the timelines progressed along with them, so that by the time of *A Walton Easter*, the incidents took place in 1969. Only *Perry Mason* and *The Rockford Files* had more reunion TV-movies than did *The Waltons*.

In Eddie Lucas' book *Close-Ups: Conversations with Our TV Favorites*, Jon Walmsley, who played the second-eldest son Jason Walton, offered this opinion why *The Waltons* clicked with television audiences: "It meant something to them. It enriched their lives and, in a lot of cases, helped them through hard times. I've heard a few stories about that that were really touching. We never even thought about that when we were doing it."

I would just add that *The Waltons* is a great series to watch no matter what your circumstances are.

---

68 — *The Red Skelton Hour*

Feb. 19, 1963. **Rating:** 34.5. **Share:** n/a.
Aired on CBS Tuesday 8:30–9:30 P.M. Eastern and Pacific, 7:30–8:30 P.M. Central
Competition: *Hawaiian Eye* on ABC, *Empire* on NBC
Cast: Red Skelton (Host), David Rose and His Orchestra, the Skeltones, the Skelton Dancers. **Guests:** Jayne Mansfield, the Lettermen, Virginia Grey, Mary Treen. **Crew:** Guy Della Cioppa (executive producer), Cecil Barker (producer), Seymour Berns (director), Ed Simmons, Mort Green, Arthur Phillips, Martin Ragaway, Larry Rhine, Hugh Wedlock, Dave O'Brien (writers).

Synopsis. After a quick sketch with Red, the Skeltones sing about marriage and introduce the regulars and guests, ending with Skelton. He comes out for his monologue about riding on his daughter Valentina's horse in a parade in Palm Springs and ends with a pantomime of a tired majorette leading a band who eventually throws her girdle off.

A medley of wedding songs by the Skeltones follows, including the Lettermen singing "Get Me to the Church on Time." In the main sketch, "Advise to the Loveworn," buxom TV marriage counselor, Dr. Joyce Sisters (Mansfield) tells meek, bespectacled George Appleby (Skelton) to be more assertive with his wife, Clara (Grey). They have a brawl that puts George in the hospital, and Joyce loses her job. George eagerly agrees to Joyce's idea they pretend to be having an affair to make Clara jealous and mend their marriage. Her efforts fail to sway Clara, and George accepts that he's stuck in a loveless union.

The Lettermen perform "You'll Never Walk Alone" from the musical *Carousel* and Mansfield sings the Benny Goodman hit "Glory of Love" before Red does his "Silent Spot." He pantomimes an accident-prone artist in Paris who has a cleaning woman serve as his subject for a picture. Red paints only her hand, prompting her to smash the egg she holds in it on his face. The show ends with Red telling the studio and home audience, "So until we meet again, I say goodbye for now and God bless."

Backstory. No other performer has been as successful in and yet largely ignored or disrespected by television than Red Skelton. Think about it: If you were on CBS during the 1960s, when it was #1 overall, and your series was its third most popular program for three of those seasons — not to mention the highest-rated CBS series for the 1966-1967 season — don't you think your name and/or program would figure more prominently than, say, than one passing mention in Erik Barnouw's *The Image Empire: The History of Broadcasting in the United States from 1953* (1970)?

Yet that's the fate that has befallen *The Red Skelton Hour*, and much of the blame for the situation is the fault of its star.

Coming to national prominence as a radio comedian in the 1940s, Red began his TV series on Sept. 30, 1951, on NBC. He was a smash in his first season, ranking #4. But he wanted to film his variety series the second season. The spark and spontaneity disappeared, leading NBC to can him in 1953.

CBS allowed him to return to the airwaves, but put him up against Milton Berle's popular show. The series languished until CBS moved its starting time in 1955. That is when the series took hold, finishing in the top 20 every season through 1970, often in the top 10.

Unlike most other comedy variety hosts, Red had no supporting cast, and as his guests were mainly B-level celebrities, it was apparent that he definitely was his show's main attraction. Apart from some known eccentricities, as well as a general avoidance of the press, Red's offstage image was favorable with everyone except his writers, who felt he disrespected them by rarely performing their scripts as written.

For example, on the 13th annual Emmy Awards (see 98), when the series won for its comedy writing, head scribe Sherwood Schwartz accepted for the team by saying only, "First, thank you, and second, to give credit where credit is due, that speech was written by all of us." It took producer Cecil Barker, serving as proxy for Skelton, to shout a word of thanks about the star as the orchestra played the group off the stage. (That was the last Emmy for the show following two wins in 1951 for best comedy show and Red as best comedian. The show received its last nomination in a major creative category as best variety series in 1963.) Schwartz was replaced as head writer by Ed Simmons while Barker remained as producer.

This Valentine-themed episode was part of the first season where Red's show ran 60 rather than 30 minutes. The changeover was so successful that it would have been the #1 show on television had it not been for the introduction of *The Beverly Hillbillies* (see 12) the same season.

This has all the hallmarks of Red's 1960s shows: unsophisticated humor with some bawdiness (Red reacted the way you would expect to Jayne Mansfield's busty physique), and the star constantly interrupting skits with asides and anything that amused him. He giggles often during the main sketch, and when a balsa wood chair collapses behind Virginia Grey's head before she is able to slam him with it, he falls to the floor in laughter. When he mistakenly references his real-life wife at the time and says, "What would you do to make Georgia jealous?" he has a fit of chuckles.

Grey (first seen on the show in 1955) and the Lettermen (making their debut on Red's show here) were frequent guests on the series, with Grey seen 12 times through 1966 and the Lettermen seven times through 1970. In '70, CBS shocked him and the entertainment world by canceling the top 10 hit because costs were projected to rise while his audience was expected to continue to remain mainly old, poor and less educated — demographics that most advertisers viewed as anathema then as now.

When news of the CBS decision hit, Red's executive producer Guy Della Cioppa swiftly convinced NBC to hire Red, but he could only secure a half-hour slot. Running against *Gunsmoke* (see 24) on CBS, Red finished a far second place in his time slot, so NBC ended the series just a month shy of its 20th anniversary, on Aug. 29, 1971.

In an interview with *Variety* before a personal appearance in Omaha, Nebraska, on Feb. 4, 1975, Skelton claimed that CBS removed him, Ed Sullivan and Jackie Gleason from the air because they refused to do off-color and unpatriotic material. A CBS official denied the charge. Sullivan did some specials for CBS after his 1971 cancellation, while Gleason was in negotiations to do the same with CBS following his series ending in 1970 (he later did *Honeymooners* specials with ABC), which makes Red's claim hard to accept. And anyone who saw one of his series' rehearsals, known in the industry as "the dirty hour," realizes that Red was hypocritical in his claim, as he indulged frequently in routines so blue and profane that they could not have been shown on CBS even in 1975.

Skelton went on to make fleeting guest shots on specials and talk shows, headlining only a handful of taped comedy specials on HBO from 1981 to 1983, none of which were too well received by viewers or critics. He also rarely allowed clips of his old series to appear in retrospectives, making viewers largely forget his legacy.

In the spring of 1981, stations were offered the chance to repeat *The Red Skelton Hour* in 60-minute form, but there were no takers. A year and a half later, edited 30-minute versions of old episodes were submitted for consideration to broadcasters. Even with test surveys indicating that audiences liked the reruns and data that showed that Red was a popular attraction on the college campus concert schedule, there remained little interest.

After Red died on Sept. 17, 1997, his estate finally officially released his TV series on DVD — but only the NBC years from 1951 to 1953 and 1970 to 1971. The grudge against CBS remained, and apparently the feeling was mutual. When CBS aired the special *50 Years from Television City* in 2002, there was no sign of the man who had been the biggest attraction in the network's Television City studios for eight years in the 1960s. The only reference was Tommy Smothers waving to a picture of him on a backstage wall, rather ironic given how Red disliked *The Smothers Brothers Comedy Hour* and its liberal-slanted humor.

Red is a member of the Television Hall of Fame (inducted in 1989). Judged by either length of network run or overall ratings, *The Red Skelton Hour* is TV's most successful comedy variety show. It takes talent on some level for that to happen. For future generations to discover what it had to be a

success, *The Red Skelton Hour* deserves commercial release.

---

67 — The Rose Bowl

Jan. 1, 1964 (the 50th edition). **Rating:** 34.6. **Share:** n/a.

Aired on NBC Wednesday 4:45–7:30 P.M. Eastern, 3:45–6:30 P.M. Central and 1:45–4:30 P.M. Pacific

Competition: *Trailmaster* (*Wagon Train* repeat) on ABC, news on CBS

Hosts: Lindsey Nelson, Rod Belcher (play-by-play announcers), Bill Symes (analyst). **Crew:** Perry Smith (executive producer).

Synopsis. The Fighting Illini of Illinois (7–1–1) met the Washington Huskies (6–4) in this year's main college football contest. This was the second appearance for Illinois at a Rose Bowl, and the seventh for Washington. The first quarter was a defensive struggle, and both teams finished with no score. The rather messy game included five fumbles on each side. An Illinois fumble on its 27-yard line gave the Huskies its only score of the game. Quarterback Bill Siler moved the team downfield before he pitched the ball to halfback Dave Kopay, who made a seven-yard run for a touchdown for Washington. The Illini could manage only a field goal before intermission. The teams went to the locker room with Washington up over Illinois 7–3.

In the second half, it was all Illini, though not a complete stomping. The team scored a touchdown on a two-yard run before the end of the third quarter to put them up 10–7. Future Pro Football Hall of Fame member Dick Butkus played for Illinois at both center on offense and linebacker on defense, making some key interceptions in the latter position to keep Illinois ahead.

The Huskies had a chance to come back in the fourth quarter, but when the Illini scored another touchdown, Washington lost 17–7. Running back Jim Grabowski of Illinois was named player of the game for rushing 125 yards and scoring the team's last touchdown.

Backstory. The Rose Bowl is an outgrowth of the Tournament of Roses Parade, which began in 1889 after members of the Valley Hunt Club in Pasadena, California, decided to celebrate the abundant flora and fauna it had at the start of each year while many Americans back east shivered in the bitter cold winter. Six years later, the Tournament of Roses Association took over the expanding event, and more bands and floats were involved in the parade.

In 1902 the group decided to draw countrywide attention to the city by staging a post-parade college football game between squads representing the top of the eastern and western halves of the country. It was the first of its kind, making it the oldest bowl game in America.

Unfortunately for western pride, that first meeting saw Michigan wallop Stanford 49–0. In the interest of saving face, the tradition of a season-ending game was not revived again until 1916, again with one team from the east and the other from the west. Whenever Jan. 1 fell on a Sunday, however, the bowl game took place on Monday, Jan. 2.

Six years after the restart, Harlan "Dusty" Hall, a writer with the Pasadena *Star-News*, dubbed the 1922 game "The Rose Bowl" in honor of the new 57,000-seat stadium built to showcase the contest. The designation stuck, and the popularity of the game led to its first coast-to-coast coverage on radio in 1927 by Graham McNamee on NBC. By the 1930s the Rose Bowl came to be thought of as the game that decided the national collegiate champion in football, even though that was not always the case, particular as other bowl games flourished.

In 1947 the Rose Bowl established the rule that the winners of the Pacific Coast Conference (later known as the Pac-8 and Pac-10) and the Big Ten Conference in the East would face off every year. That setup was still in place when this game was played.

Several factors made the 1964 game very appealing to viewers. The first was the appearance of ex–President Dwight D. Eisenhower as grand marshal for the Tournament of Roses parade earlier that day. Coming just a few weeks after the assassination of President John F. Kennedy, the presence of a beloved commander in chief reassured many Americans and put them in a relaxed mood to escape their troubles with the game following the parade.

As she had been hosting since 1955, Betty White covered that Tournament of Roses parade for NBC, this time with Arthur Godfrey as her co-host. Unlike White, Godfrey refused to do any preparation for the event, and it showed on the air. "The real low point came when a float [appeared,] carrying the University of Illinois football team, who would be playing in the Rose Bowl later that afternoon," White recalled in her memoirs *Here We Go Again*. "The Illini (Ill-eye-nigh),

as they were known, were touted as the hottest team in the country at the moment, and Arthur took off, describing, in great detail, the float carrying the 'Illeeny.' I tried to be subtle about correcting his pronunciation, but I must have overdone the subtlety, for Arthur continued to go on and on about 'the Illeeny' this and 'the Illeeny' that." Godfrey was never invited back to cover the parade again for NBC.

The Rose Queen that year was 19-year-old Nancy Kneeland, who dated one of the Huskies' stars of the bowl, Dave Kopay, after the game. Kopay, a senior at Washington, went on to play ten years in the NFL before becoming the first professional football player to acknowledge he was gay. In his 1988 update of his autobiography *The Dave Kopay Story*, he wrote that Kneeland approached him for an autograph when his memoirs came out more than a decade earlier. She was married with three kids and told Kopay she was still cheering for him.

Another advantage for the program was the timing of the game itself. Earlier that day, the Orange Bowl (ABC), the Cotton Bowl (CBS — see 81) and the Sugar Bowl (NBC) all aired against each other, leaving the football game competition clear for the Rose Bowl by the time it aired. Most of the time through the 1980s, in fact, there was no major bowl game that aired against the Rose Bowl, given its pre-eminence in the field.

And then there was a new play-by-play announcer for the affair. Lindsey Nelson first worked in a Super Bowl for NBC radio in 1939, as a spotter (a person who locates what players are on the field following changeovers in each down) for announcer Bill Stern. He performed that duty so well for the Tennessee Volunteers during the regular season that he received the opportunity to do it for NBC at the Rose Bowl as the Vols played. Nelson eventually went to work at NBC under Stern, and when the network obtained rights to college football in 1953, he went on TV announcing the regular season games along with Mel Allen. From 1955 through 1959, he and Red Grange hosted the games. ABC aired the game in 1960 and 1961 and did not use him, but CBS obtained control of college football in 1962 and put Nelson back in charge of the main games.

Nelson noted in his autobiography that the Rose Bowl football game "was the one event I wanted so badly to do and had never done. The Rose Bowl was very special for all announcers." However, NBC held rights to the season-ending game and planned to use Mel Allen to call it instead, following the end of Bill Stern's reign. Allen had been covering every single Rose Bowl on network TV since coverage began in 1952.

But Allen had lost his voice covering the fourth and final game of the 1963 World Series, and that fact unnerved Rose Bowl sponsors. Executive producer Perry Smith approached Nelson about replacing him. Nelson, ever the loyal employee, said he would do so only if his boss, CBS sports director Bill MacPhail, agreed to let him appear. At that point, Nelson had not been assigned a collegiate post-season game to cover. MacPhail acquiesced, and Nelson was there, although ironically he fought off a cold that could have cost him his voice a day before the game. He hosted the Rose Bowl three more years for NBC before CBS wanted him to do the Cotton Bowl instead for them. Curt Gowdy assumed his duty for the Rose Bowl in 1968. NBC hosted the game another 20 years. Effective with the Jan. 2, 1989, game, ABC received the rights to air the contest, which continued through 2010 before ESPN won the rights.

As for the teams that competed in 1964, while Washington lost, it would return to the bowl 14 years later and win against Michigan 27–20, as well as win a few other games thereafter. The Illini did not come back to fight at the Rose Bowl until 1984, when they endured a shellacking by UCLA (45–9). However, Illinois fans can take heart in the fact that Grabowski and Butkus were inducted into the Rose Bowl Hall of Fame in the 1990s due to their excellent play in 1964.

For the other 364 days of the year, the Rose Bowl Stadium does host other events, from flea markets to religious services.

66 — Candid Camera

Jan. 1, 1961. **Rating:** 34.6. **Share:** n/a
Aired on CBS Sunday 10–10:30 P.M. Eastern and Pacific, 9–9:30 P.M. Central
  Competition: *The Islanders* (last half-hour of 60-minute show) on ABC, *The Loretta Young Show* (repeat) on NBC
  Cast: Allen Funt, Arthur Godfrey, The Irwin Kostal Orchestra. **Guest:** Frank Fontaine. **Crew:** Bob Banner (executive producer), Julio DiBenedetto (producer-director).

Synopsis. Recorded live before a studio audience, this edition featured in one segment comedian-singer Frank Fontaine. He plays John C.C. Sivoney, who tries to convince a Boston cabbie to allow him to take an unclothed store window

dummy in the back seat across town with him in the taxi. Beyond that information, I could find no additional information about this episode.

Backstory. Is it America's longest-running national pop psychology experiment, a series of pranks designed to make people look foolish on TV, or something else entirely? However you define *Candid Camera*, it has been a part of the medium in some form every decade since the start of network telecasting (it debuted on ABC Aug. 10, 1948). For the next 60 years, the series would pop up on four networks (the others were NBC, CBS and Pax), appear in syndication in its early days (1951) as well as in the 1970s and 1990s, be one of the first series on cable (HBO, 1980), and even receive two theatrical versions, *What Do You Say to a Naked Lady?* (1970) and *Money Talks* (1972). It is so thoroughly identified as visual humor that some are surprised to learn it began on radio as *Candid Microphone* on June 28, 1947. It clearly has a durable premise, but no version to date has been as successful as the one that ran on CBS Sunday nights from Oct. 2, 1960, through Sept. 3, 1967.

That version succeeded because it had a crucial element missing from its earlier incarnations, namely a studio audience to laugh at everyday people's reactions to such situations as, say, cars splitting in half fore and aft, without knowing that it is a setup and they are being filmed surreptitiously. *Candid Camera* was a cult hit, at best prior to 1960, although it should be noted that in most versions seen on the networks during its first seven years, the series had no advertisers and thus could not be measured in the ratings.

After being reduced to an insert as part of NBC's *Pontiac Presents Playwrights 56* in 1955, *Candid Camera* appeared to be a lost cause in making it on TV. But in 1958, Jack Paar asked Funt to show some of his films on *The Tonight Show.* The response was favorable, and a year later the producer of *The Garry Moore Show*, Bob Banner, included a weekly spot with Funt's funnies on the series, sometimes with the regulars on the show participating in the scenarios. Then as now, many viewers found it hard to believe that recognizable celebrities could be assumed to be everyday folk as they often portrayed themselves in the segments, but Funt insisted that people often found it hard to believe they were interacting with an actual TV personality and consequently and unconsciously did not recognize them.

CBS revived *Candid Camera* as a series the following year, with Banner in charge (Banner brought over not only the studio audience concept for the return but even Irwin Kostal, the musical director on *The Garry Moore Show*, to conduct the house band). Network executives felt Funt lacked the confidence to be its sole host, and that is where the problems began behind the scenes.

First, actor Eddie Albert was set to be co-host. Then CBS programming head Mike Dann told Bob Stahl in *TV Guide*, "Certain contractual difficulties arose between the program and Albert" that prevented him from participating. A spokesperson for Albert was more specific when contacted by Stahl, saying a producer with the program was concerned that Albert's recent appointment as a vice-president of Kaiser Industries Corp. would present a possible conflict of interest for him as host.

Replacing Albert in a hurry was Arthur Godfrey, who had been off television as a regular performer since having lung cancer surgery in 1959. Fully recuperated, Godfrey apparently thought he was more than just the host of the series, as he came out first, often introduced a segment by himself, then a commercial and finally introduced Funt but did not let the latter say much before going to the next segment. Godfrey even did a few commercials. Funt had an ego as big as Godfrey's, and soon word leaked out that the two men were barely cooperating with each other.

"They just had very difficult agendas, basically," said Bill Funt, Allen's son, in a 2009 interview with Stu Shostak. "I mean, Arthur, as far as he was concerned, it was his show, and you can almost see the logic in that — he was the host of it. And in the meantime, my dad, I mean, it was his show creatively and otherwise, and he wanted to do it his way. And so they were sort of out there doing two different shows at the same time."

By the time this episode aired, the feud between Godfrey and Funt was in full bloom and the public knew it. But that standoff did not affect the ratings negatively at all: *Candid Camera* was the second-highest rated new series of the 1960-1961 season behind *The Andy Griffith Show* (see 79), thanks in part to weak competition (Loretta Young's series was in its eighth and final season on NBC; the adventure drama *The Islanders* on ABC faltered opposite the lead-in to *Candid Camera*, *The Jack Benny Program*).

What made this installment more popular than others was probably the fact that New Year's Day 1961 fell on a Sunday; that meant most children had no school the following day and thus could stay up later to watch *Candid Camera*.

Funt and Godfrey remained civil to each other on the air, so viewers unaware of the industry scuttlebutt probably thought things were fine. But at the end of the season, Godfrey was gone, not surprising since Funt basically was *Candid Camera* and the show was under his production company as well as Banner's. Godfrey never had another regular network TV series job. Durward Kirby, a regular on *The Garry Moore Show*, became the new *Candid Camera* co-host while continuing to appear on the former.

Candid Camera earned its only Emmy nomination in 1961 for Outstanding Program Achievement in the Field of Humor, losing to *The Jack Benny Program*. The series stayed in the top 10 the next four seasons through 1964, including its highest finish of #2 for the 1962-1963 season tied with *The Red Skelton Hour* (see 68) and just behind *The Beverly Hillbillies* (see 12). But it dropped dramatically out of the top 10 in the 1964-1965 season. Replacing Kirby with Bess Myerson as co-host in 1966 could not save it from cancellation a year later. CBS reran *Candid Camera* on weekday mornings starting in the fall of 1966.

A 2004 *USA Today* article estimated that nearly a dozen *Candid Camera* clones were then littering the airwaves, including most notoriously *Punk'd* on MTV hosted and produced by Ashton Kutcher. Asked about the trend, Funt's other son Peter, then co-hosting a revival on Pax, noted, "Other shows seem to think it's like they're representing some alien force that doesn't think humans are very interesting. In fact, they think they're stupid, and the entertainment comes in underscoring that stupidity."

I cannot think of a better way to explain how *Candid Camera* differs from reality TV. At its best, the series had viewers laugh *with* other's foibles, not *at* them. The fact that more TV series do the latter nowadays is a sad commentary on the medium today.

---

65 — *Mork & Mindy*

Feb. 8, 1979 ("Mork Goes Erk"). **Rating:** 34.6. **Share:** 52.

Aired on ABC Thursday 8–8:30 P.M. Eastern and Pacific, 7–7:30 P.M. Central

Competition: *The Waltons* on CBS, *Little Women* (series debut) on NBC

Cast: Robin Williams (Mork), Pam Dawber (Mindy McConnell), Conrad Janis (Frederick McConnell). **Guests:** Tom Poston (Mr. Bickley), Morgan Fairchild

(Susan), David Letterman (Ellsworth). **Crew:** Garry Marshall, Tony Marshall (executive producers), Dale McRaven, Bruce Johnson (producers), Howard Storm (director), Lloyd Turner, Gordon Mitchell (writers).

Synopsis. Mork, an alien from the planet Ork, is living with Mindy McConnell in the latter's apartment in Boulder, Colorado, to study the habits of Earthlings. He eats a meal with a chimp and makes small talk with the creature ("How about that new pope?"). Mindy arrives and tells Mork he needs to take the chimp back to the zoo. Mork counters by telling her his boss, Orson, has transferred him to examine another planet, which depresses Mindy.

Mindy's father, Frederick, is visited in his record store by Mr. Bickley, a tipsy curmudgeon who writes greeting cards in the apartment below Mindy. Bickley said he is tired of hearing Mindy crying lately. Overhearing this, Mindy's vain pal, Susan, tells them they can feel better with a self-help program called ERK (Ellsworth Revitalization Konditioning). After Mindy learns that Orson has allowed Mork to stay with her, but he Mork wants to leave anyway, she gives ERK a shot.

Joined by Mork and Mr. Bickley, Mindy attends an ERK session at Susan's apartment. Its founder is a jerk in a brown leisure suit with a gold medallion who humiliates and abuses his subjects. Mork puts Ellsworth in his place, and when he talks to Mindy at her apartment, he agrees with her that "Human feeling is good" after she kisses him. Mork reports back to Orson his plan to learn more about emotions on this planet before signing off with his customary wiggling of his ears and saying "Na-nu, na-nu."

Backstory. Now that viewers have had decades to get accustomed to his shtick on talk shows and specials, it may be hard for younger generations to realize how truly revolutionary Robin Williams appeared to most TV viewers when he starred in *Mork & Mindy.* His rapid-fire delivery gave the impression he was improvising his dialogue, and his manic gestures, body tics and inflections effectively complemented his efforts. Watching him as Mork was akin to riding a roller coaster: fun with a lot of unexpected twists and turns. There was no one like him on TV at the time, and very few since, for that matter.

The science fiction craze of 1978 inspired the creation of the character of Mork, although he was not written as far-out as Williams played him. Executive producer Garry Marshall's nine-year-old son was a fan of the movie *Star Wars*, so to interest children, he crafted the alien Mork as a

guest role on his hit series *Happy Days* (see 64). Williams outshone the other applicants for the job when he was told to take a seat and put his head instead of his fanny in the chair. Then he really turned it on for the taping of "My Favorite Orkan," which aired Feb. 28, 1978, and generated a huge amount of laughs (plus strong numbers of 32.7/50) as Ork's otherworldly attributes stunned Richie Cunningham. (The character returned as a guest on *Happy Days* on March 6, 1979, while *Mork & Mindy* was on the air.)

ABC approved a spin-off. Created by Marshall, Dale McRaven and Bruce Johnson, *Mork & Mindy* was a series whose potential seemed uncertain against an expected top-rated new sitcom slated to run against it on CBS, *WKRP in Cincinnati*; ABC executives consequently moved the series from Monday to Thursday nights for its debut on Sept. 14, 1978.

The setup for the series did seem rather weak. Ork went from 1950s America in *Happy Days* to 20 years later with no change in age, and he received refuge from pleasant Mindy McConnell when his egg-shaped spaceship landed on Earth. He is there to study the planet's customs and report each week to his leader, Orson. Mindy reveals his alien origins only to her father, Frederick, a music shop owner who is naturally suspicious why his single daughter would suddenly be harboring a man in her apartment's attic, and her hip grandmother (aren't they all hip in TV comedies?), Cora. Everyone else just assumed Mork was an odd person when he drank with his fingers and spoke gibberish. It sounds basically like the same premise used in a lot of fantasy sitcoms from the 1960s.

What put *Mork & Mindy* into another stratosphere was the clowning of Williams. He would play with the show's props and sets as soon as each week's new script came out, thinking of ways he could add touches that could generate more laughter. Watching any episode, particularly in the first season, you can see quizzical reactions from other actors in scenes with Williams as they try to get their bearings and continue following the script.

Williams roamed the sets so much during his improvisations that Marshall had to add a fourth camera to capture all his activities (the standard on sitcoms filmed before a studio audience was three at the time). The executive producer did try to rein in his star by forcing him to watch the dailies of the show's rehearsal to see where the cameras missed him and make him realize that while some of his comic bits could leave the studio audience in hysterics, home viewers would be missing them because he was out of range. That curbed Williams somewhat, although the show's camera operators probably thought they were covering a live news event given the way Williams continued to flee from his marks.

This episode is full of the typical zest and humor, although nowadays the funniest albeit apparently unintentional line has Morgan Fairchild saying the bright side of the ERK class was that David Letterman's character was handsome. Not that the future talk show host was homely, but to say he is a looker in a leisure suit is, well ... indicative that this episode was filmed in 1979. It also has the unfortunate tendency to swerve toward schmaltz in imparting life's little lessons to Ork, but since they were aiming this show toward children, that can be understood.

The show finished #1 this week, as it did a few other times in 1978 and 1979. It ended up at #3 for the season, tied with *Happy Days*. And then ABC killed the golden goose. First, the network relocated the series to Sundays at 8 on Aug. 12, 1979, thinking it could make inroads there against one of the top CBS hits, *All in the Family* (see 25). To blunt the impact, CBS aired a special 90-minute retrospective on the 200th episode of *All in the Family* that same night. The battle was on, and *All in the Family*—or rather its successor, *Archie Bunker's Place*—proved to be the bigger draw. By the start of 1980, ABC returned *Mork & Mindy* to its original Thursday night, but it was no longer a breakout hit, finishing the season at #27. The relocation was not the only bad move. The series replaced Frederick and Cora with Mindy's friends, deli shop operator Remo DaVinci (played by Jay Thomas) and his sister Jean (Gina Hecht). Audiences never warmed to their replacements.

Realizing how the series had erred, *Mork & Mindy* brought back Conrad Janis as Frederick for the 1980-1981 season. His return did not halt the downward momentum, as the series finished in 49th place. Desperate to prop up ratings, the show entered the 1981-1982 season with just Mindy, Mork and Frederick as regulars—and Jonathan Winters as Mearth, the grown-looking son of the now-married Mork and Mindy.

"We thought Jonathan's presence would inspire Robin and help boost our ratings at the same time," Marshall wrote in his autobiography. "When Jonathan and Robin improvised during the warm-ups, it was brilliant. But as soon as the cam-

era started to roll and they had to censor their dirty material and stick to the script, the scenes weren't as good. Things got to the point where some people would come for the warm-up, then leave before the filming started." With the series finishing at #60 for the season, ABC canned it. The last *Mork & Mindy* aired on June 10, 1982.

Mork & Mindy earned its only Emmy nominations in 1979, for best comedy series and best comedy actor (Williams, of course), which reinforces the belief that its first season was its best.

64 — Happy Days

Sept. 21, 1976 ("Fonzie Loves Pinky"). **Rating:** 34.6. **Share:** 53.

Aired on ABC Tuesday 8–9 P.M. Eastern and Pacific, 7–8 P.M. Central

Competition: *Tony Orlando and Dawn* on CBS, *Baa Baa Black Sheep* (debut) on NBC

Cast: Ron Howard (Richie Cunningham), Henry Winkler (Arthur Fonzarelli ["The Fonz"]), Marion Ross (Marion Cunningham), Anson Williams (Warren "Potsie" Webber), Donny Most (Ralph Malph), Erin Moran (Joanie Cunningham), Tom Bosley (Howard Cunningham), Al Molinaro (Al Delvecchio). **Guests:** Roz Kelly (Pinky Tuscadero), Michael Pataki (Myron "Count" Mallachi), Ken Lerner (Rocco Mallachi), Doris Hess (Tina), Kelly Sanders (Lola). **Crew:** Thomas L. Miller, Edward K. Milkis, Garry K. Marshall (executive producer), Tony Marshall (producer), Jerry Paris (producer-director), Arthur Silver (writer).

Synopsis. Howard Cunningham tells his wife Marion, son Richie and daughter Joanie that Pinky Tuscadero, the world's greatest female cyclist, will provide a driving exhibition at an upcoming demolition derby. Richie visits the Fonz, Potsie and Ralph Malph working at Bronko's Auto Repairing to tell them the news. While Ralph and Potsie pair up with Pinky's backup duo The Pinketts (Tina and Lola), Pinky renews her relationship with the Fonz in a montage. At Arnold's Drive-In, new owner Al provides free pizza and drinks the night before the derby to the gang as Fonzie learns he needs a substitute driver. Pinky volunteers, but the Fonz nixes the idea of a woman in the derby and selects Ralph. However, when Count Mallachi of the mean Mallachi brothers demolition derby team flirts with Pinky, The Fonz drafts her on his team in response.

In retaliation for the move, the Mallachis destroy the engine in Pinky's car. Fonzie leads a massive repair overhaul that includes telling Richie to have his dad stall the start of the derby, which Howard succeeds in doing. The Fonz and Pinky arrive and the race is underway. It eventually comes down to Pinky, Fonz and the Mallachi brothers. When Pinky's engine stalls, she gets out on top of her car. Count Mallachi hits her vehicle, knocking Pinky to the ground. Pinky goes to the hospital on a stretcher. Fonzie returns to his car and vows revenge.

Backstory. An hour-long extended episode where roughly the first half was filmed before a studio audience and the second on location, this *Happy Days* season opener established it as the dominant sitcom on television, propelling it to #1 for the 1976-1977 season and knocking *All in the Family* (see 25) from the perch it had held for five years. Although it only held the top spot for this season, *Happy Days* stayed in the top three the following seasons and clung into the top 20 the next three seasons after that. Then a downward slide led to cancellation two years later. It certainly lasted as a hit longer than, say, the love affair depicted here between resident cool guy Fonzie and biker extraordinaire Pinky.

The following week, when the rest of this storyline aired, Fonzie defeated the Mallachis and won the race. He reunited with a bandaged Pinky in the hospital and proposed marriage. Yet he realized that going on the road with Pinky as her act's president and mechanic was not right for him, because she would be the center of attention, and his ego could not handle it. They parted sadly but sweetly as friends.

Ironically, in real life, the story seemed to be the other way around. Several reports claim that Pinky was set to be a regular character until her portrayer, Roz Kelly, supposedly mocked Henry Winkler's portrayal of the Fonz; the producers consequently dropped her. Kelly reprised Pinky on the Feb. 12, 1977, debut episode of *Blansky's Beauties*, starring Nancy Walker as a woman in charge of a bunch of Vegas showgirls.

The "happy days" began in 1971 when Garry Marshall, producer of the TV series *The Odd Couple*, met Michael Eisner, head of ABC Entertainment program development. Eisner told Marshall that he and Paramount development director Tom Miller, snowed in at a New Jersey airport, occupied their time by fondly remembering *Mama*, a sentimental CBS sitcom of the 1950s set in the 1930s. Marshall realized they really meant they wanted a program that was nostalgic, so he set a 1970s series in the 1950s instead.

Marshall's then-partner, Jerry Belson, recalled how he hated growing up in the decade, so he passed on the project. Instead, Marshall collaborated with Miller and another Paramount executive, Eddie Milkis, on a pilot first titled *Cool* until they discovered that no one associated that term with the Fifties. The retitled *Happy Days* was set in Milwaukee, where Miller grew up. "When ABC called back, they told us nobody cared about the 1950s.... Paramount ended up pawning the pilot off to *Love, American Style* to make some of its money back," Marshall wrote in his memoirs *Wake Me When It's Funny*. "Retitled 'Love and the Happy Day,' the show appeared in February 1972."

That might have been the end of the project, but as luck would have it, George Lucas was producing a film called *American Graffiti*, set in 1962, and wanted to see how Ron Howard looked in the 1950s in the *Happy Days* pilot (the answer was good enough to star in the movie). The tremendous box office success of *American Graffiti* prompted ABC to look at the *Happy Days* pilot again and add it to the network.

When it became a series, the only performers to transfer from the pilot were Howard, Marion Ross as his character's mother and Anson Williams as Howard's best friend. Howard's dad and mom were recast. Marshall decided to add one more character that made *Happy Days* memorable.

The inspiration for Fonzie was a childhood pal of Marshall's in Yonkers, New York, who never seemed to flinch as he drove a hot rod in a leather jacket. Marshall felt that Fonzie would be allowed on TV, but when circumstances forced him away from the series for a few episodes, he was shocked to discover when he returned that Fonzie's leather jacket was gone. Network officials feared that the character looked too menacing in the outfit; Marshall protested that was not the impression at all. The two sides reached a compromise where the Fonz could wear the jacket only when he was with his motorcycle. Naturally, Marshall made sure that the bike was near the character all the time thereafter, and with *Happy Days* becoming a success, ABC eventually dropped the demand.

Coming onto ABC as a midseason replacement on Jan. 15, 1974, for *Temperatures Rising*, *Happy Days* led off the network's Tuesday night lineup with strong ratings, finishing #16 for the 1973-1974 season and making it the second most popular series on ABC at the time (*The Six Million Dollar Man* landed at #11). Ratings dropped in 1974-1975 when its CBS opposition, *Good Times*, outperformed it, but *Happy Days* rallied in 1975-

1976 to pull ahead of *Good Times* and finish at #11. The show's theme, "Happy Days," became a top five hit for Pratt & McClain in the summer of 1976, and its popularity helped set the stage for a huge returning audience to watch the season opener. (The series' previous theme, Bill Haley and the Comets' 1955 #1 classic "Rock Around the Clock," became a top 40 hit again in 1974 thanks to its *Happy Days* exposure.)

One final note about this episode: Pinky's distinctive last name came from an incident when Marshall was on a family vacation and his car broke down in Atascadero, California. He envisioned the Pinky character while waiting for assistance, then assigned it to a writer.

Happy Days earned nine Emmy nominations, with one win, for film editing in 1978. Winkler nabbed three consecutive best lead actor in a comedy nominations from 1976 through 1978, Ross appeared twice for supporting actress in 1979 and 1984, Jerry Paris received nods for his directing in 1978 and 1981, and Tom Bosley scored a supporting actor nomination in 1978.

Happy Days ended its run on July 12, 1984, having spun off *Laverne & Shirley* (see 56), *Mork & Mindy* (see 65) and several lesser series. There was also an effort to capitalize on this episode's popularity by seven appearances of Pinky's sister Leather Tuscadero (played by Suzi Quatro), a rock star, from 1977 to 1979, but she did not have the same impact of Pinky. In fact, the series ended with the Fonz being about the only unmarried character left.

---

63 — *You Again?*

Feb. 27, 1986 ("All You Need Is Love"; debut episode). **Rating:** 34.7. **Share:** 51.

Aired on NBC Thursday 8:30–9 P.M. Eastern and Pacific, 7:30–8 P.M. Central

Competition: *Ripley's Believe It or Not* (last half-hour of 60-minute show; repeat) on ABC; *Magnum P.I.* (last half-hour of 60-minute show; repeat) on CBS

Cast: Jack Klugman (Henry Willows), John Stamos (Matt Willows), Elizabeth Bennett (Enid Tompkins). **Guests:** Tiffany Helm (Christine), Frank Marth (Christine's Father). **Crew:** Sarah Lawson (executive producer), Rick Mitz (producer), Peter Bonerz (director), Eric Chappell (writer).

Synopsis. Cranky Henry Willows, a worker at grocery store supplier Global Markets, discovers to his astonishment that his son Matt wants to be part of his life after seven years of living with his mother and stepfather. The harried executive is not thrilled that he has to re-ignite his paternal instinct, or that Matt has decided to live with him, thus infringing on the middle-aged bachelor's lifestyle. To top it off, Matt is a freewheeling sort, which in businessman Henry's mind mean he is irresponsible and needs disciplining.

In the middle of this standoff, Henry's British housekeeper attempts to smooth Henry's feathers while trying to let Matt understand the mindset of his father. Father and son reach a truce of sorts, but more misunderstandings and misadventures await them in the future.

Backstory. If you had a new sitcom in 1986 and you wanted maximum exposure, you needed to slate it to follow the biggest hit at the time, *The Cosby Show* (see 22). That's what happened to *You Again?* It became the highest-rated premiere of a series in the 1980s thanks to NBC pre-empting *Family Ties* (see 29). To find a higher-rated debut, you would have to go back to 1979 and *The Ropers* (see 49). Unfortunately for *You Again?* it shared the same fate as that earlier show, starting off strong only to disappear after about a year.

You Again? and *The Ropers* were both based on much more successful British series. The inspiration here was *Home to Roost*, a sitcom that ran on Yorkshire Television from 1985 to 1990 starring John Thaw as Henry Willows and Reece Dinsdale as his son Matthew. Playing the housekeeper Enid was Elizabeth Bennett — the same actress seen in the same role on *You Again?* In a network first, *You Again?* imported one of the *Home to Roost* regulars as part of its cast. To her credit, Bennett studiously avoided the obvious traps of making her character saucy or cutesy and created a warm, sensible portrayal. That's pretty impressive, especially given the jet lag she must have encountered flying back and forth between Hollywood and London to appear on both shows since they were in production at the same time.

As for the rest of the casting for the Americanized *Home to Roost*, well, let's just say the idea of baby-faced handsome John Stamos being the biological son of haggard Jack Klugman is almost as hard to swallow as the concept of 22-year-old Stamos claiming to be a 17-year-old in the debut episode. Still, both men tried to make their on-screen relationship credible, perhaps in the vain hopes of thinking their this series was going to be a hit.

For Klugman, *You Again?* offered a chance to return to the comfortable world of sitcoms after a tempestuous seven years (1976–1983) starring in the NBC medical drama *Quincy, M.E.,* where he freely complained about the scripts. As he had no such gripes when he co-starred with Tony Randall on ABC's *The Odd Couple* (1970–1975), and he won two Emmys in that role as well, he probably thought that *You Again?* would be a relative breeze to handle like that. However...

During the taping of the second episode of *You Again?* on a Friday night in January 1986, someone on the production crew told Klugman, "Jack, I think you might have played the part too harshly." Klugman responded, "I was doing exactly what I needed do, you [bleep]. How dare you say that to me? I've been doing this for 30 years!" And with that, he stormed out of the studio, livid at the situation. But it gnawed at him over the weekend, and finally at 3:30 A.M. Sunday he woke up, reviewed the script and determined that his interpretation was in fact incorrect for the comedy. He came back to work on Monday, apologized for his behavior and redid the scene to his (and everyone else's) satisfaction.

A former teen heartthrob as Blackie Parrish on the ABC daytime soap opera *General Hospital* (1982–1984), Stamos left that series to star in his own CBS sitcom *Dreams,* that lasted only five weeks during October 1984. That led to some concern in the industry that he lacked the chops to be a leading man, particularly in comedies. "Even I had reservations about myself in the beginning," he told Michael Leahy in *TV Guide.* "I was getting advice on how to do the role from too many people. One day, Jack just told everybody, 'If you want to tell the kid something, tell me.'" That stopped the flow of unsolicited advice and provided the actor with needed confidence.

After its big debut, *You Again?* settled into its regular time slot from March 3 through June 9. Its ratings remained strong enough that it finished #19 for the 1985-1986 season, making it the third most-successful series to premiere that season behind *The Golden Girls* and *Growing Pains.* Its success appeared assured — until NBC moved it to Wednesdays from 9:30–10 P.M. effective June 18, 1986.

This was one of NBC's few weak spots on its schedule (ABC's *Dynasty* won the time slot). With CBS planning to move its hit adventure series *Magnum, P.I.* on Wednesdays from 9–10 P.M. as well, NBC figured a sitcom would provide strong counterprogramming to the hour programs. Unfortunately for *You Again?*, the network slotted the series after the aging and faltering *Gimme a Break!*, and the decision to have it lead off the

competition did not help *You Again?* Both shows began running third in their time slots in the fall.

The series was not helped by lousy plotting, which did not use many of the British original's scripts. For example, on the Dec. 31, 1986, episode, Anita Gillette appeared as Henry's ex-wife and Matt's mother, and surprise, she and Henry became romantically involved again. If you think that resulted in a reunion, however, you definitely have not watched enough sitcoms.

When the show began its second season, Henry had acquired a secretary, Pam, who was pregnant and unmarried. For some inexplicable reason (perhaps a strong agent), Pam's portrayer, actress Valerie Landsburg, received billing as a special guest star on the show. The always reliable redhead Barbara Rhoades appeared as Henry's co-worker Maggie Davis, and she is credited as a regular on the series by most sources along with Guy Marks as Harry and Luis Avalos as Louis Robles, even though all three performers appeared in only five episodes in the 1986-1987 season.

The changes did not help in the ratings, however, and NBC decided to pull the struggling series off the air unceremoniously on Jan. 7, 1987, less than a year after its spectacular debut. (The network aired an extra episode on Dec. 27, 1986, to burn off the last of the 13 shows taped for the season.) After the special *Spitting Images* on Jan. 14 and an extra episode of *Gimme a Break!* on Jan. 21, the series was replaced on Jan. 28 by *The Tortellis,* a spinoff of *Cheers* (see 10) featuring the family of Carla's ex-husband. The series was even less successful than *You Again?* and went off in less than four months.

Meanwhile, NBC allowed *You Again?* one more appearance on Monday, March 30, 1987, at 10:30–11 P.M. Eastern and Pacific. A repeat of an episode where Matt tried to go on tour with the Beach Boys as a guitarist, it followed the TV-movie *Stone Fox* (8:30–10:30 P.M. Eastern and Pacific).

Bennett had the shortest wait after the cancellation to get another series job. She stopped working on *Home to Roost* in England so that she could become a regular on the NBC sitcom *Nothing in Common* when it started on April 2, 1987. Unfortunately, that show bombed and went off two months later. She never secured another American TV series role.

Stamos rebounded with the hit ABC comedy *Full House* from Sept. 22, 1987, through Aug. 29, 1995. Klugman contracted throat cancer in 1989 but later returned to acting, although not in any regular series.

62 — *The Lucy Show*

Oct. 1, 1962 ("Lucy Waits Up for Chris"). **Rating:** 34.8. **Share:** n/a.

Aired on CBS Monday 8:30–9 P.M. Eastern and Pacific, 7:30–8 P.M. Central

Competition: *The Rifleman* on ABC, *Saints and Sinners* on NBC

Cast: Lucille Ball (Lucy Carmichael), Vivian Vance (Vivian Bagley), Candy Moore (Chris Carmichael), Jimmy Garrett (Jerry Carmichael), Ralph Hart (Sherman Bagley). **Guest:** Tom Lowell (Alan Harper). **Crew:** Desi Arnaz (executive producer), Elliot Lewis (producer), Jack Donohue (director), Madelyn Martin, Bob Carroll, Jr., Bob Schiller, Bob Weiskopf (writers).

Synopsis. Widow Lucy Carmichael and divorcee Vivian Bagley finish dinner with their respective sons, Jerry and Sherman, feeding a bone to their neighbor Harry Connors' dog Tiger. Lucy's daughter Chris perturbs her mother by going out on a date with Alan Harper, who is 16 and can drive a car. Lucy interrupts the youngsters when they return before Chris can say goodbye to Alan — and before Lucy realizes that Alan's parents were in the car with them. Alan calls the next morning and asks Chris to go out again that night. Lucy vows she will not stay up for the end of the date. When Lucy loses track of time playing cards with Viv and the kids arrive, Lucy runs outside as Chris and Alan make hot chocolate in the kitchen.

Tiger barks at the locked-out Lucy until the latter bounces on a trampoline up to Vivian's room, telling her friend to open the front door to let her enter. But Alan and Chris thwart the plan when they move from the kitchen to the living room. Viv pulls Lucy into Viv's bedroom before Chris asks where her mom is. As Lucy hides, Viv lies that Lucy went out. Lucy dons one of Viv's coats before Viv throws her down onto the trampoline. But Lucy loses her shoes and Tiger takes them. An hour later, Lucy returns, Chris is in bed asleep and Viv's shoe has been chewed by Tiger.

Backstory. After the success of CBS's *I Love Lucy* from 1951 to 1957, Lucille Ball vowed she would never do another TV series. But in 1961, the failure of both her Broadway musical *Wildcat* and her production studio, Desilu, to sell more series to the networks resulted in her returning to the medium in *The Lucy Show.*

While Desilu rented a lot of studio space for series to use for filming in the 1961-1962 season, it had only two productions it owned on the air,

The Untouchables on ABC and *Pete and Gladys* on CBS, and their poor ratings made them possible cancellation candidates. Desilu thought it had a promising entry for the fall of 1962 with *Fair Exchange*, an hour-long comedy. CBS said it would air the series only if Lucy starred in another sitcom for the network as well.

Ball agreed to the deal on two conditions: Vivian Vance would play her comic cohort as she did on *I Love Lucy*, and the show would air on Monday nights, again as did *I Love Lucy*. Ball wanted her old Monday 9 P.M. slot, but CBS programming head Mike Dann told her he wanted to keep the successful *Danny Thomas Show* at that time, so she accepted starting a half-hour earlier. Vance had her own demands: She did not have to look fat for the series, would have no husband like she did on *I Love Lucy*, and be treated more as Lucy's equal. While Ball tolerated her ex-husband Desi Arnaz as executive producer, she did not want to act opposite him. Keith Thibodeaux (Little Ricky) played the drums in the *Lucy Show* audience warm-ups.

According to the on-screen credits, the series was an adaptation of Irene Kampen's book *Life Without George*, about two divorcees and their children living in the same house. However, *I Love Lucy* creator Jess Oppenheimer later won a lawsuit contending that the Lucy Carmichael character was based on the Lucy Ricardo character, not the novel. Meanwhile, Madelyn Martin, Bob Carroll, Jr., Bob Schiller and Bob Weiskopf, all past writers for *I Love Lucy*, made the lead widowed rather than divorced to generate more audience sympathy and avoid reminding the public that Lucy and Desi were no longer husband and wife. (Given how Vance and Frawley treated each other on and off the *I Love Lucy* set, there were no fears about keeping Viv's character divorced. In fact, she refers to her "cheapskate ex-husband" in this show.)

The first show aired was "Lucy Waits Up for Chris," a serviceable if not spectacular start. Jack Donohue's direction is the biggest flaw; he had some setups that resulted in jerky camera angles, and several response close-ups of Lucy were obviously shot after the studio audience had left. But the Lucy–Viv onscreen rapport and Lucy's always excellent physical comedy timing make it a winner.

Harry Connors, mentioned in "Lucy Waits Up for Chris," showed up in the next episode, played by Dick Martin. As half the comedy team of (Dan) Rowan and Martin, Dick was so in demand by Desi to play Lucy's next-door neighbor and occasional love interest that he flew the comic out between bookings to act on the show. But as Rowan and Martin received more club work across America, it became impossible to sustain that setup, so Martin left the show after one season. That next season (1963–1964), Gale Gordon became Lucy's banker Mr. Mooney, and remained through the end of the series, as he nimbly blew his top at Lucy's antics while trying to maintain some dignity.

Audiences turned out in droves to see the new antics of their favorite redhead comedienne in 1962, and most stayed after "Lucy Waits Up for Chris"; the series finished the season tied for fourth place while *The Rifleman* and *Saints and Sinners* were cancelled. It remained in the top 10 every season during its six-year run, matching the record set by — yep, *I Love Lucy*. But backstage turmoil affected the series.

Desi vanished after the first season due to drunkenness, according to Stu Shostak, Lucy's personal film archivist for the last ten years of her life. Elliot Lewis moved up as executive producer before leaving at the end of the 1963–1964 season, when Martin, Carroll, Schiller and Weiskopf stopped writing for the series. The latter two became head writers for *The Red Skelton Hour* (see 68), while the former duo left when they believed Ball's comment that their services were no longer needed after they delivered a script whose ending did not impress her.

Coming in as new writers were Milt Josefsberg, who was script consultant and then script supervisor, and Bob O'Brien, who became executive producer from 1966 to 1968. Shostak blames them for reducing the roles of Vance and the child actors (they all left in 1965, with Vance purposely making outrageous demands if she was to continue) and transforming Ball's character into, as he put it, "a pushy, bossy bitch" who riled Mr. Mooney even more when they both moved to Los Angeles in 1965 and she became his office assistant. "It became a sketch comedy show, with the guest star breaking out in a song and dance," Shostak said. "The show never recovered after Vivian left."

The premise boiled down to an incompetent employee driving her boss nuts, arguably the most limited sitcom setup ever, and miles away from the enjoyment of *I Love Lucy*. But Ball let the deterioration happen anyway. "She trusted the writers and they convinced her this is the way the show was going," Shostak said. "There was no one to tell her that this wasn't going to work."

That included her husband Gary Morton, who became program consultant and then production executive on the series.

The Emmys encouraged Ball by awarding her two statuettes for Actress in a Comedy Series for both 1967 and 1968 (she previously earned nominations for the series in 1963 and 1966) and nominating *The Lucy Show* as Best Comedy Series in 1968. Also nominated in this period were Gordon for Supporting Actor in a Comedy in 1967 and 1968; Maury Thompson for Directorial Achievement in Comedy in 1967; and Writing Achievement in Comedy for Josefsberg and Ray Singer's script "Lucy Gets Jack Benny's Bank Account" in 1968.

Midway through its last season, *The Lucy Show* was the #1 series. However, when NBC's *Rowan and Martin's Laugh-In* (see 53) debuted opposite it, that series ate into Lucy's audience. And yes, *Laugh-In* featured the same Dick Martin who was on the first year of *The Lucy Show*.

The Lucy Show ended on Sept. 16, 1968, after Ball had sold Desilu to Paramount. CBS aired daytime reruns from 1968 to 1972. Ball came back with a new sitcom that was almost as successful — and problematic — as *The Lucy Show*. For more details, see *Here's Lucy* at 71.

61—*A Charlie Brown Christmas*

Dec. 7, 1969 (special; first aired in 1965). **Rating:** 34.8. **Share:** 54.

Aired on CBS Sunday 7–7:30 P.M. Eastern and Pacific, 6–6:30 P.M. Central

Competition: *Land of the Giants* on ABC, *Olympic Boy* (special) on NBC

Voices: Peter Robbins (Charlie Brown), Tracy Stafford (Lucy Van Pelt), Christopher Shea (Linus Van Pelt), Cathy Steinberg (Sally Brown), Chris Doran (Schroeder), Anne Altieri (Frieda), Jeff Ornstein (Pig Pen), Karen Mendelson (Peppermint Patty), Sally Dryer-Barker (Violet), Bill Melendez (Snoopy). **Crew:** Lee Mendelson (executive producer), Bill Melendez (director), Charles M. Schulz (writer).

Synopsis. At Christmas time, Charlie Brown tells Linus he always feels depressed about the season. He hates the commercialism. Charlie's dog Snoopy is decorating his doghouse to win a neighborhood lighting display contest, and his little sister Sally wants money from Santa Claus. Charlie visits Lucy's psychiatric booth to discuss his feelings. She advises him to involve himself in directing the holiday play she and the other children are rehearsing at the auditorium.

As director, Charlie encounters difficulty rallying his cast, even with Lucy as his script assistant. He decides that a Christmas tree will set the proper mood and takes Linus with him to fetch one. Over warnings from Linus, Charlie picks a spindly pine tree on a wooden stand, because he thinks it needs a home. When he returns to the auditorium, the other children mock his selection. Doubting his abilities to understand the holiday, he cries out, "Isn't there anyone who knows what Christmas is about?"

"I can tell you what Christmas is all about," Linus responds, reciting the story of Jesus Christ's birth. Smiling, Charlie picks up his tree and walks out in the spirit, vowing to decorate it. He takes an ornament from Snoopy's doghouse, but it weighs the tree down and he is upset, believing he killed it. While he's away, the other children come and decorate it. When Charlie returns, the kids say in unison "Merry Christmas!" and all sing "Hark the Herald Angels Sing" as the credits roll.

Backstory. Since its debut on Dec. 9, 1965, one of TV's most eagerly anticipated events between Thanksgiving and New Year's Day has been *A Charlie Brown Christmas*. The first animated special to win both an Emmy (for Best Children's Program) and a Peabody award, it is loved by millions of viewers of all ages for striking the right balance of humor, sentimentality and inspiration. Considering the principals had only four months to create the show, and that certain CBS executives who originally screened it were not impressed, its triumph is all the more impressive.

Cartoonist Charles M. Schulz started his comic strip *Peanuts* in seven newspapers on Oct. 2, 1950. It stood out in its field as it focused exclusively on the humorous musings of precocious children (and Snoopy, a beagle with human tendencies), with no adults ever drawn in full form or depicted speaking coherently. Its popularity extended to the point that before the end of the decade, *Peanuts* was a regular feature in more than 350 newspapers across America as well as 40 overseas publications.

In 1962 the granddaughter of the head of the J. Walter Thompson advertising agency asked him why he did not consider using *Peanuts* to promote his account for Ford Motor Company's new car, the Falcon. Intrigued, he contacted Schulz; since that was the only car he drove, the cartoonist agreed to allow his characters to appear in TV ads.

To animate them, the agency hired veteran artist Bill Melendez.

The following year, TV producer Lee Mendelson wanted to do a documentary on Schulz and include animation. Schulz told him to check with Melendez about providing two minutes for the show. Jazz musician Vince Guaraldi had a popular instrumental hit at the time called "Cast Your Fate to the Wind" that intrigued Mendelson, and he asked Guaraldi to score it. Yet despite all the talents combined, no network wanted to air the documentary.

Then in May 1965, John Allen at the McCann Erickson Agency told Mendelson he loved the documentary, but he was calling for another reason. One of his clients was Coca-Cola, and they wanted to sponsor a half-hour Christmas special. The only problem was that Mendelson and Schulz had just five days to put together an outline for the soft drink company. But the basic story for *A Charlie Brown Christmas* formulated in Schulz's mind quickly, and by the end of their first day of collaboration, the men had finished an outline to send for review. It sold.

During production, Mendelson and Schulz set some ground rules unusual for TV animated specials at the time. There would be no laugh track, and Snoopy would not speak, even though he did in "thought bubbles" in the comic strip; the beagle would pantomime his thoughts. For parts where Snoopy growled, Melendez suggested he should just talk and then speed up the tape so it was incomprehensible, thus becoming the "voice" of Snoopy.

The crew tried using adults for the voices, but didn't get what they wanted. "So we began using little kids' voices and we happened to get some real gems," Schulz told Leonard Maltin in 1984 during a presentation for the Museum of Broadcasting. "I think in *A Charlie Brown Christmas* the Linus voice [provided by Christopher Shea] was a marvel."

Guaraldi composed and conducted a delightful original score, using in the auditorium dance sequence a lively piece, "Linus and Lucy," that he had created for the 1963 documentary. It later became the unofficial theme for *Peanuts* specials. The soundtrack album has become one of the top holiday collections ever, selling more than a million copies.

The special was completed a week before it was to air on a Thursday from 7:30–8 P.M. Eastern and Pacific. "When we saw the finished show, we thought we had killed it," Melendez recalled. "It had so many warts and bumps and lumps and things." That was nothing next to the comments from two CBS executives who saw it and told Mendelson they thought it was slow and warned that CBS would not air any more *Peanuts* specials.

All that talk ended when the ratings and reviews — veritable hosannas — came in. The special finished second for the week behind *Bonanza* (see 20), with a huge 45 share. A typical critical reaction was that of Harriet Van Horne of the *New York World-Telegram*: "Write CBS and say all you want for Christmas is a repeat."

Viewers got that, along with many more *Peanuts* specials over the years. *A Charlie Brown Christmas* remained the favorite of them all, and it peaked in its popularity during its fourth repeat (preempting *Lassie*) at a time when *Peanuts* was at its zenith as a force in popular culture. I cannot improve upon how Mendelson phrased it in *A Charlie Brown Christmas: The Making of a Tradition*: "There was a single night in December of 1969 when a *Peanuts* movie was playing to a sold-out audience at the Radio City Music Hall, *You're a Good Man, Charlie Brown* was playing to a sold-out audience off–Broadway, and *A Charlie Brown Christmas* was being watched by half of the American television audience — after a hundred million of us had read his comic strip earlier that day!"

The 1969 repeat was the #1 show of the week. It finished half a point ahead of its previous high rating of 34.3 when it aired on Dec. 10, 1967. According to a compilation of the 100 highest-rated TV specials from 1964 to 1979, *A Charlie Brown Christmas* made the list five times from 1967 through 1975. It was a testament to how beloved *A Charlie Brown Christmas* had become with American TV viewers.

A Charlie Brown Christmas —and the *Peanuts* characters themselves — became so popular with annual appearances on CBS that it was a shock when ABC gained the rights to air the specials in 2001. More disturbing was the way ABC treated them: Following the 2009 showing of *A Charlie Brown Christmas*, many viewers complained how the network edited out some of the story to fit in more commercials. "Good grief!" Charlie Brown might have said in response.

By the way, the second-highest rated *Peanuts* special is *He's Your Dog, Charlie Brown*, which scored a 32.3 rating when CBS debuted it on Feb. 14, 1968. The network reran it the next five years. But whether going by ratings or quality, no other *Peanuts* special can touch *A Charlie Brown Christmas*.

60 — *Holocaust*

April 19, 1978 (Part 4 of four-part miniseries). **Rating: 34.9. Share: 49.**

Aired on NBC Wednesday 8:30–11 P.M. Eastern and Pacific, 7:30–10 P.M. Central

Competition: *Eight Is Enough* (last half-hour of 60-minute show), *Charlie's Angels* and *Starsky and Hutch* on ABC; *The Amazing Spider-Man* (last half-hour of 60-minute show) and *Posse* (repeat of 1975 theatrical movie) on CBS

Cast: Tom Bell (Adolph Eichmann), Joseph Bottoms (Rudi Weiss), Tovah Feldshuh (Helena Slomova), Marius Goring (Heinrich Palitz), Rosemary Harris (Berta Palitz Weiss), Anthony Haygarth (Heinz Muller), Michael Moriarty (Erik Dorf), Deborah Norton (Marta Dorf), George Rose (Lowy), Robert Stephens (Uncle Kurt Dorf), Meryl Streep (Inga Helms Weiss), Sam Wanamaker (Moses Weiss), David Warner (Heydrich), Fritz Weaver (Dr. Josef Weiss), James Woods (Karl Weiss). **Crew:** Herbert Brodkin (executive producer), Robert Berger (producer), Marvin Chomsky (director), Gerald Green (writer).

Synopsis. The Inga Helms-Karl Weiss wedding in 1935 Berlin is marred by Helms family friend and Nazi Heinz Muller's distaste for the Jewish Weisses, including Karl's father and mother, Josef and Berta; Karl's brother, Rudi; Josef's brother, Moses; and Berta's father, Heinrich. As anti–Semitism rises in Germany, Josef treats Marta, who talks her husband Erik into joining the SS, where he reports to Heydrich. In 1938 the Nazis imprison Karl in Buchenwald and deport Josef, his friend and patient Lowy and other Jews to Poland to join Moses. When the state takes over Josef's office and home, Heinrich and his wife commit suicide rather than move with Berta and Rudi next door to Inga and her family. Rudi runs away and romances a benefactor, Helena, in Prague.

By 1941 Berta joins Josef in Warsaw, now a walled Jewish ghetto. Inga reluctantly has sex with Muller, now an official at Buchenwald, to keep Karl alive. Erik leads a plot to exterminate Jews and other "undesirables" on the Russian front; his Uncle Kurt despises the Nazis.

As years pass, Inga reunites briefly with Karl; Rudi and Helena marry and fight Nazis; and Erik serves under Eichmann after Heydrich's assassination. Eventually Josef, Berta, Karl and Lowy die in Auschwitz, Moses is murdered in the Warsaw uprising, Helena is killed in the Ukraine, and Erik commits suicide when caught by the Allies. Inga gives birth to Karl's son, Josef, as World War II ends. Rudi considers living in Palestine.

Backstory. Some people have argued that the horrors of the Final Solution are so evil that no drama can adequately capture them. That has not stopped Hollywood from making pictures on the subject, of course. The first, most in-depth treatment on television was *Holocaust*, and it remains the medium's definitive dramatization of the topic.

The idea for *Holocaust* came to Irwin Segelstein when he was head of programming at NBC in 1976. He discussed it with an agent, Sy Fisher. Fisher's client, TV producer Herbert Brodkin, recruited novelist and playwright Gerald Green, who had written two books discussing the Nazis' persecution of Jews, to write a treatment. The success of *Roots* (see 3) in early 1977 convinced NBC to approve the project. After Green created a screenplay, the miniseries received a $6 million budget. It was shot in 18 six-day weeks on location in Austria and Germany, with 150 speaking parts.

NBC executive vice-president for ratings Paul Klein insisted to *Variety* that the miniseries "wasn't produced to get big ratings," citing several reasons why he expected it would not be a blockbuster. "It's not loaded with sex and violence like *Roots*," he argued somewhat inaccurately. "People's legs aren't cut off, there are no sexual threats."

Actually, there were plenty of scenes of killings and flashes of side and back nudity as victims faced firing squads or went to the gas chambers. And some actors playing Nazis spouted the then–forbidden derogatory phrases "bitch" and "whore" as an indication of their characters' hatred for the Jews. It was a gritty, uncompromising drama that pressed the limits of TV censorship at the time, but did not break all taboos.

Producer Robert "Buzz" Berger disagreed with NBC censoring two scenes of naked Jewish women being forcibly marched to the gas chambers, but he conceded the cuts by noting to *Variety* that "I don't want to give any NBC affiliate an excuse for not carrying the miniseries." He added that he had received anti–Semitic death threats for participating in the project.

He was not the only person in his religion to whom *Holocaust* was an important project, although some worried more about economics. One rabbi reportedly warned an NBC executive not to run the miniseries during the February sweeps month because ABC president "Fred Silverman will counterprogram it into the ground." As it turned out, it faced mostly reruns at the tail end of the 1977-1978 season, and that probably helped its numbers, as did several other factors.

Courtesy of the Anti-Defamation League of B'nai Brith, daily newspapers across America carried a 16-page tabloid supplement discussing the Nazis' extermination of Jews from 1933 through 1945. The National Education Association endorsed the miniseries and encouraged schools to have students watch it, with one million study guides printed. Green adapted his screenplay into a novel that sold well in advance of the miniseries too.

NBC also previewed *Holocaust* to more than 40 religious and organization leaders, and most praised it rapturously. "I have seen it three times, and I have found myself crying each time," Rabbi Marc Tannenbaum, director of national interreligious affairs at the American Jewish Committee (as well as a consultant to the miniseries), told Richard F. Shepard in *The New York Times*. "The impact of the series is greater than anything I have witnessed since the end of World War II."

But in that same issue, another preview attendee, Elie Wiesel, a prominent Holocaust survivor and professor at Boston University, denounced it: "Untrue, offensive, cheap: as a TV production, the film is an insult to those who perished and those who survived." He felt it possessed stereotyped characters and historical inaccuracies. Accompanying his article was a pan by *New York Times* TV critic John J. O'Connor, virtually the only unfavorable critique the miniseries received in a major publication.

The latter two comments prompted a mini–*cause celebre* in several issues of the newspaper. Many letters to the *New York Times* editor defended the miniseries, including ones from theatrical impresario Joseph Papp and former movie studio president and playwright Dore Schary. Even Wisconsin Sen. William Proxmire wrote in favor of the presentation and cited it as a reason for the U.S. Senate to pass the Genocide Convention treaty. "Let's make sure there is never another 'Holocaust' like that of the Nazis or the Communists in Cambodia," he wrote.

Also chiming in was Gerald Green, who responded to Weisel by saying that while he "admired, indeed venerated" the Holocaust expert, most critics liked the miniseries he wrote. "The viewing of *Holocaust* will create a surge of new interest in the subject," he argued. "More of Elie Wiesel's books will be sold than ever."

To Wiesel's complaint that *Holocaust* tried to cover too much ground, Green responded, "Mr. Wiesel objects that we try to tell it all. Why not?" (Indeed, the expansive nature of *Holocaust* is one of its strengths. Its major flaw is too rosy an ending, with Rudi playing soccer with youngsters.

Considering the horrors early depicted, it rings false and pat.) Green concluded his piece by asking Wiesel to reconsider his opinion. Wiesel responded in print saying he remained unmoved.

NBC told advertisers to expect an average audience share of just 31 or 32. All were stunned when the ratings results came out. The first three parts airing April 16–18, 1978, finished with 27.1/43 (Part 1), 32.7/51 (Part 2), and 30.3/49 (Part 3) before peaking at its finale. It ended with an average 31.1/49.

At the Emmy Awards, *Holocaust* won statuettes for Outstanding Limited Series, Writing, Film Editing, Directing, Costume Design, Lead Actor (Michael Moriarty), Lead Actress (Meryl Streep) and Single Performance by Supporting Actress (Blanche Baker as Anna Weiss, the family's youngest daughter, who is raped, left mentally unbalanced and then killed by the Nazis in Part 1). Also-ran Emmy nominees were Lead Actor (Fritz Weaver), Lead Actress (Rosemary Harris), Supporting Actor (Sam Wanamaker and David Warner), Supporting Actress (Tovah Felshuh), Art Direction and Music Composition.

When *Holocaust* appeared in overseas markets, reaction was generally positive. In Israel the Camp David "Framework for Peace" occurred opposite its third part, which drew attention away from it. In West Germany, there were two bomb explosions at TV transmitters as five regional stations aired it. In France the weekly newsmagazine *L'Express* raised money to run it on TV after the country's three networks rejected it. An anti–Semitic tract appeared in distribution in Toulouse the first day after it aired, and some surviving Nazi collaborators called into question the accuracy of the show.

Holocaust was rerun on NBC Sept. 10–13, 1979, with the best numbers being 16.4/27 for the opening night. It was sold to local TV stations afterward. It has since been surpassed in dramatic terms by the stunning *Schindler's List*, the 1993 Oscar Best Picture winner. Still, *Holocaust* remains a proud and affecting landmark in TV's history.

59 — *The Dick Van Dyke Show*

Jan. 1, 1964 ("The Third One from the Left"). **Rating: 35.0. Share:** N/a.

Aired on CBS Wednesday 9:30–10 P.M. Eastern and Pacific, 8:30–9 P.M. Central

Competition: *Ben Casey* on ABC; *Espionage* on NBC

Cast: Dick Van Dyke (Rob Petrie), Mary Tyler Moore (Laura Petrie), Rose Marie (Sally Rogers), Morey Amsterdam (Buddy Sorrell), Richard Deacon (Mel Cooley). **Guests:** Cheryl Holdridge (Joan Delroy), Jimmy Murphy (Ernie). **Crew:** Sheldon Leonard (executive producer), Carl Reiner (creator-producer), Jerry Paris (director), John Whedon (writer).

Synopsis. TV writers Rob, Buddy and Sally receive a visit from Mel, their show's producer. Mel is displeased because Rob has usurped his duty of finding new talent for the show by singling out an 18-year-old chorus girl, Joan Delroy, to be on next week's program. Joan gives Rob a big hug — just as Rob's wife, Laura, arrives. Rob apologizes at home for the way the situation appeared, but Laura understands because Joan has a crush on him. He attempts to end it the next day but fails miserably.

Back at home, Laura suggests that when Rob told Joan he was old enough to be her father in his gentle, self-effacing manner, it only made her want him more. So the following day he suggests to Joan that they run off to Mexico so he can divorce Laura and marry her. Joan excitedly tells this news to her boyfriend, Ernie. This prompts Rob to decide to be honest with Joan the next day, but Ernie shows up first and punches him in the gut. Hearing about this action from Rob, Joan realizes that Ernie loves her and runs to him. But Rob is facing the other way and unknowingly announces their breakup to a quiet Sally, Buddy and Mel who have entered behind him, giving all a good laugh.

Backstory. While there is universal acclaim for Erik Barnouw's three-part book survey of the history of broadcasting in the United States — *A Tower in Babel*, *The Golden Web* and *The Image Empire* — he really missed the boat in the latter by lumping *The Dick Van Dyke Show* with *Father of the Bride* and *The New Bob Cummings Show*, among other lesser sitcoms, when describing the 1961-1962 season. Anyone who has seen *The Dick Van Dyke Show* recognizes that it is so much more intelligent, realistic and (most importantly) funnier than almost all the other sitcoms on the air during the early to mid–1960s.

The Dick Van Dyke Show stands out so far from the pack that one shudders to think that it could have lost any of its four consecutive Emmy wins as best comedy series from 1963 to 1966 (a record in the category until *Frasier* won it five times in a row in the 1990s) to the unworthy likes of *McHale's Navy*, *The Bill Dana Show*, *The Farmer's Daughter* or *Hogan's Heroes*, among others. Since that time, it has become enshrined in all quarters as one of TV's classic series of any genre.

Carl Reiner created the series based in part of his experiences writing for and working with Sid Caesar on the 1950s comedy variety series *Your Show of Shows* and *Caesar's Hour*. He was unable to sell it with himself in the lead (the 1960 Reiner-starring pilot was called *Head of the Family*). Sheldon Leonard, then hot with *The Danny Thomas Show*, saw the show and felt it would have potential — with a different leading man. The two men agreed on Dick Van Dyke after seeing him star on Broadway in the musical *Bye Bye Birdie*.

Debuting Oct. 3, 1961, *The Dick Van Dyke Show* had terrible ratings its first year partly because it was a sophisticated domestic sitcom airing part of the season in the early evening. But the next season, where it immediately followed *The Beverly Hillbillies* (see 12), it became a huge hit. The series also had a considerably better critical reputation than its lead-in.

During the early to mid–1960s, *The Dick Van Dyke Show* was *the* series that writers wanted to work on, according to Garry Marshall in his autobiography *Wake Me When It's Funny*. He and his partner Jerry Belson took a fair amount of time to break through because Reiner saw them as good only for writing one-liners, which in fact was their primary job during the early 1960s. Learning that the key to success was selling a funny incident, along with character development, Marshall and Belson finally wrote several scripts during the series' last two seasons. They liked writing for Moore in particular and based several scripts on incidents that came out of Marshall's own life with his wife. "By writing for *The Dick Van Dyke Show*, we learned how to write the detailed visual and physical humor that would help set us further apart from many other writers," Marshall wrote.

The cast also developed a reputation as one of the best in the business. "They rehearsed as though they had worked together forever," director John Rich recalled of doing the pilot in his memoirs *Warm Up the Snake*. "The rehearsal went so well that as the day ended, I realized we staged the entire 30-minute piece." The setup was in fact *too* fast for Rich's taste — the cast would not film the episode until six days later — so he made sure to make changes in stages in blocking for future shows.

Still, the professionalism shone through. The series shot each episode with one taping, usually from 8–9:30 P.M., to allow for set changes. "Because the show was filmed, postproduction enhancements were possible," Rich noted. "But since the cast was so well rehearsed, the episodes never needed extensive editing."

This episode is not one of the series' best, but it does a serviceable job of generating laughs. Sally makes cracks about Joan's young age, calling her Gidget and Tammy at various points in reference to the teenage characters then seen on screen. Buddy jests repeatedly that he has first shot at Laura whenever Rob leaves her. And Mel is his usual square self.

At home, Laura has some droll lines about his dilemma. (Rob: "She's nuts about me." Laura: "Ah, she'll get over it. I did.") But Van Dyke shines as Rob with a good comic bit. As he tells Joan of his Mexico rendezvous plans, he lights two cigarettes and offers one to Joan *á la* Paul Henreid with Bette Davis in the 1942 movie classic *Now Voyager*, only to be rebuffed and have to smoke both briefly in response.

The Dick Van Dyke Show finished second this week behind *The Beverly Hillbillies*; the two series would end the 1963-1964 season at #3 and #1 respectively. But *The Beverly Hillbillies* was no match for this sitcom when it came to Emmys. This season alone, the show won statuettes for humor program, lead comedy actor (Van Dyke), lead comedy actress (Mary Tyler Moore), comedy direction (Paris), and comedy writing (Reiner, Sam Denoff and Bill Persky for various episodes). It wound up winning 16 Emmys before ending its run on Sept. 7, 1966.

The series' lead personnel — Van Dyke, Reiner and Moore — made a decision to call it quits at the end of the series' five-year contract, as they all had movie offers that would pay them more for less work, and they wanted to leave with the show on top (it finished the 1965-1966 season at #16). There was also going to be additional expense for converting the show to color if it continued into the 1966-1967 season. In the early 1970s, *The Mary Tyler Moore Show* (see 58 — *Rhoda*) was a hit while *The New Dick Van Dyke Show* struggled to last three seasons, with Reiner exiting as a writer-producer before it ended. Meanwhile, *The Dick Van Dyke Show* did well in reruns, particularly for a black-and-white series.

In 1991 Nick at Nite added reruns of *The Dick Van Dyke Show* to its nightly lineup. In '92 the network appointed Van Dyke its honorary chairman to honor America's "TV heritage," and in 1993 Van Dyke picked his favorite episodes for a special airing.

Today *The Dick Van Dyke Show* is readily available on DVD. It's just as fresh and funny as it was

50 years ago. It's not just a classic sitcom, it's a classic series. Period.

58 — *Rhoda*

Oct. 28, 1974 ("Rhoda's Wedding"). **Rating:** 35.2. **Share:** 52.

Aired on CBS Monday 9–10 P.M. Eastern and Pacific, 8–9 P.M. Central

Competition: *Monday Night Football* (Atlanta Falcons vs. Pittsburgh Steelers) on ABC; *Shamus* (1973 movie debut) on NBC

Cast: Valerie Harper (Rhoda Morgenstern), David Groh (Joe Gerard), Julie Kavner (Brenda Morgenstern) **Guests:** Edward Asner (Lou Grant), Georgia Engel (Georgette Franklin), Harold Gould (Martin Morgenstern), Cloris Leachman (Phyllis Lindstrom), Gavin MacLeod (Murray Slaughter), Mary Tyler Moore (Mary Richards), Nancy Walker (Ida Morgenstern), Bernard Barrow (The Judge), Bella Bruck (The Neighbor), Paula Victor (Joe's Mother), Lorenzo Music (Voice of Carlton the Doorman). **Crew:** James L. Brooks, Allan Burns (executive producers-creators), David Davis, Lorenzo Music (producers-developers), Robert Moore (director), James L. Brooks, Allan Burns, David Davis, Lorenzo Music, Norman Barasch, Carroll Moore, David Lloyd (writers).

Synopsis. Rhoda Morgenstern, who recently returned to her native New York City from Minneapolis, plans to marry architect Joe Gerard. She wants a small ceremony, but her meddling mother Ida has invited people over to her apartment at the same time, forcing Rhoda to reluctantly accept the plan. Rhoda greets her old friend Mary Richards, who flies from Minnesota for the event. To Rhoda's surprise, Mary's colleagues and her old friends, Lou Grant and Murray Slaughter, have decided on a drunken whim to go along with Mary on the trip, as does Phyllis Lindstrom, Rhoda's old verbal sparring partner in Minneapolis.

Mary enjoys meeting Joe, which pleases Rhoda. Rhoda and Joe go out on their last date the night before the wedding while Rhoda's former coworker, Georgette Franklin, arrives at Ida's Bronx apartment where the others are eating. Mary asks Georgette why she didn't fly with the rest of them, and she says she drove to see people along the way and recounts her trip. Phyllis interrupts her and tells her the tale is boring. Joe and Rhoda join the gang, and Rhoda and Mary recall a few of their bad dates.

The next day, Phyllis forgets her promise to pick up Rhoda from the Manhattan apartment

Rhoda shares with her sister, Brenda. Rhoda has to ride the subway in her wedding gown to get to her mother's place. She pretties herself up and exchanges vows with Joe before the judge pronounces them husband and wife. Everyone hugs the happy couple.

Backstory. It seems odd that *Rhoda* makes this top 100 list while the classic, better-remembered series that spawned it, *The Mary Tyler Moore Show*, failed to make the cut. Then again *Rhoda* was a bigger hit in its debut season (1974-1975), finishing at #6, than *The Mary Tyler Moore Show* was in any of its seven seasons on the air. It appeared unstoppable at the time, particularly in the wake of this episode, which I would argue is the best dramatized TV wedding ever, full of unexpected yet delightful turns, warm and yet quite funny. If only the later episodes of *Rhoda* could have been the same.

The idea of spinning off Mary Richards' apartment mate who delivered ready wisecracks grew out of several elements. One was the success of spin-offs from other CBS sitcoms of the period such as *All in the Family* (see 25); another was the popularity of other series from Moore's production company such as *The Bob Newhart Show*.

To show that Rhoda could carry her own program, the second episode of the 1973-1974 season of *The Mary Tyler Moore Show* was a quasi-pilot where Mary and Rhoda flew to the wedding of Rhoda's sister, Debbie, played by Liberty Williams. Debbie was never mentioned again, but Nancy Walker and Harold Gould returned in the series as Rhoda's pushy mom and supportive father respectively. Other *Rhoda* regulars were her sister Brenda; Carlton, the never-sober apartment house doorman; and Joe, an architect with whom Rhoda fell in love.

When CBS programming head Fred Silverman heard about plans to have Rhoda marry Joe just seven weeks after its debut on Sept. 9, 1974, he thought it ought to be an event, and he told the series' production team to make it the first special one-hour episode of a half-hour sitcom in order to draw a huge audience. He pre-empted the series' lead-in, *Maude*, so that *Rhoda* would start a half-hour earlier than its usual 9:30–10 P.M. Eastern and Pacific slot on Mondays, and virtually all the regular writers at the MTM production company collaborated on this unprecedented event.

The resulting episode was superb, with choice lines for every major cast member, great performances and smooth transitions between scenes, particularly the montage shot on location in New

York City with Valerie Harper running the streets and in the subway system. (David Davis supervised that filming.) Here are some of its most memorable moments:

• Phyllis describes her luggage to tipsy Lou and Murray: "I have several pieces, all brown." "Brought everything in paper bags, huh?" retorts Rhoda.

• When Phyllis said she forgot to pick up Phyllis for the wedding, Nancy Walker's visibly pained look of horror and delivery of "I'll kill you" was enough in itself to earn an Emmy nomination.

• When Phyllis apologizes profusely for leaving Rhoda behind, only Georgette forgives her. She adds, "But if I were you, I'd get my tail out of here before Rhoda shows up."

• When Ida's neighbor comes out of her apartment clutching some items as Rhoda walks the processional from the elevator in her gown, she says, "Hi, Rhoda. What's new?" "Nothing much," says a bemused Rhoda. "Same here," says the neighbor before leaving.

• Learning that Rhoda and Joe have written their own wedding vows, Ida looks at Lou and kvetches, "What's wrong with the one God wrote?" A flustered, uncomfortable Lou shakes his head with no answer to that.

This episode had fairly weak competition from the other networks. For example this was the first year that Alex Karras manned the booth on *Monday Night Football*, and not all viewers warmed to him. (Karras and his co-analyst, Howard Cosell, actually joked on the air that night about going to the reception at Rhoda's since they missed her wedding.) Its rerun on April 14, 1975, did pretty well too, with a 21.8/42.

At the Emmys, *Rhoda* won one out of five nominations in its first season, with Harper being the only victor (and yes, she won over her former co-star Mary Tyler Moore). The other nominations were for comedy series, losing to *The Mary Tyler Moore Show*; two for supporting actress in a comedy (Walker and Julie Kavner lost to Betty White on *The Mary Tyler Moore Show*—sense a theme here?); and the writers of "Rhoda's Wedding," losing to, you guessed it, *The Mary Tyler Moore Show* (for an episode written by none of them). Robert Moore did not receive a directing Emmy nomination, but he did finish among the top three contenders in the Directors Guild of America awards for best direction in a comedy series for this episode.

Rhoda later won another Emmy, for Kavner as supporting actress in 1978 (she beat out Walker in the category). But by that time, after finishing

at #7 in the 1975-1976 season, *Rhoda* seemed adrift. Grant Tinker, head of MTM Productions, blamed the downturn on this episode in his autobiography. "That episode drew a mammoth audience, but in the long term the marriage was a mistake, as even Fred [Silverman] has since admitted," he wrote. "People preferred the single, anxious Rhoda to the happily married one. Ultimately, in an effort to revive the flagging show, we put her through a divorce, but the audience didn't like that either."

As a separation led to a divorce in the 1976-1977 season, Rhoda gained new single friends who never sparked with her the way she did with Mary Richards, even with talented types such as Anne Meara and Ron Silver portraying them. CBS moved it to Sundays in the middle of the season, where it performed so-so. A switch to Saturdays to lead off that night in the fall of 1978 proved fatal. Ratings fell so drastically (it finished the 1978-1979 season at a weak #67) that CBS was compelled to cancel it before the end of the year, on Dec. 9, 1978.

---

57 — Planet of the Apes

Sept. 14, 1973 (*CBS Friday Night Movies*; first released theatrically in 1968). **Rating:** 35.2. **Share:** 60.
Aired on CBS Friday 8:30–11 P.M. Eastern and Pacific, 7:30–10 P.M. Central

Competition: *The Odd Couple, Room 222, Adam's Rib* (debut) and *Love American Style* on ABC; *The Girl With Something Extra* (debut), *NFL Players Association Awards* (hour special) and *The Dean Martin Show* on NBC

Cast: Charlton Heston (George Taylor), Roddy McDowall (Cornelius), Kim Hunter (Dr. Zira), Maurice Evans (Dr. Zaius), James Whitmore (President of the Assembly), James Daly (Dr. Honorious), Linda Harrison (Nova), Robert Gunner (Landon), Lou Wagner (Lucius), Woodrow Parfrey (Dr. Maximus), Jeff Burton (Dodge), Buck Kartalian (Julius). **Crew:** Arthur P. Jacobs (producer), Franklin J. Schaffner (director), Michael Wilson, Rod Serling (writers).

Synopsis. Time-traveling in deep space, astronauts Taylor, Landon and Dodge arrive in the year 3978 when their spaceship crashes. They escape and find mute savages. A growl is heard, and talking apes round up the humans. Taylor and Landon are separated, while Dodge dies. Held in a cage with a female he dubs Nova, Taylor writes to Zira, an animal psychologist, as his vocal cords are damaged. Zira's boyfriend, Cornelius, thinks Taylor can prove his theory about a missing link between humans and apes. Zira's superior, Dr. Zaius, dismisses the idea until Taylor finally can speak, cursing his captors after an escape attempt.

The shocked apes hold a tribunal finding Zira and Cornelius guilty of scientific heresy, with the president and Drs. Zaius and Maximus as jurors and Dr. Honorious arguing for the state. They disbelieve Taylor and plan to give him a lobotomy, as they did with Landon. Lucius, Zira's nephew, helps Taylor and Nova overpower Julius the guard, and Zira and Cornelius join them in going to the ocean. When Zaius arrives, he cannot explain why they find a human doll from earlier centuries that can talk.

Taking Zaius hostage, Taylor receives a horse and supplies and intends to set out with Nova. Zaius warns Taylor he may not like what he finds. Taylor breaks down when he sees the Statue of Liberty is halfway sunk in the ground. He had been on Earth all the time, in a future after mankind had wiped out its own civilization.

Backstory. In 1963, a novel by French author Pierre Boulle caught the attention of film producer Arthur P. Jacobs, who bought the movie rights for the book before it was published. Boulle, who also wrote *The Bridge on the River Kwai* (see 38), thought it was a lesser work unsuitable for a good motion picture, but Jacobs believed otherwise, and so did Rod Serling, who spent nearly a year writing 30 drafts of a screenplay for Jacobs. The producer also commissioned seven artists to draw scenes of how the film would look. Despite all these efforts, he spent a year unsuccessfully trying to convince studios to make the project a reality.

Knowing that what would really sell the project would be to have a star behind it, Jacobs met with Charlton Heston in June 1965, and the actor loved the idea. He recommended hiring Franklin J. Schaffner as director. With those elements in place, Jacobs began pitching his plans again and found an interested party in Richard Zanuck, the newly installed head of 20th Century–Fox.

While knowing that the script needed work, Zanuck's main concern was that the makeup for the apes be realistic, so that people would not laugh while watching it. A $5,000 screen test was shot in March 1966 with Edward G. Robinson as Dr. Zaius, James Brolin as Cornelius and Linda Harrison (a Fox contract player dating Zanuck at the time; later Nova in the film) as Zira. Ben Nye's makeup was crude compared to the final job, but it convinced Zanuck to give the project the go-ahead.

Schaffner saw that Serling's script calling for a technologically advanced ape society would be too costly to film, so he suggested a more primitive one. Jacobs drafted Michael Wilson to do a rewrite. At the same time, Robinson dropped out of doing the film, as he hated the time and effort needing to do the makeup for Dr. Zaius.

With filming set to start on May 21, 1967, veteran makeup artist John Chambers had four months to figure out how to make expressive facial prosthetics for nearly 200 actors playing apes and keep it under $1 million. Chimps, who favored people, had to appear more sympathetic and human-like, while gorillas, who were against them, were more rugged and fearsome. Orangutans were aristocratic and thus looked noble.

For the main ape actors, it took about six hours in makeup for appliances, wigs, fur on their hands and even brown nail polish. The process decreased down to three hours toward the end of the shoot, but the actors had to stay in refrigerated in dressing rooms to preserve the appliances (with new ones used daily for the leads) and eat soft foods to prevent damaging their makeup. The results were impressive enough that Chambers received an honorary Oscar for his outstanding achievement.

Planet of the Apes earned two Academy Award nominations, for Morton Haack's costume design and Jerry Goldsmith's original score. Goldsmith used odd instruments, such as metal mixing bowls and a ram's horn, to provide an eerie, otherworldly background.

The film was a particularly rough shoot for its star. "Barefoot and all but naked in most of the scenes, I was ridden down by gorillas, whipped, chained, gagged, stoned (even rubber rocks hurt), fire-hosed and finally trapped in a net and jerked upside down," Heston recalled in his autobiography *In the Arena*. He ended up getting a cold, something he never had while acting. It played in his favor, however — it gave him a memorably raspy deliver of the first line he says in captivity, "Take your stinking paws off me, you damn dirty ape!" The theatrical movie included nude scenes of Heston's buttocks, both when he and the other astronauts went skinny dipping and when he appeared before the orangutan court to argue his case. (CBS censored those moments from its broadcasts, even though they were so fleeting that the film earned a G rating.)

Shooting ended on Aug. 10, 1967, on time and on budget, even with Fox cutting ten days out of the planned filming schedule. Filming locations included the Glen Canyon Dam, where the ship "landed" in the Colorado River. The film was released six months later and proved to be one of the biggest box office hits of 1968.

With that success, 20th Century–Fox demanded that a sequel be made, thanks in part to the studio's finances being in trouble due to a series of dud releases, including Jacobs' own poorly performing *Doctor Doolittle* (1967). Jacobs had not anticipated this development, but he managed to make one anyway, and the final product was called *Beneath the Planet of the Apes*. The 1970 sequel included the last three and a half minutes of the first film as the introduction to it. That movie was a hit as well.

Jacobs had considered a TV series adaptation of the concept as early as 1971, but the movie sequels were doing so well that he nixed the idea until after the release of the fifth movie in the series, *Battle for the Planet of the Apes*, in the spring of 1973. A few months later, the big numbers generated by this movie, which opened the 1973-1974 season of the highly rated *CBS Friday Night Movies*, and by *Beneath the Planet of the Apes*, which aired six weeks after the original movie and scored similarly high numbers of 32.6/54, amazed the TV industry.

Then on Nov. 6, 1973, CBS aired the second movie sequel, *Escape from the Planet of the Apes* (1971). Although not quite as big a hit as the previous two, its numbers still remained very impressive (29.1/50), so it was not surprising then that CBS programming head Fred Silverman announced plans for a weekly *Apes* TV series for the following season.

But *Planet of the Apes* as an hour-long weekly series was far less appealing, even with Roddy McDowall playing an ape named Galen, and viewers flocked to its competition on NBC, *Sanford and Son* (see 72). *Apes* ran from Sept. 13 through Dec. 27, 1974. CBS reran the original *Planet of the Apes* movie on April 25, 1975, to so-so ratings (14.1/26), before it was sold to local TV stations, as were episodes of the series (recut to make several two-hour TV movies). If that was not enough, NBC even ran a Saturday morning cartoon rendition, *Return to the Planet of the Apes*, from Sept. 6, 1975, through Sept. 4, 1976.

In 2001 a remake *Planet of the Apes* appeared in theaters, but despite being a box office hit, most viewers rated it poorly in comparison with the original. Another relaunch of the franchise in 2011 fared much better with critics as well as audiences. It appears the apes are here to stay with us for now.

56 — *Laverne & Shirley*

Jan. 16, 1979 ("Who's Papa?"). **Rating:** 35.3. **Share:** n/a.

Aired on ABC Tuesdays 8:30–9 P.M. Eastern and Pacific, 7:30–8 P.M. Central

Competition: *CBS Reports* special "The Boat People" on CBS, *Grandpa Goes to Washington* (last show) on NBC

Cast: Penny Marshall (Laverne DeFazio), Cindy Williams (Shirley Feeney), Michael McKean (Leonard "Lenny" Kosnowski), David L. Lander (Andrew "Squiggy" Squiggman), Phil Foster (Frank DeFazio), Betty Garrett (Edna Babish). **Guests:** Ed Begley, Jr. (Robert "Bobby" Feeney), Dee Marcus (Reception Nurse), Rance Howard (Doctor), Lindsay Bloom (Nurse Krevsky), Wendy Cutler (Mrs. Plout). **Crew:** Garry Marshall, Thomas L. Miller, Edward K. Milkis (executive producers), Tony Marshall, Marc Sotkin, Chris Thompson (producers), Maurice Bar-David (director), Al Aidekman, Zoey Wilson (writers).

Synopsis. Shirley Feeney is excited because her brother Bobby is coming to visit her after a two-year absence. Her roommate and co-worker at the Shotz Brewery in Milwaukee, Laverne DeFazio, is more concerned about preventing break-ins of her locker at work to steal her gum (the culprits are another worker-roommate pair who irritate her, Lenny and Squiggy). At their apartment, Laverne and Shirley greet Bobby, who is tall, blond and handsome. Laverne's cranky, protective father Frank vows that Bobby will not stay with his daughter to prevent any hanky panky. Their landlady and Frank's girlfriend, Edna Babish, calms him down but notes how different Shirley and Bobby look. Laverne tells Shirley she may be adopted, making Shirley realize that she does not resemble the other members of her family. Her worries increase when Squiggy suggests maybe they are related, given their similar appearance.

Laverne and Shirley visit the hospital where the latter was born to retrieve Shirley's birth records, but the haughty reception nurse informs them that only doctors and pregnant can access that information. Shirley disguises herself as a male obstetrician and Shirley pretends to be an expecting brunette. Nurse Krevsky flirts with Shirley before they are caught by a doctor when trying to trespass. He gives her the records after he tells her he has an adopted child that he loves unconditionally. Shirley is relieved to know she is not adopted.

Backstory. The first ABC series to be #1 for a season more than once was *Laverne & Shirley*, which held the top spot for the 1977-1978 and

1978-1979 seasons. This followed its impressive finishes of #2 in 1976-1977 and #3 in 1975-1976, its inaugural season (it began on Jan. 27, 1976). Its overwhelming popularity is even more extraordinary when you consider that this sitcom started at the bottom of the hour, usually a time not conducive to #1 series; the only other ones with this status are *Arthur Godfrey's Talent Scouts* in 1951-1952 and *Wagon Train* (see 48) in 1961-1962.

The combination of weak competition (a CBS documentary and the final episode of a loser sitcom on NBC), as well as the fact this was the first new episode of the series to air in four weeks, resulted in this being the highest-rated *Laverne & Shirley* show ever, although it finished #2 for the week in the ratings behind the perennial powerhouse Super Bowl (see 4). With those factors in mind, it must be said this was a limp episode for the series to employ for its return.

The guest stars and supporting cast members have very little to do; the talented Ed Begley, Jr., for one, has no funny lines to deliver as Shirley's brother, just the chance to appear presentable in a sailor suit. Potential plot points pop up and disappear with no follow-up, such as Lenny and Squiggy's thefts of gum and Frank's concern about Bobby staying in the apartment. And the tiresome main plot of Shirley's birth status would probably spark the wrath of today's adoption advocates as being in questionable taste. The one distinguishing element was the casting of Rance Howard as the doctor. He was the father of Ron Howard, the star of the show that gave birth to *Laverne & Shirley* and preceded it on ABC Tuesday nights, *Happy Days* (see 64).

As for the beginnings of the series: A *Happy Days* episode was written with two ladies dating Richie and Fonzie. With time tight to cast the roles, executive producer Garry Marshall enlisted his acting sister, Penny, and her then-writing partner, Cindy Williams, to portray the visiting females. During rehearsal, cameraman Sam Rosen told Marshall that they had the makings of their own show. The studio audience loved them as well. ABC's new programming head Fred Silverman liked the success *Happy Days* had at 8 P.M. and thought something from the same producer should follow it at 8:30. (*Welcome Back, Kotter* aired after *Happy Days* for the first few months of the 1975-1976 season.) Marshall pitched Silverman *Laverne & Shirley* and the latter bought it, although to be safe Marshall and company made a ten-minute pilot on Fonzie's apartment set.

A writing veteran of a few episodes of *The Lucy*

Show (see 62) Marshall incorporated lots of physical comedy (in the style of Lucille Ball) into *Laverne & Shirley*. Joining them were Lenny and Squiggy, two greasers who got on the girls' nerves because they thought they were hipper than they really were; Laverne's father Frank, a pizza restaurateur; and Edna. The other regular not seen in this episode was their pal Carmine, a short but sleek actor and dancer.

Laverne & Shirley debuted with a 35.1/49, making it the highest-rated series premiere since *Mayberry, R.F.D.* (see 50). It stayed near that peak the next four seasons. Its hit status extended to the music charts as well. The show's theme "Making Our Dreams Come True" was a top 30 hit sung by Cyndi Grecco in the summer of 1976.

But amid its popularity, *Laverne & Shirley* gained a reputation as an uncomfortable set, thanks largely to the insecurity of its two stars. Williams felt she was at a competitive disadvantage for lines because Marshall's brother was executive producer. Several sources confirm this belief. In his memoirs *Cue the Bunny on the Rainbow*, Alan Rafkin termed *Laverne & Shirley* "one of the most unpleasant series I have ever directed." He said Williams and Marshall resisted rehearsing to the point where they had to be forced out of their dressing rooms and would often complain about scripts.

Phil Mishkin recalled to Tom Stempel in *Storytellers to the Nation* that when he became a producer there, he not only was excoriated by Marshall and Williams for the series' scripts, but even forced to light their cigarettes. "Whenever one got more jokes than the other, they would fight," Garry Marshall wrote in his memoirs *Wake Me When It's Funny*. Marshall said Williams once had her manager measure the length of time she was on screen compared to Penny. Scribes were considered lucky if they could survive one season of the series. Marshall claimed that Penny and Cindy realized how unpopular they were with the crew and even gave them dart boards with their faces as bull's-eyes one Christmas. Part of the tension may have stemmed from critical disdain for the series. Like *Happy Days*, the series never earned an Emmy nomination for best comedy. It only competed once for TV's highest honor, for outstanding costume design for a series in 1979.

More distress came the following season. In 1979-1980, ABC unwisely moved the show to Thursdays in the slot formerly held by *Mork & Mindy* (see 65). The shift resulted in a huge loss of audience, as the series not only fell from #1 but also struggled just to make the top 50. Relocating it to Mondays in December 1979 did not help either, so ABC returned it to its original slot two months later.

The series wound up at #39 for the season, which could have resulted in cancellation. But ABC had faith in the producers' plans to revamp the sitcom by having the characters leave for Hollywood and start living in the 1960s. Ratings went back up somewhat so that the show finished in the top 20 in 1980–1981 and 1981–1982.

When Cindy wed Bill Hudson and became pregnant in the summer of 1982, she started arguing with Paramount over working conditions, walked off the set and filed a $20 million lawsuit against the studio (later settled out of court). The rest of the 1982–1983 season, *Laverne & Shirley* no longer had the latter on the show, and the effect was so deadly that the producers decided to end it. It last aired on ABC May 10, 1983.

Regardless of whatever you may think of this series, it is miles better than the cartoon version of the same name that aired on ABC Saturday mornings from Oct. 10, 1981, through Sept. 3, 1983. Unless, of course, you think the idea of Laverne and Shirley serving in the military under a sergeant who is a pig is hilarious.

---

55 — Gomer Pyle, U.S.M.C.

Jan. 29, 1965 ("Love Letters to the Sarge"). **Rating:** 35.4. **Share:** n/a.

Aired on CBS Friday 9:30–10 P.M. Eastern and Pacific, 8:30–9 P.M. Central

Competition: *F.D.R.* on ABC, *The Jack Benny Program* on NBC

Cast: Jim Nabors (Pvt. Gomer Pyle), Frank Sutton (Sgt. Vince Carter), Ronnie Schell (Pvt. Gilbert "Duke" Slater), **Guests:** Larry Hovis (Larry), Buck Young (Sgt. Whipple), Elizabeth Fraser (Salesgirl), Jean Carson (Shirley), Patty Regan (Adelaide), Jackie Joseph (Marilyn), Mary Lansing (Librarian), Tommy Leonetti (Corp. Cuccinelli), Charles Thompson (Old Man), Robert Buckingham (Mail Caller). **Crew:** Aaron Ruben, Sheldon Leonard (executive producers), Coby Ruskin (director), Art Baer, Ben Joelson (writers).

Synopsis. At Camp Pendleton in California, privates Gomer Pyle, Duke Slater and Larry receive several love letters from women back home while Sgt. Carter has none. Gomer is particularly concerned, so he goes to the library to read books on how to write love poems and buys perfume to spray on the letter he intends to write. When Sgt.

Carter looks at the anonymous note, he beams and wonders who the "mysterious Miss X" is who wrote it. Encouraged by his response, Gomer writes more of them. The sergeant asks Gomer who Miss X might be, and Pyle provides several suggestions.

The first possibility Carter visits is Shirley the waitress at the PX, then Adelaide the coat check girl and finally Marilyn the U.S.O. worker. None fit the bill. When Gomer overhears Vince's buddies Sgt. Whipple and Corp. Cuccinelli tell him he should invite the mystery lady to the USO dance on Saturday night so they can see what she looks like, Gomer decides to write a "Dear John" letter. The correspondence arrives, but disappointment changes to elation for Sgt. Carter when he receives mash notes from Shirley, Adelaide and Marilyn as well. At the end of the episode, Carter reviews a prosaic letter Gomer is writing for his hometown sweetie, Ida, and tells him he would have more dates if his words were poetry.

Backstory. The character of Gomer Pyle was based on a simple-minded mechanic who once worked on the car of writer Everett Greenbaum. Greenbaum and his collaborator Jim Fritzell crafted an *Andy Griffith Show* (see 79) episode that introduced the character, whose casual approach to repairing a car incenses its owner. "Man in a Hurry" originally aired on Jan. 14, 1963.

Before the role was cast, the star of *The Andy Griffith Show* went to a nightclub in Santa Monica and thoroughly enjoyed the booming vocals of a little-known performer named Jim Nabors. Griffith raved about this talent from Alabama to his producer, Aaron Ruben, who took a chance and had Nabors play Gomer. The result was electric. Gomer was added to the cast as the perfect comic foil for Barney Fife, who vented exasperation at the slow-on-the-uptake Pyle for not following his orders.

A year later, Greenbaum and Fritzell learned that Aaron Ruben, then producer of *The Andy Griffith Show*, decided to pitch Gomer as a starring character for his own series. He wrote the pilot as the final episode of the 1963–1964 season, with good-natured Gomer joining the U.S. Marine Corps with the help of Sheriff Andy Taylor. However, Gomer's new boss, Sgt. Carter (played by Frank Sutton, who reprised the role for the series), finds Gomer one challenging private to understand and handle. (Gomer would be replaced as the mechanic on *The Andy Griffith Show* the following season by George Lindsey playing his equally dimwitted cousin, Goober Pyle.)

General Foods, the sponsor of *The Andy Griffith Show*, bought *Gomer Pyle* "on no more than a description of the proposed format," executive producer Sheldon Leonard wrote in his autobiography *And the Show Goes On*.

The premise sounded familiar to many critics. With Gomer constantly exasperating his gruff superior, Sgt. Carter, many thought it was simply a redo of *No Time for Sergeants*, the TV and later stage play that became a big hit in the 1950s for none other than Andy Griffith as the yokel private. In fact, ABC aired a TV series version of *No Time for Sergeants* the same season as *Gomer Pyle*, but the network ran it against Griffith's show. It ran for just one year.

Gomer Pyle, U.S.M.C. debuted on CBS Friday nights beginning Sept. 25, 1964. When the series aired, both Greenbaum and Fritzell disliked it, feeling Gomer had become dumber than they had envisioned him. But a majority of TV viewers felt otherwise, and soon *Gomer Pyle, U.S.M.C.* passed its popular parent series in the weekly ratings to become the third most popular series in the 1964-1965 season as well as occasionally the top-rated one for some weeks, as in this case.

Reviewing this episode, one can understand Greenbaum and Fritzell's sentiments. The humor on this series was weak: Pyle offers Sgt. Carter the chance to go with him to see *Godzilla Goes to a Beach Party*, a play on two popular genres that was so bad even the laugh track could barely muster a titter for it. The plotting was thin as well. The summary at the start of this entry contains virtually every action that occurred rather pokily during the show.

The Marine Corps thought the series was a positive portrayal of their military division and that it might even help with recruitment. To help out, they allowed the production company to use the base at Camp Pendleton in California as the main outdoor set, and they even employed real-life troops in the background for some scenes.

When *Gomer Pyle, U.S.M.C.* became a series, Ruben thought Pyle needed a buddy on the base. "Now, Aaron Ruben explained to me that it wasn't a funny part," Ronnie Schell recalled of his character, Pvt. Duke Slater, in a 2007 interview with Stu Shostak. "His philosophy was, in television, you have to have somebody representing the audience or else the audience will run away."

Slater's purpose on the show was to serve as someone who couldn't believe what Gomer was saying or doing. This was Schell's first network TV acting job, and he was scared he would not pull it off. He obtained an audition for the part thanks to his manager, Richard Linke. In 1963 Linke, who was the manager for Griffith and Nabors, saw Schell perform as the opening act for the Kingston Trio in San Diego and was so impressed that he offered to represent the comedian. Somehow, Schell overcame his fright and delivered a performance that led to him being the most frequently seen actor in the first season of the series after Nabors and Sutton. Other men showed up a few times in the corps that year, including Tommy Leonetti and Larry Hovis seen in this episode. They appeared because their manager was — you guessed it — Richard Linke.

In 1965-1966, a few more military men started appearing regularly, chief among them Ted Bessell as Pvt. Frankie Lombardi and Roy Stuart as Corp. Chuck Boyle. The ratings remained high with these changes; in fact, like *The Andy Griffith Show*, *Gomer Pyle, U.S.M.C.* finished in the top 10 every season it ran. Bessell left after one season to star in *That Girl*. The following year Schell departed for *his* own sitcom, *Good Morning World*, which ran from Sept. 5, 1967 through Sept. 17, 1968.

When that series ended, Linke approached Ruben about having Schell return to *Gomer Pyle, U.S.M.C.* According to Schell, "Aaron said, 'Well, you know, we enjoyed having him on the show, so I'll write him in. This time, he's gonna come back as a corporal, and he'll be Sgt. Carter's right-hand man in the office.'" Unfortunately for actor Roy Stuart, that meant the writers had to drop his character in favor of Schell's return.

Schell stayed with the series until Nabors said he would not continue due to his plans for other projects (for more details on them, see 87 — *Friends and Nabors*). The series was still incredibly popular at #2 in the ratings for the 1968-1969 season, but CBS executives knew that no Nabors meant no Gomer, so *Gomer Pyle, U.S.M.C.* aired the last time on CBS nighttime on Sept. 19, 1969.

CBS started rerunning *Gomer Pyle, U.S.M.C.* afternoons daily shortly before its nighttime stint ended. It proved popular enough to force its ABC competition, the five-year-old ghostly soap opera *Dark Shadows*, off the air during its two-and-a-half years in that slot. CBS also ran *Gomer Pyle* reruns in the summer of 1970 as a replacement for *Hee Haw*. It went into reruns on local stations in 1972, where it did well for most of the 1970s before dying out.

Still, demand was strong enough for *Gomer Pyle, U.S.M.C.* that the Season 1 black-and-white episodes were released on DVD in 2006. Nabors recorded audio introductions for each episode, including this one.

54 — *The Andy Griffith Special*

Feb. 21, 1967 (variety special). **Rating:** 35.5. **Share:** n/a.

Aired on CBS Tuesday 8:30–9:30 P.M. Eastern and Pacific, 7:30–8:30 P.M. Central

Competition: *The Invaders* on ABC, *Occasional Wife* and *The War of the Worlds* (1953 theatrical movie) on NBC

Cast: Andy Griffith, Don Knotts, Tennessee Ernie Ford, The Back Porch Majority, Maggie Peterson, The Bruce Davis Quintet, The Nick Castle Dancers, The Alan Copeland Orchestra. **Crew:** Aaron Ruben (producer-writer), Jack Donohue (director).

Synopsis. This hour of entertainment is rather evenly split between comedy and musical segments, most of them involving the host, Andy Griffith. The central humorous sketch has Griffith being psychoanalyzed by Tennessee Ernie Ford because the former is a farmer who has an irrational dislike of animals that naturally hinders him from getting his chores done on time (for example, he can only milk his cow in the dark of night). Adding to the fun, Don Knotts arrives to play Ford's "wife" in pink curlers. Andy also reprises his nightclub act with Knotts and discusses the success of a small-town boy named "Willie" Shakespeare and what he has written. Knotts has his own routine of a playing a TV show host who finds himself awkwardly stuck live on camera with nothing to say and trying to make the best of the circumstance without having a nervous breakdown.

On the musical side, Andy sings several country tunes with Ford, including "Maple on the Hill," "Singin' the Blues," "I Walk the Line" and "Just a Little Lovin' (Will Go a Long Way)." Andy performs "Let the Good Times Roll" accompanied by the Nick Castle Dancers, while Ford solos on "I'm Just a Country Boy." The male-female folk group the Back Porch Majority (which would be disbanded by founder Randy Sparks later in 1967) lends its voice to "This Little Light," while Maggie Peterson joins the Bruce Davis Quintet on "South Rampart Street Parade."

Backstory. Pre-empting *The Red Skelton Hour* (see 68), and using that series' regulars the Alan Copeland Singers, *The Andy Griffith Special* was

officially titled *Andy Griffith's Uptown-Downtown Show*. Most sources record it by the former name, probably because there seems very little "uptown" about it. Designed to showcase the star of *The Andy Griffith Show* (see 79), the #3 series for the 1966-1967 season, it apparently was meant to show viewers and network executives that Griffith had singing and dancing talent in addition to being a fine comic actor. Ironically, however, this pitch toward showing the leading man's versatility proved more beneficial to a member of the special's chorus line.

Goldie Hawn had arrived in Los Angeles after stints as a go-go dancer in New York City and Las Vegas. She gave herself nine months to try and succeed in the city, and if it did not pan out, she would head back to her native Maryland and open up a dance studio. Hawn found an open call in the trade papers for dancers for *The Andy Griffith Special*. Veteran choreographer Nick Castle, who was between being a regular dancer leader on *The Andy Williams Show* from 1963 to 1966 and *The Jerry Lewis Show* starting in the fall of 1967, had groups of ten terpsichoreans try out for the available jobs, and Hawn was one of the 20 girls finally picked for the show.

The schedule for the dancers was the usual tight one for television. They rehearsed four days and then taped numbers for three days in advance, so they could be edited into the final show. (The same process of doing songs and dances in the studio without an audience and inserting them later was employed on *The Red Skelton Hour* as well.) Yet even in that brief time frame, Hawn made an impact beyond most of the others in the chorus line. "I arrive on the set the first day, and Tennessee Ernie Ford, the statuesque country-and-western singer who shares the show with Andy Griffith, stares down at my old dancing shoes, which has holes in them," Hawn recalled in her autobiography *A Lotus Grows in the Wind*. Ford jokingly asked her, "You going for extra ventilation?" She responded by telling him, "These are my lucky shoes." Ford then walked away.

"Later that day, he stops the rehearsal in front of the whole cast to make an announcement. 'Everyone chipped in,' he tells me with a grin, presenting me with a brand-new pair of shoes," Hawn added.

Now Hawn really felt lucky, especially when Castle took her aside and vowed that he would use her in all of his future shows. She took a break and met Art Simon with the William Morris Agency, who thought she had potential. Using his connections, he obtained for her an interview with executive producers Bill Persky and Sam Denoff about a part on their new TV series for CBS, *Good Morning World.* Hawn was so adorable that even though she was not right for the role, the duo created another character for her to play as a regular. The sitcom lasted one year. Simon later got her onto a hit show that made her a star, *Rowan and Martin's Laugh-In* (see 53).

The Andy Griffith Special was not the first special starring the performer. That honor fell to *The Andy Griffith–Don Knotts–Jim Nabors Show* that ran on Oct. 7, 1965. Like this special, it included regular *Andy Griffith Show* scribe Aaron Ruben as its writer and Knotts as a performer. Knotts revealed to Richard Kelly in *The Andy Griffith Show* how important appearances on these specials were to him: "I was careful to do a lot of guest appearances on variety shows during the hiatus period because I didn't want to get stuck with the name Barney, although some people continue to call me that," he said. "I wanted to be sure that people knew *my* name. I wanted my own identification."

As *Variety* reviewer "Mor." noted, "One of producer-writer Aaron Ruben's minor triumphs was to somehow prevent Ford from stealing the show as he has on previous occasions. Don Knotts was excellent, but his performance was marred by a tendency to gape at the cue cards."

The special's comedy sketches were taped two weeks in advance of its air date on Sunday, Feb. 5, 1967, from 8–9:30 P.M. in front of an audience at Studio 43 in the Television City complex in Hollywood. It finished #1 for the week, with *The Andy Griffith Show* at #2. Its big audience also did little for record and concert sales for the featured vocalists, although Maggie Peterson and the Bruce Davis Quintet did manage to play Las Vegas later in 1967 before splitting up. (Peterson is better known to *Andy Griffith Show* fans for her role of Charlene Darling.)

CBS reran *The Andy Griffith Special* on Feb. 21, 1970, pre-empting *Green Acres* and *Petticoat Junction*, which were losing in the ratings opposite movies on NBC Saturday nights. By that time, Griffith had left *The Andy Griffith Show* because he was physically and mentally tired of playing Sheriff Andy Taylor, and he and his manager, Richard Linke, thought that his popularity could generate some new opportunities for him in TV, movies or the stage as shown by this special.

But the expected offers never arrived. All Griffith could manage in two years was to star the unpopular 1969 feature film *Angel in My Pocket*, along with guest visits to *Mayberry R.F.D.* (see 50). He returned to series television in 1970 with the CBS drama *Headmaster*, but when that failed, he went back to playing a small-town Southerner in the sitcom *The New Andy Griffith Show* by midseason. Viewers preferred the comedy opposite it on ABC, *The Partridge Family*, so the latter program went off after a few months in 1971.

For the next 15 years, Griffith received mainly guest star roles in dramas, comedies and TV-movies before he starred on the hit lawyer series *Matlock*, which ran from 1986 to 1995. He never had the chance to headline another variety special, however.

Given the continuing love for *The Andy Griffith Show*, it seems odd that this special has yet to come out on DVD.

53 — Rowan and Martin's Laugh-In

March 24, 1969. **Rating:** 35.5. **Share:** n/a.
Aired on NBC Monday 8–9 P.M. Eastern and Pacific, 7–8 P.M. Central
Competition: *The Avengers* (last half-hour of 60-minute show) and *Peyton Place* on ABC; *Gunsmoke* (last half-hour of 60-minute show) and *The Lucy Show* (repeat of 1962–68 series) on CBS
Cast: Dan Rowan, Dick Martin, Chelsea Brown, Ruth Buzzi, Judy Carne, Henry Gibson, Goldie Hawn, Arte Johnson, Dave Madden, Alan Sues, Dick Whittington, JoAnne Worley, Gary Owens. **Guest:** Tony Curtis. **Cameos:** Werner Klemperer, Ann Miller, Garry Moore, Flip Wilson. **Crew:** George F. Schlatter, Fred Friendly (executive producers), Paul W. Keyes (producer), Gordon Wiles (director), Chris Bearde, Phil Hahn, Paul W. Keyes, Marc London, Allan Manings, David Panich, Hugh Wedlock, Digby Wolfe, Jim Carlson, David M. Cox (writers).

Synopsis. This installment of fast-paced merriment includes the traditional introduction of the cast by Gary Owens' humorously bombastic narration, followed by a brief comic dialogue by the show's hosts Dan Rowan and Dick Martin. In sketches that recur throughout the show, guest star Tony Curtis portrays Hamlet enduring some amusing takeoffs on the play's narrative, an aging performer and the chairman of a Senate committee holding a hearing on how to control rodents. Other features include the Party, where the regulars and Curtis gyrated to music on a swank apartment set before it stopped and one or two of them spouted one-liners while everyone else froze; "Laugh-In Looks at the News," with anchors Rowan and Martin offering jokes about events in the past, present and future; and innumerable snippets of funny shots, some lasting less than a second.

Cast members also read letters from viewers and gave their comic responses as part of a new segment on the series. This latter feature may have served as the inspiration for the daytime game show *Letters to Laugh-In*, which ran from Sept. 29 through Dec. 26, 1969. In any event, the show concluded as usual with the regulars and Curtis dispensing set-ups and punch lines to Rowan and Martin by sticking their heads out of doors on the joke wall, followed by a few more gags and finally the sound of one pair of hands clapping.

Backstory. The conventions of TV variety series were upended by the debut on *Rowan and Martin's Laugh-In* on NBC on Jan. 22, 1968. Viewers no longer had to endure long comedy sketches or endless medleys here. Instead, the series took advantage of the ability to edit videotape to speed up the tempo of the entertainment, and comic bits were written very short on purpose to keep the momentum quick. With this approach, *Rowan and Martin's Laugh-In* caught the freewheeling spirit of the late 1960s better than any other TV comedy at the time, and it turn influenced other shows to be just as sprightly. It was the first series to beat Lucille Ball regularly, and it appeared to be invincible before too many copycats (and not enough adjustments in its presentation) finally ended it on May 14, 1973, after lots of laughs, awards and big audiences.

The series grew out of a comedy special hosted by Rowan and Martin on Sept. 9, 1967, which they secured after years of guest shots on TV. It employed a supporting cast of mostly unknown actors, several of whom would return as regulars in the series, such as rubbery-faced, firm-jawed Ruth Buzzi. Rowan wrote to his pal, author John D. MacDonald, a month in advance of the special's debut, "I think we have a really good hour show, one that most people will be able to watch and smile and laugh out loud a couple of places.... This one is *different*. Now we are all hoping that it's different good."

Critical reception and the ratings were favorable, so with an option to make it a series, NBC put it in a problematic time slot in the 1967–1968 midseason: 8 P.M. Eastern and Pacific Monday nights, which had been so disastrous for the network that it had been nearly ten years (*The Restless*

Gun, 1957–1959) since a series ran more than a year in the slot. Against all odds, the series became popular quickly and ended its run at #21 for the season. The next two seasons, it was the #1 series, thanks to endlessly repeated catchphrases like "Here come da judge!" and "Look that up in your Funk and Wagnalls" and routines like Judy Carne getting soaked with buckets of water after saying "Sock it to me!" It sounds silly — and it was — but it provided refreshing laughter at a time when the American public needed it amid social strife, civil rights protests, anti–Vietnam War activities and so on.

Helping the series become a favorite was the identification of many of the supporting players with certain types. For example, Henry Gibson played meek types such as poets and priests, JoAnne Worley favored loud, brassy ladies and Alan Sues emphasized men with effeminate overtones. And then there was Goldie Hawn, the show's favorite dumb blonde (and many fans' favorite *Laugh-In* regular). With her adorable, devil-may-care delivery, she was hard to resist, and her training as a dancer paid off well as she shimmied in a bikini with wild designs and phrases painted on her body. She seemed such a natural for the show that it is odd to report she signed to join it without knowing what she could or should bring to its comedy.

What happened was Hawn was mildly dyslexic, so she had some difficulty reading a cue card with an introduction on it during the first taping. "I started to laugh because I felt so stupid," she recalled in her autobiography. "I mean, how simple could this be and I screwed up? The more nervous I got, the more I giggled. The more I laughed, the more we all laughed." She apologized and said she would correct it, but executive producer George Schlatter insisted the error would remain.

The probable reason why this episode was popular, with due respect to the drawing power of Tony Curtis (still a movie star in 1969), was the decision by CBS to replace *Here's Lucy* with reruns of *The Lucy Show*. *Here's Lucy* was an even match for *Rowan and Martin's Laugh-In* during the year, but the decision to repeat Ball's previous series at the same time it could be seen daily on the CBS morning lineup was overkill, and disaffected viewers changed the channel. This made one of the last *Rowan and Martin's Laugh-In* episodes the highest-rated one ever.

The *Rowan and Martin's Laugh-In 25th Anniversary Reunion* special on Feb. 7, 1993, included a clip from this show. In it, Curtis said, "Wherever

I go, all over the world, people are always asking me about *Laugh-In*. And they all ask me the same question — 'Why?!'"

At the end of the 1968-1969 season, *Rowan and Martin's Laugh-In* earned Emmys for outstanding musical or variety series, as it had in 1968, and individual achievement for Arte Johnson, who came across as the troupe's most versatile member due to a variety of characters, from Wolfgang the German soldier ("Verrrry interesting!" he would purr after peering into the camera) to Tyrone, the dirty old man on the bench who would sexually harass Ruth Buzzi's homely character Gladys until she pummeled him with her handbag. The series earned two other Emmys in 1968 (for writing and editing) and one more in 1971 (for directing). It had 20 other nominations.

But all good things must come to an end, and in this case, it was overexposure of its style by other shows ranging from *Hee Haw* to *Sesame Street* as well as a turnover in talent (apart from the hosts, only Buzzi and Gary Owens were on the series in its final season). Even though regular Jud Strunk had a top 20 hit with "Daisy a Day" in 1973, that was not enough to keep the series from sliding, and it went off after six seasons. After a couple of failed efforts, NBC came up with another winner in the time slot in 1974: *Little House on the Prairie*, which is about as far from *Rowan and Martin's Laugh-In* as you can go.

Rowan and Martin's Laugh-In was syndicated in the fall of 1983 with half-hour edits, which were not successful. They showed up again on the Trio cable channel in the early 2000s and did somewhat better. It was a product of its time to a certain extent, but I think it's still a fun show to watch in reruns.

52 — *The Wizard of Oz*

Jan. 26, 1964 (first released theatrically in 1939). **Rating:** 35.9. **Share:** 59.

Aired on CBS Sunday 6–8 P.M. Eastern and Pacific, 5–7 P.M. Central

Competition: *The Travels of Jaimie McPheeters* (first half-hour of 60-minute show, 7:30–8 P.M.) on ABC; *Meet the Press*, local half-hour shows, *The Bill Dana Show* and *Walt Disney's Wonderful World of Color* (first half-hour of 60-minute show, 7:30–8 P.M.)

Cast: Judy Garland (Dorothy Gale), Frank Morgan (Professor Marvel/The Wizard), Ray Bolger (Hunk/The Scarecrow), Bert Lahr (Zeke/The Cowardly Lion), Jack Haley (Hickory/The Tin Woodsman), Billie Burke (Glinda the Good Witch), Margaret Hamilton (Miss Gulch/The Wicked Witch of the West), Charley Grapewin (Uncle Henry), Clara Blandick (Auntie Em). **Host:** Danny Kaye. **Crew:** Mervyn LeRoy (producer), Victor Fleming (director), Noel Langley, Florence Ryerson, Edgar Allan Woolf (writers).

Synopsis. Dorothy Gale pines for a life away from the Kansas farm where she lives with her Uncle Henry and Auntie Em. After mean Miss Gulch takes away Dorothy's dog, Toto, for biting her, Toto escapes and joins Dorothy in their house as a tornado propels it skyward. When it lands, Dorothy and Toto find a place inhabited by little people called Munchkins. Glinda, the Good Witch of the North, tells Dorothy she killed a witch when her house fell. The deceased's sister is the Wicked Witch of the West. Glinda transfers the dead witch's ruby red slippers to Dorothy and casts a spell preventing the Wicked Witch from obtaining them. Dorothy simply wants to get home, so the Munchkins and Glinda tell her to follow the Yellow Brick Road to reach the Wizard of Oz.

With Toto in tow, Dorothy meets the Scarecrow, who needs a brain; the Tin Man, who needs a heart; and the Cowardly Lion, who needs courage. They arrive to see the Wizard. He says he wants the Wicked Witch's broom before granting their wishes. The witch tries to kill Dorothy but winds up melting after the latter throws a bucket of water on her. They bring the broom back to find the Wizard is a fraud, although he does help Dorothy's friends. Glinda reappears and tells Dorothy to click her slippers and say "There's no place like home." She awakes and learns it was a dream, but she is glad to be back in Kansas.

Backstory. No other movie has ever had repeatedly high ratings in reruns as has *The Wizard of Oz*. Its January 1964 airing marked its sixth showing on TV. By the time it stopped airing regularly on network TV in 1998, *The Wizard of Oz* held (and still holds) the record for most number of appearances (15) on *Variety*'s list of movies receiving a 24.0 or higher rating on television.

L. Frank Baum wrote the novel *The Wonderful Wizard of Oz* (1900), which was so popular it was adapted into a Broadway musical in 1902, *The Wizard of Oz*. In 1925 it became a silent film, but it was not a hit. What inspired the sound movie version was the massive success of Walt Disney's 1937 cartoon movie *Snow White and the Seven Dwarfs*. Wanting to emulate it, MGM's Louis B. Mayer assigned Mervyn LeRoy, who loved the book since he was a child, to produce the film

(LeRoy had begged him to do it for five years). Arthur Freed, a songwriter and later producer at MGM, also claimed he was the one who encouraged Mayer to buy the book.

Ten writers worked on the script, beginning with Herman J. Mankiewicz, who came up with the idea of the Kansas scenes being shot in black-and-white and Oz in color. He turned in an incomplete script at the same time that two other writers, Ogden Nash and Noel Langley, were assigned to write treatments. Langley's outline was judged best, and he spent three months revising scripts for the movie. When his fourth script was finished, he assumed it would the final shooting one. But it was felt that Dorothy still was not as involved in the plot as she should be.

A few other writers tinkered with the screenplay, but only the team of Florence Ryerson and Edgar Allan Woolf received credit for their work along with Langley. A few others polished spots in the script before it was ready to roll — even lyricist E.Y. "Yip" Harburg, who would supply unforgettable music for the film along with composer Harold Arlen.

LeRoy had loved Judy Garland ever since seeing her in *Pigskin Parade*. He fixed her teeth and made her Dorothy over Shirley Temple, who MGM wanted. Buddy Ebsen, had an allergic reaction to the aluminum dust used on his face, so he left the production and Jack Haley replaced him as the Tin Woodsman. Billie Burke wrote in her autobiography *With a Feather on My Nose* that Glinda the Good Witch was her favorite role in Hollywood because "this role is as close as I have come in motion pictures to the kinds of parts I did in the theater."

LeRoy was also a director, but Mayer convinced him it would be too elaborate a production to do both jobs. Richard Thorpe originally held the post, but after two weeks, LeRoy felt he was not capturing the essence of the story. He was replaced by George Cukor, who made costume and makeup tests for ten days before Victor Fleming came aboard as the permanent replacement for four months. Fleming was taken off completing the last two weeks of shooting *The Wizard of Oz* in order to replace Cukor immediately for *Gone with the Wind* (see 6). King Vidor replaced Fleming on *The Wizard of Oz* and shot "Over the Rainbow," but he insisted on no screen credit despite ten days' work on it.

When it came out in 1939, despite strong box office results and six Academy Award nominations, the movie actually lost money during its first run due to its costs (more than $3 million, high in those days). It finally recouped its cost during a re-release in 1949, when critics also looked more favorably on the film. The Oscar nods were for Best Picture, Color Cinematography, Interior Decorations, Special Effects and Song and Score. It won in the latter two categories, with "Over the Rainbow" becoming a classic.

In 1956 CBS signed a contract to run *The Wizard of Oz* twice at $225,000 per showing, with an option for seven more airings at $150,000 apiece. The movie ran as the last presentation of the Saturday night anthology series *Ford Star Jubilee* on Nov. 3, 1956, but some parents complained that its 9–11 P.M. scheduling (Eastern and Pacific) made it too late for their children to stay up to watch it. CBS never made that mistake in future showings, running it early in the evenings thereafter.

For its 1964 appearance, CBS had Danny Kaye introduce the film not only to push his TV series at the time, but also to reassure children not to be scared, that this was just a fantasy and not really fact about a witch. With no real competition at its start, it was no wonder this became the second-highest rated show of the week, behind *The Beverly Hillbillies* (see 12) with a 41.9 rating for its Jan. 29, 1964, show.

The Wizard of Oz seemed to grow stronger every year — for example, by its second showing on Dec. 3, 1959, it had a 58 share. It remained a steady performer for CBS in the early to mid–1960s. In fact, no other movie that aired on CBS through 1966 did as well ratings-wise as *The Wizard of Oz*. Its numbers during this period, from highest to lowest ignoring this entry, were 34.7/49 on Jan. 17, 1965, 33.0/55 on Dec. 9, 1962, 32.7/52 on Dec. 11, 1960, 32.5/53 on Dec. 10, 1961, and 31.1/49 on Jan. 9, 1966.

Seeing CBS's high ratings, including 28.6/50 when the movie ran for its maximum ninth time on Feb. 12, 1967, NBC signed a deal in the summer of that year to have it air the next five seasons exclusively on the network. (CBS felt MGM wanted too much money.) NBC also dropped the idea of having a host, feeling that children could understand that the film was fantasy. It renewed the contract through 1975, then CBS won the rights back in 1976 and aired it through 1998. Thereafter it aired occasionally on Turner Classic Movies and other cable channels.

Though no longer an annual TV event, *The Wizard of Oz*'s influence on pop culture remains pervasive. Its tunes have become top 40 hits (e.g.,

"Over the Rainbow" by the Demensions in 1960, "Ding Dong! The Witch is Dead" by the Fifth Estate in 1967, "Themes from the Wizard of Oz" by Meco in 1978). Another song was paraphrased to provide the title for *Off to See the Wizard*, a 1967-1968 ABC children's series using animated characters seen in the movie as hosts. The movie has inspired other films as well, including *Under the Rainbow* (1981). It was an ABC Saturday morning cartoon in 1990 and 1991. Most recently, it has served as the basis for the hit Broadway musical *Wicked*, told from the Witch's point of view.

Undoubtedly more knockoffs will come. But none will have the magic of the original, which will remain an unforgettable children's fantasy for future generations.

51— The Burning Bed

Oct. 8, 1984 (*NBC Monday Night Movie*). **Rating:** 36.2. **Share:** 60.
Aired on NBC Monday 9–11 P.M. Eastern and Pacific, 8–10 P.M. Central
Competition: *Monday Night Football* (San Francisco 49ers vs. New York Giants) on ABC; *Kate & Allie* and *The Country Music Association Awards* on CBS
Cast: Farrah Fawcett (Francine Hughes), Paul LeMat (Mickey Hughes), Richard Masur (Aryon Greydanus), Grace Zabriskie (Flossie Hughes), Penelope Milford (Gaby), Christa Denton (Christy, age 12), James Callahan (Berlin Hughes), Gary Grubbs (District Attorney). **Crew:** Jon Avnet, Steve Tisch (executive producers), Carol Shreder (producer), Robert Greenwald (director), Rose Leiman Goldemberg (writer, co-producer).

Synopsis. March 9, 1977, Dansville, Michigan: Francine Hughes calmly drives her two daughters and one son away from a fire she set in her ex-husband's bedroom. Arrested and jailed, she tells Aryon, her court-appointed attorney, what led to the incident. She met Mickey in 1963, married him and had their first child, Christy, but they had to live with his parents because he could not hold a job. He beat her after one fruitless job search, and more beatdowns followed, so she left him. Despite sporting bruises, her mom encouraged her to return to him. He still hit her after Jimmy was born, but she rationalized it as Mickey being a good husband.

She finally separated from him and planned to get a divorce while pregnant with their third child. After she gave birth, Mickey visited her, but the reconciliation failed. She moved next door to

Mickey to help him recuperate from a near-death accident in 1971. He recovered and attacked her again, but they reconciled and seemed okay.

In 1976, she went to school for a job, which enraged Mickey. The police and other agencies couldn't help her. As she recounts tearfully in court, after he demanded she leave school, violently beat her and forced her to have sex, she waited for him to pass out, then poured gasoline around his bed and lit a match. The jury's verdict is not guilty on account of temporary insanity. Francine's children hug her to celebrate.

Backstory. Based on a true story made into a book by Faith McNulty, *The Burning Bed* debuted on television the same day National Domestic Violence Awareness Week began, and it's hard to think of a more stark presentation that network television in 1984 could present to dramatize how husbands abuse their wives and how those women try to rationalize their mistreatment due to their low self-esteem. The production has a documentary-style feel to it, which makes you flinch as you see Farrah Fawcett's character repeatedly smacked, kicked, choked and shoved down to the ground.

It is clear from watching closely that those scenes of staged beatings involved Fawcett and not a double; in fact, in one scene Paul LeMat accidentally caught her face with his hand and chipped her tooth. "Paul held me for a half-hour before we could begin again," Fawcett told Jane Hall in *People*.

While Fawcett filmed the true-life story, Francine Hughes was adamant about not meeting the actress playing her. Fawcett said she understood Hughes' position. "I thought it would be painful for her to visit the set," she told Hall. "And I needed to play her at her lowest point, not as she is today."

Where Hughes was at in 1984 was a better place than seven years earlier, although still not what one would term a happily-ever-after fairy tale following her release after nine months in prison before her trial. After she received an $11,000 advance for her contribution to McNulty's book about her case, she tried to establish herself as a productive mother of four children, but after being laid off as a forklift operator, she descended into drinking alcohol and taking speed until she finally quit, realizing that she was harming her two sons and two daughters by her activities.

Then she met and fell in love with Robert Wilson, an erstwhile country musician who had served ten years of a maximum 30-year sentence for armed robbery. The two married and bought a 15-acre plot in Shelbyville, Tennessee, to build a home financed with the $8,000 payment Hughes received from the TV rights for *The Burning Bed*.

The Burning Bed was adapted into a teleplay in 1981. Fawcett received a copy and wanted to star in it, but all three networks turned her down, saying no one wanted to watch a woman be beaten for two hours, particularly if the woman was Fawcett.

But in 1983, Fawcett received the best reviews of her career for starring off–Broadway in *Extremities*, a play about a rape victim who turns the tables on her attacker and imprisons him. It showed to the world that she was more than just the beautiful blonde who leapt to fame sporting a great figure and flowing hair as one of the three stars of ABC's *Charlie's Angels* in 1976. She left that series after one year to play in movie parts which did not impress the public nor critics. Still, Fawcett had a vivacious personality that still captivated many TV viewers, and seeing she could handle the physically and mentally draining drama onstage, NBC executives relented and allowed her to star in *The Burning Bed*.

To get a sense of who Hughes was, Fawcett watched her in a 1980 interview conducted by Phil Donahue on his daily syndicated talk show. She also listened repeatedly to seven hours of taped interviews between Hughes and the telemovie's writer Rose Leiman Goldemberg. Fawcett said the most difficulty she had in the role was adapting Hughes' mindset during the marriage. "I kept saying to the *Burning Bed* director, 'I want to hit back. I would never let a man treat me that way. Why does Francine stay?'"

"I learned that if I fought back, it only made him more angry," Hughes told Gioia Diliberto in a separate article for *People*. She said Mickey's moods and beatings would vary greatly, sometimes hitting her for hours, other times lasting just a few minutes before he would go out to the bars, drink and return to hurt her some more. The time when he destroyed the family dinner and then raped her, as depicted in the TV-movie, caused Francine to lose it and set his mattress aflame.

Besides the violence portrayed in *The Burning Bed*, the TV-movie had what appears to be a network first in allowing the young actress who played Christy to say "whore" and "bitch" in describing what Mickey yelled at Francine. As this occurred during court testimony, it was judged allowable in the movie. The program also carried this disclaimer: "This story is based upon actual events; however, some of the characters and incidents are fictitious, and some of the events have been condensed for dramatic purposes."

Although Hughes made it clear in advance that she was not looking forward to seeing the TV-movie, she was in the minority among people watching the set the night it debuted. NBC promoted it heavily, and it won raves from those who reviewed it in advance. "Don't miss it," reviewer Judith Crist urged readers in *TV Guide*. "Fawcett's finely muted portrait of an intelligent woman in constant fear for her life" was the highlight of excellent performances by all involved.

The Burning Bed attracted the highest audience ever for an NBC-TV movie, more than three ratings points ahead of the runner-up, *A Case of Rape* (see 86). Its massive numbers helped boost *NBC Monday Night Movie* to #18 for the 1984-1985 season, its highest peak ever and almost tying it with its opposition on CBS, *Kate & Allie*. At the same time, ABC's *Monday Night Football* dropped to its worst showings in the 1980s. NBC repeated it on March 17, 1985, to okay figures of 17.1/27.

At the Emmys, *The Burning Bed* had eight nominations, including ones for outstanding drama/comedy special, actress (Fawcett), supporting actor (Richard Masur), directing and writing. LeMat was notably and unaccountably overlooked in the best actor category. None of the TV-movie's nominations resulted in a win. Fawcett would earn one more Emmy nomination (for the 1989 ABC miniseries *Small Sacrifices*) before she died in 2009 at age 62.

As for Hughes at the time *The Burning Bed* aired, her situation turned out to be one of those listed as "it's complicated" on Facebook profiles. She left Wilson in Tennessee and took her daughters Christy and Nicole to live with her in Jackson, Michigan, not long after charges surfaced that Wilson may have made sexual advances toward Nicole. She became a certified practical nurse and started working at a nursing home. One of her sons, Jimmy, moved to Jackson to join the rest of the family, while her other son, Dana, decided to keep living with his stepfather in Shelbyville. Francine and Robert remained in a long-distance marriage and occasionally visited each other.

On Sept. 27, 2009, *The Lansing State Journal* in Michigan profiled the 25th anniversary of *The Burning Bed* and people's reactions to it. It reported that Francine was quietly living with Robert in Alabama, with all her children living on their own. She refused to give an interview, and her sister told the paper that "it's just not something we discuss" nowadays. But she did note approvingly of *The Burning Bed*, "That movie has helped a lot of people."

50—*Mayberry R.F.D.*

Sept. 23, 1968 ("Andy and Helen Get Married"). **Rating:** 36.3. **Share:** 52.

Aired on CBS Monday 9–9:30 P.M. Eastern and Pacific, 8–8:30 P.M. Central

Competition: *The Outcasts* (series debut) on ABC; *The Art of Love* (first half-hour of two-hour theatrical movie released in 1965) on NBC

Cast: Ken Berry (Sam Jones), Frances Bavier (Aunt Bee Taylor), George Lindsey (Goober Pyle), Jack Dodson (Howard Sprague), Paul Hartman (Emmett Clark), Buddy Foster (Mike Jones). **Guests:** Andy Griffith (Sheriff Andy Taylor), Don Knotts (Barney Fife), Ronny Howard (Opie Taylor), Aneta Corsaut (Helen Crump Taylor), William Keene (the Rev. Hobart M. Tucker). **Crew:** Andy Griffith, Richard O. Linke (executive producers), Bob Ross (producer), Christian Nyby (director), John McGreevey (writer).

Synopsis. Sheriff Andy Taylor plans to wed his girlfriend Helen Crump, and *almost* everyone in the small town of Mayberry, North Carolina, appears to be excited. Andy's Aunt Bee declines to stay as Andy's housekeeper, fearing she will get in the way of him and Helen. Sam Jones, a local farmer and member of the Mayberry Town Council, needs someone to clean and care for the home that he shares with his son Mike and offers her the job. But Bee insists she will live with her sister in West Virginia.

At the ceremony, the Rev. Tucker unites Andy and Helen as husband and wife despite some typical unintended bumbling by Andy's former deputy Barney Fife, such as momentarily losing the ring and then handing it to the pastor rather than Andy. The Rev. Tucker reminds Bee during the reception afterward what a fine reputation she built in the community taking care of Andy and his son Opie when they needed a housekeeper eight years earlier. Touched by that memory and seeing Sam face a similar situation, she agrees to help him.

But the cows, hens and other aspects of country living so perplex Bee that she announces she is leaving. Before she goes, Mike talks with her about his ancestors, unafraid to face anything thrown at them. Inspired by the spirit of the story, she gathers her first egg from a chicken and decides to stay with the Joneses.

Backstory. Many TV series have spun off successors designed to retain the audiences of the original, usually with poor results (for a good example, see 72—*Sanford and Son*). *Mayberry R.F.D.* (the initials stood for Rural Free Delivery, a now-antiquated postal term) was the rare exception to this rule, and it started with a bang. In actuality, this debut for the series actually was to be the final episode of *The Andy Griffith Show* (see 79), but CBS programming head Mike Dann, seeing its potential to attract a big audience, made sure that it was held back to open *Mayberry R.F.D.* instead. It was a shrewd move on his part: With solid promotion, it left its unimpressive competition on ABC and NBC far behind.

No effort was spared to make *Mayberry R.F.D.* appear to be basically *The Andy Griffith Show* without Griffith. Four characters who were regular supporting ones on the latter series transferred to this program: Aunt Bee; Goober Pyle the gas station attendant; Howard Sprague the county clerk, milquetoast and eternal bachelor; and Emmett Clark the fix-it man. And the story of Bee bumbling on the job before the love of widower Sam Jones and his prepubescent son, Mike, convince her to stay virtually mirrors the opening episode of *The Andy Griffith Show* in 1960. This may well have been the most risk-averse spin-off ever concocted. *Mayberry R.F.D.* did not go to the length of having an opening theme that was whistled as the leads went walking to go fishing, although the scene of Sam and Mike throwing a baseball back and forth until it shattered a window shared a certain theme of enjoying the slow country life like *The Andy Griffith Show*.

The producers even recycled the love interest for this series in later first-season episodes. Millie Swanson, played by Arlene Golonka, had dated Howard a few times in the 1967-1968 season of *The Andy Griffith Show*, but her heart now belonged to Sam. Or at least it did after an early episode when Goober took her as a date to a party and saw that she responded with more ardor to Sam when dancing with him. Sam and Millie spent years dating without getting married.

In this episode, Griffith was billed as "special guest star," as was Don Knotts. Griffith and Aneta Corsaut returned to the show in the 1969 season opener, where Sam, Emmett, Goober and Howard argue about who should be the godfather of the couple's baby boy, Andy Jr. (a compromise is reached where all four men share in the honor). Opie was nowhere to be seen, and Andy was now said to be living in Charlotte, North Carolina, working for the State Bureau of Investigation — heresy to anyone who thought he would ever stop living and working in Mayberry. He moved once again, out of state to Cleveland, according to the reunion TV-movie *Return to Mayberry*— see 90 for more details on that.

Airing in the same slot previously held by *The Andy Griffith Show*, this strong debut by *Mayberry R.F.D.* did not lose much of an audience during subsequent episodes, and it finished at #4 for the 1968-1969 season, being the second-most popular show on CBS behind another *Andy Griffith Show* spin-off, *Gomer Pyle, U.S.M.C.* (see 55). In the 1969-1970 season, it retained the same #4 spot and was the runner-up in popularity on CBS behind only *Gunsmoke* (see 24).

The following season, Frances Bavier pretty much retired from acting to live in Siler City, North Carolina (an actual small town often compared to Mayberry), until her death in 1989. Her character was said to have followed through on her first promise after Andy wed and moved to West Virginia to live with her sister. Alice Ghostley became the new housekeeper, Alice Cooper, who was also Sam's cousin retired from the Army. Ratings dropped somewhat to #15 in 1970-1971 (were there that many people who watched the series just for Aunt Bee?), but *Mayberry R.F.D.* still usually won its time slot against fairly tough competition — movies on NBC and the newly installed *Monday Night Football* on ABC. It appeared to be a shoo-in for a fourth season.

However, with Mike Dann out of power as CBS programming head and Fred Silverman installed as his replacement in 1970, there was an increased emphasis on demographics as part of the consideration for the nighttime schedule by advertisers. The network had far too many series like *Mayberry R.F.D.* with audiences composed mostly of older, less educated and more rural viewers, the sorts of groups that few national companies felt were worth their advertising dollars when compared to younger, more educated, affluent and urban types. As part of a policy to purge such series from the lineup, *Mayberry R.F.D.* received the ax. The highest-rated series to be cancelled in the 1970-1971 season, it aired its last show on Sept. 6, 1971.

"That was a nice, relaxed, fun show to do, and very much like, strangely like, *The Patty Duke Show*," director Hal Cooper said in a 2003 interview with Karen Herman for the Archive of American Television. He noted that the show tried to take advantage of Ken Berry's stage training

when it could. "Because of his talents, we were able to work into the show musical stuff so he could dance every once in a while."

One big difference between *The Andy Griffith Show* and *Mayberry R.F.D.* were no Emmy nominations for the latter series during its three-year run. Another was that its reruns were not as popular as the original even though all of them in color (*The Andy Griffith Show* stayed in black-and-white until its last two seasons).

The existence of this series was virtually ignored when the reunion TV-movie *Return to Mayberry* aired on NBC in 1986, except for the supporting characters like Goober, perpetually single and shy Howard Sprague (who was still trying to get a date with a woman 15 years after *Mayberry R.F.D.* ended), and Aunt Bee, who was said to have died. Sam, Mike and Millie were neither seen nor discussed, and the same applied to Emmett, although that was understandable, since actor Paul Hartman passed away in 1973.

To be fair, Ken Berry may have been approached to appear but turned it down due to a conflict preparing to star in the syndicated version of *Mama's Family*. That was a sitcom set in a small Southern town. The more things change....

---

49 — *The Ropers*

March 13, 1979 ("Moving On"). **Rating:** 36.3. **Share:** 56.

Aired on ABC Tuesday 10–10:30 P.M. Eastern and Pacific, 9–9:30 P.M. Central

Competition: *Zorro* (1975 movie debut, second half-hour of two hours) on CBS, *Checkered Flag or Crash* (1977 movie debut, second half-hour of two hours) on NBC

Cast: Norman Fell (Stanley Roper), Audra Lindley (Helen Roper), Jeffrey Tambor (Jeffrey P. Brookes III), Patricia McCormack (Anne Brookes), Evan Cohen (David Brookes). **Crew:** Don Nicholl, Michael Ross, Bernie West (executive producers), George Sunga (producer), Dave Powers (director), Johnnie Mortimer, Brian Cooke (writers).

Synopsis. After selling their interest in an apartment building (see *Three's Company* at 37), Helen and Stanley Roper are divided as to where to move and reside in the Los Angeles area. Stanley is looking at a mobile home, while Helen favors something more upscale. One of the places under consideration is a townhouse at 46 Peacock Drive in Cheviot Hills. Leading them in an inspection of the place is the pretentious neighbor who lives next door, balding Jeffrey P. Brookes III. He has a perky wife, Anne, who enjoys deflating her husband's detours into pomposity, and a cute son, David.

Brookes is apoplectic about the Ropers' unrefined manners and fashions as they tour the vacant unit, not to mention how Stanley cavalierly checks out the vacant unit to test its amenities. The Ropers expressed their usual feelings about each other while reviewing the property as well. Helen cracks, "Bedrooms don't interest Stanley," in reference to her husband's uninterested nature regarding their sex life. Needless to say, such repartee dismays Brookes even more.

Helen adores the townhouse and demands that Stanley buy it. Stanley is not as impressed, but he agrees to purchase it for Helen's sake. As the transaction goes through, Jeffrey shudders as he wonders what havoc his new, déclassé neighbors will wreak on the value of his own townhouse, not to mention how they will affect his future sanity.

Backstory. The idea of spinning off some of the cast of *Three's Company* had its basis in what happened with the British series *Man About the House*, which inspired *Three's Company*. When *Man About the House* ended its run in 1976, another sitcom was created based on the former landlords of its setting. *George and Mildred*, starring Brian Murphy as George Roper and Yootha Joyce as his wife Mildred, aired for three years. A sixth season was planned but Joyce died on Aug. 26, 1980. A movie version came out after her death, by which time the American equivalent of the series — *The Ropers* — had also died.

Something very wrong happened in this transatlantic translation: In terms of both artistic and commercial success, *The Ropers* is one of the least impressive spin-offs ever on television. True, there have been shorter-lived spin-offs (the briefest ever was CBS's *Checking In* [1981], a four-week effort that took Marla Gibbs from playing Florence the maid on *The Jeffersons* to a posh hotel). And there have been several other series that, like *The Ropers*, finished in the top 10 one season only to fall so dramatically in the ratings the following season that they were cancelled (e.g., *Flo, Angie, Room for Two, The Naked Truth, Veronica's Closet, Who Wants to Be a Millionaire* and *Joe the Millionaire*). But the flameout of *The Ropers* on nearly every level was particularly surprising given that the leads and much of the backstage personnel came from *Three's Company*, then the #2 show in America. With that pedigree, and the United Kingdom original being a hit, how did it go wrong?

I believe a key problem was the characterization of Helen Roper. While Helen remained her gaudy self when she and Stanley moved to a bigger residence, *George and Mildred*'s Mildred Roper put on airs as she attempted to be high class in her new digs, making her funnier and more sympathetic. That's the biggest difference one notices between *George and Mildred* and *The Ropers*; otherwise they were similar in every way, including the family next door. Surprisingly, the uptight husband-warm wife-adorable son combo was not an invention of Americans but came directly from *George and Mildred*.

That points to another possible problem with *The Ropers*: It too slavishly followed the English original without making substantial changes. This episode was the same as the one written by the creators of *George and Mildred*, Johnnie Mortimer and Brian Cooke, and future episodes used the same later characters introduced on that show, such as Helen's sister and her mother. *Three's Company* did not hew anywhere nearly as much to stories that were written for *Man About the House*, and if it had, it might have faced the same fate as *The Ropers*.

The series started strong — this episode finished #2 for the week behind the *Three's Company* episode showing the Ropers leaving Jack, Chrissy and Janet. Airing on Tuesdays at 10 P.M. Eastern and Pacific, its five following shows remained popular enough for it to average eighth place for the 1978-1979 season. The sitcom following it, *13 Queens Blvd.*, finished at #26 for the season, but the loss of several million viewers who watched *The Ropers* led ABC to think another series could retain more viewers, so it was not renewed. After the program's successful six-week spring run concluded on April 17, ABC repeated it Sundays at 8:30 Eastern and Pacific from Aug. 12 through Sept. 2.

The Season 2 opener (Saturday, Sept. 15 at 8 P.M.) featured the old *Three's Company* gang of Jack, Chrissy and Janet showing up at their former landlord's place as part of Stanley's surprise party activities for Helen. But the guest appearance was for naught. In its new time slot, *The Ropers* lost to NBC's top 20 adventure hit *CHiPs* each week. Other ABC series that season suffered similar downturns due to changes in time slots (for example, see 56 — *Laverne & Shirley*). While those series were allowed to return to their original slots, *The Ropers* was not. The network took it off on Dec. 15, then bumped its starting time on Jan. 26 to a half-hour later, following *One in a Million*, a sitcom starring Shirley Hemphill, formerly the comic relief on *What's Happening!* The Jan. 26 episode introduced Jenny Ballinger (played by Louise Vallance), an 18-year-old art student who had been living in the Ropers' store room for weeks before they discovered her. Naturally, as any logical homeowner would do, they allowed her to keep living there as a boarder. The character, apparently installed to give the series some "youth appeal," added little in terms of comedy or interesting plot lines as the Ropers served as her surrogate parents.

The *One in a Million—The Ropers* combo bombed, and both shows were off the lineup after their March 15 telecasts. ABC burned off three remaining first-run episodes of *The Ropers* after *Barney Miller* Thursdays at 9:30 on May 1, 8 and 15, by which time the network had cancelled the series. A total of 28 shows were produced.

While Audra Lindley liked having her own series ("The Ropers on *Three's Company* were supporting roles, and they'd be stars in their own show," she told Chris Mann in *Come and Knock on Our Door*), Norman Fell demanded a guarantee in his contract that he could return as a regular on *Three's Company* if *The Ropers* flopped within a year. "Because my own show could be cancelled in a month. Who knows? I didn't care about fame," Fell told Mann.

Unfortunately for him, ABC canned *The Ropers* after more than a year had passed, leaving him and Lindley without regular jobs by the fall of 1980. They did get to reprise their roles one more time in a guest shot on *Three's Company.*

The Ropers faded into TV history, brought up only as a brief mention in lengthier obituaries for Lindley in 1997 and Fell in 1998 — and as an entry on *TV Guide*'s 2002 list of the 50 worst shows of all time, finishing at #49.

---

48 — *Wagon Train*

Nov. 23, 1960 ("The Colter Craven Story"). **Rating:** 36.9. **Share:** n/a.

Aired on NBC Wednesday 7:30–8:30 P.M. Eastern and Pacific, 6:30–7:30 P.M. Central

Competition: *Hong Kong* on ABC, *The Aquanauts* on CBS

Cast: Ward Bond (Major Seth Adams), Frank McGrath (Charlie Wooster), Terry Wilson (Bill Hawks). **Guests:** Carleton Young (Colter Craven), Anna Lee (Alarice Craven), John Carradine (Park Cleatus), Ken Curtis (Kyle Cleatus), Cliff Lyons (Creel), Dennis

Rush (Jamie), Paul Birch (Ulysses S. "Sam" Grant), John Wayne (Gen. William Tecumseh Sherman; cameo, billed as "Michael Morris," a variant of his birth name of Michael Morrison). **Crew:** Howard Christie (producer), John Ford (director), Tony Paulson (writer).

Synopsis. Driving the lead wagon westward, Charlie Wooster tells Major Seth Adams that the caravan's water supply is low. Along with scout Bill Hawks, Adams locates Dr. Colter Craven and his wife Alarice, who left a nearby fort because of Colter's refusal to operate on a man facing certain death. They join the wagon train, but Colter's self-confidence is so low that Alarice helps a sick woman there instead. The group finds the Cleatus family, whose patriarch, Park, tells Adams he can have water from his well for $25 a barrel. Refusing to be gouged, Adams drops some supplies in order for the horses to reach a river to be replenished. Colter mends the leg of a boy named Jamie, but he remains shaky.

When another passenger, Creel, needs help, Colter declines and confesses to Adams that he began drinking during the Civil War when only 38 percent of the soldiers he treated survived. To bolster the doctor's spirit, Adams said when he was in Helena, Illinois, in 1855 in the lumber business with Bill Hawks, a pal named Sam was kicked out of the Army; Sam then began working in the Illinois governor's office as a clerk. In the war, Sam became a leading officer, and promoted Adams from lieutenant to major due to his battlefield skills. Adams tells Colter that that man is now known as President Ulysses S. Grant, and like him, Colter has a second chance to redeem himself. Inspired by the tale, Colter helps Creel's wife give birth.

Backstory. Legendary film director John Ford (*Stagecoach*, *The Searchers* and many other great westerns) made a rare foray into television with this show, which was appropriate for him because he directed its star, Ward Bond, in the film that inspired this series, *Wagon Master* (1950). Coincidentally, it was Ford who advised Bond to take the lead of *Wagon Train* after the actor rejected previous offers to be a regular on other TV series. But it was not as easy for Bond to coerce his friend to join him behind the camera for it. Ford had a loathing for television in general; as he groused to Douglas Whitney in *TV Guide*, "It's a fine thing if you don't like to eat and sleep. You can't build a scene the way you can in the movies. There's no time."

But he did take time to watch *Wagon Train* and often called Bond to criticize the presentation of an episode. Bond, who served as unofficial script editor, writer, associate producer and casting director as well as star of *Wagon Train*, grew weary of this process and finally called Ford on it by saying several times, "Why don't you try directing it then?" (or words to that effect).

Finally, Ford relented, but to accommodate his pace of directing, he received six days to film the episode rather than the usual five. Ironically, Ford wound up delivering a 72-minute film to the production company, which made them consider making the program into a two-part episode before deciding it would work better shorn of 15 minutes.

During the last day of filming, John Wayne turned up on the set to revisit his old friends Ford and Bond. (The trio first worked together in 1928 on the movie *Salute* and became frequent collaborators on screen thereafter.) Wayne even made a rare TV acting appearance in the episode, delivering one line in shadows, but there was no mistaking that voice of his.

Truth be told, it's hard to claim this show's script was worthy of Ford's time. Charlie Wooster's wagon overturns in a great action sequence, but otherwise the backstory of how Seth Adams became a major is ploddingly told and cliché-ridden. Charlie the cook supplies occasional comic relief.

This was the second TV episode Ford directed following his debut with the NBC anthology *Screen Directors Playhouse* in 1955. Though he professed to enjoy his stint with *Wagon Train* enough that he promised to do more TV, he directed just one other show, a 1962 episode of the ABC anthology *Alcoa Premiere*. Bond was not able to enjoy watching this episode, as he died of a heart attack at age 57 in Dallas on Nov. 5, 1960, while preparing to make a halftime appearance at a Cowboys pro football game.

Wagon Train ambled onto TV to set several precedents during its eight-year run. It was TV's first hour-long weekly western, preceding the debut of *Maverick* by five days when it premiered on Sept. 18, 1957. It was the first NBC series to finish #1 for a season (in 1961-1962) since Milton Berle's *The Texaco Star Theatre* in 1950-1951. It also was the first #1 series to switch networks (which it did in the fall of 1962, moving to ABC).

What attracted ABC was the series' continued huge success since its debut. This occurred even in the wake of Bond's death, when John McIntire became new leader Chris Hale, and despite the fact that Bond had been alternating weekly as its lead, with the other episodes starring Robert Horton as scout Flint McCullough. Through it all, *Wagon Train* finished an impressive #23 its first season followed by three seasons at #2 behind *Gunsmoke* before passing the latter for the top spot in its fifth season. ABC thought it had a winner on its hands that would finally bring it to number one in the ratings.

Unfortunately, ABC did not count on the series' producer, MCA, to develop an even bigger western to compete against it on NBC. *The Virginian* was 90 minutes and in color, and it fought *Wagon Train* to a virtual tie in the ratings at the #25 mark in 1962-1963. This was a considerable disappointment to ABC even though it was the network's second-highest rated series that season behind *Ben Casey* (see 88) at #7 — that's how bad the network fared at the time.

In fact, the drop was the biggest falloff in ratings ever for TV's top-rated series from one season to the next until the 1979-1980 season, when *Laverne & Shirley* (see 56) sunk to #39 when ABC moved it from its regular Tuesday time slot for most of the season. But while *Laverne & Shirley* returned to the top 20 in 1980-1981 before going off two years later, *Wagon Train* had no such luck.

Thinking that the solution was to emulate *The Virginian*, ABC made *Wagon Train* from 1963-1964 a color 90-minute series. However, it ran opposite CBS's *The Lucy Show* (see 62), *The Danny Thomas Show* and *The Andy Griffith Show* (see 79), all of which remained in the top 10 while *Wagon Train* slid further. The show declined more next season when it shrank back to an hour in black and white and lost badly against *The Ed Sullivan Show* (see 11) and Disney on NBC. By January 1965 it ranked among the bottom 10 shows on television. It went off the air on Sept. 5, 1965.

ABC believed *Wagon Train* reruns would be an afternoon ratings draw but, airing under the title *Trailmaster*, the repeats trailed *The Secret Storm* on CBS and *The Match Game* on NBC. It went off after two sluggish years and was the last western ever rerun daily by a network, with its repeats ending on ABC 19 days after its nighttime cancellation. Along with the nighttime decline, it confirmed insiders' belief that ABC was the one network that could snatch defeat from the jaws of victory.

Wagon Train was available to local stations for repeats in the fall of 1965, but as westerns were becoming less popular each year, it did not perform particularly well. I imagine if you ask most *older* people to name the three westerns that finished #1 in a season on TV, they could easily guess *Gunsmoke* and *Bonanza* before this one, maybe even naming *Rawhide, The Rifleman, The Wild Wild West* or others in its place.

47 — *Little Ladies of the Night*

Jan. 16, 1977 (*ABC Sunday Night Movie*). **Rating:** 36.9. **Share:** 53

Aired on ABC Sunday 9–11 P.M. Eastern and Pacific, 8–10 P.M. Central

Competition: *Switch* (in a new time slot) and *Entertainer of the Year Awards* (special) on CBS; *McCloud* (last half-hour of 90-minute episode) and *Stonestreet: Who Killed the Centerfold Model?* (TV-movie) on NBC

Cast: David Soul (Lyle York), Lou Gossett (Russ Garfield), Linda Purl (Hailey Atkins), Clifton Davis (Comfort; billed as "Special Guest Star"), Carolyn Jones (Marilyn Atkins; billed as "Special Guest Star"), Paul Burke (Frank Atkins), Lana Wood (Maureen), Kathleen Quinlan (Karen Brodwick), Vic Tayback (Finch), Katherine Helmond (Miss Colby), Dorothy Malone (Maggie), Bibi Osterwald (Matron), Sandra Deel (Mrs. Brodwick), David Hayward (Brady). **Crew:** Aaron Spelling, Leonard Goldberg (executive producers), Hal Sitowitz (producer-writer), Marvin J. Chomsky (director).

Synopsis. Hailey Atkins breaks into a car at Hollywood to get some sleep. Nearby, prostitute Karen Brodwick meets Finch, a middle-aged potential client who turns out to be a cop and busts her. Coincidentally, Finch owns the car where Hailey is resting. Det. Garfield and ex-pimp Lyle York determine that Karen is under 16. York bonds with Hailey. Hailey's distraught dad, Frank, takes her home, where she tells her mother, Marilyn, that she ran away because Marilyn picked on her. They make peace, but when Hailey overhears them argue about whether Frank loves her more than Marilyn, she returns to Los Angeles. A pimp named Comfort picks her up.

Comfort's "number one lady," the older Maureen, oversees Hailey's first trick. Afterward, Hailey meets Karen at ex-hooker Maggie's bar and says she is leaving Comfort and Maureen. Karen warns her it is a bad idea. Stealing to stay alive, Hailey calls home to return, but Marilyn answers and refuses to take her back, as she wants to control Frank.

Hailey goes to York, who gets her into Miss Colby's detention facility. She dislikes its restrictions and escapes. Maureen lets her return to Comfort after beating Hailey. York tracks Hailey

down, but she rejects him because of his ineffective earlier actions. He pays Comfort $1,000 to release Hailey to his care, but she nixes that as well. York then fights Comfort, who knifes him. Hailey saves York's life and leaves with him, promising not to return to walking the streets.

Backstory. Resident *TV Guide* critic Judith Crist called *Little Ladies of the Night* "pure exploitation masquerading as socially significant drama." (Interestingly, almost the exact same wording was used when it was reviewed in Leonard Maltin's movie guides in the 1980s and 1990s. Hmmm....) But one of its executive producers says otherwise. "The movie wasn't about teen prostitution, as critics said, but it was really about runaway children," Aaron Spelling wrote in his autobiography. "It wasn't an exploitative film. We got interested because there were so many runaway kids out here living in empty buildings. We wanted to explore why they ran away, what they were running from, and what they wanted to do with their lives."

Spelling's explanation does not hold up too well when later in his book he refers to *Little Ladies of the Night* as "the first of the 'teenage hooker' movie, but ours really said something about teen runaways." He does not specify what that message was, but he does gloat about how it is the second-highest rated TV movie of all time behind *The Day After* (see 8), which is true if you average both nights of the two-part TV-movie *Helter Skelter* (see 41) rather than use the individual nightly ratings. That fact more than any inherent quality in *Little Ladies of the Night* probably encouraged Spelling to list it as one of the 11 highlights among nearly 140 TV-movies he produced.

The fact of the matter is that *Little Ladies of the Night* is one sordid, poorly done feature where hardly anyone involved in front of or behind the cameras comes off particularly well. Indeed, it seems like everybody would rather forget their participation in it.

The opening narration sets the tone of an instruction film, condescending and artificial: "This is Hailey. She's a runaway. The number of teenage kids who've run away from home in this country each year numbers close to one million. It has become a major social issue. The story of their life on the street is not a pretty one, but it's one our society must cope with. This film is a warning to teenagers, and to you parents, because you don't want to find your kid here."

From there onward, *Little Ladies of the Night* is as leering as can be for a 1977 TV show with a

"Viewer discretion is advised" warning. There are plentiful shots of Linda Purl and Kathleen Quinlan naked from the back, with shoulders exposed and with legs unclothed, whether it is on the job or showering in juvenile detention hall. All in the name of "realism," of course.

It's also preachy, with Det. Garfield in one sequence spouting off statistics about child prostitution at a governmental hearing to impart information. Later, when York spews out all the reasons he wants Garfield to help him pay off Comfort to save Hailey, and Garfield cuts him short with "It's worth the 400 bucks just to get you off the soapbox," you agree with him.

Besides its prurient theme, the movie is offensive in the way it depicts as a sleazy black man (Comfort) preying on and manipulating an innocent young Caucasian female, relying on racist fears in the name of bad drama.

The fashions are horrible as well. Soul's character sports a blond perm and mustache that have dated badly, as has his open shirt with jewelry, not to mention Comfort's white leisure suit. The score by Jerry Fielding is inappropriately cheesy, sounding like something you would hear in a softcore sex movie (which may have been the intention).

Finally, there is just bad writing. The motivations of many characters are murky, and York's explanation on how he became a pimp is particularly hard to comprehend.

Little Ladies of the Night was not the first depiction of child prostitution on television. That distinction goes to *All My Children*, which in 1976 introduced 16-year-old Donna Beck (played first by Francesca Poston, Tom Poston's daughter, and then by Candice Earley). Producer Agnes Nixon told Irv Broughton in *Producers on Producing* the inspiration came from a Ted Morgan article that ran in the *New York Times* Sunday magazine section on Nov. 16, 1975, titled "Little Ladies of the Night." There, the title referred to runaway girls who sold their bodies for money on the Minnesota Strip in New York.

Spelling said the same article inspired the script as well as the title for the TV-movie *Little Ladies of the Night*, and in fact Morgan did receive on-screen credit for suggesting the idea for it. Too bad the TV-movie substituted the elegant writing, stark realism and unpleasant truths contained in Morgan's piece with a phony veneer of concern while reveling in titillation in covering a troubling problem that remains just as serious 35 years later, maybe even more so.

ABC originally planned to show *Little Ladies*

of the Night on Sept. 18, 1976. But less than a month before the air date, the network decided to try to steal the thunder from NBC's debut of *Airport 1975* on Sept. 20, 1976, by airing two similar "plane in jeopardy" films, the TV-movie *Murder on Flight 502* on Sept. 18 and then *Sky Terror*, a new name given to the 1972 theatrical film *Skyjacked*, on Sept. 19. While the moves did not stop *Airport 1975* from being a hit, *Sky Terror* did fantastically well, getting a 32.0/51 and just missing inclusion in this top 100 list. But *Murder on Flight 502* compiled much lower numbers than that of *Airport 1975*. Had *Little Ladies of the Night* run in the Saturday 9–11 P.M. slot as originally planned, it could very well have suffered the same fate as that TV-movie.

The promise of dramatizing a TV taboo, sold well by ABC's publicity department, made *Little Ladies of the Night* the highest-rated TV-movie of the 1976-1977 season and helped considerably in allowing the *ABC Sunday Night Movie* to finish #8 for the season, its highest ranking ever.

One of this production's stars, Kathleen Quinlan, appeared in another TV-movie about teenage prostitution, *Children of the Night*, which aired Oct. 26, 1985. She played a sociology graduate helping victims of this crime. It was not as bad as *Little Ladies of the Night*, but that's not saying much.

In 2004, after generally drifting into obscurity, *Little Ladies of the Night* was released on DVD by a company that specialized in lurid horror, action and martial arts movies such as *I Eat Your Skin* and *Samurai Reincarnation*. The name of the outfit, Dollar-DVD, appropriately references about the right amount you should expect to pay to see this film nowadays, although even that number may be overpriced by about 99 cents.

46 — Shogun

Sept. 17, 1980 (Part 3 of a five-part miniseries). **Rating:** 36.9. **Share:** 57.

Aired on NBC Wednesday 9–11 P.M. Eastern and Pacific, 8–10 P.M. Central

Competition: *Charlie's Angels* and *Vega$* (both repeats) on ABC; *Rodeo Girl* (TV-movie) on CBS

Cast: Richard Chamberlain (Maj. John Blackthorne), Toshiro Mifune (Lord Yoshi Toranaga), Yoko Shimada (Lady Mariko), Frankie Sakai (Lord Yabu), Alan Badel (Father Dell'Aqua), Michael Hordern (Friar Domingo), Damien Thomas (Father Martin Alvito), John Rhys-Davies (Vasco Rodriguez), Vladek

Sheybal (Capt. Ferriera), George Innes (Johann de Vinck), Leon Lissek (Father Sebastio), Yugi Meguro (Omi), Hideo Takamatsu (Buntaro), Hiromi Senno (Fujiko), Nobuo Kaneko (Ishido), Orson Welles (Narrator). **Crew:** James Clavell (executive producer), Eric Bercovici (producer-writer), Jerry London (director).

Synopsis. In 1600, Maj. John Blackthorne crashes his Dutch ship in Japan. Spanish priest Father Sebastio tells the major that Lord Yabu and his subordinate, Omi, have power over him and his crew. Pilot Vasco Rodriguez rescues John from slavery and directs him to meet Toranaga, lord of the eight provinces who is battling Ishido for control of Japan. With his ship confiscated and navigation charts stolen, John reluctantly goes with Vasco.

Father Alvito, a priest under Father Dell'Aqua, translates for Toranaga, but the major distrusts him, so Lady Mariko serves as John's translator. To save the major from Ishido, Toranaga temporarily imprisons John. John meets Friar Domingo, who teaches him Japanese while warning him about the Jesuits' abuse of power. John tells Toranaga about how the Spanish Jesuits exploit the country for financial gain by their silk trade monopoly, putting Dell'Aqua and Alvito on the defensive along with ship Capt. Ferriera.

Lady Fujiko becomes John's consort as he learns the Japanese language and customs at Toronaga's request. But his heart lies with Mariko, even though she is wed to Toronaga's soldier Buntaro. John becomes a Shogun (chief samurai) fighting for Toronaga with his freed crew. But plans to sail home collapse as Mariko and mate Johann de Vinck die and his ship is burned. John builds a new ship without realizing that Toronaga had destroyed his vessel and plans to keep him in Japan, now that the lord has defeated Ishido and needs his help to rule the country.

Backstory. Officially titled *James Clavell's Shogun*, this miniseries was based on the third novel written by Clavell following *King Rat* and *Tai-Pan*. The author's inspiration was the true story of William Adams, the first Englishman to visit Japan when storms blew him off course. Adams later established a trade route with the country.

Released in 1975, *Shogun* became a best seller like the other two Clavell books. But as with the author's previous entries, the sprawling saga with multiple viewpoints (the reader knows what every character is thinking) proved to be hard to condense into a movie. Nonetheless, the plan was to make it into a two-hour movie with Robert Redford, until it was learned that it simply would not work that way.

Finally, NBC and Paramount shared the rights, and the head of the latter company, Gary Nardino, contacted writer Eric Bercovici on Feb. 9, 1979, to meet with Clavell (who was also serving as executive producer on the project). Bercovici told Clavell he intended to turn the book inside out and tell the story from the perspective of Blackthorne, leaving out most of the discussions between the Japanese characters. Clavell was leery, but after taking a copy of his book and tearing out the parts Bercovici planned to omit, he realized it would still be an effective story and backed the screenwriter.

"The first thing I did was I read the book from beginning to end four times.... The story was so complex, I tried to memorize it," Bercovici said in the DVD documentary *The Making of Shogun*. The final script was nearly 600 pages long.

Bercovici and Clavell searched for a director willing to spend months on location and chose Jerry London, in part because he had directed several miniseries such as *Wheels* (1978). London asked Bercovici to join him while shooting in order to do rewrites when needed on location, and that led to Paramount appointing Bercovici as producer.

When NBC obtained the movie rights, Clavell wanted an Englishman in the role, but Sean Connery, Roger Moore and Albert Finney turned down the part. NBC cared less about the nationality and just wanted a recognizable name in the lead, and they found one with Richard Chamberlain. The actor read the book and was enthralled by the romantic tragedy as well as the setting (he had been an Army sergeant in the Korean War and had sex with a woman in Japan on one visit there). Chamberlain won the role only after two meetings with Clavell, with the author warily approving him. Still, Clavell insisted on watching Chamberlain perform the first 14 days of the production before leaving, apparently satisfied. The other major name in the cast was Japanese star Toshiro Mifune, who was thrown from his horse in a sequence, causing him to miss two days of shooting.

The miniseries was a tough shoot, with participants working 18 hours a day in oppressive heat and bone-chilling cold, and Chamberlain as the star endured it all. He and most of the rest of the crew spent nearly six months on location. The myriad disasters that befell the production included:

• The crew failed to learn Japanese customs and used female translators, irritating the Asians and leading to delays.

• An earthquake sequence nearly turned deadly when a trench collapsed on four crewmen. It took an hour to rescue them.

• To top it off, the crew just missed a typhoon when they finished production at the start of September 1979.

The castle sets were handmade and hand-painted and looked beautiful onscreen. The costumes were handmade as well. And amusingly, Lord Buntaro's double for his master archery shooting was none other than a steady 80-year-old man, according to London. Plus, everyone got weekends off to recuperate from it all.

But the setbacks wound up pushing the miniseries over budget, and there was a furious race to complete post-production work in time for its air dates. In the midst of it, NBC officials disapproved of having the Japanese characters speak in their native tongues (without dubbing or subtitles) so that the audience would sense Blackthorne's frustrations in trying to understand them. It stayed, as did many elements that had been taboo on network TV in 1980: a beheading, a display of men's buttocks, the words "whore," "bastard" and "goddamn," and even Imo urinating on a supine Blackthorne as a sign of disrespect in their initial meeting.

Designed to kick off NBC's fall season in high fashion, *Shogun* was helped by the fact that there was an actors' strike at the time, which meant that most of its competition would be repeats. Besides its top-rated episode, the show's ratings for its other nights were impressive: 29.5/44 for Sept. 15, 31.7/48 for Sept. 16, 35.6/56 for Sept. 18 and 31.5/53 for Sept. 19. Its overall average numbers were 32.6/51.

Within a week after ratings for *Shogun* appeared, Fremantle Corp. announced it would sell 78 episodes of a Nippon TV adventure series from Japan dubbed into English and titled *I, Samurai*, about a man seeking vengeance for the killing of his wife. But the excitement over the NBC miniseries did not translate into enthusiasm for *I, Samurai* by American TV executives, and the series failed to sell.

Shogun went on to win three Emmys (Outstanding Limited Series, Costume Design, and Graphic Design and Title Sequences). It racked up 11 other Emmy nominations, for Actor in a Limited Series or Special (Chamberlain and Mifune competed against each other), Actress (Yoko Shimada), Supporting Actor (Yuki Meguro and John Rhys-Davies in the same category), Director, Writing, Cinematography, Art Direction, Film Editing, and Film Sound Editing.

Eight months after the Emmys, NBC aired another Asian-themed miniseries, *Marco Polo*, from May 16 to 19, 1982. It led the listings for the week with overall average numbers of 21.3/36, but it did not overwhelm the critics nor general public the way *Shogun* did.

NBC repeated *Shogun* from Jan. 31 through Feb. 4, 1983, scoring its best numbers with the first part, 19.6/29. It finished with an 18.2/27 average, very good when compared to average audiences for reruns of a miniseries. For the initial repeat, NBC requested Bercovici to write more narration for Orson Welles and add some subtitles.

There were still more revisions set for *Shogun*. A near-incomprehensible two-hour version appeared, then a three-hour one. The version that appears on DVD today is the complete version that ran 12 hours with commercials on NBC back in 1980 (three hours the opening and closing nights, two hours the other three nights).

45 — *Rocky*

Feb. 4, 1979 (first released theatrically in 1976). **Rating:** 37.1. **Share:** 56.

Aired on CBS Sunday 8–10:30 P.M. Eastern and Pacific, 7–9:30 P.M. Central

Competition: *The Bad News Bears* (second hour of two-hour 1976 theatrical movie repeat) and *The Way We Were* (repeat of 1973 theatrical movie) on ABC; *Centennial* on NBC

Cast: Sylvester Stallone (Rocky Balboa), Talia Shire (Adrian), Burt Young (Paulie), Carl Weathers (Apollo Creed), Burgess Meredith (Mickey), Thayer David (Jergens), Joe Spinell (Gazzo), Jimmy Gambina (Mike). **Crew:** Gene Kirkwood (executive producer), Robert Chartoff, Irwin Winkler (producers), John G. Avildsen (director), Sylvester Stallone (writer).

Synopsis. November 1975, Philadelphia: Boxer Rocky Balboa, aka "The Italian Stallion," finds little respect as a boxer or as a person beyond pet shop employee Adrian. An opportunity arrives when star fighter Apollo Creed asks boxing promoter Jergens to solicit Balboa to face off against him on Jan. 1, 1976. Balboa accepts, even though he knows he has no business fighting Creed. Adrian's brother Paulie, a loan shark, agrees to help Rocky train, but Adrian is the only one who thinks he can be a contender.

Mickey, the boxing gym operator who has grown disillusioned with Rocky (he thinks the pugilist threw away his career to work for Paulie), asks to be his manager. Balboa is incensed because he thought Mickey should have helped him years earlier and rejects him. Rocky trains by running the streets and pounding raw meat hanging in a freezer. When footage of this airs on a TV station, Creed and his handlers realize that Balboa is serious about beating their guy. Balboa also decides to put aside his differences with Mickey and work with him. Adrian moves in with the fighter after an argument with Paulie.

At the fight, Balboa is all business and goes the distance, taking his opponent to the 15th round in a bloody bout. Creed wins and reporters swarm Balboa asking about a rematch. All he wants is Adrian, and the two hug in the ring and profess their love for each other.

Backstory. The network TV debut of the 1976 Best Picture Oscar winner had its own drama with shows preceding and following it. CBS was showing the Bing Crosby National Pro-Am golf tournament when the competition went into sudden death at 7 P.M. Eastern time. As the contest could have lasted an additional 90 minutes and thus delayed the start of *Rocky* a half-hour or more, and thus potentially lose viewers who did not want to wait for it to start, CBS decided to drop its coverage and return to its regularly scheduled programming of *60 Minutes* (see 89) followed by the movie. There were relatively few complaints from viewers about this action.

At the other end of the schedule, CBS scheduled a special preview of its new sitcom *Co-Ed Fever*, a ripoff of the popular 1978 movie *National Lampoon's Animal House*, to air from 10:30 to 11 P.M. Eastern and Pacific and 9:30–10 P.M. Central. *Co-Ed Fever* scored a 21.0/36, which placed it 19th for the week. It was supposed to start on CBS on Mondays on Feb. 19, 1979, but its premiere performance was so disappointing, given the huge drop-off from the audience that watched *Rocky*, that the network decided not to continue it. It is without a doubt the highest rated show ever to be cancelled after just one airing.

Rocky is one of the great "underdog in sports" movies, a positive vehicle that says that with hard work and determination, you can meet your goals even if others don't believe in you. In an America battered by inflation and post–Watergate malaise in 1976, it struck a chord of confidence with millions of viewers and became the highest-grossing film of the year.

The struggle of the film's star-writer to make the project a reality somewhat mirrored the title character's efforts as well, although Sylvester Stallone was nowhere nearly as down-and-out as Rocky Balboa was. Stallone was doing fine as a supporting movie actor when he decided to write a script based on the circumstances that allowed the unknown Chuck Wepner to receive the opportunity to meet Muhammad Ali in a championship fight. Producers Irwin Winkler and Robert Chartoff agreed to work on it as a film. Stallone, Winkler and Chartoff kept rewriting even while director John G. Avildsen was filming.

Stallone rejected several offers for considerable amounts of money to produce his script without him starring in it. He did the boxing choreography as well as many of his own stunts. The one that freaked out most viewers was not an athletic one, but rather the sight of him swallowing a raw egg for breakfast. Avildsen had Stallone and Carl Weathers start rehearsing the boxing before shooting began. The fight sequences were filmed last.

The production had a low budget that included a non-union crew and a tight schedule of 28 days. The first shots were on location in Philadelphia, including the iconic one of Stallone climbing the steps of City Hall and jumping for joy at the end of a training montage sequence. That scene has become immortalized with a statue of Stallone as Balboa at City Hall.

Eventually, word came out about *Rocky* using a non-union crew, and it prevented the cast and crew from filming Rocky and Adrian's date sequence in an ice skating rink. They filmed the scenes at a rink in Santa Monica, California, instead and told interested people the rink was closed to save having to pay for extras. The gym training scenes were photographed in an actual old facility, with many extras there being fighters in real life. Originally Rocky's trainer, Mickey, was not supposed to be a one-time pugilist, but this was changed with Stallone's permission.

Composer Bill Conti created the movie's dynamic theme with an emphasis on horns. The song "Gonna Fly Now," with lyrics by Carol Connors and Ayn Robbins, played during Rocky's training scenes and became a #1 hit in 1977. Maynard Ferguson also made the top 30 with his cover of it. (Ferguson also had a minor chart entry doing a version of the theme during the 1979 release of the sequel, "Rocky II Disco," about which the less said the better.)

The originally planned ending called for Rocky to be carried out of the ring on people's shoulders, and he would pick up Adrian. There weren't enough extras available to carry him out, so Stallone suggested Rocky that leave down the aisle after all had left the building to rejoin Adrian in a rather low-key reunion. But Conti's music at the end was so vibrant that Avildsen said what should happen is to keep Rocky in the ring and have Adrian fight her way to him. They created a crowd with 20 extras and had just four hours to shoot the last 20 seconds of the film, with Rocky bellowing "Adrian!" from the ring.

Released in November 1976, *Rocky* had enough momentum going into the Oscar race to win the Academy Award over a strong field of contenders that some critics argue was better than the winner: *All the President's Men, Bound for Glory, Network* and *Taxi Driver.* Besides Best Picture, *Rocky* claimed two more Oscars from ten nominations, for Best Directing and Film Editing. The other categories where it was in contention were for lead actor (Stallone), lead actress (Talia Shire), supporting actor (Meredith and Burt Young), writing, music (for "Gonna Fly Now") and sound.

With only a few swear words needing to be deleted, and running nearly two hours, the PG-rated *Rocky* aired on CBS with little editing. It also provided United Artists with an excellent way to promote the sequel coming out in theatres that year, *Rocky II.*

Avildsen disagreed with Stallone on how to do *Rocky II,* so they split and Stallone became its director. Avildsen returned a few sequels later to direct *Rocky V* in 1990, but when the studio decided that Rocky should survive at the end rather than die as planned, he viewed his participation in the movie as a mistake. He liked it better when dealing with Stallone before *Rocky.* "The moral of this story is, there's nothing like a starving actor," Avildsen said in *The Directors Take Two.*

CBS repeated *Rocky* on Nov. 13, 1980 (18.9/29), April 2, 1983 (15.4/27), Feb. 19, 1985 (9.9/15) and Aug. 30, 1985 (10.2/19). *Rocky II* made a strong debut on the network on Feb. 14, 1982 (21.8/33). The other follow-ups had lower ratings.

The sixth and most recent installment in the series is *Rocky Balboa,* released in 2006. Moviegoers have learned since 1976 that as long as Stallone is alive and has an ego, there is always a chance there will be another Rocky film, whether we need one or not.

44 — Ben-Hur

Feb. 14, 1971 (first released theatrically in 1959). **Rating:** 37.1. **Share:** 56

Aired on CBS Sunday 7–11 P.M. Eastern and Pacific, 6–10 P.M. Central

Competition: *The Young Lawyers, The F.B.I.* and *Fantastic Voyage* (1966 theatrical movie; repeat) on ABC; *Wild Kingdom, Disney, The Bill Cosby Show, Bonanza* and *The Bold Ones* (*The New Doctors*) on NBC

Cast: Charlton Heston (Judah Ben-Hur), Jack Hawkins (Quintus Arrius), Haya Harareet (Esther), Stephen Boyd (Messala), Hugh Griffith (Sheik Ilderim), Martha Scott (Miriam), Cathy O'Donnell (Tirzah), Sam Jaffe (Simonides), Finlay Currie (Balthazar/Narrator), Frank Thring (Pontius Pilate). **Crew:** Sam Zimbalist (producer), William Wyler (director), Christopher Fry, Gore Vidal, Karl Tunberg (writers).

Synopsis. Prince Judah Ben-Hur, a Jew, dislikes the anti–Semitic mindset of his childhood friend Messala, now a leader in Rome. Sensing the rift, Messala has Ben-Hur, his mother Miriam and his sister Tirzah arrested under false pretenses. Ben-Hur escapes from prison but does not retaliate against Messala, for he knows that Miriam and Tirzah will be harmed if he takes any action. He ends up enslaved as a rower on a sea galley under the command of Quintis Arrius. When the ship is rammed, Ben-Hur frees himself and saves Arrius on a raft. The gesture leads Arrius to adopt Ben-Hur by the time they head back home.

Ben-Hur meets Balthazar, one of the Three Wise Men who witnessed Jesus Christ's birth, and Sheik Ilderim, who shows him four white horses he wants Ben-Hur to drive in a chariot race against Messala. Ben-Hur returns home four years after his arrest and finds beautiful Esther and her father Simonides living there. Esther lies to Ben-Hur that his sister and mother are dead before he participates in the race. In a heated match, Ben-Hur wins and Messala dies, but not before he tells Ben-Hur the truth: His mother and sister have become lepers.

Ben-Hur confesses his true identity after accepting the race crown from Pontius Pilate. Pilate banishes him and puts Jesus on trial. After Christ's crucifixion in a howling storm, which Ben-Hur witnesses, Miriam and Tirzah are cured of their leprosy. They reunite with Ben-Hur and Esther.

Backstory. Ben-Hur holds the record for most Oscar wins by one film — 11 in all, for Best Picture, Actor (Heston), Supporting Actor (Hugh Griffith), Director, Cinematography, Art Direction-Set Direction, Sound, Score, Editing, Costumes and Special Effects (it also earned a nomination for Screenplay). Yet despite its initial success on TV, it has not become an annual event like *The Ten Commandments,* even though it scored a higher rating than the latter on its debut.

The property had a long history. While serving as governor of the New Mexico territory, Lew Wallace found time to write the novel *Ben-Hur,* first published in 1880. A fictional story that many readers thought was real due to its vivid characterizations, it became a hit. The saga was adapted for the stage across America in the early 20th century, with treadmills used for creating the chariot race at the centerpiece of the adventure. In 1907 the first film version of *Ben-Hur* emerged, a silent which managed to include the chariot race within its 15-minute running time. A much more lavish $4 million silent version (1925) finally turned a profit in 1932 from a re-release.

Then 22 years later, MGM decided to revive the property, as Biblical epics were in vogue and the company needed a hit to improve its flagging box office numbers (it finished 1953 without having a movie among the year's top 10 moneymakers, the first time that had happened to MGM). They approached producer Sam Zimbalist, who gave them a hit in 1951 with a similarly themed remake of a silent, *Quo Vadis*, and told him the company's future was staked on this remake.

Zimbalist decided to shoot the film in Italy like *Quo Vadis* and drafted Sidney Franklin as his director, but the main studio there was held up by the filming of *War and Peace* (1956). Franklin decided to drop out of the project. Zimbalist then offered King Vidor, the director of *War and Peace*, a shot at the job, but Vidor was tired of working in the country. Zimbalist's next pick was veteran director William Wyler, who was finishing up *The Big Country* (1958) with Heston. (Executive turmoil at MGM management during this period also hampered Zimbalist's efforts to make the film for five years.)

Wyler claimed he took the job after being told it was something Cecil B. DeMille should handle, not him. As an epic was virtually the only film genre which Wyler had not directed, he took the project in part to prove his versatility. He liked how, in the story, Judeans were fighting for freedom in the same way Jews were doing in the present day in Israel. The fact that Zimbalist was willing to pay him $1 million for the job, making him the first director to receive that high a paycheck, did not hurt either.

For the title role, Zimbalist had wanted Paul Newman, but the actor said no. Marlon Brando, Rock Hudson, Kirk Douglas and Burt Lancaster were considered at various points before Heston won the role.

Wyler had American actors portray the Jews and British ones play the Romans. (He replaced an English actress playing Ben-Hur's mother with Martha Scott for that reason. It was her second time playing Heston's mother, after *The Ten Commandments*, although the actress was only ten years older than him.) There were some exceptions, notably American Stephen Boyd as Messala. Wyler also believed there was no need to see or hear Jesus Christ, so all viewers witnessed were other characters' reaction to the obscured figure.

After Karl Tunberg submitted his script, Zimbalist asked Gore Vidal to rewrite it. Vidal agreed to do so only if MGM released the writer from his contract, which Vidal hated. He said he rewrote the scene of Ben-Hur and Messala meeting ten times before he told Wyler it would work only if Messala previously had a gay relationship with Ben-Hur; Wyler responded by telling Vidal he could tell Boyd but not Heston about it. (Wyler later said that discussion did not occur.)

In his autobiography, Heston pooh-poohed Vidal's contributions and was indifferent to the author's claim about the past gay dalliance being portrayed without his knowledge. Heston was more impressed with British playwright Christopher Fry making the dialogue sound like the period it took place, and so was Wyler, who lobbied to have Fry receive solo credit for writing the script. The Writers Guild refused, crediting Tunberg instead.

For the chariot race, Yakima Canutt and Andrew Marton directed the second unit. They spent four months setting it up. Wyler at one point asked David Lean (see 38 — *The Bridge on the River Kwai*) to direct the sequence before handling it himself. Wyler told the American Film Institute in 1975, "It was my idea to make them go around once in formation. That part of it I shot, showing the set and the chariots parade around."

No men or horses died in the shooting, but there were two accidents, one of which injured Canutt but ended up being used in the final nine-minute sequence. Canutt also spent a month and a half teaching Heston how to drive a chariot. Canutt's son Joe served as Heston's double when needed. Four thousand extras watched the shooting.

The elaborate production took eight months to film and cost $15 million in 1950s dollars. Zimbalist died after seven months of filming and did not get to view the final picture. Heston said he worked more than 30 weeks, six days a week, sometimes shooting with two units simultaneously in Italy. His last shot was Ben-Hur looking at the crucified Christ; Heston unexpectedly found himself weeping.

There was $3 million budgeted for promotional activities, which meant that *Ben-Hur* merchandise proliferated in the build-up to the film. There were clothing lines dedicated to Ben-Hur polo shirts, sandals, even diapers. Schrafft's came up with Ben-Hur candy, its first new chocolate bar since the 1940s. Four paperback publishers released new versions of the 1880 novel. The saturation campaign worked; a survey found that 50 percent of Americans had heard of the film before it was released on Dec. 10, 1959.

Ben-Hur became the top moneymaking movie of 1959 — in fact, one of the biggest hits ever if figures are adjusted for inflation. It was re-released in 1969 to more success before going to TV.

In 1970, CBS bought the rights to show the movie three times. But the network's first repeat in two parts on Feb. 13 and 20, 1972, scored a blah 15.7/24 for part one and 18.0/27 for part two, and another shot on May 22, 1977, notched a similarly weak 17.2/31, which may have discouraged future network showings. Its reputation as a classic remains intact, however, and in 2004 it was selected by the National Film Preservation Board.

43 — Ali-Spinks Fight

Sept. 15, 1978 (sports special). **Rating:** 37.3. **Share:** 73.

Aired on ABC Friday 8–11 P.M. Eastern, 5–8 P.M. Pacific

Competition: *The Incredible Hulk* (repeat) and *Grand Theft Auto* (debut of 1977 theatrical film) on CBS; *Starship Invasions* (debut of 1978 theatrical film) and *Quincy, M.E.* on NBC

Cast: Muhammad Ali, Leon Spinks, Howard Cosell, Chris Schenkel, Frank Gifford. **Crew:** Roone Arledge (executive producer), Chet Forte (producer), Alex Wallau (assistant producer).

Synopsis. A year prior to this fight, defending his title in 1977 for the 19th time in 13 years, heavyweight boxer Muhammad Ali took on bald Earnie Shavers in New York City's Madison Square Garden and entered the ring with the crowd on his side as the electronic-laden instrumental version of "Theme from *Star Wars*" by Meco played in the background. Commentator Ken Norton, a pro boxer himself, told the home audience that Ali looked "a little flabby," but most observers predicted that Ali would not need a full 15 rounds to

dispense with Shavers. But Shavers displayed surprising power and stamina to last the entire fight, and even knocked Ali down a few times. Still, the three judges all scored nine rounds in favor of Ali.

Ali's triumph was short-lived. Two months later he lost his title to 1976 Olympic gold medalist Leon Spinks. Vowing revenge, he received a chance for a rematch in the fall of 1978.

Before the fight, Ali told Howard Cosell that he was in better shape than when he defeated Joe Frazier in "the Thrilla in Manila" in 1975 and pledged, "I will destroy Spinks." After Frazier sang the National Anthem(!), the fight was on. Ali did not exactly live up to his words, as the match went 15 rounds, but he disoriented Spinks enough that in a unanimous decision, Ali was declared the winner. For an unprecedented third time, Ali held the world heavyweight championship crown and fulfilled his claim of saying, "I am the greatest!"

Backstory. Television's fascination with Muhammad Ali, the "black Superman" (as he was dubbed in a 1975 hit reggae record by Johnny Wakelin), began in 1964 when he was 22 and knocked out Sonny Liston in six rounds. Known then as Cassius Clay, he announced the day after the fight that he henceforth would be called Muhammad Ali, as he had become a follower of the Nation of Islam. The change in name as well as religion stunned the public, and many members of the press refused to address him by his new moniker. The notable exception was Howard Cosell of ABC Sports, whose rise at that network coincided with that of Ali.

In 1967 Ali incensed some people even more by his refusal to serve in the military, claiming he had conscientious objector status. Professional boxing leaders stripped him of his title and banned him from the sport, while Ali received a five-year federal sentence for draft evasion. The U.S. Supreme Court later reversed that decision, and Ali was able to return to fighting in 1971. However, he lost a chance to win back the heavyweight title when Joe Frazier defeated him that year.

Ali persevered, and he became heavyweight champion again in 1974 by beating George Foreman. His defeats of Frazier in 1974 and again in 1975 in the aforementioned Frazier "Thrilla in Manila" solidified his standing internationally. His popularity did not go unnoticed by the networks. When Ali fought English pugilist Richard Dunn on May 24, 1976, and knocked him out in the fifth round, NBC carried the event; the network was rewarded with jaw-dropping numbers of

35.0/53. Those were the highest figures for a fight on television as well as the fifth-highest rated special for the year. Ali defended his title successfully on Sept. 28, 1976, against Ken Norton and on May 16, 1977, against Alfredo Evangelista before going against Earnie Shavers on Sept. 29, 1977.

The Norton and Evangelista bouts did not match the audience levels set by the Dunn one with Ali, and Shavers was not a well-known challenger to the champ. But NBC promoted the match very well, as it had with Dunn, and the numbers were even more impressive: an average 37.3/57 for the whole presentation, which started with a 27.6/44 and grew to an astounding 43.8/71 in its last 30 minutes. NBC claimed about 70 million viewers watched at least part of the bout, five million more than the Ali-Dunn contest.

For the honor to be the next challenger to Ali, Leon Spinks beat Alfio Righetti on Friday, Nov. 18, 1977, in a match that aired starting at 11:30 P.M. Eastern on CBS. When Spinks and Ali first met on Feb. 15, 1978, at Las Vegas airing on CBS, the show finished number two for the week (behind *Three's Company*) with a 34.4/51. That event earned the Emmy for live sports special.

Ali's loss to Spinks gave rise to the idea that Ali needed to retire, even though it was a 15-round split decision. Despite the score, most observers felt the man who boasted that could "float like a butterfly, sting like a bee" was much more lumbering than in the past and was in no condition to try to avenge his previous loss to Spinks. "An aging fighter who has already lost to a strong young fighter almost never wins the rematch — and, at 36, Ali is by every account an aging fighter," wrote Gregg Simms in *Ebony*. He quoted associates of Ali telling the ex-champ, "Leon kicked your butt good."

But Ali assured Simms he would be in better shape for the rematch and boasted to Simms, "I will stop him.... This time I am hungrier. I only really fight when I'm an underdog or when somebody's good." The second Ali-Spinks bout drew 70,000 spectators and $5 million in ticket sales at the New Orleans Superdome. With jazz music playing everywhere, the fighters entered with a swarm of policemen surrounding them, adding to the spectacle.

Since this match occurred as part of a Roone Arledge production in the late 1970s, there was plenty of overkill here. There were shots of celebrity attendees such as Larry Holmes, Pele and Mr. T, who was one of Spinks' bodyguards before leaving the entourage for acting in the 1980s. ABC even planted a couple of its series stars in the audience, forcing ringside reporter Frank Gifford to interview Judd Hirsch of *Taxi* and Robin Williams of *Mork & Mindy* (see 65). Williams barely spoke (possibly a first for him on TV), while Hirsch delivered the very telling statement, "I don't know what we're doing here." Despite the inanity of such moments, the interest in the fight was so great that its audience share was 16 points more than the Ali-Shavers fight even though it had the same rating, meaning that nearly three-fourths of viewers who had their TV set on at the time were watching this match.

Cosell, serving as lead analyst, was as bombastic and loud as ever, calling Spinks a befuddled fighter while yelling statements like "Ali's giving him a boxing lesson!" Actually, many speculated that Spinks stumbled because he was having family strife during his training for this rematch and was doing a lot of drinking during the lead-up to the bout.

Ali's trainer, Angelo Dundee, basked in the outcome even though it was not as thorough a thrashing of Spinks as his man predicted, and he was upset that referee Lucien Joubert penalized Ali one round for holding Spinks. "It was gorgeous sloppy, wonderful sloppy," he told Pat Putnam (*Sports Illustrated*) about the match. "And it was the only damn way we were going to beat Spinks."

Several in Ali's camp now urged him to retire from the sport. He officially did so on June 27, 1979, but then he unwisely attempted a comeback. His losses against Larry Holmes on Oct. 2, 1980, and Trevor Berbick on Dec. 11, 1981 confirmed to everyone (including finally Ali) that his days in the ring were over.

In 1984 Ali announced he was diagnosed with Parkinson's disease. Though it could not be proven, general speculation arose that his lengthy time in the ring, particularly in the late 1970s and early 1980s, contributed to his condition. He has become a symbol of many things to many people since that time.

I will give the last word to Cosell, the man who championed Ali the most on television. "Ali's life touched the civil rights movement," he noted in *I Never Played the Game*. "He became a hero to the anti–Vietnam War movement when he refused to serve in the army and endured an unjust three-year exile from the ring. He changed the financial structure of sports, demanding multimillion-dollar paydays and getting them.... Ali was always larger than the ring in which he floated."

42 — *Jeremiah Johnson*

Jan. 18, 1976 (*ABC Sunday Night Movie*; first released theatrically in 1972). **Rating:** 37.5. **Share:** 56.

Aired on ABC Sunday 9–11:10 P.M. Eastern and Pacific, 8–10:10 P.M. Central

Competition: *Kojak* and *Bronk* on CBS; *McMillan and Wife* on NBC

Cast: Robert Redford (Jeremiah Johnson), Will Geer (Bear Claw), Delle Bolton (Swan), Josh Albee (Caleb), Joaquin Martinez (Paints His Shirt Red), Stefan Gierasch (Del Gue), Allyn Ann McLerie (Crazy Woman). **Crew:** Sydney Pollack (director), Joe Wizan (producer), Edward Anhalt, John Milius (writers).

Synopsis. Aspiring mountain man Jeremiah Johnson suffers in the Rockies' winter snows during the 1800s until Bear Claw teaches him how to hunt as well as deal with Crow Indians. He ventures westward as seasons change and spots a woman hysterical after a Blackfeet Indian killed her son. She makes him take her surviving son with him on his trek. Jeremiah dubs the mute boy Caleb.

Caleb and Jeremiah rescue Del Gue, who the Blackfeet buried in sand up to his neck. He joins the duo to regain his horse, gun and pelts stolen by the Indians, and he takes pelts from some warriors after they try to ambush the trio. When they meet a tribe of Flathead Indians, Jeremiah offers his pelts and horse to placate them. Feeling they must return an equal gift in kind, they give Jeremiah the chief's daughter, Swan. He reluctantly weds her while Del Gue rides off.

Jeremiah, Swan and Caleb settle comfortably in Crow territory until the Third Cavalry demands that Jeremiah lead them to a wagon train isolated in the dangerous area. He gets them there safely but returns home to find his wife and Caleb have been killed in the interim. Jeremiah goes on a rampage against the Crows in retaliation, along the way meeting Bear Claw and Del Gue again and finding that the crazy woman was killed. The narrator informs us that legend has it that Jeremiah stayed in the mountains and never died.

Backstory. The biggest box office blockbusters that starred Robert Redford were the Best Picture Oscar nominee *Butch Cassidy and the Sundance Kid* (1969) and the Best Picture winner *The Sting* (1973), both co-starring Paul Newman. Yet surprisingly both finished in second place in the ratings when shown on TV to a dark horse, *Jeremiah Johnson*. (Both earned a strong 31.9 rating for their debuts on ABC, with *Butch Cassidy* airing first on Sept. 26, 1978, followed by *The Sting* on Nov. 5, 1978.)

The huge turnout for *Jeremiah Johnson* can be explained by three elements: the popularity of Redford; the lack of any westerns on network TV at the time; and what I believe was the most crucial one — the failure to plan adequately for compelling carryover programming following the Super Bowl, which aired earlier that day. In this case, CBS dropped the ball (sorry for the pun) by giving little reason for the immense Super Bowl X audience — its rating was 42.3, and its audience share was an incredible 78 — to continue watching the network afterward. It simply programmed its normal, ratings-challenged lineup, and a sizable number of bored viewers changed channels in response.

Also, viewers were starving for a theatrical hit to watch on *The ABC Sunday Night Movie*. The previous two weeks, the network aired its prestigious but often low-budget *ABC Theatre* presentations that were not big ratings-getters. (For example, on Jan. 11, 1976, the network aired the first of two parts of the classic TV-movie biography *Eleanor and Franklin*.)

Jeremiah Johnson derived from a 1965 novel by Vardis Flesher called *Mountain Man*. John Milius, a hot name at the time due to his uncredited contributions to the script of the 1971 crime action film *Dirty Harry*, began writing the adaptation under the working title *The Crow Killer*. The latter was taken from a name of a 1958 book written by Raymond W. Thorp and Robert Bunker (*Crow Killer: The Saga of Liver-Eating Johnson*) that provided background material for the script as well. All were inspired by the legend of a man living in the mountains in Montana, Wyoming and other Western states, John "Liver-Eating" Johnson.

An enthusiast of he-man adventures, as later borne out by his writing and directing such swaggering 1980s hits as *Conan the Barbarian* and *Red Dawn*, Milius planned to be faithful to the book, including the lead killing 200-plus Crow Indians and eating their livers in retaliation for killing his adopted wife and child. After Warner Bros. bought the script, Edward Anhalt, an Oscar winner twice for his screenplays for *Panic in the Streets* (1950) and *Becket* (1964), rewrote the property, softening its violent story. Anhalt had a reputation within the industry of salvaging what were deemed as problematic scripts. "I thought it was brilliant, but I don't know how many people would have paid to see it," Anhalt said of Milius' script crafted to William Froug in *The Screenwriter Looks at the Screenwriter*.

Milius claimed that David Rayfiel did a draft as well, but the latter received no screen credit. (Rayfiel earned an Emmy nomination for dramatic writing for an episode of *Bob Hope Presents the Chrysler Theatre* in 1964 and wrote screenplays for 1969's *Castle Keep* and *Valdez Is Coming*.) Even so, Milius has maintained that his contribution to what finally appeared on screen was most important.

"But nobody could write the mountain men dialogue," Milius said of the script's later writers in *Backstory 4: Interviews with Screenwriters of the 1970s and 1980s*. "The point of being a mountain man is that he's out there alone and he doesn't see anybody or talk to anybody, and when he *does* see somebody, the guy more than likely wants to kill him."

The original plan was for Sam Peckinpah to direct and Clint Eastwood to star, but Peckinpah bailed after meeting with Eastwood, and Eastwood was drafted to replace Frank Sinatra as the lead in *Dirty Harry* (yes, the film where Eastwood read dialogue written by the same man who wrote some of *Jeremiah Johnson*). Redford and director Sydney Pollack took their places on the production instead.

Anhalt said he made all the creative talent on the film agree on one common summary of *Jeremiah Johnson* in order to revamp the screenplay. That statement was, "This is the story of the inevitable destruction of every man's dream, and the spine of the film, the comment that it makes, is that the measure of a man is the grace with which he survives that destruction."

But Pollack had a slightly different take on its theme. "It's the classic fable of the man who tried to escape society and went up into another civilization, and then that old society followed him up the mountain and said, 'You can't get away from us,'" he told Robert Emery in *The Directors Take One*. Pollack also noticed how all the characters had problems communicating with each other and emphasized that fact in every scene when Jeremiah met a new person and both sides talked enigmatically with one another initially.

Much of the filming was done on location at Utah's National Forests and Zion National Park. The snow and wintry weather was real, and it made conditions for shooting challenging. Yet Redford managed to cope with it all, very impressive given that much of the film involved only himself on screen.

Making its U.S. theatrical premiere on Sept. 10, 1972, with a three-minute overture, intermis-

sion and 90-second *entr'acte*, *Jeremiah Johnson* finished among the top films at the box office that year. It also was the first western ever to be screened at the Cannes Film Festival.

ABC ran *Jeremiah Johnson* again on Dec. 19, 1976 to good ratings (22.3/36), and then NBC showed the movie twice, on May 10, 1977 (17.5/30) and March 4, 1979 (19.2/29).

Robert Redford loved the Utah mountains where *Jeremiah Johnson* was filmed and later established a yearly film festival in the town of Sundance, attracting filmmakers from around the world to participate. He is also known for being a committed environmentalist, dedicated to protecting the natural beauty of his adopted homeland. That's certainly more admirable than, say, eating the livers of more than 200 people.

41—*Helter Skelter*

April 2, 1976 (*CBS Friday Night Movies*, second of two parts). **Rating:** 37.5. **Share:** 60.

Aired on CBS Friday 9–11 P.M. Eastern and Pacific, 8–10 P.M. Central

Competition: *A Fistful of Dollars* (1964 theatrical movie; repeat) on ABC; *The Rockford Files* and *Police Story* on NBC

Cast: George DiCenzo (Deputy D.A. Vincent Bugliosi), Steve Railsback (Charles Manson), Nancy Wolfe (Susan Atkins), Marilyn Burns (Linda Kasabian), Christina Hart (Patricia "Katie" Krenwinkel), Cathey Paine (Leslie Van Houten), Alan Oppenheimer (Assistant D.A. Aaron Stovitz), Rudy Ramos (Danny DeCarlo), Sondra Blake (Ronnie Howard), Vic Werber (Lt. Sam Brenner), Jason Ronard (Paul Watkins), Howard Caine (Everett Scoville), Skip Homeier (Judge Charles Older). **Crew:** Lee Rich, Phil Capice (executive producers), Tom Gries (producer-director), J.P. Miller (writer).

Synopsis. Actress Sharon Tate, eight months pregnant, and four others are murdered at her residence in Los Angeles County on Aug. 9, 1969. A day later, Leno LiBianca and his wife Rosemary suffer the same fate. Two months later, Susan Atkins is arrested and tells inmate Ronnie Howard that she is part of the Charles Manson "family" (followers) that killed Tate.

On Nov. 18, 1969, Vincent Bugliosi becomes the case's co-prosecutor. Susan graphically testifies before the grand jury that she, Katie and Tex Watson committed the Tate murders while Linda Kasabian stood outside, and that Manson and Leslie Van Houten joined them for the LiBianca ones. When it is leaked and appears in *The Los Angeles Times*, Bugliosi cannot use it.

Bugliosi keeps digging and gets information from ex–Manson procurer Paul Watkins plus a plea bargain for testimony from Linda. Manson's attorney Everett Scoville repeatedly objects as Linda details the crimes, including how Manson intended to frame black militants for the murders. Manson, Susan, Katie and Leslie disrupt the trial a few times before Judge Older bans them from the courtroom. The jury finds the defendants guilty. They shave their heads before they are sentenced to die in 1971. The California Supreme Court abolishes the death penalty the next year, so all remain in jail without remorse for their actions.

Backstory. The Beatles recorded "Helter Skelter" for their 1968 double LP *The Beatles*, also known as "The White Album." The song might have been forgotten except among Beatles collectors were it not for Charles Manson, who thought the Beatles were sending messages through their album.

According to Manson's warped mind, "Helter Skelter" was to be the last war on Earth, where every man takes vengeance against his fellow human beings. He believed it would result in victory for the black man after a third of the population died, but that Manson and his "family" would be needed to provide leadership for the black man after that victory. To spark the "war," Manson devised murders of mainstream establishment, or as it he put it, the "pigs" (inspired by another cut on *The Beatles*, "Piggies").

To achieve his goals, Manson created a commune for his followers at the Spahn Movie Ranch in Simi Hills following a messy life. He was raised by his mother (along with a succession of her boyfriends) in several rundown motels, after she served time for armed robbery in state penitentiary. (He adopted the surname of one of his mom's companions.) Manson ran away at age 12 and committed several robberies and other crimes, leading him to spend 17 years in various boys' homes, jails and federal penitentiaries. He married and divorced twice and fathered at least two children.

Vincent Bugliosi, Manson's co-prosecutor, offered these details and much more in the 1974 best seller *Helter Skelter*, which he wrote with Curt Gentry. While some may have had a morbid curiosity about the story, *Helter Skelter* stood out because Bugliosi did not sugarcoat the facts. The book acknowledges that the Los Angeles Police

Department did not follow up adequately in locating the revolver used by Manson (the Van Nuys police department had it for months without connecting it properly to the killings), nor in using Susan's grand jury testimony to locate the gang's bloodied clothes (a local ABC-TV news team followed her statements in the *Los Angeles Times* and spotted the items).

When CBS adapted the book, the case's notoriety led some "name" actors to shy away from the project. The horrible crimes also disgusted the Beatles, who refused the use of their vocals (a group called Silverspoon substituted for them). Bugliosi, who served as technical advisor on the production, had George DiCenzo (the actor playing Bugliosi) redo the climactic confrontation with Manson, feeling that DiCenzo was not as flamboyant in his portrayal as Bugliosi was in real life.

The relatively unknown Steve Railsback became Manson and provided a chilling portrait of the madman, despite barely having any dialogue in Part One. Marilyn Burns told an interviewer with the Terror Trap website that all the actors playing Manson family members agreed to have their heads shaved for their last scenes, but director Tom Gries spared their locks and gave them skull caps to wear instead. She added that while filming a scene at the Manson ranch, an extra who apparently had ties to the "family" put her nails in Burns' arm and said, "Linda wasn't there that day."

In the movie, Susan Watkins is allowed to say "bitch" without bleeping, probably a network TV first. "Bastard" is heard twice, also highly unusual then. Hearing about the details of the butchery of Sharon Tate and others remain hard to stomach. (CBS warned viewers that the program may not be suitable for all family members.)

When it was finished, the project's subject matter and realism scared away many advertisers. CBS asked for $35,000 per 30-second commercial, but settled for some under $20,000.

CBS affiliates in San Francisco, Pittsburgh, Bellingham, Washington and Portland, Maine refused to air the miniseries (another station picked it up in the Golden Gate City). Twelve other stations postponed airing it until later in the evening. In Los Angeles, Bugliosi's candidacy for district attorney in the June 8 election was seen as a problem that could have his opponents demand equal air time on KCBS, so it was delayed airing there until June 10 and 11.

Helter Skelter was the top-rated show of the

week, even beating the Academy Awards. While it lost money initially, it helped CBS win for the 1975-1976 season. *Helter Skelter* received three Emmy nominations, for directing, music composition (Billy Goldenberg, whose electronic sounds in scenes depicting Manson's "family" are effectively unnerving) and film editing. The directing nod was the last for Gries, who died less than a year after *Helter Skelter* ran at age 54 from a heart attack. Railsback got no nomination as supporting actor, even though he proved more memorable than all the other Emmy contenders that year (the winner was Howard Da Silva in the forgotten "Verna: USO Girl" on public television's *Great Performances*). In fact, Railsback was so effective that he became typecast as a psycho. He has remained fairly busy since then, but no role has had the same impact. Asked by Elaine Lamkin for the Bloody Disgusting website in 2005 how he felt about playing Manson, he said, "I have no problem if that's how people want to remember me. I'm proud of all my work."

CBS reran *Helter Skelter* to a much smaller audience on Jan. 24, 1977 (12.7/18) and Jan. 26, 1977 (16.2/24). The movie then encountered a battle of ownership between Lorimar Productions and TV distributor Viacom along with another 1976 TV-movie, *Sybil*, when they were sold in syndication to local stations and overseas markets. Eventually the rerun rights were resolved, and both productions are now available on DVD.

CBS decided to remake *Helter Skelter* as a TV-movie with Jeremy Davies as Manson. It focused on the criminals this time, with Bugliosi (played by Bruno Kirby) in a lesser role. Airing May 16, 2004, it was a critical bomb with so-so ratings of 4.1/11. It received an Emmy nomination for Outstanding Musical Composition

The original *Helter Skelter* has held up well except for its stilted opening. It has DiCenzo (as Bugliosi) walk out of a court building and address the camera by saying the following:

> Good evening. You're about to see a dramatization of actual facts, in which some of the names have been changed. The story is true. If it were not true, it would not be believable, for it is surely one of the most bizarre chapters in the history of crime. We may not like to accept the fact that people like some of those in the history of *Helter Skelter* exist in our life. And yet they do. And while they do, we cannot say that the story of *Helter Skelter* has ended.

That part remains true. As of this writing, Manson and most of his followers are still in jail.

40 — *Marcus Welby, M.D.*

Jan. 5, 1971 ("Another Buckle for Wesley Hill"). **Rating:** 37.7. **Share:** n/a.

Aired on ABC Tuesday 10–11 P.M. Eastern and Pacific, 9–10 P.M. Central

Competition: *60 Minutes* on CBS, *First Tuesday* (second of two hours) on NBC

Cast: Robert Young (Dr. Marcus Welby), James Brolin (Dr. Steven Kiley), Elena Verdugo (Nurse Consuelo Lopez). **Guests:** Glenn Corbett (Wesley Hill), Chill Wills (Clayton Hill), Michael F. Blake (Bobby Hill). **Crew:** David Victor (creator-executive producer-writer), David J. O'Connell (producer).

Synopsis. Working out of an office in Santa Monica, California, kindly Dr. Welby and his young, hip assistant, Dr. Kiley, help their patients meet their mental and emotional needs as much as their physical ones. Nurse Lopez also doubled as secretary at the office.

In this episode, rancher Wesley Hill undergoes treatment for kidney disease and worries that he will no longer be as active physically as he becomes dependent on a dialysis machine. His father Clayton and son Bobby try to be supportive.

Backstory. On *All in the Family* (see 25), Edith Bunker occasionally mentioned something she saw on *Marcus Welby, M.D.* as a defense of her beliefs. By doing so, the sitcom's writers were making a sly jab at the quality level of the drama, as Edith was not known for profound introspection. Looking back 40 years later, I would say the portrait is right on the mark, for despite four Emmy wins (all in 1970, for lead actor Robert Young, supporting actor James Brolin, cinematographer Walter Strenge, and the series itself as best drama) and six other Emmy nominations, this is one rather mediocre medical program, certainly less impressive than *St. Elsewhere*, *ER* or *House*— or *Medic* or *Ben Casey* (see 88) before it, for that matter.

Originally Universal Studios developed *Marcus Welby, M.D.* as a pilot for CBS, who rejected it, then pitched it to NBC, who turned it down as well. The original leading man changed in the process too.

Len Goldberg, head of programming at ABC at the time, wanted Lee J. Cobb to play the part but could not get him. The person picked instead was Ralph Bellamy — or so thought Grant Tinker, the recently installed head of television for Universal Studios, until another actor became involved. "I came into my office one morning, and sitting there was Robert Young, whom I knew only by sight," Tinker recalled in his autobiography. "Someone had given him the script, and his opening words to me were 'I want to be Marcus Welby.'"

Young was semi-retired in Rancho Santa Fe, California, when he made the pitch to Tinker. A mainstay with MGM studies in the 1930s, Young had acted with many of its top stars in movies without becoming one himself, then freelanced for other studios in several interesting films, particular the 1947 Oscar nominee for Best Picture, *Crossfire*, where he was a dogged detective investigating an anti–Semitic murder. In 1949 he agreed to star in a radio sitcom, *Father Knows Best*, which transferred to TV in 1954 and became more popular each year until Young resigned from it when it was #6 in the ratings in 1960, as he was weary of the grind and the format.

After the follow-up sitcom *Window on Main Street* (CBS, 1961-1962) flopped, Young struggled most of the rest of the 1960s, securing only rare guest shots. One was on *Dr. Kildare*, whose producer David Victor would later perform the same honors on *Marcus Welby, M.D.* and was willing to test Young for the role after the latter begged him and Tinker. Young's screen test impressed both men and ABC executives, and Bellamy was out of the role that could have enhanced his already impressive résumé.

When the TV-movie pilot *Marcus Welby, M.D.* (later retitled *A Matter of Humanities*) scored well in the ratings when it aired on March 26, 1969, to become a series in the fall of that year, Young went with it. So did James Brolin as Dr. Kiley. However, Elena Verdugo replaced Penny Stanton as their nurse-secretary.

Installed as the concluding show for ABC's Tuesday lineup, where it would stay for its entire seven-season run, *Marcus Welby, M.D.* debuted on Sept. 23, 1969, against the sophomore newsmagazine series *60 Minutes* (see 89) on CBS and movies on NBC. The series finished its first season at #8, making it ABC's top-rated program for the 1969-1970 season as well as ABC's first top 10 series since 1966-1967.

NBC and CBS stuck with their same lineups against *Marcus Welby, M.D.* in the 1970-1971 season, which only made the latter more popular. The series finished the season at #1, the first time ever that an ABC series managed to reach that summit, and this episode was the most popular of them all. Ironically, the show at #2 this week was *Medical Center*, the top hospital drama on CBS.

Taking a cue from the TV audience, CBS and NBC started putting mostly entertainment programs up against *Marcus Welby, M.D.* thereafter, but the series still managed to make the top 20 the next two years before falling considerably thereafter. Although it still generally won its time period, it did so by a smaller margin from the 1973-1974 season onward, and ABC aired it for the last time on May 11, 1976.

Throughout it all, *Marcus Welby, M.D.* followed mostly a "disease of the week" pattern where a guest star or two would be afflicted by a condition that usually affected their family life or love interest, and sometimes Dr. Kiley would on the receiving end of that romantic involvement. Dr. Welby would show compassion and urge the patient to do the right thing before the end of every pat and predictable episode.

There were efforts to exploit *Marcus Welby, M.D.* elsewhere on ABC. For example, Elinor Donahue's character Dr. Miriam Welby on *The Odd Couple* was named in honor of this series. The most obvious was *Owen Marshall—Attorney at Law*, which Victor created to be the legal equivalent of this medical drama. But it never had the same draw for viewers, as it struggled for a three-season run on ABC (1971–1974).

Frankly, I find the best drama involving this series lies less in most of its episodes than with its leading men's biographies. For Brolin, interest lies in the fact that like Young, he was one of a few men to star in two top 10 TV series (in Brolin's case, it was *Hotel* on ABC in 1983-84). And there is his marriage to superstar Barbra Streisand, still going strong as of this writing after they wed in 1998, and his fathering of Josh Brolin, one of the most promising actors in contemporary movies.

When *Marcus Welby, M.D.* was a hit, Young had grown disillusioned with his family's conservative Republican politics and became an independent, protesting discrimination and the Vietnam War. He also acknowledged that he had struggled with alcoholism for three decades. His honesty shocked some but won him over new fans as well, and after the series ended, he remained fairly busy on TV through the 1980s, including the TV-movie revivals *The Return of Marcus Welby, M.D.* (ABC, May 16, 1984) and *Marcus Welby, M.D.—A Holiday Affair* (NBC, Dec. 19, 1988). The former, with an okay but not spectacular 19.5/32, led ABC to consider a midseason revival of the show from 1984-1985 with Darren McGavin and Morgan Stevens to be regulars, but it did not pan out. Young still had personal demons that led him to try to commit suicide in 1991. He survived and died of natural causes seven years later, at age 91.

The irony of this show's triumph, as anyone who has seen American TV since the 1970s will realize, is that CBS stayed committed to *60 Minutes* despite its low initial ratings, and moved it to another day and time. While *60 Minutes* has remained on the air and doing well since then, *Marcus Welby, M.D.* faded pretty quickly after it ended in 1976. (Retitling it *Robert Young, Family Doctor* when it was syndicated to local stations in reruns may have hurt it as well.)

Until 2010, *Marcus Welby* was the only #1 scripted series that had never been released officially on home video; then a DVD of the first season came out via Shout Factory in May. It was not a particularly successful release, but nevertheless Shout Factory released the second season with this episode in October. Be prepared to be disappointed while watching it, unless you do not mind stock characters and melodrama.

39 — *John Wayne: Swing Out Sweet Land*

Nov. 29, 1970 (special). **Rating:** 38.0. **Share:** 54. Aired on NBC Sunday 8:30–10 P.M. Eastern and Pacific, 7:30–9 P.M. Central

Competition: *The Ed Sullivan Show* (last half-hour) and *The Glen Campbell Goodtime Hour* on CBS; *The F.B.I.* (last half-hour) and *The Carpetbaggers* (first hour of two-hour 1964 theatrical movie; repeat) on ABC

Cast: John Wayne (Host), Ann-Margret, Lucille Ball (Lady Liberty), Jack Benny, Dan Blocker (Indian), Roscoe Lee Browne (Frederick Douglass), Glen Campbell, Johnny Cash, Roy Clark, Bing Crosby (Mark Twain), Phyllis Diller (Belva A. Lockwood), The Doodletown Pipers, Lorne Greene (George Washington), Celeste Holm (Nancy Lincoln), Bob Hope, Michael Landon (Peter Minuit), Dean Martin (Eli Whitney), Dick Martin (Wilbur Wright), Ross Martin (Alexander Hamilton), Ed McMahon (Bartender), Greg Morris (Crispus Attucks), David Nelson (Union Soldier), Rick Nelson (Confederate Soldier), Hugh O'Brian (Thomas Jefferson), Dan Rowan (Orville Wright), William Shatner (John Adams), Red Skelton (Printer), Tommy Smothers (Printer's Apprentice), Leslie Uggams (Saloon Singer), Dennis Weaver (Tom Lincoln). **Crew:** Nick Vanoff, William O. Harbach (executive producers), Paul W. Keyes (producer-writer), Stan Harris (director).

Synopsis. Coming on stage after a fife and drum corps marches to a patriotic tune, John

Wayne informs us that this salute to America's history will be short on preaching, with levity making up the difference. After Glen Campbell sings, Wayne recounts the land's colonial days from the purchase of Manhattan in 1626 to the early 1900s, with a Cliffs Notes presentation featuring celebrities playing famous figures — or sometimes just themselves, like Bob Hope doing a monologue to weary Revolutionary War troops at Valley Forge. Wayne occasionally steps away from his stage, which includes a floor map lighting up states as they joined the union, to interact with characters for a few sketches.

Also seen are the Doodletown Pipers (singing a tribute to the Declaration of Independence), Roy Clark (playing the banjo and singing "Oh Susanna" at Andrew Jackson's inauguration), Johnny Cash (performing on a train) and Leslie Uggams (doing "My Darling Clementine" as a torch song in a western saloon). The latter comes as Wayne appears in his traditional cowboy garb, riding around a ghost town. Wayne spends the show's last five minutes thanking his sponsor and the "beautiful people" in front of and behind the camera, then telling what he believes is right with his country and what can be made be better in the future. He concludes by saying "God bless America," which leads into the song with each cast member singing a line, ending with Wayne on the map of America surrounded by actors standing on states and singing the finale.

Backstory. The actor born Marion Michael Morrison appeared in films more than two decades before becoming a top box office attraction in the late 1940s, and he remained in that position until the time of this special. He had only done a handful of TV appearances when he decided to make this special, an appeal for patriotism mixed with comedy and music.

"I'm doing this for my kids," Wayne told Joseph Finnegan in *TV Guide*. "Before I get too old, I want to do something on television that will give them an idea of how the country developed, even if it is played for laughs." Wayne's Batjac Productions company was part of the production team.

The show cost an estimated $2 million, with Wayne receiving the bulk of that in what was reported to be the highest salary for a TV special up to that time. He used his clout to get the stars on the show, all of whom were paid anywhere from union scale ($210 at the time) to $1,000.

One of those invited, comedian Tom Smothers of the Smothers Brothers comedy duo, debated for a week whether he would be "selling out" by appearing on it. After mulling it over, he decided it might make a nice statement for him to be discussing dissent with right-wingers Wayne and Red Skelton.

"The logistics were unbelievable," producer-writer Paul Keyes told Joseph Finnegan in *TV Guide*. "We had to fit everything into everybody's schedule. Dan Blocker came in from Switzerland the night before we shot him. We had Dean Martin for only a few hours. Johnny Cash was brought in from Nashville for only five hours. And for that Washington inauguration scene with [Jack] Benny, Bill Shatner, Ross Martin, Lorne Greene and Hugh O'Brian, the schedule was predicated on Hugh having to leave by two o'clock to do another show."

Unfortunately, the production that emerges is a spotty affair at best. There is a lot of canned applause and laughter that harms it, plus some pretty pretentious narration. It is jarring how the dramatic and comedic elements were jammed next to each other. The tones even changed within songs, if you can believe that. As for camerawork, there were jumbled shots outside and inside, some on location and some on studio. (The location shots included the Bodie, California, State Historic Park, Knotts Berry Farm, and Ports O'-Call, Whalers Wharf, in San Pedro, California.)

Bob Hope's routine was amusing, but it was out of place. It is hard to take a special seriously when Hope is followed by Ann-Margret shimmying and belting out a tune in her 1770s bodice outfit along with boogying Continental soldiers. Then there's the scene where George Washington and his cabinet of John Adams, Thomas Jefferson and Alexander Hamilton ruminate on the meaning of their new jobs; then Washington walked to another room to encounter Jack Benny, joking about his parsimonious nature when he was thrilled that a dollar he found near the Potomac was not the one that Washington threw and thus he could claim it. (In the same scene George Burns appeared in an unbilled cameo. Crossing from stage right in modern clothes with a cigar in hand and espying Benny, he said, "Hello, Jack. Working?" and then left the stage.)

Each comic sketch with Wayne involved — including the ones with Dean Martin, Red Skelton and Tommy Smothers (co-existing in the same shot despite Skelton loathing *The Smothers Brothers Comedy Hour*) and Rowan and Martin — all included this same line: "How he ever got that horse on the seventh floor, I'll never know." It was not funny the first time Wayne said it with one

of his guests, nor was it on the third. Nor was it clever to Dean Martin as Eli Whitney say, "Everybody picks some cotton sometime." Wayne's five-minute concluding speech was pretty powerful, however. It included the line, "I believe there's time in my life and yours to get this country in such shape that God would be proud of it."

The critics hated this. Jack Gould of *The New York Times* judged it "a sorry cavalcade that mixed TV celebrities in disconcerting incidents of miscasting, inspirational flag-waving and sermonizing, perfunctory attempts of video humor and repulsively intrusive commercials." At the end of the year, *Time* magazine dubbed it the year's Most Embarrassing Special along with Raquel Welch's *Raquel!* on CBS.

There were only two Emmy nods for the special a few months later. Marshall King lost his bid to claim the statuette for live or tape sound mixing for a program. Dominic Frontiere won an Emmy for his conducting of a variety, musical or dramatic program. Frontiere also arranged music for the special, but Ray Charles (not the blind superstar, but the one who gave us the Ray Charles Singers with the top five 1964 hit "Love Me with All Your Heart") provided special music material and choral direction. Jaime Rogers provided choreography, including a somewhat ridiculous male ballet on building railroad tracks.

NBC reran this on April 8, 1971, where it scored a 24.1/39. NBC repeated the special on Jan. 15, 1976, and drew an 18.2/28.

In 2007 MPI Home Video acquired rights to the special and released it on DVD as *John Wayne's Tribute to America*. It included the Budweiser commercials seen during the original airing, plus Wayne's "mystery guest" appearance on the CBS game show *What's My Line?* in 1960.

38 — *The Bridge on the River Kwai*

Sept. 25, 1966 (*ABC Sunday Night Movie*; first released theatrically in 1957). **Rating:** 38.3. **Share:** 61.

Aired on ABC Sunday 8–11 P.M. Eastern and Pacific, 7–10 P.M. Central

Competition: *The Ed Sullivan Show, The Garry Moore Show, Candid Camera* and *What's My Line?* on CBS; *Walt Disney, Hey Landlord!, Bonanza* and *The Andy Williams Show* on NBC

Cast: William Holden (Shears), Jack Hawkins (Maj. Warden), Alec Guinness (Col. Nicholson), Sessue Hayakawa (Col. Saito), James Donald (Maj. Clipton), Andre Morell (Col. Green), Peter Williams (Capt. Reeves), John Boxer (Maj. Hughes), Percy Herbert (Gorgan), Harold Goodwin (Baker), Ann Sears (Nurse). **Crew:** Sam Spiegel (producer), David Lean (director), Carl Foreman and Michael Wilson (writers).*

Synopsis. "Commander" Shears digs graves in a POW camp in Burma in 1943 when British Col. Nicholson and his troops arrive. Col. Saito tells the prisoners they will build a bridge over the River Kwai to get Japan a train route to invade India. Shears, a survivor of a ship sinking, tells Nicholson that men at the camp have died from disease, famine, overwork and suicides. Yet Nicholson agrees with Saito that trying to escape is unreasonable, to Shears' consternation.

When Saito dislikes how Nicholson insists his men will be under his command in the prison, a battle of wills begins, with Saito locking Nicholson in a box outside for days. After his men refuse to follow Saito's order to finish the bridge, Nicholson takes command of them. Sensing that his battalion has no order (while failing to comprehend that he is aiding the enemy), he usurps Saito to complete the bridge with his men.

Shears escapes from camp and tells Maj. Warden of Force 316 about the bridge. The major blackmails him for impersonating an officer to force Shears to join their group in invading the construction area and blowing up the bridge. Shears, Warden and others make it to the now-completed bridge and plant explosives. Nicholson and Saito notice the wires to the detonator before the train crosses. They, along with Shears, die in the ensuing battle. The bridge blows up, but Maj. Clipton, the British doctor who witnessed the scene from a hill, concludes it was all "Madness!"

Backstory. The immensely successful TV premiere of *The Bridge on the River Kwai* signified the increasing importance of theatrical features on network TV schedules. The season it debuted, viewers could watch previously released films an unprecedented five nights a week (none on Mondays or Wednesdays) on ABC, CBS and NBC in 1966–1967. Noting the rush, *TV Guide* devoted a section to upcoming movies for the first time in its 1966 fall season preview and enlisted critic Judith Crist to review each week's offerings in every issue, while *Variety* ended the season by listing the ratings of every regularly scheduled movie of 1966–1967. (Since *The Bridge on the River Kwai*

started an hour earlier than the standard two-hour length of ABC's Sunday movie, it was not included there.) The fever for motion pictures was underway, as shown when *Saturday Review* quoted CBS programming head Mike Dann in 1966 saying, "The biggest crisis faced by the TV networks is that we're running out of movies."

Apart from perennially popular repeats of *The Wizard of Oz* (see 52), movies had performed variably for the networks up to the fall of 1966. That all changed with the debut of *The Bridge on the River Kwai*, a classic study of the insanity of war. A Best Picture Oscar winner, it also won in six other Academy Award categories: directing, writing, Guinness as best actor, cinematography, score and film editing. (Hayakawa lost supporting actor to Red Buttons in *Sayonara.*) Helping its appeal to TV viewers was the facts that it was well known (it was a top grossing movie).

Its director David Lean was living in New York and struggling to establish himself in America (after considerable fame in England) when his agent put him together with producer Sam Spiegel. Spiegel gave Lean a copy of the book by Pierre Boulle, which Lean loved, and the first script adaptation, which he loathed. ("I mean, the whole film when I read it started in an American submarine, the thing was being depth-charged. It really was not very good," he told Steven Ross in *Take One* in 1971.) Yet the property intrigued him and, having no other work available, he helped in reworking it. That was the easy part. It was more difficult filming the complex story in Ceylon, where Lean spent a year creating the settings.

He also encountered problems with two of his stars. He made the mistake of telling Alec Guinness, whom he did not want to play Col. Nicholson originally, that his character was to be somewhat monotonous, devoting himself to building the bridge. "And we fought pretty well all the way through that film," he told David Ehrenstein at the American Film Institute in 1990. (The men later worked together in 1984's *A Passage to India.* In his memoirs, Guinness quoted himself telling an interviewer in later years, "Let me make it clear that I am very fond of David, admire his work enormously, know him to be extravagantly generous, and all is well between us.")

ABC paid the unprecedented sum of $1 million for two runs of the film, but it had a sponsor ready to foot the bill in anticipation of a large audience.

*Pierre Boulle, author of the novel, received screen credit initially because Foreman and Wilson were blacklisted in 1957; nowadays, Foreman and Wilson are credited for it officially.

The Ford Motor Company used the presentation to introduce its new Cougar line of cars. It was not too difficult for ABC to have the firm advertise on the movie, as its first hour pre-empted Ford's regularly sponsored series *The F.B.I.*

William Holden sued unsuccessfully to prevent ABC from airing the film, arguing that the exposure would impact the box office take of future theatrical rereleases. His personal interest in the film was deep because he earned $50,000 annually for it in a deferred salary arrangement.

Only one other film on *ABC Sunday Night Movie* came close to matching *Kwai*'s blockbuster status during the season: *The Robe* notched a 31.0/53 on March 26, 1967. *Kwai*'s rating was 12 points higher than the week's #2 entry, an episode of *Green Acres*. The movie series wound up finishing in the top 30 for its first time that season.

A few months later, in a letter in *Variety*'s Aug. 2, 1967 issue, Paul Sonkin, ABC's director of research, called *The Bridge on the River Kwai* "TV's all-time hit movie" while reeling off statistics about its demographics and its audience of 72 million viewers. In the wake of its success, the average sales price of a movie running on network TV was now double ($800,000) what it was in 1965.

ABC repeated the film on March 10, 1968, with a disappointing 20.2/32. CBS reran it as a two-part feature on its Thursday and Friday movie slate Jan. 7 and 8, 1971, to solid ratings (part one was 23.9/36 and part two was 24.1/39). It fared slightly less well on its next rerun on CBS, getting a 17.8/26 for part one on Jan. 16, 1972, and 16.9/25 for part two on Jan. 23, 1972.

The success of *The Bridge on the River Kwai* led ABC and Ford to try a similar approach the next season, and they paid $1.1 million to run the 1962 *Mutiny on the Bounty* as a special Sunday feature on Sept. 24, 1967. But that bloated remake starring Marlon Brando was a commercial and critical dud, even though it had received an Oscar nomination for Best Picture, and its numbers of 23.0/38 was a definite comedown from *Kwai*. Its relative failure made network heads scale back expectations of a highly promoted movie being omnipotent ratings bait — until four months later, when NBC surpassed the ratings of *The Bridge on the River Kwai* with *The Birds* (see 35).

---

37 — *Three's Company*

March 13, 1979 ("An Anniversary Surprise"). **Rating:** 38.5. **Share:** 58.

Aired on ABC Tuesday 9–9:30 P.M. Eastern and Pacific, 8–8:30 P.M. Central

Competition: *Zorro* (1975 movie debut, first half-hour of two hours) on CBS, *Checkered Flag or Crash* (1977 movie debut, first half-hour of two hours) on NBC

Cast: John Ritter (Jack Tripper), Suzanne Somers (Chrissy Snow), Joyce DeWitt (Janet Wood), Audra Lindley (Helen Roper), Norman Fell (Stanley Roper). **Guests:** Ruta Lee (Mrs. Dawson), Paul Ainsley (Bartender). **Crew:** Don Nicholl, Michael Ross, Bernie West (executive producers), Roger Shulman, John Baskin (producers-writers), Dave Powers (director).

Synopsis. Janet and Chrissy try to write songs to celebrate the anniversary of their landlords, Stanley Roper and his wife, Helen, but both dismiss each other's efforts. Their roommate Jack says they should bake them a cake instead. Meanwhile, at the Regal Beagle bar, Stanley closes the deal to sell his apartment building with his real estate agent, Mrs. Dawson, and tells her to bring the check by his place tonight as an anniversary surprise for Helen. As Mrs. Dawson leaves, Helen arrives and asks Stanley why he had her at his booth. Stanley dismisses her concerns, then goes to fix the roommates' refrigerator and drops hints about how someone will be moving out soon. Janet, Jack and Chrissy think this means Stanley will leave Helen after 22 years of marriage.

While Janet and Chrissy visit Helen to reveal their suspicion, Jack drags Stanley down to the Regal Beagle. He misinterprets Stanley's derogatory comments about the apartment as references to Helen and convinces frigid Stanley to make a move on Helen. She rejects his advances based on what Janet and Chrissy told her. The roommates and Mrs. Dawson arrive to surprise Helen, and after the confusion clears, Helen is thrilled to leave with the money after 14 years. Jack is happy too, as he thinks will no longer have to pretend he is gay to stay there. Unfortunately, Stanley already has told the new landlord Jack is gay, causing Jack to fall out of his chair.

Backstory. For all but the last of the seven years it aired on ABC, *Three's Company* somehow managed to stay in the top 15 every season despite a tiresome formula used in every episode, including this one. One of the show's principals (usually Chrissy, the stereotypical dumb blonde) would overhear a statement involving another regular, leading to complications when he or she misconstrues the context and makes an incorrect assumption, often regarding a matter of a sexual nature. This assessment leads to complications involving the others until somehow everything is straightened out, sometimes with Jack, Chrissy or Janet — or all three — on the losing end of the predicament.

Yet millions of Americans tuned in faithfully every week to witness these shenanigans once it premiered on March 15, 1977, as a midseason replacement on Thursday nights. (That fall it moved to the Tuesday night slot where it stayed most of its run.) Some of the creative talent behind the much superior sitcoms *All in the Family* (see 25) and *M*A*S*H* (see 1) were involved in its creation.

From 1973 to 1976, Thames Television in the United Kingdom aired a sitcom called *Man About the House*, featuring a single man living with two female roommates in one apartment (or flat, as the British would call it). To pacify his landlords, he pretended to be gay to imply that no hanky panky would occur between himself and the lasses. It was a hit, and the U.S. representative for Thames, Don Taffner, contacted producer Ted Bergmann about modifying the program for American audiences, as had been done with *All in the Family*.

ABC, CBS and NBC all turned down his pitch initially. "They said, 'You can't have a boy living with two girls in the same apartment! Not on our network!'" Bergmann recalled to Chris Mann in *Come and Knock on Our Door*. Finally, when Fred Silverman became ABC head of programming in 1975, he was willing to give it a shot.

Peter Stone (creator of the hit Broadway musical *1776*) wrote the first adaptation and set it in New York City. Silverman told Bergmann to redo it and make it more accessible to people not living in (or loving) Gotham. Bergmann enlisted Larry Gelbart, who had launched *M*A*S*H* a few years earlier, to rewrite the pilot. On Silverman's recommendation, Bergmann cast Ritter as the lead, with Audra Lindley and Norman Fell as the married landlord and landlady, the Ropers — and Valerie Curtin and Suzanne Zenor as the other roommates.

This time, Silverman liked everything except the latter two actresses, so he held off plans to install the series on the 1976 fall lineup until they were recast. The network also drafted the team of Don Nicholl, Michael Ross and Bernie West, who had been writing and producing almost all the episodes of *All in the Family* from the fall of 1971 through the fall of 1975. Nicholl, Ross and West thought the show could have more appeal with sexual overtones, so with that in mind, they decided to make Chrissy a blonde bimbo.

The final version, set in Los Angeles, arrived as six shows (airing in the spring of 1977) that did remarkably well, finishing #11 overall for the 1976-1977 season. Ratings were even better the following season, when *Three's Company* ended at #3.

In 1978 the show added Jack's swinging pal Larry (played by Richard Kline) to the mix, and its popularity remained steady. With that in mind, the network and the producers decided to spin off the Ropers in their own series. And what better way to do that than have this episode air before the premiere of that series?

With heavy on-air promotion about this "big event," this episode ranked #1 for the week, with *The Ropers* (see 49) a strong #2. It also was the last non-repeat episode of *Three's Company* for the season until May 8. It helped the series finish the 1978-1979 season at #2 overall, just slightly behind its lead-in, *Laverne & Shirley* (see 56).

Ritter's idol, Don Knotts, joined the gang as the new landlord, Ralph Furley, in the fall of 1979. His character, always on the prowl for ladies, was an acceptable substitute for the Ropers, although many fans of *The Andy Griffith Show* (see 79) moaned that his comic talents were being wasted here.

That was nothing compared to the media storm that emerged in 1980 when Suzanne Somers demanded a huge hike in financial compensation, believing she was the real star of the show. The producers denied her request and forced her instead to tape her scenes separately at the end of each show, saying that her character was out of town, until she was replaced by Jenilee Harrison as Chrissy's klutzy cousin, Cindy, then by Priscilla Barnes as the less ridiculous Terri Alden. Yet through it all, ratings barely fell at all, with the show averaging no less than #8 for any season from 1980 to 1983.

By the 1983-1984 season, however, the cast and many viewers noticed how plots were becoming repetitive. Ratings dropped dramatically, particularly with the competing action series *Riptide* on NBC regularly making the top 20 while *Three's Company* struggled to crack the top 50. ABC Entertainment president Tony Thomopoulos told producers privately that the network planned to cancel the show; they convinced him to let them do a spin-off with Jack moving into another apartment with his girlfriend, as had occurred on the finale of *Man About the House* in England. The project sold.

Three's Company last aired on ABC on Sept. 18, 1984. Five days later, Ritter finally won an Emmy as lead actor in a comedy following nominations in the category in 1978 and 1981. The show had only two other Emmy nominations besides those, for outstanding comedy series in 1978 and video tape editing, also in 1978.

Ritter starred in *Three's a Crowd* from Sept. 25, 1985, through Sept. 10, 1985. ABC officials decide not to renew it after it finished #38 for the season. However, it was included in some *Three's Company* rerun packages sold to stations in 1986. There were talks about a *Three's Company* reunion, but Somers' demands in 1980 so upset Ritter that he vowed never to work with her again. The two finally reconciled in 1995, but their work commitments prevented any reteaming. Ritter's unexpected death in 2003 at age 54 ended any reunion hopes.

36 — *Patton*

Nov. 19, 1972 (*ABC Sunday Night Movie*; first released theatrically in 1970). **Rating:** 38.5. **Share:** 65.

Aired on ABC Sunday 9–11 P.M. Eastern and Pacific, 8–10 P.M. Central

Competition: *The New Dick Van Dyke Show* and *Mannix* on CBS; *McMillan and Wife* (last hour) and *Night Gallery* on NBC

Cast: George C. Scott (Gen. George S. Patton, Jr.), Karl Malden (Gen. Omar Bradley), Michael Bates (Field Marshal Montgomery), Karl Michael Vogler (Field Marshal Rommel), Edward Binns (Gen. Bedell Smith). **Crew:** Franklin Schaffner (director), Frank McCarthy (producer), Francis Ford Coppola, Edmund H. North (writers).

Synopsis. Fearless Gen. Patton barely follows protocol while leading his men to repeated victories in the European theater during World War II. His approach alternately exasperates and impresses Gen. Bradley, who witnesses Patton destroy Field Marshal Rommel's Nazi troops across Africa, then pursue his own course through Italy to steal the thunder from English Field Marshal Montgomery's successful campaign in the same country.

Patton's star dims when he slaps a shell-shocked patient in an Army hospital and suffers substantial casualties while in Italy. He is personally reprimanded and forced to apologize in public for the former act, then relieved from commanding the 7th Army. Put on probation through D-Day, he does himself no favors by failing to mention Russia as an ally during a war speech. Ordered to serve under Bradley, Patton promises to watch his

tongue while commanding the 3rd Army across France. Bradley tells him he performs brilliantly but does not know when to shut up.

Despite a lack of supplies, Patton pushes his troops 100 miles against the Nazis to win the Battle of the Bulge. Germany surrenders, but Gen. MacArthur declines to bring Patton to fight on the Pacific front. Patton begins spouting off again, and Gen. Smith warns him to stop comparing Russians to American politicians and refusing to follow de–Nazification policies. Patton does not care, and he is relieved of duty permanently. In a voiceover at the end, Patton says he realizes he is out of place in diplomacy, and all glory is fleeting.

Backstory. As fearless as Gen. George S. Patton, Jr., was in war, so was Barry Diller, ABC's vice-president for feature films, in the summer of 1971 in pursuit of blockbuster films to air on the network. Despite finishing the 1970-1971 season with TV's #1 series (*Marcus Welby M.D.* — see 40), ABC remained in third place overall. Diller thought the practice of following CBS and NBC in buying films in packages from movie studios did not aid ABC, so he managed to secure $50 million from the network to spend on individual blockbusters, many of which made this book's list.

Diller's acquisitions over five days included *The Ten Commandments* (see 83), *Love Story* (see 17) and others that aired in 1972 and 1973, mainly on ABC's Sunday movie lineup. These proved to be popular with advertisers: *Patton* brought $150,000 per minute from General Motors to sponsor half of the movie, for example. It was a successful plan, and ABC was wise to schedule *Patton* one week after airing *True Grit* (see 34), as it was believed they drew the similar pro-patriotic audiences. (Some fans of *Patton* would argue that it was anything but a flag-waving tribute.)

The idea of telling Patton's story on screen first went into motion in 1951, when two filmmakers who knew him in World War II, 20th Century–Fox vice-president in charge of production Darryl Zanuck and producer Frank McCarthy, planned to enact the story of a man who made a great impression in their lives. But his family objected to the move, so plans were placed on hold.

In 1968 McCarthy secured the rights to two books, *Patton: Ordeal and Triumph* by Ladislas Farago and *A Soldier's Story* by Omar Bradley, in order to bring the tale to the screen. He hired a young screenwriter named Francis Ford Coppola to do the script, which was faithful enough to allude to Patton's staunch belief in reincarnation mentioned in both books. Veteran writer Edmund H. North also made contributions, but Coppola received the bulk of the credit, and its favorable reception gave him the clout to create his own masterpiece, *The Godfather* (see 27). Franklin Schaffner won the directing job because of his efficient handling of *Planet of the Apes* (see 57). The immense scope of the story needed someone with his talent to keep it on time and on budget.

The first choice to play Patton was Lee Marvin and then Rod Steiger before George C. Scott accepted the role. Scott drank some on the set, but he was considered very professional otherwise. It is a mark of his talent that some viewers believe he treats the character reverentially, while others think he captures the flaws of the general so perfectly as to show the folly of that notion. In an interview with Scott during the production that appeared in the 1997 documentary "The Making of *Patton*," the actor made clear his opinion about his approach to the role and the man he was portraying. "As to glorifying him, I don't think that's what I've set out to do," said Scott. "I certainly didn't set out to make any glorification of war, of which I disapprove."

Also distinctive was the movie's score, which was unique for the period (only about a half-hour of the picture's running time had music behind it.) As composer Jerry Goldsmith later said, "Frank [Schaffner] and I spent a great deal of time deciding where the music was going to be and where it didn't go. And I know there were a couple of places where he hated music and when it came to writing, I just couldn't come up with it." Schaffner did come up with a distinctive fanfare heralding Patton's appearances from Goldsmith's work. The sound came from taping horns with an echo effect added to them.

The unforgettable first scene with Patton addressing an audience with an oversized American flag in the background was the last scene filmed. It originally was to open the film's second act after the intermission, but McCarthy and Schaffner thought it would introduce the character better at the front. It took only half a day to film.

The production wrapped up on schedule in May 1969, very impressive given it depicted four battles in six countries and encountered weather delays during shooting. Location filming took place primarily in Spain and a few other European countries, from England to Greece.

The movie debuted on Feb. 4, 1970. It won box office success, rave reviews and seven Oscar wins out of ten nominations. *Patton* received Academy Awards for Best Picture, Actor (Scott), Director, Original Story and Screenplay, Art Direction-Set Decoration, Sound and Film Editing. The other nominations were for cinematography, original score and special visual effects.

Scott refused to accept his Oscar. He had said he would not take the statuette in the past, but this was the first time he won an Academy Award and followed through on his promise. Some thought Scott declined not just due to his principles about competing against fellow actors for the award, but also because he felt his acting was not up to the part, as he said in some interviews. He may be the only person ever to see *Patton* to feel that way.

ABC editors replaced the foul words spoke by Patton at the beginning with milder words that Scott spoke on other parts of the soundtrack. ABC censor Alfred R. Schneider allowed the general to say "bastards" in his opening address to the troops and "son of a bitch" to the soldier he accuses of cowardice. *Patton* also included the seldom allowed off-color term "frigging" as well.

For a network that just a few weeks earlier had Ali MacGraw saying "bull" with the second profane syllable dropped out of the soundtrack in *Love Story* (see 17), this was a major accommodation. Some speculated it was allowed because President Richard Nixon said he loved the film, and if the leader of the country could handle it, so could its TV watchers. (Nixon later received criticism for revealing that the heroic battles of *Patton* inspired him to have America invade Cambodia, a move that exacerbated rather than resolved the Vietnam War.)

ABC reran *Patton* on Nov. 14, 1976 (22.9/35), then it went to NBC Nov. 28, 1978 (19.6/30), where it ran into trouble because it began airing at 8 P.M. Eastern and Central, allowing younger viewers to hear profanities. It returned to ABC on April 13, 1980 (18.9/31) and March 22, 1981 (17.3/27).

On Sept. 14, 1986, CBS presented a TV-movie sequel, *The Last Days of Patton*, which did well with a 15.2/32, although critics found it sluggish. Scott reprised the Patton role, detailing the general's death following a car crash. The TV-movie won an Emmy for Outstanding Makeup.

That production was long forgotten when the Library of Congress added *Patton* to the National Film Registry for preservation in 2003. And decades after it was first proposed, members of Patton's surviving family loved the film, and they take pride in being associated with it today.

35 — The Birds

Jan. 6, 1968 (*NBC Saturday Night at the Movies*; first released theatrically in 1963). **Rating:** 38.9. **Share:** 59.

Aired on NBC Saturday 9–11:30 P.M. Eastern and Pacific, 8–10:30 P.M. Central

Competition: *The Lawrence Welk Show* (last half-hour of 60-minute show), *The Iron Horse* (last episode) and *ABC Scope* on ABC; *Hogan's Heroes, Petticoat Junction* and *Mannix* on CBS

Cast: Tippi Hedren (Melanie Daniels), Rod Taylor (Mitch Brenner), Jessica Tandy (Lydia Brenner), Suzanne Pleshette (Annie Hayworth), Veronica Cartwright (Cathy Brenner), Ethel Griffies (Mrs. Bundy), Charles McGraw (Sebastian Sholes), Ruth McDevitt (Mrs. MacGruder), Lonny Chapman (Deke Carter). **Crew:** Alfred Hitchcock (director-producer), Evan Hunter (writer).

Synopsis. At a San Francisco bird shop, Mitch asks Melanie for help in buying a pair of love birds. The playful socialite pretends to be a store employee until he tells her he knows who she is and leaves. Intrigued, she tracks him down at Bodego Bay, takes a boat, gets inside his home and leaves two love birds. She rows back to the dock, but Mitch spies her, and a gull suddenly attacks her. Mitch gets Melanie treated, then takes her to the residence he shares with his daughter Cathy and his mother Lydia.

Melanie recuperates while staying with Annie, Mitch's ex-girlfriend, as bird attacks continue. They swoop down at a children's birthday party, then invade Mitch's place and a nearby farm. A rampage at a school forces students to flee, and Melanie takes cover at the Tides Cafe on the pier, where another flock of birds cause more havoc. Melanie and Mitch later reunite with Cathy, who tells them the birds killed Annie when she could not take cover.

Mitch boards up his house as night falls, to protect himself, Melanie, Lydia and Cathy. But Melanie wakes up and investigates a noise in the attic. It is the birds again, pecking at and nearly killing Melanie until Mitch saves her. He puts everyone in his car as the radio reports more destruction by the creatures. Birds as far as the eye can see coo ominously as the car quietly heads off into the distance.

Backstory. *The Birds* was the last hit movie directed by Alfred Hitchcock that was admired by audiences and critics alike. Although *Marnie* (1964) and *Torn Curtain* (1966) performed decently at the box office, reviewers were lukewarm

to them, and *Topaz* (1969), *Frenzy* (1972) and *Family Plot* (1976) were commercial and critical disappointments.

The Birds was the director's third adaptation of a Daphne DuMaurier story, following *Jamaica Inn* (1939) and *Rebecca* (1940), the latter his first film in America. It was planned to be an episode of his dramatic anthology series *Alfred Hitchcock Presents*, which alternated running on CBS and NBC twice from 1955 through 1965, but the costs involved in depicting the ambushes dissuaded "Hitch" from making it a TV episode in the 1950s.

In 1961 writer Evan Hunter received the assignment of taking the DuMaurier novella and re-fashioning it into a screenplay. (Richard Matheson was under consideration at one point for the job as well.) After reading Hunter's draft, Hitchcock had him remove extraneous scenes of Melanie with her father, as well as her shopping for clothes and looking for a hotel in Bodego Bay (an actual seaside community north of San Francisco). He then passed the script for review to Hume Cronyn, who in the 1940s had written two of Hitch's films (*Rope* and *Under Capricorn*) and acted in two others (*Shadow of a Doubt* and *Lifeboat*). Cronyn admired how the screenplay contrasted the pastoral seaside setting with the ambushes by the birds, but he said it needed more humor plus more vulnerability for Lydia, to show how she was worried about losing her son to any new woman in his life. (Coincidentally or not, Cronyn's wife Jessica Tandy co-starred as Lydia.)

Hitchcock sent the script along to British writer V.S. Pritchett, who thought it was superb, but warned about the lack of characterization for the principals. For example, Mitch was said to be a criminal lawyer, but there was little indication that he possessed a savvy mind, and the same could be said about mentioning Melanie's supposedly wild former life as an upscale prankster. He also cautioned that the opening was slow, but Hitchcock retained most of the first scenes.

"I believe it was Fellini who said, 'Hitchcock made them wait for the birds to come on. I wouldn't have the nerve to do that.' But I think it is a matter of figuring it out and then gradually, one bird just hitting the girl. And the gradual slow buildup," the director told the American Film Institute of his plans with *The Birds*.

Hitchcock had spotted Tippi Hedren in a TV commercial and considered her for the role of Melanie. He had several meetings with the inexperienced actress where he dictated how she should play her character. Her rather flat performance is cited by most critics as the movie's weak link, with some suggesting that if Hitchcock had employed, say, Eva Marie Saint as Melanie, the byplay between the character and Mitch probably would have worked better.

As was typical for Hitchcock, almost all of the film was storyboarded. Birds were matted into the movie after principal photography had ended, with rear projection used in close-ups. Hitchcock insisting on no musical score, which added to the suspense.

One of 1963's top moneymakers, *The Birds* received one Oscar nomination, for Special Visual Effects regarding the matte process used to give the illusion of hundreds of birds on screen at one time. It lost to *Cleopatra*.

NBC cut out much of the footage of birds attacking when the film arrived on TV, leaving only the pained expressions of the victims intact. Also gone was the gruesome shot of farmer Fawcett with his eyes plucked out, leaving his corpse with two gaping eyeholes. (This was enough to get the film rated PG-13 when it came out on DVD.)

The network promoted *The Birds* so much that it made the film an appealing alternative to the dying western series *The Iron Horse* on ABC and the then-struggling detective drama *Mannix* on CBS. One viewer wrote to *TV Guide* that when the NBC peacock mascot appeared before the movie, the bird "seemed to have a wide grin on his face." The movie easily finished as the highest-rated show of the week.

Behind *The Birds*, the second-highest rated Hitchcock film on network TV was *North By Northwest*, which aired on CBS Friday, Sept. 29, 1967, and pulled down a 27.8/50. Finishing third was *Marnie*, which ran on NBC Saturday, Nov. 4, 1967, and earned a 26.4/47. (CBS bought *Psycho* to air in the fall of 1966, but as affiliates thought it was too violent even when edited, it did not get a network showing.)

NBC Saturday Night at the Movies was so dominant in the 1967-1968 season that the series ended at #10, the first time ever a motion picture series finished that high. It was rather appropriate, being that it was the first series to show motion pictures made after 1948 on network television when it began on Sept. 23, 1961. *The Birds* and *Marnie* were the highest and third-highest rated weekly entries on the series that season, with *The Thrill of It All*, which aired Nov. 25, 1967 with a 26.7/46, finishing between them.

The network repeated the film on Saturday, March 8, 1969, where it earned a strong 24.0/40.

NBC Saturday Night at the Movies remained on the schedule until Sept. 3, 1978. No other movie that aired on NBC Saturday surpassed the ratings of the debut of *The Birds*, and that includes part one of *The Godfather* (see 27).

On March 14, 1994, Hedren appeared as a supporting character — not Melanie Daniels — in *The Birds II: Lands End*, a 90-minute Showtime movie which despite its title was a remake rather than a sequel. Filmed in and around Wilmington, North Carolina, this version was crass in all departments, and director Rick Rosenthal removed his name from it.

Meanwhile, *The Birds* remains a fan favorite, with the American Film Institute ranking it #7 in its "100 Years ... 100 Thrills" survey of exciting movies in 2001. There has been talk of a full-blown theatrical remake, in the future.

---

34 — *True Grit*

Nov. 12, 1972 (*ABC Sunday Night Movie*; first released theatrically in 1969). **Rating:** 38.9. **Share:** 63.

Aired on ABC Sunday 9–11 P.M. Eastern and Pacific, 8–10 P.M. Central

Competition: *The New Dick Van Dyke Show* and *Mannix* on CBS; *The Trouble with People* (special) and *Night Gallery* on NBC

Cast: John Wayne (Reuben J. "Rooster" Cogburn), Kim Darby (Mattie Ross), Glen Campbell (La Beouf), Robert Duvall ("Lucky" Ned Pepper), Jeremy Slate (Emmett Quincy), Dennis Hopper (Moon), Jeff Corey (Tom Chaney). **Crew:** Hal B. Wallis (producer), Henry Hathaway (director), Marguerite Roberts (writer).

Synopsis. Impetuous, precocious tomboy Mattie pursues Tom Chaney, who killed her father in Texas. She learns that Tom has escaped to Indian territory, and that eyepatch-wearing, semi-drunk Rooster Cogburn is the meanest U.S. marshal patrolling the area. She piques his interest by telling him that Tom is in cahoots with Cogburn's nemesis "Lucky" Ned Pepper. But La Beouf, a Texas Rangers sergeant who has been tracking Tom for four months, offers Cogburn a reward bigger than Mattie's from the family of a state Senator that Tom killed.

A determined Mattie tags along with La Beouf and Cogburn. The trio find a hideout where outlaws Quincy and Moon tell of Ned's planned rendezvous before they are killed. Ned and his gang arrive, but Ned escapes the trio's ambush. They continue onward. At a stop, Mattie goes to fetch water and runs into Tom. She wounds him, but he abducts her. Ned and his posse join them, and he tells Cogburn and La Beouf he will kill her unless they leave.

The two pretend to go, then La Beouf rescues Mattie while Cogburn kills Ned's three men. Ned nearly kills Cogburn, but La Beouf gets him in his gunsights and shoots him dead. Tom hits La Beouf in the head and Mattie falls into a pit full of snakes. Cogburn kills Tom. A rattlesnake bites Mattie, and he goes down to save her. La Beouf pulls both up with his horse before dying. Cogburn gets her treated safely. He accepts Mattie's grateful offer of a burial plot before riding away.

Backstory. Best known today as the movie that finally won John Wayne an Oscar, *True Grit* began its life as a serialized story in *The Saturday Evening Post* in 1968 before its writer, Charles Portis, modified it into a novel. Veteran film producer Hal B. Wallis won the rights to put it on screen, but he said it was an unusual process.

"When the book came out, the agent sent seven copies of galleys to seven different people in Hollywood," Wallis told the American Film Institute in 1974. "I got one. The response was so great that he sent out a wire stating he would send a telegram on a certain day, giving the price, and if more than one company met the price, the author reserved the right to choose whom he wanted to have it." Wallis believed Portis picked him among the qualifying applicants because of his previous successful film westerns. (Wayne's company Batjac Productions was one of the losers to Wallis in the bidding war for movie rights to *True Grit.*)

Wallis assigned Marguerite Roberts to adapt the property, without telling her he had John Wayne set to star. Roberts was blacklisted for nearly a decade after refusing to name names before the House Un-American Activities Committee in 1952, and she was worried about the reaction of Wayne, a conservative who had supported the blacklist, when he learned she wrote it.

But Wayne loved her work, calling it the best-written script he had seen in years, and accepted the role. Roberts did a fine adaptation, focusing on the book's themes while improving on some plot points (for example, in the novel, La Beouf simply disappears without explanation). Her script earned a Writers Guild of America nomination.

Wayne agreed to put on an eyepatch; crewman Luster Bayless used a wire screen covered with gauze painted black to give "The Duke" the ability to see through it and not have his vision impaired. There was some concern about Wayne's physical condition (he was overweight and had a lung re-

moved a few years earlier), but director Henry Hathaway wisely knew how to work around him. Some beautiful outdoor scenery was captured by cinematographer Lucien Ballard, although the mountains shown behind Mattie at home in Fort Smith, Arkansas, were obviously out of place to anyone familiar with the Razorback State's geography.

Hathaway suggested Kim Darby for the female lead after the original pick, Mia Farrow, drove Wallis crazy with her contractual demands. The director had seen Darby guest on a two-part *Gunsmoke* episode and thought she would be perfect as the plucky heroine. She was 21 when she played 14-year-old Mattie and happy to do the role. "I read the book and, well, I liked her a lot, you know?" Darby said on the movie's 2007 DVD commentary. "I mean, she was her own person and was authentic and was passionate, strong."

Darby's dedication to the source and the way it reflected how people in the 1880s spoke without contractions and other patterns rankled Wayne, according to Jeremy Slate on the same DVD commentary. "I figured while we were making the movie that several times, Duke was somewhat puzzled by Kim Darby. He was sort of like, 'What's she trying to do?' You know, that kind of attitude. Well, Kim was doing [it] the way the book was written, you know. She was doing that language, and Duke wasn't used to that."

To sell to a youth audience, Wallis added popular singer Glen Campbell as La Beouf. (Originally he wanted Elvis Presley, but the latter's controlling manager Col. Tom Parker wanted too much money.) Hathaway thought Campbell was a wooden actor but reluctantly accepted him. Wayne agreed to do two relatively rare TV guest shots on *The Glen Campbell Goodtime Hour* in 1969 and 1971 as a show of appreciation for his work.

Campbell also sang the title tune, which earned the film's only other Oscar nomination for Best Song; the record made the top 40. Its lyrics were by Don Black and its music was by Elmer Bernstein, who contributed his traditionally rousing score for *True Grit* too.

Filmed in the summer of 1968, the movie was a financial success when released a year later. When it came out, supporting cast member Dennis Hopper could be seen in movie theaters at the same time in the far different lead role of a hippie in *Easy Rider.*

Although it was rated G (after having been re-edited after failing to receive the family-friendly rating its first go-round), there were elements in

True Grit that did not survive the ABC censor's scissors, at least in terms of language. La Beouf called one character a bastard, while Rooster called Ned a son of a bitch before their final shootout. There was also a scene involving a public hanging of four men that may have been edited somewhat, particularly seeing their twitching legs once the platform beneath them fell out. (Jay Silverheels, better known as faithful Indian sidekick Tonto on TV's *The Lone Ranger* [1950–1957], played one of the hanged men.)

Wayne's well-remembered recent Oscar win (see 13 — The Academy Awards) drew viewers to watch the movie's TV debut, as did some weak programming decisions by the other networks. The NBC competition was a collection of five sketches written by Neil Simon that replaced *The NBC Sunday Mystery Movie*. It was the highest-rated movie featuring Wayne on television, with the runner-up being *McLintock!* on CBS Nov. 3, 1967 (31.2/54). It even outperformed Wayne's high-rated special from two years earlier, *John Wayne: Swing Out Sweet Land* (see 39). ABC reran *True Grit* on Jan. 13, 1974 (24.1, 36), Oct. 11, 1974 (15.3/26), and Sept. 2, 1979 (14.2/28). The last airing was a poignant one: Wayne had died three months earlier.

Wallis reunited Darby and Campbell in *Norwood* (1970), again based on a Charles Portis novel and adapted by Roberts; it was a flop with critics and the public. (It scored a so-so 15.4/28 when it premiered on ABC on April 19, 1975.) The producer then tried to recapture the magic with a *True Grit* sequel, 1975's *Rooster Cogburn*, teaming Wayne with Katharine Hepburn, but it suffered the same fate as *Norwood*. When it debuted on NBC Sept. 17, 1977, however, it performed quite well, with a 20.3/39.

On May 19, 1978, ABC presented the tele-movie-series pilot *True Grit (A Further Adventure)*, with Warren Oates as Rooster and Lisa Pelikan as Mattie. Its unimpressive numbers of 11.6/22 nixed any potential for it to become a regular series. In 2010, directors Joel and Ethan Coen filmed an excellent, Oscar-nominated remake with Jeff Bridges as Rooster and Matt Damon as La Beouf.

33 — *Carol & Company*

Feb. 24, 1963 (comedy special). **Rating:** 38.9. **Share:** n/a.

Aired on CBS Sunday 10–11 P.M. Eastern and Pacific, 9–10 P.M. Central

Competition: *The Voice of Firestone* and *Winston Churchill—The Valiant Years* on ABC; "The Problem with Water Is People" (news special) on NBC

Cast: Carol Burnett, Robert Preston, The Ernie Flatt Dancers, The Irwin Kostal Orchestra. **Crew:** Bob Banner (executive producer), Ernest Chambers (director), Mike Nichols (writer, credited under his birth name of Igor Peschkowsky).

Synopsis. Addressing a New York studio audience, Carol Burnett clears her throat in the opening monologue and says, "This is one of the very first times I get dressed up like a girl" and "I smell di-*vine*!" She recalls that when she was a child (just five years earlier), she and her cousin played Tarzan and Jane, and she always had to be the ape man. (She does her classic Tarzan "yodel" after saying this.) Her cousin also liked to portray Jeanette MacDonald, which leads Carol to bemoan in a comical torch song that "I Don't Want to Be Nelson" (Eddy). Six male dancers join her to be Nelson instead during the number.

Carol introduces her guest Robert Preston with leering comments. Making his entrance to "76 Trombones," the tune from his hit musical *The Music Man*, Preston tells her he wants to sing with her. This starts a manic round that includes "Row Row Row Your Boat," "Frere Jacques," "The Man on the Flying Trapeze" and more. Preston does a solo patter number recalling his stereotyped film roles.

Preston and Carol's main sketch is "Stereo," where a woman who has never been in a man's apartment hopes he will seduce her, but he is more fascinated with his a hi-fi system. Carol then performs a burlesque turn with the "Charwoman Strip" that includes the song "Let Me Entertain You" from the musical *Gypsy*. The ending number is the rousing "Just Can't Say Goodbye."

Backstory. Could *Carol & Company* be The Great Lost Carol Burnett Special? Consider this: It was not reviewed by *Variety* or *The New York Times*. She made no mention of it in either of her memoirs, *Once Upon a Time* (1986) or *This Time Together: Laughter and Reflection* (2010). Biographies on Burnett on A&E and public television have ignored it as well.

Yet it did exist, as I can attest to it from hearing an audiotape of the soundtrack. And there *was* a review of the special (after it ran) in *TV Guide*. Henry Harding commented, "Miss Burnett made the most of her opportunity ... Robert Preston helped make Carol's show a delight." There was a snippet of it in *Carol Burnett: The Special Years* on CBS on May 20, 1994, as well.

Finally, there was the Emmy nomination for Outstanding Program Achievement in the Field of Variety. Burnett won the Emmy for Outstanding Performance in a Variety or Musical Program or Series in part due to this special — and in the other part due to *Julie and Carol at Carnegie Hall,* her second TV special (it aired on CBS June 11, 1962). *Julie and Carol* is better remembered even thanks in part to Julie and Carol doing reunion specials thereafter, whereas there was none for *Carol and Company.* (*Julie and Carol at Carnegie Hall* also won the Emmy for Outstanding Program Achievement in the Field of Variety.)

Carol and Company, the first TV special starring Burnett, stemmed from when she announced on Feb. 13, 1962, that she would not be returning to *The Garry Moore Show.* Burnett had one of the most publicized mentoring relationships in television. While a struggling actress in New York City, she first performed a comic routine on *The Garry Moore Show* on Nov. 9, 1956, when it was a CBS weekday morning show. Moore loved her as did his audience, and she returned several times until he decided to end the series on June 27, 1958, to start a nighttime variety series.

Airing on CBS Tuesday nights starting Sept. 30, 1958, the new version of *The Garry Moore Show* struggled to find the right format as well as its audience during its first year. In midseason Bob Banner became executive producer and implemented changes. Martha Raye, set to guest star in an episode, fell sick one week in 1959. She withdrew on Sunday when the show was to air live on Tuesday. Banner tried to get Nanette Fabray as a replacement but she had previous work commitments. Then, at Moore's suggestion, he sought to hire Burnett, but CBS officials said no to that idea, that Burnett was not a name. When Moore held his ground and said it was either Burnett or they would not do that week's show, CBS acquiesced. Burnett was an immediate hit, which led to another guest shot. On Nov. 19, 1959, Burnett officially became a regular on *The Garry Moore Show.*

Burnett's appeal was that she had no shame in mugging as much as necessary to get a laugh, whether it was to make herself look homely or play a woman with a sex drive in overdrive once she saw a handsome eligible man. Her arrival on the show coincided with its increase in ratings; it peaked at #12 in the 1961-1962 season. Burnett gave much of the credit to Moore along with the show's writers. "If Garry has a very funny line in a sketch and he thinks it would be funnier if I said

it, he gives it to me.... Moreover, he kind of rations me to the public, and he's right," Burnett told Pete Martin in *The Saturday Evening Post.* "He doesn't use me to the point where the audience tires of me."

This strategy paid off during the 1961-1962 season, as his series won the Emmy for Outstanding Variety or Music Program, and Burnett was named Outstanding Performer in a Variety or Musical Program or Series. Unfortunately for Moore, by that time Burnett had announced that she would be leaving his show to consider other ventures. Her departure caused the show to slide in the ratings, as audiences were not as enthralled with her replacement Dorothy Loudon. Even though Moore voluntarily ended his program on June 14, 1964, the fact of the matter was that his new ABC competition, *The Fugitive* (see 9), was out-rating him during the final season.

Meanwhile, six months after saying she was leaving *Garry Moore,* Burnett signed a $1 million contract with CBS in August 1962 to do a series of specials for the network over the next decade. The first was *Carol and Company.* It pre-empted two series which usually made the top 15 in the 1962-1963 season, *Candid Camera* (which Banner also produced — see 66) and *What's My Line?* But it turned out to be far more popular than either as it finished #1 for the week. That development had to please Lipton Tea, the sponsor of the special, which employed George Fenneman introducing the commercials.

Burnett acquitted herself very well here, proving she could carry a show on her own. Some might think she pushes too hard to get the laugh, but the important thing is that she gets one, whether it involves unexpected squealing jags in the middle of a song or just delivering double entendres about Preston which were rather risqué for 1963 television.

The specials deal for Burnett lasted five more years. On March 22, 1966, CBS aired *Carol + 2* with Lucille Ball and Zero Mostel as her guests, and Burnett topped the ratings that week with her second-best performance, a solid 32.8. Burnett did another special with the *Carol and Company* title, with Rock Hudson, Frank Gorshin and Ken Berry, on Oct. 9, 1966, in the same Sunday 10-11 P.M. Eastern and Pacific slot, but it was not as popular.

The following year, Burnett followed through with an option in her contract to star in her own weekly variety series. *The Carol Burnett Show* ran on CBS from 1967-1978 with a great critical and popular reception. Not bad considering that Burnett had vowed she would never be tied to a series a few years earlier.

In 1991 Burnett starred in a NBC comedy anthology series titled *Carol and Company*, but it had no relation to the old specials. And though Robert Preston never appeared on Burnett's series, he did reunite with her professionally at least once: He competed against her on the TV game show *Password* on Jan. 9, 1964.

---

32 — *Danny Thomas Special: Wonderful World of Burlesque*

March 14, 1965 (special). **Rating:** 38.9. **Share:** n/a. Aired on NBC Sunday 9–10 P.M. Eastern and Pacific, 8–9 P.M. Central

Competition: *The Happy Thieves* (debut of 1962 theatrical movie) on ABC, *For the People* on CBS

Cast: Danny Thomas, Mickey Rooney, Jim Nabors, Lee Remick, Frank DeVol and His Orchestra. Cameo **Guests:** Frank Sinatra, Andy Griffith, Don Knotts, Sid Melton, Carl Reiner, Sheldon Leonard, Edie Adams, Dean Martin, Jack Benny. **Crew:** Danny Thomas (executive producer), George Schlatter (producer), Alan Handley (director), Coleman Jacoby, Arnie Rosen (writers), Marc Breaux, Dee Dee Wood (choreographers).

Synopsis. "People do not really know what old-time burlesque was like," Danny Thomas says in this special. Danny does the routines of comics like his idol, Yiddish-spouting Abe Reynolds. He then introduces guests Lee Remick, Mickey Rooney and Jim Nabors, and the show becomes the "Wonderful World of Burlesque."

Danny and Mickey do a song and dance, then come the chorus girls, joined by Remick singing. Next is a man-on-the-street sketch, with Danny meeting Sinatra, Griffith, Knotts, Melton and Reiner for jokes. Nabors sings in his fine, "regular" voice. A few more comic bits follow, alternating with songs by Remick, Nabors and Danny. The show's sponsors appear in the former: Sheldon Leonard pitches Dutch Masters while acting as a concessionaire in the aisles, and Edie Adams plays a nurse testing Danny as a stuntman for Timex watches. (Edie also appears in a separate commercial for Muriel Cigars.)

The show's centerpiece has Remick (as exotic dancer Bubbles LaMore) in court accused of indecency. Danny is the district attorney, Rooney is the judge and Nabors is the bailiff. Rowdiness

ensues, including the inevitable joke about the size of Danny's nose.

Danny appears in black tie with chorus girls, and Nabors, Remick and Rooney come out for a final bow and to sing goodbye.

Backstory. NBC had a pronounced case of "starlust," if you will, regarding comedian Danny Thomas. Having left the network in 1952 after being frustrated as one of the recurring hosts on the *All Star Revue* variety series, he created his own ABC sitcom, *Make Room for Daddy*, which became a huge hit when it moved to CBS to take over the slot previously held by *I Love Lucy*. *Make Room for Daddy* defeated everything NBC threw up against it, and the network was afraid it would have an even bigger impact if CBS employed the same tactic it used with *I Love Lucy* and reran it in daytime. Swallowing its pride, the network shelled out the unprecedented sum of $7 million for exclusive rights to repeat *Make Room for Daddy* starting in the fall of 1960, while the series remained on CBS nighttime as the *Danny Thomas Show*. *Make Room for Daddy* held its own on NBC daytime until its run there ended on March 26, 1965.

A year prior to that, Thomas announced he was ending the series after seven years of being a regular top 10 hit or thereabouts, because he and his staff had run out of storylines. With the popular star a free agent, NBC pounced, signing him to a deal to star in five variety specials in the 1964-1965 season. It was a testament to his popularity that all the specials were sold out to sponsors in advance of the season's start.

A curious event happened prior to the specials airing, however. CBS was losing badly in the ratings to NBC's *Bonanza* (see 20) on Sunday nights, so it planned to start running a half-hour series it would call *The Best of Danny Thomas* Sundays at 9 (62 episodes from the last two seasons that were not part of NBC's daytime package) in January 1965. But when Thomas pointed out to CBS that his special would pre-empt *Bonanza* and thus leave him competing with himself, the network backed off the plan, especially given how his production company had two big hits on the network at the time, *The Andy Griffith Show* (see 79) and *Gomer Pyle, U.S.M.C.* (see 55).

Thomas' first special was a revival of his old TV series: *The Danny Thomas TV Family Reunion* aired on Feb. 14, 1965, and received a very good rating of 27.4. For the next special, Thomas decided to revisit his early days in show business as a source for its humor. The result was *Danny Thomas Special: Wonderful World of Burlesque.*

Two of the guests were naturals: Nabors was starring in the aforementioned *Gomer Pyle, U.S.M.C.*, the hottest new show on TV. Rooney was born to vaudeville trooper Joe Yule and followed his dad in the act. "I saw him perform in my hometown when I was young," Thomas told his audience. The two did some good-natured self-deprecating banter, with Rooney telling Danny, "Three of my wives were taller than you! And one of them was prettier too!"

The revelation here to many viewers was Remick, previously best known as an intense dramatic actress in movies such as *Anatomy of a Murder* (1959) and *Days of Wine and Roses* (1962). She sang on Broadway in *Anyone Can Whistle* in 1964, but that musical was a flop, and she rarely had sung in public elsewhere. Looking spectacular in ornate costumes (including one risqué mermaid outfit with bikini top), Remick acquits herself well singing "By the Light of the Silvery Moon" on a crescent-shaped piece that hovered over the studio audience. Danny introduces her as "one of the most exciting women in show business," and she lives up to the billing.

In my opinion, the opening with Danny reminiscing about the old days was the weakest part of the show, but the audience ate it up. Much better done was the man-on-the-street segment, which included stars from Danny's production company (all from CBS, probably to NBC's chagrin), namely Griffith and Knotts from *The Andy Griffith Show* (see 79) and Carl Reiner from *The Dick Van Dyke Show* (see 59). Griffith and Knotts cross, one with umbrella open, the other with one closed. They look at each other and the sky, then they change the status of their umbrellas before walking off. Reiner appears as a cop threatening to arrest Nabors when he vocalizes in his "Gomer voice."

Best of all, Sinatra appears as a bum to do one-liners with Danny, then shows up to donate money to Nabors after hearing the latter massacre Sinatra's 1957 hit "All the Way." It's briskly handled, and one can see touches of the pace Schlatter would later fine-tune on *Rowan and Martin's Laugh-In* (see 53). Herbie Faye, formerly on *The Phil Silvers Show*, served as comedy consultant as well as a bit player in the special. *Wonderful World of Burlesque* received Emmy nominations for Outstanding Program Achievements in Entertainment and its writing. It won a statuette for technical direction.

Thomas did three more NBC specials on the "Burlesque" theme, on Dec. 8, 1965, Dec. 11, 1966, and Sept. 11, 1967; all were highly rated (e.g., a 32.7 for the 1966 one), but none performed as well as this special, even with big guest stars (Lucille Ball, Shirley Jones, Jerry Lewis and Jimmy Durante in the first, followed by Dean Martin, Bill Cosby and Mickey Rooney in the second).

The last special kicked off NBC's variety-anthology series *The Danny Thomas Hour*, which ran for a year and only did well with reunion specials of his *Make Room for Daddy* cast. It ended on June 10, 1968. As it appeared the public wanted to see him only in his old sitcom role, Thomas did a handful of specials before launching *Make Room for Granddaddy* on ABC on Sept. 23, 1970. But the revival sputtered out; its last episode ran on Sept. 2, 1971.

After *Make Room for Granddaddy* flopped, his TV career ebbed to the point where producers of the 1976 sitcom *The Practice* wanted him to audition for the lead role. He refused and won the job anyway, but it only ran from Jan. 30, 1976, through Jan. 26, 1977. Another one-year bomb for Thomas was ABC's *I'm a Big Girl Now* (Oct. 31, 1980, through July 24, 1981).

None of these failures can erase the legacy of Thomas as one of TV's best early comedians. This special shows his ability both to appreciate what he had learned and apply it successfully to a mass audience years later. He deserves congratulations for that.

---

31 — *The Poseidon Adventure*

Oct. 27, 1974 (*ABC Sunday Night Movie*; first released theatrically in 1972). **Rating:** 39.0. **Share:** 62.

Aired on ABC Sunday 9–11 P.M. Eastern and Pacific, 8–10 P.M. Central

Competition: *Kojak* (last half-hour) and *Mannix* on CBS; *Columbo* on NBC

Cast: Gene Hackman (the Rev. Frank Scott), Ernest Borgnine (Det. Lt. Mike Rogo), Red Buttons (James Martin), Carol Lynley (Nonnie Parry), Roddy McDowall (Acres), Stella Stevens (Linda Rogo), Shelley Winters (Belle Rosen), Jack Albertson (Manny Rosen), Pamela Sue Martin (Susan Shelby), Arthur O'Connell (Chaplain John), Eric Shea (Robin Shelby), Leslie Nielsen (Captain). **Crew:** Irwin Allen (producer–co-director), Ronald Neame (co-director), Stirling Silliphant, Wendell Mayes (writers).

Synopsis. As passengers celebrate New Year's Eve, the luxury liner S.S. *Poseidon*, bound from New York to Athens, is turned upside down by a tidal wave. Regrouping from the incident, nine people follow the advice of the Rev. Scott that the only way to survive the rising waters is to go to the upturned hull (where the metal is one inch thick) and hope rescuers can hear their cries for help. They are Mike, a cop who argues with the Rev. Scott; Linda, Mike's wife; Belle, an obese, spirited woman; Manny, her husband; Susan and Robin, a sister and brother planning to reunite with their parents on the mainland; Acres, a waiter on the ship; Nonnie, a singer whose brother died in the accident; and James, a middle-aged bachelor who befriends the younger Nonnie.

The group endures a hellish trek, losing three members along the way. The most poignant is when Belle expires from a heart attack after rescuing the Rev. Scott from drowning. When Linda falls to her death from an explosion, Mike unleashes his fury at the Rev. Scott for all the suffering they have witnessed. Shortly thereafter, the Rev. Scott loses his life. The stunned Manny, Susan, Robin, Nonnie and James follow new leader Mike to the hull, where they are saved. They are the tragedy's sole survivors.

Backstory. Any doubts that the "disaster movie" was here to stay following the success of *Airport* (see 16) were washed away by *The Poseidon Adventure.* Released in late 1972, it was 1973's biggest grossing film and sparked a wave of releases that had stars battling catastrophic elements to stay alive.

Apart from lead Gene Hackman, following his popular, Oscar-winning star turn in *The French Connection* (1971), there was little to suggest *The Poseidon Adventure* would be a hit. It was based on a 1969 novel by Paul Gallico that was not as much a runaway success as was Arthur Hailey's *Airport,* and producer Irwin Allen had been away from theatrical films for a decade, returning after a string of diminishingly successful science fiction TV series culminating with *Land of the Giants* on ABC (1968–1970).

Allen bought the novel and began casting. He put Ernest Borgnine and Red Buttons under contract, to be paid until filming began (Buttons took his part after Gene Wilder rejected it).

For the property's transfer to film, Allen enlisted writer Wendell Mayes, who asked Allen to replace him after a couple of rewrites. His successor, Stirling Silliphant, was delighted that Allen supplied his office with models of upside-down ship compartments to view for research. In his script, Silliphant emphasized the clash between the Rev. Scott's spirituality—and his struggles to accommodate it, as

he discussed with Chaplain John prior to the capsizing—and Mike Rogo's earthiness.

The real star was the special effects. The sequence depicting the ship turning upside down remains spectacular today. The filming went pretty well thanks to Allen's precautions, such as making sure that using a hydraulic lift to tilt the main ballroom set 45 degrees did not hurt stuntmen. However, there was at least one time where the camera crew ended up in the water when a set did not stop tilting as planned. In Ernest Borgnine's autobiography, the actor with more than 200 movie credits called *The Poseidon Adventure* "one of the most personally satisfying films I've made." He enjoyed talking about it as a guest on actual cruises, although he acknowledged at least one man didn't want to see the film on board!

The movie earned deservedly a Special Achievement Academy Award for Visual Effects, along with eight other Oscar nominations, for Supporting Actress (Shelley Winters, in her most endearing screen role), Art Direction, Cinematography, Costume Design, Film Editing, Music and Song ("The Morning After" by Al Kasha and Joel Hirschhorn, which became a #1 hit following its Oscar win). Twentieth Century–Fox wanted Irwin Allen to include a song in the movie, believing it would help spur ticket sales. He, Ronald Neame and Lionel Newman, the studio's musical director, met with Kasha and Hirschhorn, gave them a copy of the script and just one day to come up with a tune. While Allen was indifferent to "The Morning After," Neame said, "I believe it has something," and that led to hiring Maureen McGovern to sing it.

"'The Morning After' speaks of a common anxiety—that love affairs won't work beyond one night of sex," Kasha and Hirschhorn wrote in *If They Ask, You Can Write a Song.* "In an uncertain time, it can be read as an expression of hope, that tomorrow will be better, that national disillusionment will vanish." In the movie, Carol Lynley lipsyncs to McGovern's vocal as Nonnie (her musician brother) and their band practice the song for the New Year's Eve festivities, then reprise it during the party itself. (It's unintentionally funny seeing a black-tie crowd dance upbeat to it.) Nonetheless, it served the movie's theme very well, so it is not surprising that Kasha and Hirschhorn wrote "We May Never Love Like This Again" for Irwin Allen's next disaster film *The Towering Inferno* (1974)—and won the Best Song Oscar again. (But this time the record only cracked the top 20 on the pop charts, even with McGovern singing.)

The *Poseidon Adventure* was the quickest transfer of a film from theaters to TV since *Love Story* (see 17). ABC paid an unprecedented $3.2 million to run it once. This came after an auction 20th Century–Fox held with all three networks which started with ABC's bid of $2 million — the amount ABC paid for *Patton* (see 36). After the deal, Barry Diller, ABC's prime time vice-president, announced that the network would not participate in such auctions in the future.

Expectations were high that it would perform well, given its huge box office, the continuing popularity of disaster films and ABC's own track record. In the network's 1974 fall presentation special, announcer Ernie Anderson said, "ABC has presented the four most widely viewed movies in the history of television," as the names of *Airport, Love Story, True Grit* (see 34) and *Patton* came up in marquee lights. "ABC will present the spectacular to top them all — Irwin Allen's *The Poseidon Adventure.*"

The movie did not top them all, but it did finish in the middle of that quartet. What prevented it from reaching the summit was competition. NBC altered its rotation schedule for its weekly mystery movie series so that *Columbo,* the most popular element by far, aired its third episode of the season against the movie one week ahead of schedule.

The *Poseidon Adventure* is one of a few theatrical movies to air on ABC, CBS and NBC. CBS ran it on Nov. 4, 1978 (13.3/24), followed by NBC on May 6, 1979 (13.5/23). It then was sold to local TV stations. In New York City, independent station WPIX played it opposite the networks' Democratic convention on Aug. 11, 1980, and won the night in Manhattan with an impressive 15.1/27. Some might argue that the convention, where challenger Ted Kennedy never embraced winner Jimmy Carter (who lost his re-election bid to Republican Ronald Reagan three months later), was more of a tragedy than the movie itself.

The WPIX airing came a year after the sequel *Beyond the Poseidon Adventure* ran in movie theaters. More than one observer joked that they thought the ship would be turned right side up in it. Actually, it told of other survivors in the ship trying to get out through the open hull. Boring and uninvolving, the box office flop scored a so-so 16.0/25 when it debuted on ABC May 17, 1981.

Still, the impact of *The Poseidon Adventure* was so strong that it resulted in a rare double remake 30 years later, as a TV-movie on NBC in 2005 and a theatrical edition called *Poseidon* in 2006.

Neither was as popular as the original, which remains to many the ultimate "disaster movie," as proven by its inclusion in the American Film Institute listing it at #90 on its "100 Years ... 100 Thrills" survey in 2001.

30—*Jaws*

Nov. 4, 1979 (*ABC Sunday Night Movie*; first released theatrically in 1975). **Rating:** 39.1. **Share:** 57.

Aired on ABC Sunday 8:30–11:15 P.M. Eastern and Pacific, 7:30–10:15 P.M. Central

Competition: *One Day at a Time, Alice, The Jeffersons* and *Trapper John, M.D.* on CBS; *20,000 Leagues Under the Sea* (last half-hour; repeat of 1954 theatrical film) and *MacArthur* (second of two parts; 1977 theatrical film) on NBC

Cast: Roy Scheider (Martin Brody), Robert Shaw (Quint), Richard Dreyfuss (Matt Hooper), Lorraine Gary (Ellen Brody), Murray Hamilton (Mayor Larry Vaughn). **Crew:** Richard D. Zanuck, David Brown (producers), Steven Spielberg (director), Peter Benchley, Carl Gottlieb (writers).

Synopsis. Police chief Martin Brody wants to close the beach at Amity Island, New York, after a great white shark attacks and kills a swimmer. Mayor Vaughn overrules him, as the town relies on the upcoming July 4 celebration for tourism dollars. When the shark kills a boy on June 29, the town offers a $3,000 bounty. Grizzled fisherman Quint says he can catch and kill the shark for $10,000. His offer is ignored. Matt Hooper from the Oceanographic Institute arrives as boaters kill and bring back a tiger shark. An autopsy by Hooper finds it was not the killer. Vaughn ignores their pleas to close the beach, and a man is eaten alive. Vaughn then signs a contract hiring Quint.

Brody, Hooper and Quint set out aboard Quint's vessel the *Orca.* Seeing the shark is 25 feet long, Brody wants a bigger boat. He shoots a line attaching a barrel to the shark with rope but cannot reel it in. The shark rams the boat that night, attacks again the next morning, damaging the boat. Hooper goes down in a cage to shoot strychnine in the shark, but the shark busts the cage, and Hooper barely escapes. The shark destroys the boat and eats Quint before Brody shoves a compressed air tank into its mouth and shoots a bullet into it, blowing up the shark. Brody and Hooper swim back to shore using the barrels.

Backstory. A monster movie in more ways than one, *Jaws* established Steven Spielberg as a director of note in Hollywood, and eventually a household name. For a time, it was the most successful movie ever made. It even became part of the ride on the Universal Studios tour. Pretty impressive.

In 1964 author Peter Benchley read a story about a fisherman who caught a 4,550-pound shark off the coast of Long Island. In 1971 he submitted an outline for a shark novel to Doubleday and delivered the final draft to the publishing company two years later. The title was a last-minute one; after rejecting dozens of them, Benchley said in frustration to his editor that all they could seem to agree on was that the word "jaws" should be in the title.

Producers Richard D. Zanuck and David Brown bought the novel for development as a movie before it was published. When Spielberg met with Zanuck and Brown to discuss the final cut of his first feature film *The Sugarland Express* (1974), he noticed the unpublished galleys for *Jaws* on their secretary's desk. He asked to read it over the weekend, even though he thought it dealt with dental work(!). They told him they already had another director assigned to it.

"I just went nuts, especially the last 150 pages, which was the sea hunt for this great white shark," Spielberg said in *The Directors Take Three*. He told Zanuck and Brown that if the director dropped out of the project, he wanted to replace him. And he did.

Benchley adapted his novel into a screenplay, which Spielberg thought was good but not the film he wanted to make. Spielberg wrote his own version to get his vision into place, but he knew he was not a screenwriter. Zanuck and Brown enlisted Howard Sackler to do a rewrite. Spielberg thought it was more on the money.

With the looming possibility of a July 1974 strike by the Screen Actors Guild, Universal told the crew they had to finish filming by the end of June. Yet in the spring of 1974, the script was still not finalized. Spielberg invited his colleague, writer-actor Carl Gottlieb, to offer some comments. Hired first as an actor in a minor role in the film, Gottlieb suggested streamlining the story, making the characters more human and adding more tension. His critique led Spielberg to successfully lobby Zanuck and Brown to hire him as the project's last writer just prior to commencing shooting.

The rest of the creative team found that their plans to present a realistic shark on screen was more difficult than anticipated. Art director Joe Alves came up with a design for a mechanical model that was considered unfeasible by special effects experts. Then Bob Mattey came out of retirement to show how to build it.

Later dubbed "Bruce" (after Spielberg's attorney Bruce Ramer), the 12-ton replica took 15 men to operate and caused much trauma when put into action. The mechanical shark and two replicas kept breaking down during shooting, putting the production behind schedule (the film took more than 150 days to complete). It also exceeded its original budget by $2.5 million, a considerable amount in 1974. But the director used the difficulties with the shark to his advantage. "The film was actually scarier because the shark didn't work that well," Spielberg said. "With the absence of the shark I had just the ocean and the power of suggestion. I let the audience use their imaginations instead of always seeing the shark. I think that really ramped up the suspense of the picture tenfold."

For Quint, Lee Marvin said no, and Sterling Hayden wanted too much money, so Brown suggested Robert Shaw, who had done a marvelous job as the antagonist in Brown's last hit picture *The Sting* (1973). Shaw, also a playwright, contributed to the script, including one famous scene (his description of the USS *Indianapolis* tragedy) which he filmed both drunk and sober, with the final version on screen being a combination of both takes (now that's acting!).

On June 21, 1974, Benchley joined the cast on location (Martha's Vineyard) to play a bit part as a TV reporter. After his scenes, all that was left to film was the mechanical shark, and that was problematic. The saltwater, algae and seaweed gummed up the mechanics and caused it to malfunction more often than anticipated; it also had to be washed and repainted every night. "Everything that could go wrong with a shark went wrong," Brown said in the documentary *The Making of Jaws*.

On March 26, 1975, a sneak preview in Dallas went so well that Universal decided to open it wide. The picture became a smash hit, and effects of *Jaws* on pop culture during its first year of release were myriad: spoofs on TV (Chevy Chase played the "land shark" on *Saturday Night Live*), imitation movies and much more. On the radio, John Williams' "Theme from *Jaws*" was an unlikely top 40 in 1975. *Jaws* won Oscars for best sound, original score and film editing, but lost Best Picture to *One Flew Over the Cuckoo's Nest*.

After its hit debut, ABC repeated *Jaws* on Oct. 5, 1980 (21.9/33). It ran the 1978 sequel *Jaws 2* on Feb. 15, 1981 (20.9/31).

Jaws succeeds because it combines shocks with lots of effective humor, like when Matt Hooper flinches when viewing the remains of the first victim and when a Louisiana license plate is taken out from the tiger shark's digestive system during the autopsy. The biggest laugh, "We're going to need a bigger boat," was a Roy Scheider improvisation. It's great fun now as it was in 1975.

29 — *Family Ties*

Jan. 22, 1987 ("Higher Love"). **Rating:** 39.2. **Share:** 53.

Aired on NBC Thursday 8:30–9 P.M. Eastern and Pacific, 7:30–8 P.M. Central

Competition: *Our World* on ABC, *Shell Game* on CBS

Cast: Meredith Baxter Birney (Elyse Keaton), Michael Gross (Steven Keaton), Michael J. Fox (Alex P. Keaton), Justine Bateman (Mallory Keaton), Tina Yothers (Jennifer Keaton), Brian Bonsall (Andrew "Andy" Keaton), Marc Price (Irwin "Skippy" Handelman), Scott Valentine (Nick Moore). **Guests:** Jonathan Emerson (Colin Spencer), Penelope Ann Miller (Joyce), Chad McCann (Delivery Boy). **Crew:** Gary David Goldberg (creator–executive producer), Alan Uger (supervising producer), Marc Lawrence (producer), Debbie Allen (director), Susan Borowitz (executive story editor–writer).

Synopsis. College student Mallory want to impress her fellow poetry reading class members who are visiting her family's house, but her smart-alecky older brother Alex hinders her efforts with his comments. The group leader Colin Spencer, a graduate student in English literature, considers Mallory his best pupil, even though her critiques of poems are rather shallow ("It's really neat, but it's really sad" she says of one poem). That was at least better than Skippy, her friend and classmate, who has a problem with poems not rhyming. Colin asks Mallory out; she has a biker boyfriend, Nick, but his uncouth behavior makes her question staying with him. Ever-helpful Alex tells her sister to dump both of them and start new in the morning.

Mallory confesses to Nick that she is thinking about dating Colin. Joyce, Mallory's classmate, warns her that Colin woos a freshman girl and then drops her every year—as he did with her. Colin runs true to form, so Mallory leaves him in a huff. Mallory tells her mother Elyse how upset she is that she was feeling appreciated intellectually only to discover Colin's ulterior motives. Elyse urges Mallory not to give up her new interest in poetry just because of Colin. Mallory agrees, then calls Nick to go out to pick up some tacos.

Backstory. *Family Ties* is best remembered as the series that introduced the charming actor Michael J. Fox. But the initial emphasis of this family sitcom was on the liberal parents, Alyse and Steven Keaton, as they coped with their differences with their offspring, particularly their eldest son, the very conservative Alex. But fate—and talent—have a funny way of changing plans for any TV series.

Originally creator Gary David Goldberg thought he had a great actor to portray Alex. But Matthew Broderick preferred to stay in New York rather than go to Hollywood, so Goldberg auditioned others. The first person he saw was Fox, an actor from Canada with few credits in America. Goldberg was not impressed by Fox's audition, but Goldberg's casting director, Judith Weiner, saw something in it and implored him to ask the actor to read again. He refused and looked at other actors until Weiner finally convinced him to try Fox again.

The second audition was a winner, and Goldberg hired Fox—or rather, he attempted to hire Fox. The actor was so poor he could not afford a home phone, so he checked in with his agent by phone from a chicken restaurant instead. Fox was nearly ready to move back to Canada before winning the role of Alex.

CBS programming head Harvey Shephard turned down the series based on the script, telling Goldberg that both families and comedies were dead on TV in 1982. But NBC Entertainment president Brandon Tartikoff loved everything about the series' concept—except for Fox as Keaton. Tartikoff wanted him replaced, thinking he was too short and did not have the kind of face that would appear on a lunch box. Yet Goldberg insisted on the man he once rejected for the role, and Tartikoff relented.

Then, to everyone's surprise, audience research and reaction indicated that Keaton was the show's breakout character. More stories began to revolve around him—although in later seasons, other members of the family could take the spotlight, such as this one featuring Mallory, the under-achieving, often ditzy daughter. (Jennifer, the younger daughter, managed for the most part to stay out of those skirmishes between her brother and sister.)

The series started out slowly in the ratings—actually, almost all series on NBC were doing poorly in the dark days of 1982. NBC switched *Family Ties'* time slot twice in its first season, which did not help matters. But in 1983-1984, following yet two more changes on the lineup, it eventually rose to be a fairly strong number two in its time slot against *Magnum, P.I.* on CBS, even though it just ranked #42.

Then, at the start of the 1984-1985 season, NBC moved it back 30 minutes to follow another family sitcom, *The Cosby Show* (see 22). The pairing was very beneficial for both in the ratings; *Family Ties* was #5 that season. The series stayed in the top 10 the following two seasons as well.

When Meredith Baxter became pregnant, so did her character Elyse in the 1984-1985 season. Steve and Elyse's son Andrew appeared as a four-year-old in this season, in which Alex engaged in a battle for control over his little brother's political beliefs with his parents.

Luckily for the portrayer of Andrew, Brian Bonsall, the first on-site, employer-supported day-care center in the entertainment industry had been created by Goldberg at Paramount Studios; this allowed Bonsall a chance to enjoy childhood away from the show. Goldberg and his wife had been involved in day-care centers since their days in Berkeley, California, in 1972. When Goldberg negotiated a new contract with Paramount, he insisted the studio provide a state-of-the-art day-care arena and a basketball court.

"Those were the two things I wanted most in the world," Goldberg told Natalie Gittlesen in *McCalls* in 1987. The day-care center accommodated Baxter's child as well as those of several other actors and actresses on the lot, such as Rhea Perlman on *Cheers* (see 10). It helped cement *Family Ties'* reputation as one of the friendliest sets in Hollywood.

Family Ties also was considered one of the best-written family sitcoms, but you might not guess that from this lesser outing. Mallory is gullible enough to think her professor likes her only as a student, but his motives are transparent to the viewer. It's a tired situation and none too funny in execution.

The subplot in this episode is extremely trivial: Andy wants a dog, but his parents make him compromise and get a fish for a pet instead. When Andy gets a second fish for his bowl, he is not impressed until the new fish eats the old one. It's a waste of lines and time for Michael Gross and Tina Yothers in particular. And as for the character of Skippy, the stupid family friend who loves Mallory but always said or did something idiotic to

prevent them from clicking as a couple, the less said the better. Despite these deficiencies, this episode finished #2 for the week behind its lead-in, *The Cosby Show*.

There were two Emmy wins for *Family Ties* this season (Fox for best actor and for Goldberg and Alan Uger for writing of another episode). Fox also claimed statuettes as best actor in 1986 and 1988. The series had 19 Emmy nominations total, including five for Fox alone (the first time for supporting actor, in 1985) and four consecutive years for best comedy (1984–1987).

Family Ties' high ratings and Emmy nominations fell off considerably the next year as NBC switched its slot to allow a spin-off of *The Cosby Show*, *A Different World*, to follow its parent series. Now airing Sunday nights at 8 P.M. Eastern and Pacific, *Family Ties* sunk down to #17 while its competition on CBS, *Murder, She Wrote*, topped it at #9 for the season. *Family Ties* wrapped up production the next season and aired its last show Sept. 17, 1989.

Since then, times have been rather eventful for the *Family Ties* cast. Fox has been coping with Parkinson's disease since 1991, and Baxter came out as a lesbian in 2009, while she was a grandmother. Fox, Baxter, Yothers, Gross and Justine Bateman reunited on *The Today Show* on Feb. 7, 2008, to promote Goldberg's memoirs. It was a warm occasion, even though there was a sad note. When asked if *Family Ties* could be on network TV today, Goldberg responded, "I would say no, because I don't think the network executives are smart enough to put it on and give it the kind of attention it would need to stay on."

28 — Michael Jackson Talks to ... Oprah

Feb. 10, 1993 (interview special). **Rating:** 39.3. **Share:** 56.

Aired on ABC Wednesday 9:30–11 P.M. Eastern and Pacific (tape delay for latter), 8:30–10 P.M. Central

Competition: *In the Heat of the Night* (second half-hour of 60-minute episode) and *48 Hours* on CBS; *Melrose Place* (second half-hour of 60-minute episode) on Fox; *Homicide* (second half-hour of 60-minute episode) and *Law & Order* on NBC

Cast: Oprah Winfrey, Michael Jackson. **Crew:** Oprah Winfrey (executive producer), Debra Di Maio (producer), Wendy Roth (coordinating producer), Roger Goodman (director).

Synopsis. In his first live TV interview in 14 years, music superstar Michael Jackson opens up his house to Oprah Winfrey to address a wide variety of topics without any restrictions, as Winfrey notes at the outset. The two talk in the living room for the first half of the show, with the smoke alarm going off at one point. That prompted a commercial break; when the show returned, Winfrey informed viewers that the heat from all the TV lights caused the ruckus.

Around the halfway point, another entertainment icon, Elizabeth Taylor, appears to supply a few comments about why she considers Jackson a friend. "He is the least weird man I've ever known," she tells Winfrey as Jackson listens stoically. She says they bonded because they both became stars when they were children and share experiences that way, and she emphasizes that he is a caring and generous person.

After that, Jackson and Winfrey tour the grounds of his estate, including his movie theater with seats and a stage, where Jackson performs his moonwalk dance. As the show winds down, Oprah asks him how he wants to be known. "I just simply want to be loved wherever I go, all over the world, because I love people of all races from my heart, with true affection," he says. After agreeing with Winfrey that the interview was fun, the two go outside for a ride on the Ferris wheel on Jackson's property as the credits roll.

Backstory. How very fitting that the most extensive interview by arguably the most successful and best known black male entertainer of the 20th century should be conducted by the female equivalent. Michael Jackson had been in front of the public much longer than Oprah Winfrey by 1993, having his first #1 hit, "I Want You Back," in 1970 with his brothers as part of the Jackson 5. In contrast, Winfrey became a household name later (her daily talk show went on local TV stations in 1986 followed by worldwide distribution) by shrewdly expanding her empire into other entertainment venues. It was a meeting of giant equals.

For her part, Winfrey was thrilled to have the exclusive. "Michael Jackson has always been at the top of my list of people I am most interested in interviewing," she told *Jet* magazine. "The excitement of this interview being live and unedited is certainly a special event for me and all of Michael's fans." She and Jackson agreed that doing it live would work best for both of them.

Although there was no official reason given for his decision to break his silence, many entertainment industry observers believed that Jackson was disappointed that his album *Dangerous*, released in late 1991, was losing its popularity quicker than had his two previous best sellers, *Thriller* (which stayed on the chart from late 1982 through 1985) and *Bad* (which had a chart stay of nearly two years, from 1987 through 1989). By putting his face before the general public, he hoped to boost those numbers.

The special included the world premiere of Jackson's newest video for "Give In to Me," a song he recorded with hard rock guitarist Slash, who also appeared in the clip. That song was not released as a single in North America in order to prompt more album sales of *Dangerous*, on which it appeared. (It did become a huge hit as a release overseas for Jackson, however.)

Winfrey asked Jackson about the challenge of creating a new album every few years with hopes that it will be a hit in the face of his immense previous successes. "It does make it harder each time," he acknowledged.

The interview occurred at Jackson's Neverland Valley Ranch in Santa Ynez Valley, on the outskirts of Santa Barbara. The show began with roughly three minutes of clips of TV appearances by Jackson before he walked into his living room (his 1982 #1 hit "Billie Jean" playing in the background), kissed Winfrey and said, "I'm not nervous. I never get nervous."

Winfrey's initial round of questions focused on Jackson's personal life. He acknowledged that he had been lonely since he was young. Suzanne de Passe, former creative director for Motown, confirmed that in a taped interview seen on the show: she said that Michael did not have a real childhood and now compensated by having kids around him all the time.

Jackson said he was not jealous of his sister Janet's success in the music world and that he was on good relations with everyone, although he said he had not read his sister LaToya's recent book that made unflattering statements about his clan. Above all else, Jackson emphasized that he considered his mother perfection.

Other insights from the special included the following:
• He confirmed that his father beat him and that he remained scared of him even as an adult. Describing their present relationship, he said, "I love my father, but I don't know him."
• He hated his press coverage and felt it was full of lies.
• He dismissed notions that he bought an oxygen chamber, wanted to buy the bones of the Ele-

phant Man or demanded to be the sole entertainer at the presidential inauguration of Bill Clinton.

• Regarding the reason why he grabbed his crotch in his performances, which upset many parents whose children were his fans, Jackson said, "It's the music that does it — I'm slave to the rhythm." He apologized to anyone who was offended by it and said it was instinctual.

• He claimed he dated Brooke Shields and that they usually stayed at his home. He said he had been in love with another woman before her.

• He refused to say whether he was a virgin, but he said he did plan to raise a family.

• When showing the beds at his house where visiting children could sleep, he stressed that they were sick and needed them to rest there.

• He strongly denied that he wanted a Caucasian boy to play him in his 1984 Pepsi commercial or that he bleached his skin. He said his pigmentation lightened after he recorded *Thriller* and said he inherited the problem from his father's side. ("I am proud to be a black American," he says, later adding, "When people make up stories that I don't want to be who I am, it hurts me.")

• As for his plastic surgery operations, "You could count on two fingers."

All in all, Winfrey solicited a fairly substantial number of comments from Jackson about rumors and issues surrounding him professionally as well as personally. One could argue that there should have been more follow-ups on certain topics, but that is not Winfrey's style, which probably is why Jackson went with her for the interview.

Oprah promoted the special that day on her afternoon show. The result was TV's highest-rated entertainment program since *The Cosby Show* (see 22) six years earlier. An estimated 90 million people viewed it worldwide. After the show aired, ABC's Los Angeles affiliate KABC-TV devoted its entire newscast (except for weather and sports segments) to following up the interview. For that effort, they scored huge local numbers of 32.5/62. The show received Emmy nominations for informational special, lighting direction and technical direction. It pre-empted *Coach* and *Going to Extremes*. In a certain sense, this was the last TV hurrah for Jackson. He died unexpected on June 25, 2009, at age 50. Much of the world mourned his passing.

Reflecting on the special following Jackson's death, Oprah said on her Sept. 16, 2009, show, "It was the most exciting interview I had ever done.... What I remember about Michael the most is that he was a person who was passionate about life. He was really passionate about his work

... and [passionate about] his desire to try to be a good force in the world."

27 — *The Godfather*

Nov. 18, 1974 (second of two parts; first released theatrically in 1972). **Rating:** 39.4. **Share:** 57.
Aired on NBC Monday 9–11 P.M. Eastern and Pacific, 8–10 P.M. Central
Competition: *Monday Night Football* (Kansas City Chiefs vs. Denver Broncos) on ABC; *Maude, Rhoda* and *Medical Center* on CBS
Cast: Marlon Brando (Vito Corleone), Al Pacino (Michael), James Caan (Sonny), Richard Castellano (Clemenza), Robert Duvall (Tom Hagen), Sterling Hayden (Capt. McCluskey), John Marley (Jack Woltz), Richard Conte (Barzini), Al Lettieri (Sollozzo), Diane Keaton (Kay Adams), Abe Vigoda (Tessio), Talia Shire (Connie), John Cazale (Fredo), Rudy Bond (Cuneo), Al Martino (Johnny Fontane). **Crew:** Albert S. Ruddy (producer), Francis Ford Coppola (director), Mario Puzo, Francis Ford Coppola (writers).

Synopsis. At his daughter Connie's wedding reception in 1945, mob boss Vito Corleone, assisted by his sons, Fredo and Sonny, and his lawyer, Tom Hagen, listens to requests for help, such as singer Johnny Fontane wanting a movie role. Hagen tells producer Jack Woltz to hire Fontane. When Woltz refuses, he wakes up in bed next to his prize horse's cut off head. Kay Adams, dating Vito's other son Michael, is appalled by the mob activities, but Michael assures her that he does not participate in them.

Gunmen shoot at Vito while Hagen is held hostage by Sollozzo, who orchestrated the attack. Sonny enlists the help of Clemenza and Tessio to retaliate. Police Capt. McCluskey, suspicious of the hospitalized Vito, sets up a meeting with Michael and Sollozzo at a Bronx restaurant, where a nervous Michael kills both men. Michael flees to Italy for safety while a mob war breaks out.

Sonny beats up Connie's abusive husband, then Sonny is shot to death at a toll booth. Vito meets with other mob family leaders, including co-organizer Barzini, to call a truce. Vito brings Michael home, and he weds Kay while getting more involved in the family business, as Vito is aging and Fredo is weak. When Vito dies, Michael has men kill Barzini and his partner, Cuneo, who were moving in on the Corleones' turf. After attending the baptism of Connie's son, Michael has Connie's husband killed. To Kay's horror, she realizes that Michael has become his family's new godfather.

Backstory. Author Mario Puzo took the suggestion of an editor of his second book, *The Fortunate Pilgrim* (1965), and wrote a ten-page outline about the world of organized crime that he called *Mafia*. After getting a deal for his proposal, Puzo wrote a few chapters that impressed Paramount enough to buy the future movie rights in 1967. However, the studio did not plan to produce it until 1970, when it already was a million-selling novel for several months.

Puzo wrote a first draft screenplay that year, paring down some 300 pages from the novel and setting it in contemporary times. Meanwhile, 12 directors turned down the chance to handle the film adaptation, mainly due to worries of romanticizing the Mafia. In fact, the Italian-American Civil Rights League called the proposed movie defamatory, and many legislators joined them. Producer Al Ruddy met with the group and made some concessions to quell their anger. For example, unlike the book, the words "Mafia" and "Cosa Nostra" do not appear in the film, and he promised to hire some League members as extras.

When Francis Ford Coppola received the directing assignment, he hated Puzo's script, particularly the modernization of the setting. He proposed to rewrite and swap halves of it with Puzo to edit (Coppola already had worked on the script for *Patton*—see 36).

Coppola first rejected the book as sleazy, but after his pal, producer George Lucas, urged him to look it over again, Coppola found a metaphor in the Corleones' growth along with capitalism in America. He took the novel, sliced out the pages and pasted each one on a larger notebook page. With that system, he made notes on each page on what to emphasize and delete, broke down the scenes for the movie, and so on.

Puzo and Coppola readied two more versions of the script in March 1971. Production began at the end of the month on location in New York City. It finished three months later, but Coppola was unable during postproduction to finish it in time for a Christmas 1971 release, which added to the tension between himself and Paramount Pictures production head Robert Evans. (Coppola and Evans constantly fought during production and afterwards, with Coppola threatened with dismissal from the film five times. Even the casting of non–Italian Marlon Brando in the lead prompted fights.)

When *The Godfather* opened on March 15, 1972 in New York, raves followed, as did huge box office (it remains one of the all-time moneymakers when prices are adjusted for inflation). It collected three Oscars out of ten nominations, for Best Picture, Actor (Brando) and Screenplay. Other categories where it contended were Supporting Actor (James Caan, Robert Duvall and Al Pacino), Director, Sound, Film Editing and Costume Design.

Coppola wanted Italian composer Nina Rota to do the score; Evans reluctantly okayed Rota after favoring Henry Mancini. But after hearing it, Evans demanded it be taken out. A private test showing with members of the general public showed they liked it, so it stayed. Rota earned an Oscar nomination for his score, but he was disqualified when it was learned that what became known as "Love Theme from *The Godfather*" consisted of music he had written for the Italian film *Fortunella*. However, that piece of Rota's music, also known as "Speak Softly Love," became a hit, but not for Al Martino, who barely cracked the Hot 100 with his version. It was Andy Williams who made it to the top 40 with the song in 1972.

In July 1974, NBC announced it had paid $10 million for one showing of the film and planned to run it in a few months. The price was unprecedented and designed as a loss leader for the network, even though NBC wanted — and received — $225,000 per minute for ads for 28 minutes of the four-hour presentation, which would gross the network more than $6 million. Paramount agreed to the deal not just for the large payout, but also because it would allow the studio to promote the sequel *The Godfather Part II*, coming out in theaters on Dec. 17, 1974.

To make the R-rated film acceptable for network TV, NBC's Standards and Practices vice-president Herminio Traviesas said he made 35 changes, including new dubbed lines of dialogue from Caan and John Marley to clean up obscenities. Also, some violence disappeared, such as Luca Brasi's hand being stabbed. The alterations did not appease everyone. At NBC's Washington, D.C. affiliate WRC, 40 religious protesters appeared during the first part's airing, decrying its violence and its allegedly glamorous portrayal of the Mafia.

While Part One's ratings on Saturday, Nov. 16, 1974, were strong with a 37.0/61, Part Two (airing two nights later) was even bigger. Together, the movie finished with overall average numbers of 38.2/59.

It is hard to gauge how much the showing promoted the strong box office for *The Godfather Part II*, but it certainly did not hurt it. The sequel wound up doing even better than the original at the Oscars, winning six statuettes for Best Picture, Director, Supporting Actor (Robert De Niro, playing Vito in flashbacks), Adapted Screenplay, Art Direction-Set Decoration and Dramatic Score. The other nominations were for Actor (Pacino), Supporting Actor (twice, for Michael V. Gazzo and Lee Strasberg), Supporting Actress (Shire) and Costume Design.

Three years later, NBC combined the original movie and the 1974 sequel into a miniseries, using some deleted scenes to fill out the running time. Billed as *Mario Puzo's Godfather*, the saga grew in ratings every night from its start on Saturday, Nov. 12, 1977, culminating on the fourth and final installment Tuesday, Nov. 15, 1977, with a 28.5/43.

NBC reran the 1977 version on Nov. 13, 1980 (18.3/28), Nov. 14, 1980 (14.1/22) and Nov. 15, 1980 (14.5/24). The network repeated it again Aug. 28 through Sept. 1, 1983, getting its highest rating for the last installment (15.5/26). By that time, the miniseries had been released on home video as *The Godfather 1902–1959: The Complete Epic*, albeit with some restored scenes left out. Those missing scenes (and even more) finally appeared in a 1992 home video release, *The Godfather Trilogy: 1901–1980*. It included *The Godfather Part III*, which emerged in 1990 after years of discussion. Despite the involvement of many principals from the first two films, it did not fare as well commercially or critically. Its seven Oscar nominations were for Best Picture, Director, Supporting Actor (Andy Garcia), Cinematography, Art Direction-Set Decoration, Song and Film Editing.

"It was the most miserable film I can think of to make," producer Al Ruddy said of the original in *The Annotated Godfather: The Complete Screenplay* by Jenny Jones. "Nobody enjoyed one day of it." But no matter how tough it was to make, the end result has been a fixture on many lists of the greatest movies of all time since 1972. To paraphrase its own catchphrase, they offered us a film we couldn't refuse.

---

26 — World Series Game 6

Oct. 21, 1980 (Philadelphia Phillies vs. Kansas City Royals). **Rating:** 40.0. **Share:** 60.

Aired on NBC Tuesday 8–11:45 P.M. Eastern, 7-P.M. Central, 6-Mountain, 5-Pacific

Competition: *Flatbed Annie and Sweetiepie* (TV-movie repeat) and "CBS Reports: The Saudis" (news special) on CBS; *Happy Days, Laverne & Shirley*, *Three's Company, Taxi* and *Hart to Hart* (all repeats) on ABC

Announcers: Joe Garagiola, Tony Kubek, Tom Seaver, Ron Luciano. **Field Reporters:** Bryant Gumbel, Merle Harmon. **Crew:** Don Ohlmeyer (executive producer), Michael Weisman (coordinating producer-co-producer), George Finkel (co-producer), Harry Coyle, Ken Fouts (directors).

Synopsis. Leading three games to two, Philadelphia hoped to claim the World Series winner title at home after surviving a three-game stretch at Kansas City. The Phillies won the first two games at Veterans Stadium in the best-of-seven event, with scores of 7–6 on Oct. 14 and 6–4 on Oct. 15. But the Royals triumphed at home 4–3 in ten innings on Oct. 17 and 5–3 on Oct. 18. The Phillies prevented a sweep by eking out a 4–3 victory on Oct. 19, sending the Series back to the City of Brotherly Love.

At 11:30 P.M. Eastern, with bases loaded and two out in the top of the ninth, longtime Phillies ace Tug McGraw struck out the Royals' Willie Wilson, just like McGraw did against Jose Cardenal at the end of Game 5, which sent the Series back to Philadelphia. The Phillies won the sixth game by a score of 4–1. The other Phillies swarmed McGraw as legions of fans celebrated the franchise's first Series pennant just three years shy of its centennial. No announcer said anything for a minute and a half as NBC showed jubilation in the stands and on the field, then cut to Bryant Gumbel in the locker room interviewing the winners. One is Pete Rose, a 1978 transplant to the team who won two back-to-back World Series with the Cincinnati Reds in the mid–1970s. Asked how it felt to be a World Series champion again, Rose told Gumbel, "You never get tired of it."

Backstory. Though baseball's links with TV extend back more than 70 years, when a college contest was seen by a handful of New York City viewers in 1939, it has had an uneasy relationship with the medium. Baseball bigwigs warily considered its impact and decided it was more important to have fans come out in person to ballparks than to stay at home and watch. So, major league baseball implemented a rule wherein major markets, such as New York City and Philadelphia, could not see televised games during the regular season in order to promote attendance in person. That applied to both local and network telecasts, with the latter beginning to cover Saturday games starting in 1953.

This policy proved to be unwise in the long run, as NFL football placed no such restriction on its TV exposure, and by the 1960s that sport surpassed baseball as America's favorite pastime thanks in part to baseball's frequent absence on screen versus football's wide availability. Eventually baseball dropped its policy.

The World Series has been intertwined with TV since 1947, when its debut that year boosted sales at bars with TV sets some 500 percent, according to *Variety*. That was very impressive, especially considering that the annual October event aired in the daytime, making it difficult for working adults to view it. Strong ratings for a nighttime game in 1971 convinced baseball commissioner Bowie Kuhn to decree that henceforth all World Series games would occur in the evening. Still, no game had surpassed the 39.5 rating reached by the 1963 World Series shown in the daytime until this one.

Making this series particularly attractive to viewers was the fact that neither the Phillies nor the Royals had won a World Series previously. It was the first time Philadelphia went to the World Series since 1950, when they lost to the New York Yankees. The win clinched a 91–71 season record for the Phillies.

Kansas City won the American League Conference by shutting out the New York Yankees, while Philadelphia had to go the distance to overcome the Houston Astros 3–2 for the National League title. Both of those championships had aired on ABC. (Major league baseball made an agreement in 1976 that alternated annual airing of the World Series between ABC and NBC, with ABC having won the rights to Monday night baseball after NBC carried it from 1972 to 1975.)

The Kansas City team had been favored by some observers thanks to its long dominance during the 1980 season, which at one point included George Brett having an impressive .400 batting average. But Philadelphia had a top squad as well, including Mike Schmidt, who was named the World Series' MVP. Brett unintentionally provided his own drama during the series when he had to enter the hospital for hemorrhoid surgery between Games 2 and 3. He shook off the ribbing (along the lines of "What a pain in the butt that must have been!") from wiseacres, played in every game and batted an impressive .375 for the Series.

There was an actors' strike in the fall of 1980 that delayed the debut of new TV series episodes. Facing an avalanche of repeats and re-repeats and news specials on the networks' schedules — as was the case here — viewers often took whatever new entertainment they could find. With the World Series base audience already strong, the additional interest from casual viewers helped push this through the ratings roof.

Perhaps anticipating a strong turnout, NBC Sports had an unprecedented six announcers covering the championship games. As Joe Garagiola recalled in his autobiography *It's Anybody's Ballgame*, "Tony Kubek and I did play-by-play, Bryant Gumbel did the pregame show and a commentary from the booth, Tom Seaver analyzed pitching strategy, former umpire Ron Luciano commented on controversial calls, and Merle Harmon interviewed people in the stands during the game. Three more guys, and we could have played an Old-Timers Game."

Garagiola and Kubek were the lead team on the regular Saturday *Baseball Game of the Week* telecasts on NBC, while Luciano and Harmon became the backup crew covering games in areas where the games were blacked out the same day. Luciano provided more color commentary than he was allowed in the World Series, but his failure to do his homework before each game about, say, the proper pronunciation of players' names, led NBC to can him in 1982 after just two years on the job. "In truth, I was to baseball broadcasting what Francis the Talking Mule had been to acting," Luciano recounted in his memoirs *Strike Two*. "Although Francis had some funny lines."

Some traditionalists griped about the excessive amount of announcers and claimed that they tuned them out and instead listened to coverage on CBS Radio, where Vin Scully provided play-by-play with Sparky Anderson also contributing. But the radio ratings did not back up this assertion.

The series' averaged numbers were 32.5/56 over the six games from Oct. 14 through 21. The lowest-rated was the fourth game (Oct. 18), which was hurt by the fact it was the only one not carried in the nighttime (it aired on a Saturday afternoon). NBC's coverage earned sports Emmy nominations for live sports special and for technical direction-electronic camerawork.

With such a great 1980 showing, the World Series was expected to get even bigger numbers down the line. However, besides the increased competition from cable and home viewing, pro baseball took a huge hit the following season when a 50-day players' strike destroyed many viewers' enthusiasm for the sport. Indeed, when the World Series was played in 1981, viewership went down sharply.

Incidentally, the game pre-empted the planned

debut of a three-hour "disaster" TV-movie called *The Night the Bridge Fell Down*. It had to wait nearly two and a half years before it finally aired on NBC. As luck would have it, the film ran opposite the final episode of *M*A*S*H* (see 1). Some competitions just are not fair at all, are they?

25 — *All in the Family*

Jan. 8, 1972 ("Edith's Problem"). **Rating:** 40.7. **Share:** 62.

Aired on CBS Saturday 8–8:30 P.M. Eastern and Pacific, 7–7:30 P.M. Central

Competition: *Getting Together* on ABC, *The Partners* on NBC

Cast: Carroll O'Connor (Archie Bunker), Jean Stapleton (Edith Bunker), Rob Reiner (Mike Stivic), Sally Struthers (Gloria Bunker Stivic). **Guest:** Jeannie Linero (Waitress). **Crew:** Norman Lear (executive producer), Michael Ross and Bernie West (script supervisors), Don Nicholl (story editor), Burt Styler, Steve Zacharias (story), John Rich (director).

Synopsis. Archie Bunker tells his daughter, Gloria, and son-in-law, Mike, how he plans to surprise Edith, his wife, with a trip to the recently opened Walt Disney World in Florida. Edith reacts oddly to the news, snapping at the family, then returning from the kitchen with a pleasant demeanor. Her bizarre behavior continues, ranging from complaining how hot it is during the cold winter to singing "I'm in the Mood for Love" spontaneously. Gloria explains to her mom that she appears to be undergoing menopause, which dismays Edith because she thinks "the change" will result in Archie no longer loving her. Later, as Archie reviews the Disney World brochure with Edith, she loses composure and blurts for him to "stifle"—along with everyone in the house.

After Edith visits a gynecologist, she refuses to talk about her condition. Archie provides her with pills and tries to be understanding. Archie's "niceness act" backfires, as Edith feels he is no longer acting honestly with her. But when she tells him she wants to go to Scranton, Pennsylvania, to see her cousin Emily, who Archie loathes, her husband blows his stack and refuses—and also derides her soup. Edith rejoices in Archie's outburst because, as she put it, "He don't think I'm old! He loves me!"

Backstory. Just as CBS sitcom *The Beverly Hillbillies* (see 12) usually finished #1 in the ratings each week by a large margin over other programs from 1962–1964, so did *All in the Family* from

1971–1975. But where the former sitcom was "unreal people in unreal situations," as Gilbert Seldes described it in a 1962 *TV Guide* review, *All in the Family* came across as very real people in all-too-real situations. This episode is a perfect example of how the show brought authenticity to the often plastic world of situation comedies.

Put aside the fact that this was the first time menopause had been discussed on a comedy — or perhaps a drama, for that matter. It was a real shock at the time to hear a meek woman like Edith Bunker blurt out "Dammit!" on network television. At the same time, the show began with references to the Disney World theme park that many Americans were talking about visiting. It was all very contemporary and relatable, and that aspect — along with excellent casting, producing and directing — helped keep *All in the Family* #1 for five seasons.

As with most groundbreaking series, *All in the Family* did not start off that auspiciously. The success of the 1966 British series *Till Death Us Do Part* interested American executive producer Norman Lear, as it centered on a prejudiced blue collar worker, a character that reminded him of his father. (*All in the Family* never used any of the scripts from the British original.) He filmed a pilot in 1968 for ABC with Carroll O'Connor as the bigot, Jean Stapleton as his sometimes slow-on-the-uptake wife, and other actors in supporting roles. ABC felt the supporting players were not right for the show, so Lear recast and redid the pilot in 1969.

That second pilot did not fly with ABC either, but CBS officials heard about it and felt it could help them shed their label as a rural-oriented network. But CBS wanted another recasting of the supporting characters before committing. Joining them now were Sally Struthers as the Bunkers' petite blonde daughter, Gloria, and Rob Reiner as Gloria's husband, Michael. Michael's Polish heritage, hungry stomach and liberal politics all made him a prime target for Archie's diatribes.

CBS premiered *All in the Family* on Jan. 12, 1971, on Tuesday nights at 9:30 P.M. Eastern and Pacific, and it slowly caught on, building its audience each week as people saw current issues being discussed in an adult yet comic manner. By the time of the Emmys (May 9, 1971), *All in the Family* was TV's most talked-about series, and it was no surprise that it won several statuettes, including best comedy and actress (Stapleton). By the fall of 1971, it was leading off CBS's Saturday night lineup and topping the ratings. Everyone watched it — and that included President Richard Nixon, as tapes of conversations from the Oval Office released after his death bore out. (He thought Mike was homosexual because he had a handbag in one show.) The series even cracked the music charts. Charles Strouse created the music and his partner Lee Adams wrote the lyrics for the show's theme "Those Were the Days." The pilot's budget had only a few hundred dollars left to do the theme, which could not cover an orchestra, so Strouse suggested they record it on the set with him playing the piano (Stapleton mimed that role on screen). With Stapleton's screechy rendition and the show's popularity, it came close to being a top 40 hit in early 1972.

The popularity of *All in the Family* peaked with this episode, which is very funny along with being topical. Archie's ignorant, compassion-free statements about Edith's condition are golden. "When I had the hernia that time, I didn't make you wear the truss!" he yelled at one point. He followed that with "Edith, if you're gonna have a change of life, you gotta do it right now. I'm gonna give you just 30 seconds! Now come on, change!"

All in the Family remained strong the rest of the season (the following week's episode drew a 40/58, for example), and it ended the season with seven more Emmys, including best comedy, actress (Stapleton again), actor (O'Connor), supporting actress (Struthers), directing (John Rich) and sound mixing. Burt Styler's script for this show won the writing award as well. The series ended with 22 Emmys and 56 nominations. The award for Styler probably should have gone to the producers instead, if the show's director, John Rich, is to be believed. He said in his autobiography that Lear, Ross, West and Nicholls "either wrote or rewrote every word of the nearly 100 episodes I directed or produced during the first four years." Indeed, rewrites were so common on *All in the Family* that it led several writers to avoid doing more than one episode.

When "Edith's Problem" appeared in daytime reruns on CBS starting in 1975, the network deleted about three minutes to fit in more commercials. Lear publicly protested. He also disliked the Family Viewing Hour, which forced CBS to carry *All in the Family* at a later time beginning in 1975. That knocked the show out of the #1 position, but it stayed in the top 10.

Also in the top 10 at various points for CBS were several spin-offs, including *The Jeffersons* (1975–1978), with the black neighbors of the Bunkers "movin' on up" from the Queens neighborhood to Manhattan; *Maude* (1972–1978), with Edith's liberal cousin; and *Good Times*, a spin-off of *Maude*. *All in the Family* itself became somewhat of a spin-off itself when Mike and Gloria left in 1978 and Stapleton departed the following year. The last *All in the Family* appeared on Sept. 16, 1979, to be replaced by *Archie Bunker's Place*, in which Archie ran a bar. Nowhere near as clever or enjoyable as the original, *Archie Bunker's Place* nonetheless ran through Sept. 21, 1983, and was still in the top 25 when it was cancelled.

All in the Family is a TV classic, funny yet poignant, and trenchant yet touching. Today's TV could use a few more of its kind.

24 — *Gunsmoke*

Jan. 28, 1961 ("Love Thy Neighbor"). **Rating:** 40.9. **Share:** 65.

Aired on CBS Saturday 10–10:30 P.M. Eastern and Pacific, 9–9:30 P.M. Central

Competition: *The Fight of the Week* on ABC, *The Nation's Future* (last half-hour) on NBC

Cast: James Arness (Matt Dillon), Milburn Stone ("Doc" Galen Adams), Amanda Blake (Miss Kitty Russell), Dennis Weaver (Chester Goode). **Guests:** Jeanette Nolan (Rose Galloway), Jack Elam (Ben Scooper), Harry Dean Stanton (Harley Scooper), Ken Lynch (Leroy Galloway), Warren Oates (Jep Galloway), Nora Marlowe (Jennie Scooper), David Kent (Peter Scooper), Cyril Delevanti (Sy Tewksbury), Wayne West (Man). **Crew:** Norman MacDonnell (producer), James Arness (associate producer), Dennis Weaver (director), John Meston (writer).

Synopsis. Rose Galloway and her husband Leroy are awakened by their dog barking. Leroy and his son Jep chase and capture Peter, a young boy with potatoes taken from the Galloways' shed, and release the would-be thief with a warning. The next day Peter's mom, Jennie, tends to his damaged leg, which was cut by barbed wire on the Galloways' fence. Her husband, Ben, allows her to go into Dodge City and have Peter treated by Doc Adams, but it is too late. Ben and his other son, Harley, vow they will avenge Peter's death. A concerned Doc informs Marshal Dillon of this development.

Dillon breaks up a shootout (Ben and Harley against Leroy and Jep) on the Galloway farm. Later, Leroy is shot dead. Jep pursues Ben and Harley despite Rose's pleas to let Dillon handle the matter. He confronts a drunk Ben at Miss Kitty's saloon. Jep threatens to kill Ben on the street. Ben unwisely fires his gun at Jep, and the latter slays him. Jep plans to get Harley too, but Dillon charges him with murder. When Dillon goes to arrest Harley, the latter forcibly resists and the marshal is forced to kill him.

Dillon releases Jep from jail the next day. Rose arrives with Sy Tewksbury, who admits he stole the potatoes and gave them to Peter to take when he was chased. Rose and Jep go to Jennie to make amends with her, all caused by a sack of potatoes.

Backstory. Gunsmoke ran nearly 20 years on TV to the day, from Sept. 10, 1955 through Sept. 1, 1975, and spent much of that time being a hit (13 seasons in the top 10, with four consecutive seasons at #1 from 1957–1961). It started as a CBS radio series in 1952, and quite a successful one at that, running nine years until dramatic programming on network radio was virtually dead. (Almost all the *Gunsmoke* TV episodes in the first four seasons were adaptations of radio scripts.)

While none of the radio cast made the transition to TV, the audio Matt Dillon, William Conrad, did direct the video version. From the TV cast, it was Dennis Weaver, who played Sheriff Dillon's limping assistant Chester Goode from 1955 to 1964, who was the actor who directed the most episodes.

"This episode happens to be the first *Gunsmoke* I directed, and it was a joy, because I was able to cast some of the top talents in Hollywood, including Jack Elam and Jeanette Nolan," Weaver recalled in the 2006 DVD commentary for "Love Thy Neighbor." He believed as a director that casting is half of what makes the show a success, and he was impressed recalling that he included future favorite character actors Warren Oates and Harry Dean Stanton (billed here as Dean Stanton) as well. He took suggestions from producer Norman MacDonnell and James Arness on whom to cast, but he made the final selections himself. Weaver said he got the directing job just by asking for it. "I went to [MacDonnell], I also showed him some live theatre I was in, and I said, 'I'd like to direct.' And there was really no argument about it."

He found that preparation before filming was at least as time-consuming as the actual shooting of the episode. He met and took suggestions not only from the assistant director but also from the prop man and the makeup artist about what would work best. This was more time-intensive than when he just acted on *Gunsmoke*, although the show's production schedule was pretty rigid in the half-hour days. "We had, well, we would call it a rehearsal day, one day, and mostly it was for

the running characters, like Matt Dillon, Kitty, and Doc, and Chester," Weaver said. "What we would do is, we would read the script and say, 'Well, you know, the scene doesn't fit my character' or 'This particular thing violates my character' or 'I don't believe the story here.' And we would massage the script until we were comfortable with it. And that day at rehearsal was a very important day." After that, there were three days to film the episode, then it was on to the next one. Because of these time demands of his acting role, Weaver was unable to be with the editor when the latter cut this episode.

The hardest problem Weaver encountered during "Love Thy Neighbor" was a technical one involving filming. "Do you realize we didn't have a zoom lens when we shot this show? If you wanted a close-up, you had to move the camera and everything else, and that took time, and time is money."

He elaborated on how the limits of technology affected his directing assignments. "They were all just a lot of fun, but the only problem with directing a *Gunsmoke* or a *McCloud* [Weaver's 1970–1977 detective series], which I also did — you're directing yourself, and that's tough. It's not only, you don't have an objective eye necessarily about your own work, and you can't look at it as it's being shot. And we didn't have in those days the kind of equipment they have today, where the director doesn't even look at the actors.... You had to look at the actors in real time, and then you had to trust the cameraman and say 'What do you think?'"

"Love Thy Neighbor" is smoothly paced and acted and effectively blends outdoors scenes with ones on a soundstage (incidentally, the saloon front was an interior set, though few viewers at the time realized it). Fans may be a little disappointed that it offers the bulk of screen time to the guests; Matt does not arrive until eight minutes into the show, Miss Kitty gets only a handful of scenes, and Chester is seen briefly at the jailhouse at the end. But it makes its points effectively, and it admirably manages to avoid most western stereotypes.

Weaver said he liked directing "Love Thy Neighbor." "I think it was a strong script, had some real interesting characters in it, and that's the kind of script I wanted to direct. I wanted a script that really involved people."

People were involved intensely with *Gunsmoke* during the 1960-1961 season, in part due to the appeal of the regular characters — forthright, tall Matt, alluring Miss Kitty, no-nonsense Doc and easygoing Chester — as well as the other networks basically giving up in putting competition against it, unless you consider boxing and public affairs to be more fun to watch. Its ratings were so high (several other episodes this season had a rating of at least 40) that CBS expanded *Gunsmoke* to an hour in the 1961-1962 season. That is where a few problems began to arise. NBC, desperate to beat the show, started its *Saturday Night at the Movies* series in the fall of 1961 an hour before *Gunsmoke* ran. While it only occasionally beat the western, it provided enough competition to have *Gunsmoke* finish at #3.

Then, as Arness noted in his autobiography, "*Gunsmoke* was in its eighth season in 1963, and some of our actors and writers were getting pretty worn out." Principal writer John Meston told him, "Jim, I just don't have any more *Gunsmoke* stories in me," and left. The following season (1963-1964), *Gunsmoke* fell from #10 to #20 in its seasonal averages, and so CBS canned MacDonnell as producer. Philip Leacock, the new producer, and his successor, John Mantley, helped transform it into an anthology that put even more emphasis on the guest stars.

In 1967 CBS announced the cancellation of *Gunsmoke*, only to be overruled by the network's owner, Bill Paley, who demanded it be reinstalled. Returned at the last minute to lead off the Monday night lineup, *Gunsmoke* remained in the top 10 the next six seasons (1967-1968 through 1972-1973) before gradually slipping again and being cancelled.

Gunsmoke received no Emmy nominations during the 1960-1961 season, and won just five times (out of 14 nominations) through 1970, including best drama (1957), supporting actor (Weaver in 1959 and Milburn Stone in 1968), film editing (1957) and film sound editing (1970).

Gunsmoke is more than just awards and longevity (it ties the record with *Law & Order* as TV's longest-running nighttime drama with continuing characters). It is to many people the best TV western, and it holds up very well today.

---

23 — *The Winds of War*

Feb. 13, 1983 ("Into the Maelstrom," Part VII of seven-part miniseries). **Rating:** 41.0. **Share:** 56.
Aired on ABC Sunday 8–11 P.M. Eastern and Pacific, 7–10 P.M. Central
Competition: *Archie Bunker's Place, Gloria, The Jeffersons, One Day at a Time* and *Trapper John, M.D.*

on CBS; *The Invisible Woman* (two-hour TV-movie) and *Highway Honeys* (one-hour comedy pilot) on NBC
Cast: Robert Mitchum (Comdr. Victor "Pug" Henry), Ali MacGraw (Natalie Jastrow), Jan-Michael Vincent (Byron Henry), John Houseman (Aaron Jastrow), Polly Bergen (Rhoda Henry), Lisa Eilbacher (Madeline Henry), David Dukes (Leslie Slote), Topol (Berel Jastrow), Ben Murphy (Warren Henry), Peter Graves (Palmer Kirby), Jeremy Kemp (Brigadier General Armin von Roon), Ralph Bellamy (President Franklin D. Roosevelt), Victoria Tennant (Pamela Tudsbury), William T. Woodson (Narrator). **Crew:** Dan Curtis (producer-director), Herman Wouk (writer).

Synopsis. In 1939 Comdr. "Pug" Henry and his wife Rhoda head from New York to Germany while their son, Warren, and daughter, Madeline, wish them bon voyage. Their other son, Byron, is in Italy communing with diplomat Leslie Slote, Leslie's girlfriend Natalie Jastrow, and Natalie's uncle Aaron, whom Byron works for as a researcher. Natalie is visiting her relatives in Poland, including spirited Uncle Berel, when the Nazis attack. Byron helps save her, prompting a romance. Meanwhile, "Pug" begins an affair with the younger Pamela Tudsbury in England as the country's war with Germany heats up. Rhoda becomes affectionate with Palmer Kirby in the United States.

"Pug" is on civil terms with Nazi Armin von Roon, who realizes that the war is eventually going to encompass America. "Pug" follows orders from President Roosevelt that include him monitoring the eastern front of the war in 1941. By this time, Natalie and Byron are married and have a child, and Byron is serving as a naval officer in the Philippines. "Pug" is transferred to command the battleship USS *California* in Hawaii, but before he gets there the Japanese attack and sink it. Warren is a lieutenant who survives the bombing on the island. Natalie, her son and Aaron escape Italy as Mussolini declares war against America. "Pug" gets command of another battleship to go off to war as Rhoda re-thinks her proposed divorce.

Backstory. Officially titled *Herman Wouk's The Winds of War*, this miniseries was an adaptation of Wouk's 1971 bestseller, based in part on his experiences as a naval officer in World War II. Wouk started researching the war in 1960, eventually reading some 300 books related to the subject. He found that when he had reached the bombing of Pearl Harbor, the book was more than 1,000 pages long, and his editor agreed that the novel should end at that point.

Everybody thought *The Winds of War* would make a great movie except the author, who had been displeased with Hollywood's treatment of his previous works. "*Marjorie Morningstar* and *Youngblood Hawke* were just were trivialized, and that wasn't going to happen again with *The Winds of War*," Wouk said in the DVD documentary *Making The Winds of War*. But Paramount Pictures chairman and CEO Barry Diller won the film rights in 1977 by convincing Wouk it could be done properly as a miniseries like *Roots* (see 3).

Wouk attached several provisos to the project, such as demanding approval of the producer, director and casting. He also required limiting the amount of time allowed for commercials, their placement during the miniseries and even what sponsors would be allowed to participate. ABC wanted the project so badly that they accepted all of Wouk's conditions.

Gary Nardino, president of Paramount Television, contacted executive producer and director Dan Curtis about making the miniseries. Curtis had no idea what *The Winds of War* was at first. When he saw the size of the book, he thought Nardino was crazy to try to adapt it, but the executive insisted he look over the book. Intrigued, Curtis met with Wouk to discuss the project. The two hit it off, especially with Curtis insisting the miniseries follow the book as closely as possible, so *The Winds of War* was underway.

According to Curtis in *Making The Winds of War*, Wouk's writing of the screen adaptation (with contributions from Curtis) and preproduction work by Curtis took more than a year, with both happening simultaneously. According to Curtis, "When I got to Yugoslavia, that's where I met Branko Lustic, who ended up basically as my first [assistant director].... Without him, I never could have completed this film." Lustic had the sets prepared the way Curtis wanted for every shot; plus, he survived the Auschwitz concentration camp as a teenager, so he provided the director with an understanding of the "German mentality," as Curtis termed it.

Shooting started in Hollywood on Dec. 1, 1980, followed by Yugoslavia, with Zagreb as the base. Filming in Yugoslavia was inexpensive and the country could double for many other locations due to its buildings' grand interiors and exteriors resembling the European capitals of the late 1930s and early 1940s. There were close to 300 speaking parts. With a planned $35 million budget, Paramount president Gary Nardino called it "the largest single undertaking ever in TV" in 1980.

However, that did not mean the pace of shooting was leisurely with all this time and money.

On the contrary, locations work was often long and frenetic. Ali MacGraw estimated they did a staggering 50 setups a day for filming. "In one day, we actually shot in three different countries," said associate producer Barbara Steele, who also acted briefly in the miniseries. The three countries were Austria, Switzerland and Italy, with trucks transporting the cast and crew in the cold weather.

As for how Curtis directed *The Winds of War*, there were two schools of thought among the actors. "I always felt he was a very straight and very attentive director," Polly Bergen said in the documentary.

"He'd have kind of a short fuse, but it was wonderful, because if he blew, he blew for a very good purpose, and the whole pictures and the actors all came out better for that happening," said Peter Graves.

The Pearl Harbor battle sequences were the last segments shot, with eight cameras on location at Oxnard, California, to capture the blowing-up of naval ships, with planes flying over them. They were filmed exactly 40 years to the day of the original attack, on Dec. 7, 1981.

The Winds of War was originally set to air in the fall of 1982. But as it took Curtis a year to edit the miniseries into 18 hours, that debut had to be pushed back. When it finally emerged, some critics rightly nicknamed it "The Windy War." While a good drama overall, it slogs a lot to fill its time slot; an inordinate amount of time is spent on ceremonies like weddings and dancing. The acting was quite variable too, with MacGraw, Jan-Michael Vincent and Gunter Meisner (as a cardboard Adolf Hitler) the weak spots.

Still, the story was sturdy, and ABC's heavy promotion helped too. Its debut on Sunday, Feb. 6, 1983, scored a hefty 39.1/53. It ran on ABC every night the rest of the week (except Saturday) before its conclusion the following Sunday provided the highest ratings. Its overall numbers were 38.6/53.

The Winds of War won three out of 13 Emmy nominations, for cinematography, costumes and special visual effects. It lost for limited series, supporting actor (Ralph Bellamy, who received a "special appearance by" designation), supporting actress (Bergen), directing, art direction, film editing, film sound editing and film sound mixing (three nominations in the category for different episodes). There was no nomination for Robert Mitchum, who played "Pug" pitch perfect. ABC reran the miniseries Sept. 7–14, 1986. It finished third in its time slots most nights, with its best numbers being a weak 10.8/18 on the final part.

Wouk wrote a sequel to the book, *War and Remembrance*, in 1978, and ABC decided to adapt it as well. *War and Remembrance* was budgeted at $104 million for 30 hours, a cost that made it impossible for the network to make a profit on it. Curtis served as executive producer as well as co-writer with Wouk and Earl Wallace. It ran from Nov. 13 to Nov. 23, 1988, with less impressive ratings than the original (generally around a 30 share). Even though it won the Emmy for outstanding miniseries (beating *Lonesome Dove,* to the dismay of most critics), the endeavor's mediocre performance soured the industry on the concept of such large-scale miniseries. Few of the miniseries made since then ran more than three nights.

The irony of it all is that the most expensive miniseries ever made turned out souring the networks on the concept altogether. War is hell indeed.

22 — *The Cosby Show*

Jan. 22, 1987 ("Say Hello to a Good Buy"). **Rating:** 41.3. **Share:** 56.
Aired on NBC Thursday 8–8:30 P.M. Eastern and Pacific, 7–7:30 P.M. Central
Competition: *Our World* on ABC, *Shell Game* on CBS
Cast: Bill Cosby (Cliff Huxtable), Phylicia Rashad (Claire Huxtable), Lisa Bonet (Denise Huxtable), Malcolm-Jamal Warner (Theo Huxtable), Tempestt Bledsoe (Vanessa Huxtable), Keisha Knight Pulliam (Rudy Huxtable). **Guests:** Sinbad (Davis Sarrette), Gilbert Gottfried (Mr. Babcock). **Crew:** Marcy Carsey, Tom Werner (executive producers), Tony Singletary (director), John Markus, Carmen Finestra, Matt Williams (writers).

Synopsis. Claire Huxtable reads an article in bed to her husband Cliff, and makes him take a quiz on what makes a happy marriage. A tired Cliff tells her a good marriage would be one where there are two of him so that one could get some sleep. The next morning Cliff goes shopping for a new station wagon with his son Theo, while his youngest daughters, Vanessa and Rudy, work on Rudy's school report on mammals, reptiles and birds. Theo suggests Cliff get a sports car, what with Theo soon going to college like his older sisters, Denise and Sondra. But Cliff's main concern at the dealership is to negotiate a low price with Davis Sarrette, a salesman.

Loudmouth Mr. Babcock is at the showroom and recognizes the man who was his wife's obstetrician. He blabs to Davis about Cliff wearing de-signer sweaters and Claire becoming partner in her law firm. Cliff shakes off the disclosure and haggles successfully for an amount he and Davis agree upon.

Vanessa's suggestion that Rudy add pictures to her report led Rudy to cut out images from the encyclopedia and other valuable books in the house. To placate Cliff in advance, the three girls make him dinner, but he realizes something is up. Told the truth, he reacts in a rather low-key manner and reads Rudy's report. Resignedly, he says he likes it but, "It's very expensive."

Backstory. The Cosby Show was the #1 show for five consecutive seasons, from 1985-1986 through 1989-1990, and for four of those seasons it was a full two ratings points ahead of the #2 series, which in 1985-1986 and 1986-1987 was the show that followed it, *Family Ties* (see 29). Its average ratings those two seasons were the highest since *Dallas* (see 2) in the 1980-1981 season. Another NBC hit, *The Golden Girls*, referenced it in the episode "It's a Miserable Life" (Nov. 1, 1986), where the regulars refused to schedule a funeral for a woman on a Thursday night lest they miss *The Cosby Show.*

That reception by the public stands in stark contrast to what greeted Cosby and company when they tried to sell the series to the networks. Marcy Carsey and Tom Werner were former ABC programming executives who helped create the series. They knew that Bill Cosby remained a popular, much-loved TV comedian and personality, and they believed that with the right format, he could star in a hit the way he did with *I Spy* from 1965–1968, even though the nighttime shows he did since that time — *The Bill Cosby Show* (1969–1971), *The New Bill Cosby Show* (1972-1973) and *Cos* (1976) — did not click in the long run.

Cosby wanted a family show, so he fashioned the series in the pattern of his own home, with a wife, several daughters and one son. As Cosby told Todd Klein in *The Saturday Evening Post*, "My family life is the behavior I know best." There was discussion over what job his series character would hold, finally settling on obstetrician.

A 14-minute presentation piece was taped on the set of ABC's *Oh Madeline*, a sitcom starring Madeline Kahn that ran in 1983-1984. (Kahn would later be a regular on *Cosby*, a 1996–2000 sitcom on CBS starring you know who.) Everything was in place, with Cliff Huxtable often exasperated by the antics of his children but willing to forgive and forget if they learned from their experiences. Carsey and Werner showed it to Lou Ehrlich, then the chief programming executive at ABC, and he rejected the program twice, telling his fellow former executives, "Comedy is dead."

Undaunted, they tried CBS; it was "no sale" there either. NBC's head programmer Brandon Tartikoff loved Cosby's appearances on *The Tonight Show* and was willing to give the series a shot. But he put it in a tough slot, leading the network's Thursday night lineup against CBS's *Magnum, P.I.*, the #6 show of the 1983-1984 season.

Debuting Sept. 20, 1984, *The Cosby Show* received glowing reviews (*TV Guide* called it the fall's best new series); it became the highest-rated NBC series since *The Big Event* in 1976-1977. It finished the 1984-1985 season at #3, and it grew even bigger the next year. The Nov. 21, 1985, episode notched a 35.3/51, the best numbers for a regular series episode since *Dallas* (see 2) on Jan. 23, 1981. From there until the rest of the decade, it was rare for any week of the regular TV season not to have *The Cosby Show* atop the ratings. It also established Thursday nights as "must see TV" for NBC and led that network to #1 from 1985 to 1990.

Its phenomenal popularity caught many experts off guard, as the 1983-1984 season was the first since the days before *I Love Lucy* that no sitcom cracked the top five. Cosby offered this opinion of its appeal to Klein: "Regardless of race or social status, parents perceive themselves as people who work hard and have wisdom to hand down to their children. And they all see their children as these brain-damaged people who repel wisdom."

In the 1986-1987 season, Cosby's TV wife, Phylicia Rashad, was pregnant in real life, which limited her screen time. The show did not want to incorporate a baby into its plotlines, so Rashad did scenes (such as the opening one in this episode) with pillows and large blankets concealing her condition from viewers.

What helped push this to be the highest-rated episode was probably a combination of cold temperatures throughout most of the United States and excitement over the upcoming Super Bowl (see 4), which aired on CBS three days later and managed to top this with a 45.8 rating. This show was the highest-rated sitcom episode since *The Beverly Hillbillies* (see 12) scored a 42.2 on March 25, 1964. It was no surprise at season's end when its competition on ABC, *Our World*, wound up as the lowest-rated series among 71 ranked.

A year after this episode ended, *Variety* announced that *The Cosby Show* had become the highest-grossing series in history to sell its reruns to local TV stations. Viacom, its distributor, set minimum price bids for stations in each market to bid on it, and competition was fierce enough that the company earned a half-billion in sales. Helping to sell it was the fact that Viacom agreed not to allow NBC (or any other network) to repeat the shows on its daytime schedule before it went into daily reruns on Oct. 3, 1988.

"We parcel it out to keep it fresh," Joseph D. Zaleski, president of domestic syndication at Viacom, said in *Business Week*. "We will control the episodes, and there will be no Christmas shows in July." Not everyone took the bait, however: In 22 markets, all stations declined to offer the amount requested by Viacom, feeling it was too much of a gamble. As it happened, the series turned out to be a solid performer in reruns, although not quite reaching the blockbuster status that Viacom proclaimed it possessed.

In the 1990-1991 season, with the TV children growing older and the Fox network adding a formidable competitor with the cartoon *The Simpsons* (an anti–Cosby family show if there ever was one), *The Cosby Show* slid to #5. A year later, Cosby decided to end the series while it still had appeal. After finishing the season at #16, it ran in repeats until Sept. 17, 1992.

The Cosby Show claimed six Emmy wins during its run, all before this episode ran. In 1985 it won best comedy series, writing and directing, and in 1986 it won for directing, guest performer (Roscoe Lee Browne) and editing. Cosby kept his name out of Emmy contention, which may have had an impact on the Emmy numbers. He never had another series with the impact of this one, but then again, no other series since then has stayed at #1 longer than *The Cosby Show* except for *American Idol*. In other words, *The Cosby Show* is a TV classic.

21—Seinfeld

May 14, 1998 ("The Finale"). **Rating:** 41.3. **Share:** 58.

Aired on NBC Thursday 8:45–10 P.M. Eastern and Pacific, 7:45–9 P.M. Central

Competition: *Unforgiven* (repeat of 1992 theatrical movie) on ABC; *Promised Land* and *Diagnosis Murder* on CBS; *World's Wildest Police Videos* and *When Animals Attack* (special) on Fox

Cast: Jerry Seinfeld (Jerry Seinfeld), Jason Alexander (George Costanza), Julia Louis-Dreyfus (Elaine

Benes), Michael Richards (Cosmo Kramer). **Guests:** Wayne Knight (Newman), Jerry Stiller (Frank Costanza), Estelle Harris (Estelle Costanza), Liz Sheridan (Helen Seinfeld), Barney Martin (Morty Seinfeld), Ian Abercrombie (Mr. Pitt), Stanley Anderson (Judge Vandelay), Frances Bay (Mrs. Choate), Peter Blood (Jay Crespi), David Byrd (Pharmacist), Tony Carlin (Co-Worker), Steve Carlson (Captain Maddox), Melanie Chartoff (Robin), Brian Doyle-Murray (Mel Sanger), David Dunard (Guard), Donna Evans (Woman), Geoffrey C. Ewing (Bailiff), Richard Fancy (Lippman), Warren Frost (Mr. Ross), Brian George (Babu), Philip Baker Hall (Bookman), Teri Hatcher (Sidra), John Hayman (Bubble Boy), Richard Herd (Wilhelm), Keith Hernandez (Himself), Steve Hyntner (Bania), Carlos Jacott (Pool Guy), Scott Jaeck (Officer Vogel), Wendle Josepher (Susie), Robert Katims (Mr. Deensfrei), Scott Klace (Guard), Jane Leeves (Marla), Len Lesser (Uncle Leo), Bruce Mahler (Rabbi), Wendel Meldrum (Low Talker), Phil Morris (Jackie Chiles), Sheree North (Babs), John O'Hurley (J. Peterman), Ed O'Ross (Det. Blake), Kevin Page (Stu Chermak), James Pickens, Jr. (Det. Hudson), John Pinette (Howie), Victor Raider-Wexler (Dr. Wexler), James Rebhorn (D.A. Hoyt), Peter Riegert (Kimbrough), Geraldo Rivera (Himself), McNally Sagal (Carol), Miguel Sandoval (Marcelino), Reni Santoni (Poppy), Gay Thomas (O'Neal), Larry Thomas (Soup Nazi), Myra Turley (Foreman), Patrick Warburton (David Puddy), Jane Wells (Herself), Danny Woodburn (Mickey), Grace Zabriskie (Mrs. Ross). **Crew:** Larry David (executive producer–writer), Jerry Seinfeld, George Shapiro, Howard West, Alan Berg, Jeff Schaffer (executive producers), Gregg Kavet, Andy Robin (co-executive producers), Spike Feresten, David Mandel (supervising producers), Jennifer Crittenden, Steve Koren (co-producers), Tim Kaiser, Suzy Mamann Greenberg (producers), Andy Ackerman (producer-director).

Synopsis. NBC's new president, James Kimbrough, tells George Constanza and Jerry Seinfeld he is offering them a 13-episode commitment to do *Jerry*, the sitcom about nothing they proposed five years earlier. They also have use of NBC's corporate jet to fly anywhere in the world. Meeting with Elaine Benes and Cosmo Kramer, they all decide to go to Paris. The plane malfunctions, causing an emergency stopover in Latham, Massachusetts. When the gang mocks Howie, a stout man who is carjacked, he calls a cop to arrest them for violating the new "Good Samaritan" law. Facing a possible five-year sentence, they call their lawyer, Jackie Chiles, to defend them.

D.A. Hoyt, realizing the trial will be a media circus with Chiles involved, advises his attorneys to find out everything about the defendants to win it. He intends to prove a pattern of selfishness

runs among the quartet. He runs the video Kramer shot of the carjacking and has a parade of people testify to the court about the callous foursome over the last eight years. Longtime friends, foes and co-workers of George, Jerry, Elaine and Kramer, including George and Jerry's parents, are horrified by the revelations.

The jury finds them guilty of criminal indifference. Judge Vandelay sentences them to a year in jail. As they all share a cell, Jerry talks about George's shirt button — the same conversation the two had on the opening episode of *Seinfeld*.

Backstory. It's hard to think of a more disappointing farewell show than this. Laughter over Howie's weight during a carjacking was out of character for Jerry, George, Elaine and Kramer, and the count recounting of their misdeeds was somber, not humorous. The laugh track and supposed studio audience of friends of the show yocked it up, but others' mileage varied. Even the usual quips by the cast about the trivia of life rarely score this time around. In short, the sitcom that promoted itself as "the show about nothing" lived up to its slogan here.

This episode was clearly overstuffed in many respects. More than 50 actors appeared in addition to the regular cast. Filming occurred on 33 sets and three soundstages, much more than a typical sitcom episode.

The hype about the finale was so strong that some reporters tried bribing series personnel with cash to get exclusive information about it. To prevent that, participants on- and off-screen signed confidentiality agreements saying they would not discuss the show, and that included Geraldo Rivera and CNBC reporter Jane Wells. (The episode had *Rivera Live*, an actual CNBC series from 1993 through 2001, covering the trial.)

After an April 1, 1998, table reading of the script, filming commenced immediately. All but one script was destroyed after the reading to prevent copies from being found. These precautions seem rather incredible given how *Seinfeld* modestly started with a handful of episodes on May 31, 1990. It detailed the life of its title character with his friend George, an insecure man distraught by the littlest things in life; Jerry's apartment house neighbor Kramer, an eccentric bon vivant; and Jerry's ex-girlfriend Elaine, a woman who often spent time with these three men so she could talk with them about how wacky and/or irritating life in Manhattan could be. That modest setup allowed for some of the most inventive and intricate sitcom plotting *ever*, and typically resulted in belly laughs.

Seinfeld had basically a cult audience until it began airing after *Cheers* (see 10) in 1993; then it stayed in the top three the rest of its run, including finishing at #1 in the 1994-1995 and 1997-1998 seasons. When Jerry decided he'd had enough of doing the show, it was not surprising that viewers everywhere wanted to see how it would end, and the TV industry knew it.

During the hour the finale aired, TV Land broadcast an image of a sign on an office door that read, "Gone watchin' *Seinfeld*, be back in 60 minutes." And the May 13, 1998, episode of *Dharma and Greg* (airing one day before the finale) had the married couple having sex in public places while *Seinfeld* ran, as they were confident no one would be doing anything else that night and thus would not see them. (Nearly 76 million people in America watched the finale, in fact.)

After the 75-minute episode "The Finale" ran, nearly 15 minutes were deleted so that it could appear in reruns on local stations as two half-hour episodes. The removals included two taxi scenes with Jerry and George, first on their way to meeting Kimbrough and then discussing plans to move to California with the sale of *Jerry* to NBC. Also missing were scenes involving various interactions among the guest stars, such as the rabbi counseling the parents of Jerry and George, and several partial and full testimonies of people about their interactions with the quartet. All actors who appeared on the original long version were listed as guest stars at the end even though their scenes had been cut.

Seinfeld won none of five Emmy categories for the 1997-1998 season, including one for comedy series. The series ended Sept. 10, 1998, with 68 total Emmy nominations and ten wins, for comedy series in 1993, for Richards as supporting actor in 1993, 1994 and 1997, for Louis-Dreyfus as supporting actress in 1996, for writing in 1992 and 1993, and for editing in 1992, 1994 and 1995.

Larry David, writer of "The Finale," made amends on his HBO series *Curb Your Enthusiasm*. In the "It's Not a Reunion Show But It's the Closest You'll Get" episode in 2009, the old *Seinfeld* crew gets back together for a contemporary update special (e.g., George has lost his money as part of one of Bernie Madoff's Ponzi schemes), and David uses it as a way to try win back his ex-wife by playing George instead of letting Jason Alexander reprise the role (it's a story too convoluted to summarize here). Funny and witty, it left you with a warm feeling at the end, the way "The Finale" should have done.

20 — *Bonanza*

March 8, 1964 ("The Pure Truth"). **Rating:** 41.6. **Share:** 62.

Aired on NBC Sunday 9–10 P.M. Eastern and Pacific, 8–9 P.M. Central

Competition: *The Judy Garland Show* on CBS, *Arrest and Trial* (last hour of 90-minute episode) on ABC

Cast: Lorne Greene (Ben Cartwright), Dan Blocker (Eric "Hoss" Cartwright), Michael Landon (Little Joe Cartwright), Pernell Roberts (Adam Cartwright), Ray Teal (Sheriff Roy Coffee). **Guests:** Glenda Farrell (Lulabelle "Looney" Watkins), Stanley Adams (Sheriff Tate), Jay Lanin (Ward), Lloyd Corrigan (Jesse Simmons), Maudie Prickett (Bank Customer), Olan Soule (Herman the Telegrapher), Raymond Guth (Al the Stagecoach Driver). **Crew:** David Dortort (creator-producer), Lois Hire (writer), Don McDougall (director).

Synopsis. To undo the annual effects of spring fever on Hoss, Ben feeds his son a tonic that makes him soporific, and Little Joe has Sheriff Coffee install Hoss as a temporary deputy at Virginia City to further keep an eye on him. Due to misunderstandings while semiconscious, Hoss takes a stagecoach at night to Red Rock, where a lynch mob accuses him of stealing the local bank's money. Hoss avoids pursuit from the barely competent sheriff when he encounters Lulabelle, a grizzled prospector camping outside of town who believes in his innocence.

The inability to capture and frame Hoss gnaws at the real robbers, Ward and banker Jesse Simmons. A suspicious Ward heads towards Lulabelle's camp. Meanwhile, Hoss accidentally discovers gold at the camp, but Lulabelle fears others may exploit it. Ward arrives and makes Hoss his hostage until Lulabelle knocks Ward out with a rock thrown at his head. She brings Hoss to Red Rock to get his $500 reward and learns that Jesse provided the money she received. After claiming her camp land with the cash, Lulabelle tells Jesse she knows he did the crime, then follows him when he meets with a recovered Ward and they plan to leave town. Sheriff Tate disbelieves Lulabelle, who then frees Hoss from jail, and she and Hoss nab Ward and Simmons. Hoss returns to the Ponderosa ranch to recount his misadventures to his brothers.

Backstory. During much of the 1960s, a good amount of channel-changing took place on Sunday nights. Millions of Americans would watch *The Ed Sullivan Show* (see 11) on CBS, then switch over at the finish to view *Bonanza* on NBC. That pattern bedeviled Mike Dann, CBS head of programming, particularly since it was the only NBC series to make the top 10 every season from 1962 to 1966 which CBS otherwise dominated. As Dann recalled of that four-year period in his memoirs, "We pitted a variety of formats and more than half a dozen programs against the show: *General Electric Theatre, The Jack Benny Program, The Real McCoys, General Electric True, The Judy Garland Show, My Living Doll, The Joey Bishop Show* and *Perry Mason*. Every one of them failed."

Those failures were so big that by the 1964-1965 season, *Bonanza* became the #1 series, where it stayed for three years. But most of the series' individually highest rated episodes occurred the previous season, in February and March of 1964. In fact, only a few million viewers separated it from the stellar ratings *The Ed Sullivan Show* won with the Beatles on Feb. 9 and 16, 1964, with *Bonanza* scoring numbers of 41.0 and 41.4 respectively those nights. A few weeks later, this episode proved to be the biggest draw of them all, and it's hard to say why.

One problem is there are contrivances throughout the story. The script is not the only element at fault, however. The episode is flat in all departments, with "cute" music cues underlining the action, and even reliable character actors like Stanley Adams, Maudie Prickett and Olan Soule appear to be just going through the motions.

Part of what may have hampered "The Pure Truth" is the set of conventions established on *Bonanza* by this time. The format typically required Ben Cartwright and his sons Adam, Hoss and Little Joe (all born by different women who died, which provoked no amount of speculation among more prurient viewers as to what really happened to them) to be together at the start of an episode, usually at their massive Ponderosa ranch. Then an incident involving primarily one of them would dominate the rest of the show before they reunited at the end. Making it more difficult for the writers was that even minor character flaws were not permitted for the regulars.

Yet this concept of a happy family probably made *Bonanza* last longer than most of the westerns which were on the air when it debuted rather inauspiciously on Sept. 12, 1959, to kick off NBC's Saturday night lineup. The show floundered its first season opposite *Perry Mason*—yes, the same series that it beat decisively and drove off the air in 1965-1966—but the second season it pulled even with *Perry Mason* and did even better when moved to its Sunday slot in the fall of 1961, finishing #2 in 1961-1962 and 1963-1964 and #4 in 1962-1963. Also in 1961, guitarist Al Caiola made the driving "Bonanza" theme a top 20 hit.

For a while *Bonanza* was omnipotent, even with Pernell Roberts leaving in 1965 because he considered the role of Adam unchallenging. The character was not replaced, and to most viewers Adam was out of sight and out of mind. (In the 1987 film *Tin Men*, set in 1963, writer-director Barry Levinson had characters discuss the unrealism of the show in several amusing quotes, but he forgot that Adam was still in the cast then, as his characters talk about only the other Cartwrights.) In 1967, CBS's hit *The Smothers Brothers Comedy Hour* only succeeded in knocking *Bonanza* out of #1, as the show remained in the top 10 through 1971. But when the series came close to being tied with ABC's Sunday night movie in the 1971-1972 season at #20, NBC decided a change was in order.

On May 12, 1972, NBC started rerunning *Bonanza* episodes aired three to five years earlier under the title *Ponderosa* on Tuesdays from 8–9 P.M. Eastern and Pacific while repeating episodes from the current season in the regular Sunday night slot. This was to prepare viewers for the show's shift to the Tuesday slots that fall. At the same time, local stations could buy 260 *Bonanza* repeats from the first seven years of the series to air in the fall of 1972. *Bonanza* looked ready to stay strong.

But Dan Blocker died unexpectedly of a pulmonary embolism at age 43 just one day after the NBC *Ponderosa* repeats began. Producer David Dortort later said he knew this meant the series was finished, as no one could replace the imposing (6-foot-4, 275 pounds) yet avuncular actor. Nonetheless, production continued.

In the 1972 season opener, Little Joe got married, and his wife died tragically in the same episode. Along with the death and disappearance of Hoss, this cavalier development displeased fans greatly, and the initial strong turnout (in fourth place with a 25.1/38) dropped substantially the next time out, with *Bonanza* barely making the top 40 while its competition on CBS, *Maude* and *Hawaii Five-O*, increased substantially. They made it into the top 10, and with better demographics (upscale, well-educated audiences) than *Bonanza*.

Seeing the show as a relic of a bygone era, NBC dropped *Bonanza* midseason. The last episode aired on Jan. 16, 1973, making it the longest running series to be cancelled without completing its final season. (The runner-up is another NBC show, *Ironside*, which the network ended on Jan. 16, 1975, in the middle of its eighth season.) The only western series to appear on NBC after *Bonanza* ended were *The Quest* (1976), *The Oregon Trail* (1977) and *Bret Maverick* (1981).

Bonanza won only one Emmy out of ten times it was in contention, in 1971 for David Rose's music composition for one episode. The other nominations were one for best drama series in 1965, four for cinematography (in 1965, 1966, 1967 and 1971), one for special cinematography in 1966, one for art direction and scenic design in 1963, and one each for film editing and music in 1966.

There were TV-movie revivals of *Bonanza* in 1988, 1993 and 1995, but all of the original cast was dead except for Pernell Roberts, who refused to participate in them. There was also a series featuring detailing the characters' lives when they were younger, but this show, *The Ponderosa*, aired on the little-watched PAX network and lasted only from 2001 to 2002.

Meanwhile, *Bonanza* remains strong in reruns, making it one of the few series from 50 years ago still on the air in some markets. Long may it gallop.

---

19 — Miss America Pageant

Sept. 9, 1961 (the 35th edition). **Rating:** 41.8. **Share:** 75.

Aired on CBS Saturday 9:30 P.M.–midnight Eastern and Pacific, 8:30–11 P.M. Central

Competition: *Make That Spare* on ABC, *The Nation's Future* on NBC

Cast: Bert Parks, Don McNeill, Marilyn Van Derbur (Hosts), The Honeydreamers, The Hamilton Trio, The Glenn Osser Orchestra. **Crew:** Paul Levitan (producer), Vern Diamond (director).

Synopsis. A parade of 55 smiling ladies in gowns, representing all the states in the union plus a few other areas (e.g., Miss Washington, D.C.), appeared at the start of the festivities in the packed Atlantic City Convention Hall in New Jersey. The women are shown next in the bathing suit competition, even though the judging for that competition took place in the preliminaries prior to the show. The winner of the Preliminary Swimsuit competition was Maria Beale Fletcher, representing North Carolina. She made it to the semifinalist lineup along with several others.

In the talent competition, Fletcher performed a song-and-dance routine accompanied by her own recording. Like the swimsuit competition, this section already had been judged. Fletcher's scores were good enough to help her make it to the top five, along with Miss Arkansas, Miss Utah, Miss Texas and Miss Minnesota. They each were asked a different question, and the judges decided which answer they liked best.

Bert Parks announced that Fletcher has been picked as Miss America 1962. He placed a crown on her head and gave her a bouquet of roses before she walked down the runway. Parks serenaded Fletcher with "There She Is, Miss America," the pageant's theme song since 1955. She was the pageant's first winner from the Tar Heel State and remains the only one hailing from it as of this writing.

Backstory. It is hard to think of any other U.S. institution which has been alternately and thoroughly admired, ridiculed, emulated and castigated as much as the Miss America pageant. It has never received critical respect and has had only three Emmy nominations, all from 1996–2001, with just one win, for Best Choreography for Anita Mann and Charonne Mose in 1996. Feminists particularly held it in disregard, feeling that it belittled women by placing a premium on physical beauty; rumors swirled during the 1970s that they were going to disrupt the ceremonies. And it is hard to think of any comedy variety show from the 1950s through 1970s that did not include a sketch mocking the conventions of the spectacle, and the sketch usually envisioned the pageant with male contestants to heighten the comedy.

Yet for many of the competitors, it marks one of the high points of their lives, as many of them spent years training themselves to win this competition. It's given several women their start in show business: Bess Myerson (1945), Lee Meriwether (1955), Phyllis George (1971) and Vanessa Williams (1984) all had successful entertainment careers launched after being named Miss America. To them and dozens of others, the pageant is a glorious event they will never forget.

Begun in 1921 as a way to attract tourists to Atlantic City after Labor Day, the Miss America pageant began with just eight contestants but soon attracted women who won local events held across America. It was discontinued for six years starting in 1927, but returned stronger than ever thereafter. ABC executives wanted to telecast it in 1953, but pageant officials insisted it could not air in the Philadelphia market just an hour's drive away (they feared a drop in attendance). But the next year, with Philco TV sets lined up as a sponsor, ABC's financial offer was too great to resist. The Miss America Pageant debuted on TV Sept. 11, 1954, and it easily beat the competition on CBS and NBC, something ABC rarely did at the time.

The next year, Bert Parks replaced Bob Russell as pageant host, and he retained the job for almost 25 years. His unctuous, overpowering style added drama to the show as well as lent itself to parody. "I'm identified with it so closely that I think it may even have hurt my career on television," he acknowledged to Frank Deford in *There She Is.* "But look, I like it, and if I can speak for myself, I do a damned good job at what I'm supposed to do. I'm a catalyst, and I never forget that it is not my show. It is the girls' show. I work for them."

In 1957 the pageant's executive committee chairman, Albert A. Marks, Jr., allowed rights for the special to go to CBS. With more affiliates than ABC, the network was able to get more than half the viewing audience, and it expanded the show from 90 minutes to two hours the next year. The 1961 edition marked its longest show ever on TV to that point, at two and a half hours. Then as now, the show aired live in the East and Midwest.

Given that the regular series pre-empted by the pageant included the top shows on TV at the time, *Have Gun Will Travel* and *Gunsmoke* (see 24), and the fact that the network competition at the show's opening consisted of a bowling show on ABC and a public affairs one on NBC, it is not too surprising to report this is the highest-rated of the Miss America pageants. A little extra incentive to watch might have been the distinguished quintet of judges for this year's pageant: classic movie actress Joan Crawford; Ted Mack, host of TV's *The Original Amateur Hour;* June Taylor, choreographer for many TV series; Broadway impresario producer David Merrick; and mezzo-soprano operatic singer Blanche Theborn.

As for the winner, Maria Beale Fletcher had been a Rockette at Radio City Music Hall for a year before competing in the pageant. She considered opening a dance school following her win, but some previous pageant winners persuaded her that it was not becoming to use her scholarship money that way, so she attended Vanderbilt instead. She quietly avoided the limelight thereafter.

"Jose"'s review of the program in *Variety* was favorable, but it unfortunately reflected the sexism of the period regarding the contestants when he concluded, "It seems that beauty and brains can be combined in the young things of this era."

Wonder what the "young things" thought of that backhanded compliment.

Subsequent Miss America pageants routinely finished among the highest-rated specials on TV every year through the 1970s, typically drawing more than a third of all Americans with TV sets. In 1979, Parks was unceremoniously dropped as host; his replacement was Ron Ely, an actor best known for starring in NBC's *Tarzan* series from 1966 to 1968. Ely lasted only two years before Gary Collins, then hosting the popular syndicated daytime talk show *Hour Magazine,* took over in 1982 and stayed there the rest of the 1980s. (His wife, actress Mary Ann Mobley, was Miss America 1959.) Parks returned to the pageant in 1990 as a guest, in one of his last public appearances before dying in 1992 at age 77.

The program moved to NBC in 1966, where it stayed for 30 years until a major, continuous decline in ratings during the 1990s (it lost more than six million household viewers since 1989) led the network to drop it. ABC assumed broadcasting rights for the spectacle in 1997, but audience declines continued, and by the time that network last aired it in 2005, there were barely more than five million viewers.

The pageant went to cable channels CMT for 2006 and 2007, and then TLC since 2008, but ratings have remained small, even though the pageant moved to the more heavily watched month of January and took place in Las Vegas rather than Atlantic City. The most recent pageants have employed the youthful Mario Lopez, the first person to host the show for more than two years since Regis Philbin led the proceedings from 1992 to 1996. (Collins ended his tenure in 1991.) Recent shows have also been somewhat awful.

At the Jan. 30, 2010, ceremony, the contestants read tacky introductions of themselves in reference to their home states. The worst was Emily Woods (Miss Georgia) saying, "From the home of the Masters golf tournament, where I *didn't* meet Tiger Woods," in reference to revelations about the latter having multiple mistresses. Later, judge Rush Limbaugh, the right-wing radio commentator, embarrassed himself and the audience by dancing to Lady Gaga's "Poker Face" during a break in the competition.

Imagine the 1961 judges trying to preserve their dignity had they jived to a contemporary hit like "Tossin' and Turnin'," and you realize how pathetic the pageant has become. With such presentations, it is unlikely to regain its stature. In other words — there she *was*, Miss America.

18 — *Cinderella*

Feb. 22, 1965 (musical special). **Rating:** 42.3. **Share:** 59.

Aired on CBS Monday 8:30–10 P.M. Eastern and Pacific, 7:30–9 P.M. Central

Competition: *No Time for Sergeants, Wendy and Me* and *The Bing Crosby Show* on ABC, *The Man from U.N.C.L.E.* and a Jonathan Winters special on NBC

Cast: Lesley Ann Warren (Cinderella), Ginger Rogers (The Queen), Walter Pidgeon (The King), Celeste Holm (The Fairy Godmother), Jo Van Fleet (Stepmother), Stuart Damon (The Prince), Pat Carroll (Prunella), Barbara Ruick (Esmerelda). **Crew:** Charles S. Dubin (producer-director), Joseph Schrank (writer), Richard Rodgers (music), Oscar Hammerstein II (lyrics), John Green (music director).

Synopsis. When the Prince stops at a cottage and asks a woman to fetch him water from its well, she says she is afraid to do that because her mean Stepmother would punish her. Realizing she does not know who he is, the Prince coaxes the woman out, and he learns that her name is Cinderella (because she sleeps with the ashes). The Prince continues his trek back to the palace, where his father, the King, is disappointed he did not return with a wife after traveling the kingdom. To remedy the situation, the King announces that a ball will be held to invite all fair young maidens to present themselves before the Prince as matrimonial candidates.

The Stepmother and her ungainly daughters, Prunella and Esmerelda, are excited to attend, but Cinderella cannot go in her old clothes. While she is sobbing about her situation, her Fairy Godmother appears and magically turns a pumpkin into her coach and rodents into her horses and horsemen; she also bestows a gown and crown on Cinderella. As Cinderella heads to the ball, the Fairy Godmother warns her everything will return to normal at the stroke of midnight.

At the ball, the Prince sees Cinderella, who entrances him when they dance and talk. But she flees when the clock hits twelve, accidentally leaving behind a glass slipper. The Prince searches for its wearer and finds it is Cinderella. Her dowdy outfit matters not to him, and he marries her.

Backstory. In the summer of 1956, Charles Tucker, the agent for Julie Andrews, asked the musical team of Rodgers and Hammerstein if they wanted to write a musical based on *Cinderella* for television. The reason for this request was that Mary Martin's version of *Peter Pan* was a huge success when NBC ran it on March 7, 1955, be-coming the first show ever to beat *I Love Lucy* in the ratings, and network executives believed that a similar fairy tale with music could be just as big a smash (see 93 for more on *Peter Pan*).

Sensing the opportunity to reach a large TV audience — and perhaps smarting over the fact that their latest Broadway musical *Pipe Dreams* was their first failure, closing on June 30, 1956, after just seven months — the duo wrote their first TV musical. For the most part, the two men took a traditional approach in crafting the book for the show. "One of the major changes, though, was making the two stepsisters less frightening and more comic," Rodgers noted in his autobiography. "We also decided to make our Fairy Godmother an attractive young woman ... rather than the customary old crone."

Rodgers and Hammerstein crafted eight songs for the production, among them Cinderella's plaintive song of desire at the start, "In My Own Little Corner," the robust "The Prince Is Giving a Ball," the bubbly "Impossible/It's Possible" between Cinderella and the Fairy Godmother, and the humorous "Stepsisters Lament," where Prunella and Esmerelda grouse about why the Prince desires Cinderella. Though none of the numbers became hit records, both Vic Damone and Tony Martin made the lower reaches of the *Billboard* pop chart in 1957 with their versions of the Prince's song "Do I Love You Because You're Beautiful."

Cast in the leads were Julie Andrews as Cinderella, taking a break from her success playing Eliza Doolittle in *My Fair Lady* on Broadway, and Jon Cypher as the Prince. Heavily promoted by CBS, *Cinderella* premiered live from New York City on March 31, 1957, pre-empting *The Ed Sullivan Show* (see 11) and *General Electric Theater*. It was one of the highest rated specials of the 1950s.

In 1963 CBS announced plans to remake the musical, probably inspired by NBC's success re-running the videotaped production of *Peter Pan*. The network decided not to use the kinescope of the original production, nor employ Andrews again as its leading lady (she was too busy filming *Mary Poppins* at the time, although the fact she was now six years older than when she did the original might have dissuaded age-obsessed executives). Instead, the network announced that Anna Marie Alberghetti would assume the title role.

But Alberghetti was dropped in favor of newcomer Lesley Ann Warren, who received good notices from critics in a featured role in the Broadway musical *110 in the Shade* in 1963. Playing the Prince was Stuart Damon, who made his Broadway debut in the musical *First Impressions* in 1959. Both were essentially unknowns to TV audiences in 1965.

For the 1965 remake, Rodgers added "Loneliness of Evening," which the Prince performed as the first song in the show, lamenting his state of mind. It was a tune Rodgers and Hammerstein wrote for *South Pacific* that was cut prior to its Broadway opening in 1949. Indeed, some numbers from previous Rodgers and Hammerstein musicals appears to have colored their tunes for *Cinderella*. For example, the love theme Cinderella and the Prince sing after they meet, "Ten Minutes Ago," has echoes of "I'm Gonna Wash That Man Right Outa My Hair" from *South Pacific*, while their follow-up song, "Do I Love You Because You're Beautiful," owes a debt to "Something Wonderful" from *The King and I.*

For this go-round, the special was videotaped so it could be repeated. Production took place at CBS Television City in Hollywood. Writer Joseph Schrank, whose biggest credit up to this point had been adapting the Broadway musical *Cabin in the Sky* into a feature film in 1943, added a new beginning and changed a few other elements, but he basically kept intact most of the 1957 book for the musical.

Watching the 1965 *Cinderella* today, you may well wonder why and how this became the highest-rated special of its decade. Sure, the songs are great, the acting is fine, the sets are beautiful and director Charles S. Dubin paces it well. The problem is mainly the script — it is a rather straightforward narrative with little wit or innovation, and if you know the story, there is nothing exciting that will happen for you on screen.

Officially titled *Rodgers and Hammerstein's Cinderella*, the special replaced *The Andy Griffith Show*, *The Lucy Show* and *Many Happy Returns*, the latter a sitcom so unpopular that it lost millions of viewers on average despite following Lucille Ball's top 10 series. *Cinderella*'s huge ratings helped CBS in finishing #1 for the 1964-1965 season. It not only was #1 for the week but also for the year, outperforming even the highest ratings of the #1 series on TV, *Bonanza* (see 20).

The massive popularity of the show was expected to catapult its unknown stars to big careers, but that did not happen immediately. Warren signed with the Disney studios and starred in *The Happiest Millionaire* (1967) and *The One and Only, Genuine, Original Family Band* (1968), two feature films that failed to showcase her depth as an ac-

tress. Neither did her first regular TV series role on *Mission: Impossible*, which lasted just one season (1970-1971). She kept working steadily nonetheless and received a supporting actress Oscar nomination for *Victor/Victoria* (1982). The film's star, who earned an Oscar nod as lead actress, was the 1957 Cinderella, Julie Andrews.

When *Cinderella* debuted, Damon was rehearsing in Richard Rodgers' next musical on Broadway, *Do I Hear a Waltz?* It opened on March 18, 1965, and closed seven months later. He then went to England to work for about a decade, starring in the adventure TV series *The Champions*, which ran on NBC in the summer of 1968. He finally became somewhat known when he starred on *General Hospital* as Dr. Alan Quartermaine from 1977 through 2007.

CBS repeated the special eight times through Feb. 3, 1974. By that time, its numbers were not as impressive (a 16.2/25 for the final showing). Nearly a quarter century later, ABC decided to revive the musical. ABC's version, first telecast Nov. 2, 1997, and starring Brandy as Cinderella, finished #1 for the week. It won an Emmy for art direction as well as six other nominations, including best variety, comedy or music special.

The book for the TV *Cinderella* is available for professional and student theater groups to perform around the country. For those who want the original, the 1965 *Cinderella* came out on DVD in 2002 from Sony Pictures.

---

17 — *Love Story*

Oct. 1, 1972 (*ABC Sunday Night Movie*; first released theatrically in 1970). **Rating:** 42.3. **Share:** 62.

Aired on ABC Sunday 9–11 P.M. Eastern and Pacific, 8–10 P.M. Central

Competition: *The New Dick Van Dyke Show* and *Mannix* on CBS; *McCloud* and *Night Gallery* on NBC

Cast: Ali MacGraw (Jenny Cavellerri), Ryan O'Neal (Oliver Barrett IV), John Marley (Phil Cavellerri), Ray Milland (Oliver Barrett III), Russell Nype (Dean Thompson), Katherine Balfour (Mrs. Barrett), Sydney Walker (Dr. Shapeley), Robert Moddica (Dr. Addison), Walker Daniels (Ray Stratton), Tommy Lee Jones (Hank), John Merensky (Steve). **Crew:** Arthur Hiller (director), Howard G. Minsky (producer), David Golden (executive producer), Erich Segal (writer).

Synopsis. Jenny Cavellerri dismisses Oliver Barrett IV as a "preppie" when they meet in Radcliffe University's library. Barrett is a Harvard undergrad hockey player from a rich family (a campus hall is named after his grandfather). She is a modest Rhode Island baker's daughter and a musician. But they click, and Oliver proposes to Jenny. Their wedding plans irk Oliver's stuffy father, who cuts off his son financially. Oliver begs Dean Thompson for assistance to law school to no avail, and Jenny's dad Phil cannot support him either. Phil does attend Oliver and Jenny's secular civil ceremony; Oliver's family does not.

Jenny works to pay for Oliver's studies. They argue after she calls Oliver's dad about the latter's 60th birthday party and tells him that Oliver loves him in his own way. Oliver scolds her, as he remains upset with his dad, and she runs away for hours before they reconcile. Oliver earns his law degree and secures a job. Then they learn that Jenny is dying. Oliver lies to his father to obtain cash for her medical treatments, but it is for naught. Jenny dies at age 25 with Oliver at her bedside.

Oliver runs into his dad, who had learned the truth and wanted to help. "Jenny's dead," Oliver tells him. "I'm sorry," his dad responds. Oliver repeats what Jenny told him when they ended their big spat — "Love means never having to say you're sorry" — then wanders away in sorrow.

Backstory. People either adore or abhor *Love Story* — there seems to be no middle ground. Fans call it inspirational and moving. Naysayers term it treacly and trite. The film's final line, as well as its opening narration by Oliver — "What can you say about a 25-year-old girl who died?" — became part of pop culture as well as sources for endless parodies, from *Mad* magazine to *The Carol Burnett Show.*

The Academy Awards liked it enough to give it seven nominations, for picture, director, writer, actor (O'Neal), actress (MacGraw), supporting actor (Marley, who had to be convinced to take the role) and music (Frances Lai).

On the other hand, the *Harvard Lampoon* "Movie Worst" awards ranked it among the top 10 (or should that be bottom 10?) of the year, named MacGraw worst actress, and even suggested that her marriage to movie executive Robert Evans (which occurred a month into the filming on Oct. 24, 1969) was "The Strongest Argument for Laxer Divorce Laws." The *Lampoon* also dispensed "The It-Can't-Happen-Here Award" to the motion picture "for showing the American public that the nicest things about Harvard are Cambridge winters, low-rent housing, Winthrop House and leukemia." Ouch.

What sparked this pro and con opinion was a story that occurred to Erich Segal, a classics professor at Yale, based on his college years at Harvard dating a Radcliffe girl. (He later claimed his classmate, Al Gore, had inspired it as well with his love of his eventual wife, Tipper. In fact, Tommy Lee Jones, Gore's real-life roommate, played one of Oliver's three roommates in the film, billed as Tom Lee Jones.)

Segal wrote it as a screenplay first, then converted it into a book when all movie studios turned down the script. When Howard Minsky at the William Morris talent agency sent it to Ali MacGraw, her interest spurred Paramount Pictures to film it, as she was a top new star. Robert Evans, Paramount's production head who loved Mac-Graw, participated in the adaptation and made the female lead Italian American rather than Jewish as first identified.

Evans went through two directors before he recalled Arthur Hiller's work on *The Out-of-Towners* (1970) and felt he would be the best match for the film. He delayed production of Hiller's next directing job, *Plaza Suite,* to have him direct *Love Story.*

After eight actors rejected the lead role, Paramount tested ones who were not well known, including David Birney, Ken Howard and Christopher Walken. Ryan O'Neal was in that group, and Evans thought he had the best audition. Coincidentally, Hiller had directed O'Neal on the debut episode of *Empire,* the actor's first regular TV series, which ran on NBC from 1962 to 1963. After that, O'Neal shot to fame starring on ABC's nighttime TV soap opera *Peyton Place* from 1964 to 1969.

For the hockey scenes, Hiller found a camera operator who played the game. The technician was able to attach a camera to a hockey stick to follow the action in motion in the rink. O'Neal learned how to ice skate for his role. Likewise, MacGraw practiced playing 12 seconds of music so that she would be shown as a capable pianist in one continuous take. While Hiller was shooting in Boston, there was a huge unexpected snowstorm. Hiller persevered and filmed Ryan and Ali frolicking in the elements, including throwing a football and making snow angels. "I often think if we hadn't done that, the film would not be quite the same," Hiller said in *The Directors Take Two.* "But that's taking away from that beautiful music that Frances Lai wrote for that scene. Actually he contributed an entire score that was unbelievable."

Lai's theme became a top 40 instrumental record; Henry Mancini released his own version as a single which cracked the top 20. The most successful version came when Carl Sigman wrote lyrics and Andy Williams recorded the renamed "Where Do I Begin (Love Story)," a top 10 hit in 1971. Since the lyrics were not part of the film, it was not nominated for the Best Song Oscar. However, Lai's original score did win the film's only Academy Award.

Lai got the job after a score by hit songwriter Jimmy Webb failed to make the grade. "[Webb] fell so in love with Ali MacGraw and her character that he buried her every time she was on the screen, and I had been working so hard to keep it from being a soap opera ... so we had to drop the score," Hiller said on the *Love Story* 2000 DVD commentary.

Helping the box office was Segal's decision to adapt his screenplay into a novel, which came out in early 1970 and was still at #1 on the *New York Times* best seller list when the movie debuted at the end of the year. At the time, its transfer from theaters to television was the quickest ever for a major motion picture.

ABC reran the film on Oct. 21, 1973 (19.5/30), and July 19, 1977 (15.1/26). In 1978 Paramount released *Oliver's Story*, a sequel based on a novel by Segal. Even though Jenny had said in *Love Story* that she wanted Oliver to find another lover, it shocked viewers to see that he could and would do that, and it bombed in theaters. Its network TV debut's numbers on Feb. 22, 1982, were an unimpressive 16.2/24.

Following *Love Story*'s success came more tales of a young man and his dying sweetheart. For example, there were two TV-movie knockoffs in 1973 (*She Lives* and *Sunshine*) and hit songs ("Seasons in the Sun" by Terry Jacks in 1974, "Rocky" by Austin Roberts in 1975). An NBC-TV version of *Love Story* (1973) was just an anthology with Lai's theme music; it failed quickly opposite *Kojak* on CBS.

---

16 — *Airport*

Nov. 11, 1973 (*ABC Movie Special*; first released theatrically in 1970). **Rating:** 42.3. **Share:** 63.

Aired on ABC Sunday 7:30–10:30 P.M. Eastern and Pacific, 6:30–9:30 P.M. Central

Competition: *The New Perry Mason, Mannix* and *Barnaby Jones* on CBS; *Disney, McMillan and Wife* and a news special on NBC

Cast: Burt Lancaster (Mel Bakersfield), Dean Martin (Capt. Vernon Demerest), Jean Seberg (Tanya Livingston), Jacqueline Bisset (Gwen Meighen), George Kennedy (Joe Patroni), Helen Hayes (Ada Quonsett), Van Heflin (D.O. Guerrero), Maureen Stapleton (Inez Guerrero), Barry Nelson (Capt. Anson Harris), Dana Wynter (Cindy Bakersfield), Lloyd Nolan (Harry Standish), Barbara Hale (Sarah Demerest), Gary Collins (Second Officer Cy Jordan). **Crew:** Ross Hunter (producer), George Seaton (director-writer).

Synopsis. The man in charge of operations at Lincoln International Airport in Chicago, Mel Bakersfield, faces multiple crises during a snowy night at Chicago's Lincoln International Airport. A stuck plane closes a runway. Neighbors protest flight noise. His shrewish wife Cindy plans to divorce him. Mel's biggest challenge comes when D.O. Guerrero boards a flight to Rome with a bomb in his attaché case and plans to detonate it so that Inez, his wife, can collect the flight insurance from his death. The plane takes off with Guerrero sitting next to Ada Quonsett, a repeat-offender stowaway. Back at the airport, Inez tells Mel and his trusty aide Tanya what she has learned of her husband's plans; they relay the information to pilot Vernon, the husband of Mel's sister. The plane turns around while flight attendant Gwen enlists Ada in a failed ploy to get a-hold of the case. Despite Vernon telling Guerrero his plan will not benefit Inez, the latter detonates the bomb in a lavatory.

The plane decompresses and is structurally damaged. Gwen, who is pregnant with Vernon's child, is seriously injured. After some complications, they land at Lincoln. The passengers disembark, with Vernon caring for Gwen. The blizzard ends the next morning, and Mel and Tanya head off to her apartment for breakfast.

Backstory. *Airport* began its life as a Canadian TV drama in 1956. Its writer, Arthur Hailey, was a pilot with the Royal Air Force during World War II, but the idea for the aerial adventure did not occur to him until 1955, when he speculated on a flight within his native country what would happen if the plane was disabled. Hailey decided to flesh out the concept for a novel released in 1968. A bigger hit than his previous best seller *Hotel*, *Airport* received a big-screen adaptation in the wake of its success.

Putting together the theatrical version was Ross Hunter, a man known for opulent motion picture productions. He spared no expense, spending a then-astounding $10 million during four months of filming in the winter and spring of 1969. Along with their salaries, stars Burt Lancaster and Dean Martin received a percentage of the film's grosses, which led to many future paydays. (Ironically, considering the nature of their characters, both Lancaster and Martin were undergoing real-life marital strife while filming this movie; it resulted in divorces for both of them.)

The warm, romantic score was the last created by the prolific Alfred Newman, who died a month before the film's premiere. It earned him his 45th Oscar nomination (nine of which were wins) and his third Grammy nomination. Guitarist Vincent Bell recorded a version of the "*Airport* Love Theme" that sounded like dripping water and managed to score a top 40 record with it in the spring of 1970.

Airport earned nine other Academy Award mentions, but only one win, for Helen Hayes as Best Supporting Actress. Hayes was staying at the residence of her friend Lari Mako, a Beverly Hills designer, when the latter introduced her to Hunter, who told her he had left a copy of Hailey's book in Hayes' guest room and hoped she would consider the part of the adorable stowaway. The story and the role enchanted Hayes, and she agreed to put aside her dislike of acting in movies (she had not appeared in one since a cameo in 1959's *Third Man on the Mountain*) to do it. Hayes later commented that Mrs. Quonsett "is pretty much me, though of course I took some hints from the writers." (Hayes defeated *Airport* castmate Maureen Stapleton in the category, but I feel Stapleton's work is better; she perfectly captured every facet of her character's emotions. Like Hayes, Stapleton was primarily a stage actress, with *Airport* being only her sixth movie.)

The other Academy Award nominations for *Airport* were for best picture, writing, art direction-set direction, cinematography, costume design, film editing and sound. Many critics decried *Airport* as unworthy of celebration, believing it to be hokey, old-fashioned and manipulative. But moviegoers loved the family-friendly escapism (it was rated G), and shortly after it debuted on March 5, 1970, it became the top moneymaker for many weeks that year. In those days, that kind of public reaction often resulted in Oscar nominations no matter what any reviewer thought.

The success of *Airport* led to other successful "disaster" films putting cast members in jeopardy, such as *Earthquake* and *The Towering Inferno*. There was a knockoff of the movie on TV as well: Universal sold *San Francisco International Airport* to NBC first as a TV-movie and then as a series starting Oct. 28, 1970, with Lloyd Bridges playing the operations manager. But viewers preferred *Hawaii Five-O*, so the series ended less than a year later.

Universal re-released the movie in September 1972 (on a double bill with *The Andromeda Strain*) before releasing it to television. When *Airport* first ran on ABC, it finished #1 and put the network on top overall for that week. That was an impressive achievement, given how ABC finished third among the networks for most other weeks during the 1973-1974 season. It was billed as a movie special because its three-hour length pre-empted the series which preceded ABC's Sunday night movies in 1973-1974, *The F.B.I.*

ABC repeated the movie on Feb. 9, 1975, and it did very well: 30.0/42, making it the network's second-highest rated movie that season after another disaster flick, *The Poseidon Adventure* (see 31). The network ran it again on Dec. 19, 1976 (14.8/24), May 1, 1977 (18.2/30), and July 6, 1980 (16.5/31). The 1975 repeat was helped by the fact that a popular sequel, *Airport 1975*, came out the previous year. When the latter film aired on NBC on Sept. 20, 1976, it was a hit, earning a strong 31.6/46.

The next sequel was *Airport '77*. Last and definitely least (in terms of quality) was *The Concorde—Airport '79*. On TV, NBC added 70 minutes of outtakes and new footage to *Airport '77* to make it a four-hour event when it ran on Sept. 19 and 20, 1978 (18.9/30 for part one, 21.2/33 for part two). ABC added 19 minutes of footage to *The Concorde—Airport '79* for their May 17, 1982 telecast, getting a pretty good rating in the process (18.3/31).

15 — NFC Championship Game

Jan. 10, 1982 (Dallas Cowboys vs. San Francisco 49ers). **Rating: 41.0. Share: 55.**

Aired on CBS Sunday 5–8:30 P.M. Eastern, 4–7:30 P.M. Central, 3–6:30 P.M. Mountain and 2–5:30 P.M. Pacific

Competition: *Code Red* and *Today's FBI* (first half-hour of 60-minute show) on ABC; news, *Here's Boomer* (two repeats back-to-back) and *CHiPs* (first half-hour of 60-minute show) on NBC; these apply only to the Eastern and Central showings

Hosts: Vin Scully (play-by-play announcer), Hank Stram (color commentator), Irv Cross (sideline reporter), Brent Musberger (studio host).

Synopsis. Facing the San Francisco 49ers on the latter's home turf, the Dallas Cowboys engaged them in a furious battle for the right to meet the

Cincinnati Bengals in the Super Bowl. The lead went back and forth six times in the game. The 49ers scored first on a touchdown, but Dallas led by 10–7 at the end of the first quarter thanks to a field goal and then a touchdown. In the second quarter the 49ers struck first with another TD, but Dallas responded with a field goal that put the Cowboys up 17–14 by halftime.

San Francisco took the lead in the third quarter with an interception off Dallas, putting the score at 21–17 in favor of the 49ers by the start of the final period. The Cowboys cut the 49ers lead to one with a field goal, then another touchdown gave them the lead at 27–20. Getting the back deep in their territory, San Francisco initiated an 89-yard drive in 13 plays that consumed more than four minutes near the end of the game. With third down and 51 seconds left, San Francisco quarterback Joe Montano threw a six-yard pass to wide receiver Dwight Clark that resulted in a touchdown, followed by a successful point after conversion. The Cowboys tried to mount a comeback in the few seconds left but they fumbled the ball. In a heartbreaker for Dallas fans, their team lost to San Francisco by just one point, 28–27. It was the 49ers' first-ever NFC championship title.

Backstory. With due respect to fans of both Dallas and San Francisco, the most popular NFC championship game by a considerable margin owes some of its TV success to horrible weather. It was record-breaking cold across much of America. Chicago recorded a temperature of minus 26, while in Fargo, North Dakota, the wind chill made it feel like a deathly 98 degrees below. The severe freeze extended as far south as Dallas, Texas, where it felt like 15 below. With weather like that outdoors, who wouldn't want to stay inside and watch a football game? (For the record, it was 52 degrees at Candlestick Park in San Francisco, which is warmer than it gets sometimes in the summer there.)

It was a messy game. The 49ers had three interceptions and three fumbles, plus a pass interference call that negated a touchdown, while the Cowboys had three turnovers, one interception and two fumbles. Yet it was a win for the 49ers in the end, and a sweet one: The team had won three division titles before it finally won the right to play in the Super Bowl.

John Brodie, who the previous week served as analyst for the AFC division championship game (see 74), was a former quarterback for the 49ers in attendance at the game. So was O.J. Simpson, during the days when he was known best as a for-mer star running back. He told Dave Anderson in *The New York Times* that when the winning pass was thrown, "John Brodie was crying. And he was raving about Joe Montana, saying that there isn't a quarterback in the league who can do what he can do, especially the way he throws off balance."

"The 49ers did a great job of driving down the field at the end, and we just couldn't get any pressure on Montana," Cowboys coach Tom Landry said after the game.

With the huge audience this game brought, observers thought CBS had a good chance to set a Super Bowl ratings record when the 49ers faced the AFC champions, the Cincinnati Bengals, two weeks later. To find out what happened next, see entry 4.

14 — *The Thorn Birds*

March 29, 1983 (Part III of four-part miniseries). **Rating:** 43.2. **Share:** 62.

Aired on ABC Tuesday 9–11 P.M. Eastern and Pacific, 8–10 P.M. Central

Competition: *High Anxiety* (repeat of 1977 theatrical movie) on CBS; *The A-Team* (second hour of two-hour extended episode) and *Remington Steele* on NBC

Cast: Richard Chamberlain (Ralph de Bricassart), Rachel Ward (Meggie Cleary), Jean Simmons (Fiona Cleary), Ken Howard (Rainer Hartheim), Mare Winningham (Justine O'Neill), Piper Laurie (Anne Mueller), Richard Kiley (Paddy Cleary), Earl Holliman (Luddie Mueller), Bryan Brown (Luke O'Neill), Philip Anglim (Dane O'Neill), Barbara Stanwyck (Mary Carson), Christopher Plummer (Vittorio Contini-Verchese). **Crew:** David L. Wolper, Edward Lewis (executive producers), Stan Margulies (producer), Daryl Duke (director), Carmen Culver (writer).

Synopsis. Father Ralph de Bricassart performs a Christmas service in 1920 at Drogheda, a large ranch in New South Wales, Australia, overseen by Mary Carson. Her brother Paddy Cleary, his wife Fiona, daughter Meggie and three sons come from New Zealand to live with her. Meggie's kinship with Father Ralph burns Mary, as he rejects her advances. Mary wreaks revenge by willing Drogheda to him and the Catholic Church in 1929, forcing him to choose between denying the bequest and staying with Meggie or accepting it and receiving attention as a candidate for advancement as a result. He favors the latter. The Clearys remain as tenants.

Ralph becomes a cardinal and then archbishop

at the Vatican, with Vittorio as his superior and advisor. After Paddy dies during a fire, Meggie weds sheep shearer Luke O'Neill. As she works as a housemaid for Luddie Mueller's wife Anne, her marriage sours (she's pregnant and Luke doesn't want a child). Ralph arrives and attempts to help Meggie deliver her daughter Justine, but Meggie curses him for loving ambition more than God or her. Months later, they reconcile at an island retreat and have sex. Meggie claims their son Dane (from their tryst) was Luke's before divorcing him and returning to Drogheda.

As adults, Justine loves Ralph's friend, Rainer Hartheim, while Dane becomes a priest. He dies by drowning before Christmas 1962. Meggie tells a tearful Ralph the truth. After agreeing she was right about his foremost love for ambition, Ralph dies in her arms.

Backstory. A thorn bird, as Father Ralph explains to Meggie when she is a child, is a legendary creature that sings only once in life while fatally impaling, drowning out all other birds, and the whole world stands still to listen to it. He tells her it means "that the best is bought only at the cost of great pain."

This notion is central to the ten-hour miniseries (three hours first and fourth night, two hours second and third nights) in that every death depicted has a major impact because of the suffering that person has endured, and not just Father Ralph's at the end. For example, the passing of the youngest Cleary male, Stuart (played by Dwier Brown), forces his loving sister Meggie to become an independent woman and his other brothers to be stronger than he was.

But few remember *The Thorn Birds* for this metaphor. Most who saw it will say it's the tragic romance between a handsome priest and his beautiful younger object of obsession. That's how author Colleen McCullough envisioned it when she wrote the novel. McCullough, a native of Australia who was working at Yale University, crafted the story admiring the success (but not the content) of fellow Yalie Erich Segal with *Love Story* (see 17). Her tearjerker, however, was more epic in scope when it became a million-seller in the summer of 1977.

Warner Brothers bought the rights to the book with initial plans to adapt it as a feature film starring Robert Redford. However, no one could figure out how to condense the mammoth story down to a three-hour motion picture, and after going through three directors, the studio sold the rights to producers David L. Wolper and Stan

Margulies. Their production of *Roots* (see 3) had gripped America a few years earlier.

Wolper and Margulies planned to film the tale on location, but when Margulies went to Australia, he discovered several drawbacks. Most of the top motion picture crews were busy on other projects, the sheep ranches in the Outback were far away from most towns, and the country's film commission had regulations that allowed only two American actors in the cast; the rest had to be Australian. So the men settled instead on American locales, recreating Drogheda in Simi Valley, California (with an imported kangaroo to add atmosphere), and doing the sugar cane field scenes on Kauai, Hawaii.

The men knew who they wanted for most of the primary supporting roles and secured their services, with a few concessions for billing (e.g., Christopher Plummer was listed as special guest star). They were not as certain regarding the top roles, however.

For Father Ralph, Wolper said in the documentary *The Thorn Birds: Old Friends ... New Stories*, "We had about four or five choices. My wife suggested Richard Chamberlain." Chamberlain craved the part and acknowledged in his autobiography *Shattered Love* that he saw parallels in the character's life and his own, including his being a closeted homosexual at the time. "I was dedicated to building my glamorous career and the public image I thought the world demanded, and I regarded aspects of my quite different private self with disapproval and fear," he wrote. Chamberlain did a magnificent job, although it must be said that his scenes with the young Meggie (played by Sydney Penny) are a little disturbing to watch today, given the greater discussion about pedophilia among priests.

For Meggie, the producers auditioned ten actresses, including Michelle Pfeiffer, Kim Basinger and Olivia Newton-John (a native Australian), and arranged screen tests for two of them — Jane Seymour and Rachel Ward. The latter said in the documentary that she was not really interested in doing the miniseries because she never saw herself as the character. "If I had to visualize, I would probably find Sissy Spacek," she said. The producers thought Seymour came across too strong and lacked the vulnerability Ward projected. The latter got the job, as well as a husband from the program: Bryan Brown, who played Luke, was the only Australian in the main cast, and he was so dedicated to his character that he spent three weeks learning to shear sheep. The sparks did fly between him and Ward, and they married after the production wrapped.

Ward had difficulty filming some big scenes during the first week of the shoot, leading to rumors that Seymour would replace her. She recovered and the rest of the filming went fine — at least according to the actors.

In the end, the miniseries received Emmy awards for lead actress (Stanwyck), supporting actor (Kiley), supporting actress (Simmons), art direction, makeup, cinematography and editing. Other Emmy nominations included limited series, lead actor (Chamberlain), supporting actor (Brown and Plummer), supporting actress (Laurie), direction, music composition (Henry Mancini, whose flavorful score featuring a dulcimer prompted Wolper to tell him "You're a genius!") and costume design.

The Thorn Birds averaged a 41.9/59 for its entire run. That's very impressive, especially in light of protests from the Catholic Church about its depiction of a priest having sex outside of marriage and lusting after a woman for years (the protest received coverage on ABC's *Nightline* news program). It was repeated twice on ABC (first in four parts on Jan. 6, 7, 8 and 10, 1985, with average numbers of 18.3/27), then went into syndication and came back for one more rerun on ABC.

Due to its continuing popularity, Wolper and Margulies created a sequel, *The Thorn Birds: The Missing Years*, for CBS. Chamberlain was the only original main cast member to return. Despite location shooting in Australia, this saga of Father Ralph's World War II experiences struck many as a disappointment compared to the original. Ratings were fine, however —14.6/23 for Part I on Feb. 11, 1996, and 12.9/20 on Feb. 13, 1996, placing it first or second in its time period all but for one half-hour it aired. McCullough said she hated it — and the first miniseries too, for that matter.

Chamberlain went on to host the segment on miniseries on ABC's 50th anniversary special in 2003. By that time, Father Terence Sweeney, the technical advisor for the film's Catholic practices on screen, had left the priesthood to marry one of his own parishioners, proving once again that truth isn't stranger than fiction — it's just sometimes an extension of it.

13 — The Academy Awards

April 7, 1970 (42nd annual edition). **Rating:** 43.4. **Share:** 78.

Aired on ABC Tuesday 10 P.M.–Wednesday 12:25 A.M. Eastern, 9–11:25 P.M. Central, 7–9:25 P.M. Pacific

Competition: *CBS News Special* "Mysteries of Pain" (first half-hour); second hour of *First Tuesday* on NBC; late night programming on both networks for the Eastern and Central time zones

Hosts-Presenters: Candice Bergen, Elliott Gould, Myrna Loy, Cliff Robertson, John Wayne, Claudia Cardinale, James Earl Jones, Raquel Welch, Bob Hope, Barbara McNair, Fred Astaire, Jon Voight, Frank Sinatra, Clint Eastwood, Katharine Ross, Ali MacGraw. **Crew:** Richard Dunlap (producer-director for ABC), Mike J. Frankovich (producer for the Academy of Motion Picture Arts and Sciences), Jack Haley, Jr. (director), Hal Kanter, Frank Pierson, Mary Loos (writers).

Synopsis. Replicating the pattern from the previous year's show, 1970's award ceremonies had 16 "Friends of Oscar" doling out most of the honors for films released theatrically in 1969 in 20 categories, plus two honorary awards. The event occurred at the Dorothy Chandler Pavilion in Los Angeles. Academy president Gregory Peck introduced the proceedings before letting the "Friends" read the nominations and open the envelopes announcing the winners for each category, sometimes solo (as with John Wayne for cinematography), but usually as a duo (e.g., Claudia Cardinale and James Earl Jones for film editing).

There were also performances of the five Best Song nominees, as well as the presentations of the Jean Hersholt Humanitarian Award to George Jessel and an honorary award to Cary Grant. Frank Sinatra hogged the spotlight before he introduced Grant and talked even after the actor arrived on stage to a standing ovation. After that awkward moment, Grant was his usual charming self. Speaking nearly two and a half minutes, he thanked his directors, writers and others before noting, "Ours is a collaborative medium. We all need each other." That comment elicited approving applause.

The winners were *Midnight Cowboy* for Best Picture, presented by Elizabeth Taylor; John Wayne for Best Actor, given to him by Barbra Streisand; and an absent Maggie Smith for Best Actress, with Cliff Robertson announcing her triumph.

Backstory. Why was this the highest rated Academy Awards telecast of them all? There are several reasons:

• Anticipation was high that film superstar John Wayne finally would win the trophy for *True Grit* (see 34). It was his second Oscar nomination following one 20 years earlier for *Sands of Iwo Jima*.

• Elizabeth Taylor agreed to appear for the first time in ten years in the hopes that her then-husband, Richard Burton, would finally win an Oscar for his sixth nomination for *Anne of the Thousand Days*. He lost to Wayne, and he never won the statuette.

• Three of the Best Picture nominees—*Midnight Cowboy, Butch Cassidy and the Sundance Kid,* and *Hello, Dolly!*—were among the top box office hits of 1969.

• Jane Fonda and her brother, Peter, were competing for supporting actress and writing respectively. Jane and Peter lost here, but Jane would go on to claim several Oscars starting two years later for *Klute*.

• Four of the five tunes in contention for Best Song made the top 40 and thus were familiar to radio listeners. The last time that had occurred was in 1957. Moreover, either the writer or the performer with the top 40 hit sang all but one of the numbers, the exception being Lou Rawls for "Jean," which Oliver took to #2. The winner, "Raindrops Keep Fallin' on My Head," was the first #1 hit to claim the Best Song Oscar since "Love Is a Many Splendored Thing" in 1955.

Also, ABC did as good as a third-place network could do in promoting the gala affair. For example, the night before the ceremony, film critic Rex Reed appeared on the network's late night series *The Dick Cavett Show* to discuss his predictions. Reed made sure everyone knew his discontentment at the start by saying, "There aren't too many heroes nominated this year." He thought the best picture of the year was the non-nominated *The Damned* and feared that *Anne of the Thousand Days* would win the category due to previous critical honors, even though he was pulling for *Midnight Cowboy*.

Reed saved his strongest words for the Best Actor competition. "I really have the terrible, lurking, poisonous suspicion that John Wayne will win the Academy Award," he said (members of the studio audience groaned in response to the reviewer's disdain for one of their favorites). Reed explained why he felt Wayne's performance was not worthy of an Oscar, but it was hard to understand, as ABC bleeped part of it.

The first Oscar ceremony was in 1928. Created by movie moguls to prevent unions from wielding too much power, the Academy of Motion Picture Arts and Sciences included annual awards of merit as part of its agenda. The award categories would widen over the next 80-plus years as well as occasionally contract (there used to be categories split between color and black-and-white films, for example).

The honors soon became a source of desire,

envy and derision inside and outside the movie community. Every year some major public figure opines that at least one of the awards went to the least-deserving or even undeserving nominee due to poor voting by members of the Academy. In 1970, for example, there was much controversy over how *Hello, Dolly!* won three awards—for Best Sound, Art Direction/Set Direction and Score—plus four other nominations including Best Picture when hardly any critic put it on his or her "Ten Best" list. Many suspected that 20th Century–Fox's campaigning for the picture among Academy voters led to this situation.

The first Oscars telecast was on NBC on March 19, 1953, when RCA offered the Academy $100,000 to carry it live in exchange for sponsorship. Needing money to fund the ceremony, Academy president Charles Brackett eagerly accepted the offer. NBC carried the special until ABC snagged the rights in 1961. Bob Hope served as its sole host until 1968.

The Oscars moved back to NBC after this 1970 show, which gave the award show an even greater potential audience (NBC had more affiliates than ABC at the time). But while ratings were strong, none were as high as 1970's. The awards returned to ABC in 1976, where it has remained ever since.

The Oscars has always been the top-rated special for the week each year it airs, although it has not had more than half the audience watching TV at the time since 1998. It regularly finished with a 30 rating or higher through 1983, and like this telecast, it even passed the 40 mark with its second-highest rated show, on April 10, 1967 (41.2/75). It is much more popular than any other TV awards show, despite constant complaints that it runs too long and ends too late. To address the latter charge, it has accommodated East Coast viewers by starting earlier (at 5:30 P.M. Pacific) since 1999.

The Oscars have won several Emmys as best entertainment special since the 1980s, even though the program remains frustratingly poky and uneven. Still, as long as they are making films, the awards probably will remain a significant draw on television. One just wishes that this celebration of movie excellence was outstanding in its own way.

12 — *The Beverly Hillbillies*

Jan. 8, 1964 ("The Giant Jackrabbit"). **Rating:** 44.0. **Share:** 65.

Aired on CBS Wednesday 9–9:30 P.M. Eastern and Pacific, 8–8:30 P.M. Central

Competition: *Ben Casey* on ABC; "The Pope's Trip" (news special) on NBC

Cast: Buddy Ebsen (Jed Clampett), Irene Ryan ("Granny" Daisy Moses), Max Baer, Jr. (Jethro Bodine), Donna Douglas (Elly May Clampett), Raymond Bailey (Milburn Drysdale), Nancy Kulp (Jane Hathaway), Arthur Gould Porter (Ravenswood), Sharon Tate (Janet Trego). **Guests:** Peter Bourne (Bill Tinsman), Kathy Kersh (Marian Billington). **Crew:** Paul Henning (creator–co-writer), Wesley Tuttle (co-writer), Richard Whorf (director), Al Simon (executive producer), Joseph DePew (associate producer-assistant director).

Synopsis. Granny informs Jethro and Jed that she is out of vittles. The men recall that Mr. Drysdale told them a Beverly Caterer could cook them a meal and bring it to the estate under these conditions. Thinking Beverly Caterer is a widow, Granny orders cooked critters, which baffles Marian, the girl on the receiving end, so she hangs up on the Clampetts.

Undeterred and still hungry, Jethro takes his bloodhound Duke out hunting for a rabbit for Granny's stew. A kangaroo sent to Mr. Drysdale's estate by an Australian banker escapes its crate and hops over to the Clampetts, prompting Granny to think she is seeing a five-foot jackrabbit. She plots to capture it, prompting a boxing match with it at one point.

Mr. Drysdale learns of the Beverly Caterers misunderstanding and instructs the firm to deliver food to the Clampetts. Marian and her boss Bill arrive and apologize, but the nuttiness prompts them to leave soon thereafter. The scared kangaroo, briefly captured by Granny, returns to its crate at the Drysdale estate, while Granny accidentally traps Jethro instead.

Backstory. Prior to *The Beverly Hillbillies*, which debuted on Sept. 26, 1962, no series had so drastically divided reviewers (who hated it) from the general public (who propelled it to #1 by a wide margin). Even music critics went up the wall when the show's jangling theme song, "The Ballad of Jed Clampett," played by Lester Flatt and Earl Scruggs, became a #1 country hit in 1963 and nearly cracked the top 40 pop chart.

What prompted this consternation was cornpone humor that arose when Ozarks backwoodsman Jed Clampett struck oil, and the gusher's profits made him a multimillionaire. He relocated to a mansion in Beverly Hills, with his curvaceous blonde daughter Elly May, his feisty mother-in-law "Granny" (Jed was a widower), his strong but thickheaded nephew Jethro and, in its first season, Jethro's mom Pearl Bodine (Bea Benaderet) and

her daughter Jethrene (Max Baer, Jr., in drag, with Linda Kaye Henning providing the voice). To say there was a culture clash between the hillbillies and their rich, sophisticated neighbors is an understatement.

This concoction that ABC had rejected shocked the industry when it topped the ratings. (It led to creator Paul Henning designing a similar hit rural comedy for CBS in 1963 around Bea Benaderet, *Petticoat Junction*.) It was so incredibly popular that four episodes from January through May of 1963 still rank among the all-time top 15 highest rated sitcom episodes. By winter 1964, the series was doing even better against ABC's former hit *Ben Casey* (it went back to Mondays after the Clampetts whupped the doctor) and NBC's spy anthology drama *Espionage* for most of the season.

"There was a bit of set time to enjoy the kangaroo, but other than that, I have to tell you, it was just another show," Wesley Tuttle, the episode's co-writer, said on *The E! True Hollywood Story* in 2001. "It was getting one out. The fact that it was so widely watched, I don't know if that had to be the subject or the guest star being a kangaroo."

It was probably neither. The likely explanation is that the show followed President Lyndon B. Johnson's State of the Union address. That lead-in was better than what the show had received the four previous months from *Glynis* (a sitcom) and what replaced it on Dec. 18, 1963, *Tell It to the Camera* (a *Candid Camera* knockoff). After much of the country watch the new president's speech, viewers' next options were to watch a documentary on the Pope or Ben Casey operating on a taciturn senior citizen. As ratings for *The Beverly Hillbillies* already were strong (the 1964 New Year's Day show the previous week scored a 41.8 rating and 59 share, the highest numbers since a *Gunsmoke* episode in 1961), it was no surprise that this show performed so well.

The next week scored an equally amazing 42.8 rating and 62 share, and the shows the following three weeks through Feb. 5, 1964, generated at least a 40 rating and a 60 share. Audiences decreased slightly thereafter, but the series still had enough appeal to get a 40.1 rating and 60 share on April 8, 1964. Among half-hour sitcoms, only one episode each of *All in the Family* and *The Cosby Show* have scored as well as those seven episodes did.

With that huge drawing power in mind, CBS moved *The Beverly Hillbillies* back a half-hour on its schedule for the 1964-1965 season to establish a beachhead on its Wednesday night schedule and cut into the audience for *The Virginian*, a 90-minute western on NBC that finished #17 in

1963-1964. But airing against the last half-hour of that oater, *The Beverly Hillbillies* barely cut into its audience; in fact, Jed and all his kin dropped to #12 that season, which disappointed CBS. (It did beat *Shindig* on ABC, though.)

The Beverly Hillbillies rebounded into the top 10 for three of its next four seasons before drooping to #18 in 1969-1970 due to ABC's first successful programming against it, the contemporary comedy-drama *Room 222*. CBS moved it from Wednesdays to the Tuesday lead-off position at 7:30 P.M. in 1970-1971. Despite lagging behind *The Mod Squad* on ABC, it finished a strong second in its time slot, easily defeating *The Don Knotts Show* on NBC. But the die was already cast for its cancellation.

The series' audience was now aging, less educated and less affluent than the audiences that advertisers wanted. Creator Paul Henning understood the situation (his *Petticoat Junction* ended for that reason in 1970) and tried to make it "hip" in 1970-1971 with continuing storylines on relevant topics like Granny, Elly May and Jane demanding women's liberation, but this did not improve the situation. Moreover, CBS and the other networks were losing the 7:30-8 P.M. slot to local stations in the fall of 1971 under the Prime Time Access Rule. Though the cast of the show lobbied against it in person on Capitol Hill in hopes of staying on the air, the effort was for naught. The series ended on Sept. 7, 1971.

Since *The Beverly Hillbillies'* cancellation, the network has mostly treated it like a bumpkin it ignores at a family reunion. For example, the *CBS at 75* retrospective special in 2003 ran a clip only at the very end. The Television Academy snubbed it too; despite seven nominations, including ones for Irene Ryan for lead actress and Richard Whorf for comedy direction in 1964, *The Beverly Hillbillies* never won an Emmy. Truly, nobody seems to love *The Beverly Hillbillies* except the public.

Because this episode was in black and white, it has not been as widely rerun as later episodes. However, because someone neglected to renew the copyrights for the first two years, it is widely available from various home video companies as it is now in the public domain.

11 — *The Ed Sullivan Show*

Feb. 9, 1964 (the Beatles debut). **Rating:** 45.3. **Share:** 60.

Aired on CBS Sunday 8–9 P.M. Eastern and Pacific, 7–8 P.M. Central

Competition: *The Travels of Jaimie McPheeters* (last half-hour) and *Arrest and Trial* (first half-hour) on ABC, *Disney* (last half-hour) and *Grindl* on NBC

Cast: Ed Sullivan (Host), the Ray Bloch Orchestra. **Guests:** The Beatles (John Lennon, Paul McCartney, George Harrison and Ringo Starr), Fred Kaps, Georgia Brown, Frank Gorshin, Tessie O'Shea, Mitzi McCall, Charlie Brill, Wells and the Four Fays. **Crew:** Bob Precht (producer), Tim Kiley (director).

Synopsis. Ed Sullivan opened this episode by telling viewers that Elvis Presley and Col. Tom Parker sent a wire to the show's featured act, the Beatles, wishing the English quartet success as they made their American TV performing debut on his show. Sullivan introduced the group, who energetically performed "All My Loving," "Till There Was You" and "She Loves You." Women screamed and cried in the audience during each song. Next up was European magician Fred Kaps, who did tricks with cards and a salt shaker, followed by Georgia Brown singing "I'd Do Anything" to the young male chorus from the Broadway musical *Oliver!* and her solo "As Long as He Needs Me" from the show. Joining her at one point, playing the Artful Dodger, is Davy Jones, who two years later starred on *The Monkees*, NBC's sitcom answer to the Beatles.

Frank Gorshin impersonated several celebrities, best of all Burt Lancaster and Kirk Douglas. Then Sullivan introduced in the audience America's sole gold medalist in the 1964 Winter Olympics, Terry McDermott. Tessie O'Shea sang a medley of show tunes, followed by Mitzi McCall and Charlie Brill in a comedy routine about a producer auditioning actresses.

The Beatles returned to perform "I Saw Her Standing There" and "I Want to Hold Your Hand." Wells and the Four Fays had the unenviable task of following them with their acrobatic routine before Sullivan said good night.

Backstory. Out of the dozens of performers who made their American TV debuts on *The Ed Sullivan Show*, none had the impact of the Beatles. (Elvis Presley had appeared on other TV shows prior to Sullivan's — for a chronological list, see 75.) This show serves as a testament to its host's ability to find the hottest upcoming talent and present it in a polished package. Indeed, it holds up well as a smooth, briskly paced hour even if you are not a fan of John, Paul, George and Ringo.

Sullivan was a New York newspaper columnist not generally known across the United States when he began hosting a live TV variety series initially called *Toast of the Town* on June 20, 1948. It typically billed five to ten entertainment acts per show, and with Sullivan's keen eye for what worked on it, the program became a top hit by its seventh year, when it was renamed *The Ed Sullivan Show*.

In late 1963 Sullivan visited England and saw massive crowds waiting for the Beatles to return home amid their explosive popularity. Meeting with the quartet's manager, Brian Epstein, Sullivan struck a deal for the band to appear on his show. In January 1964, Capitol Records signed the quartet for America and started a massive publicity campaign. More reporters started writing about the group as its records received plenty of airplay and sales. By the time the Beatles debuted on Sullivan's show, they had the top two records in America ("I Want to Hold Your Hand" at #1 and "She Loves You" at #2), a feat accomplished previously only by Presley.

Crowds formed around Sullivan's theater for a week in hopes of glimpsing the mop tops, and the New York police had to send extra men to patrol the streets. All this was lost on the acting team of Mitzi McCall and Charlie Brill, who came from writing *The Edie Adams Show* in Hollywood to do a routine on the program. "We didn't know who they were," Brill told Stu Shostak in 2009.

After McCall and Brill finished dress rehearsal, Sullivan told them their material was too sophisticated for the largely young audience expected for the show and told them to restructure it. While trying to figure out how to do that in their dressing room, Lennon came by to get a drink. McCall took him over to a small window to see the commotion outside and asked him, "Do you believe this is all for you?" Lennon responded, "No, I think it's for Ringo," which made no sense to them. "We didn't know who he was talking about," Brill said.

Their segment generated few laughs, and McCall and Brill felt they had bombed. Realizing that the show had a huge audience, the duo went to Florida to stay with Brill's grandparents to avoid being recognized in its wake. Incredibly, one night after leaving a nightclub there, they saw a limo following them, and it contained the Beatles. "They were getting ready to do their second show from Florida, and they said, 'What are you doing here?'" Brill recalled. "And I said, 'Escaping from you. You ruined our careers.' They were very nice and wanted us to hop in and see Florida."

The Beatles' niceness was what Sullivan sold on the show, calling them "tremendous ambassadors of goodwill." He introduced them by saying, "Now yesterday and today, our theater has been jammed with newspapermen and hundreds of photographers from all over the nation. And these veterans agreed with me that the city has never witnessed the excitement stirred by these youngsters from Liverpool who call themselves the Beatles." The Beatles acquitted themselves by being photogenic, energetic and engaging, and they cemented a fan base in America that remained dedicated to them even after they broke up in 1970 after having set many records in the music industry worldwide.

After the first set, Ed cautioned the audience to quiet down ("You promised!") before telling everyone, "Those three first songs were dedicated to Johnny Carson, Randy Paar and Earl Wilson." The latter was a leading newspaper columnist, while Paar was the daughter of Jack Paar, star of a Friday night NBC series which showed the first clips on an American TV entertainment program of the Beatles performing on Jan. 3, 1964. Carson asked McCartney on *The Tonight Show* in 1984 if he knew why Sullivan dedicated the performance to him, and the ex–Beatle said he had no idea.

The following week, the Beatles returned to Sullivan's show in Miami (where McCall and Brill ran into them), and the encore drew a 43.8/60, just a little bit below the stellar numbers of the previous outing. The Beatles had one more turn the next week (Feb. 23, 1964), then made a final live appearance on the show on Sept. 12, 1965. Their high ratings in 1964 helped bump the ratings average for *The Ed Sullivan Show* in the 1963-1964 season to #8 overall, its first top 10 finish since its highest-rated season in 1955-1956, when it ended at #2.

Sullivan's series continued through the 1960s but began to slip as the competing Disney series on NBC and *The F.B.I.* on ABC started outrating it regularly by the 1968-1969 season. Sullivan no longer was able to win over the younger generation with his "something for everyone" format, and this was no more apparent than when he presented a Beatles tribute on his show near the end of its run. Rather than have the Fab Four play again, or even just say hey on film or tape, Sullivan allowed other artists to perform the group's songs. For Beatles fans, it was a letdown.

Sensing that Sullivan was no longer relevant, CBS programmers canned his show in 1971, with its final episode appearing two weeks shy of its 23rd anniversary on June 6. Sullivan returned with a couple of highlight specials on the network, including *Ed Sullivan's TV Comedy Years* on Feb. 20, 1973 (24.5/40), and *Ed Sullivan's Broadway* on March 16, 1973 (15.2/26), before he died in 1974.

Meanwhile, Sullivan's first show with the Beatles had so well remembered that it inspired the 1978 film *I Wanna Hold Your Hand*, about teenagers going to attend the program. Impressionist Will Jordan recreated Sullivan. The Museum of Broadcasting's 1986 survey of the most requested programs in its collection placed this show at the top of the list.

On July 16, 2009, McCartney appeared again in the Ed Sullivan Theater as a guest on *Late Night with David Letterman*. He said that "just the memory of being here is great" before he performed the Beatles' hit "Get Back" on top of the marquee. For people of a certain age, it felt just a little bit like the excitement they first witnessed 45 years earlier.

10 — *Cheers*

May 20, 1993 ("One for the Road"). **Rating:** 45.5. **Share:** 64.

Aired on NBC Thursday 9–11 P.M. Eastern and Pacific, 8–10 P.M. Central

Competition: *Matlock* (second hour of two-hour extended episode) and *Prime Time Live* on ABC; *The Color Purple* (last two hours of three-hour 1985 theatrical movie) on CBS; *America's Most Wanted* on Fox

Cast: Ted Danson (Sam Malone), Kirstie Alley (Rebecca Howe), Rhea Perlman (Carla Tortelli LeBec), John Ratzenberger (Cliff Clavin), Woody Harrelson (Woody Boyd), Kelsey Grammer (Dr. Frasier Crane), George Wendt (Norm Peterson). **Guests:** Shelley Long (Diane Chambers), Tom Berenger (Dan Santry), Kim Alexis, Mike Ditka (Themselves), Mark Harelik (Reed Manchester), Anthony Heald (Kevin), Jackie Swanson (Kelly Gaines Boyd), Paul Willson (Paul), Mitchell Lichtenstein (Waiter), Tim Cunningham (Tim), Steve Gianelli (Steve), Alan Koss (Alan). **Crew:** James Burrows, Les Charles, Glen Charles, Dan O'Shannon, Tom Anderson, Dan Staley, Rob Long (executive producers), Tim Berry (producer), Glen Charles, Les Charles (writers), James Burrows (director).

Synopsis. The gang at Boston's Cheers bar — bartender Woody, waitress Carla, and regular patrons Cliff, Norm and Frasier — watch a cable TV awards show where model Kim Alexis and Chicago Bears coach Mike Ditka present an award for Best Writing of a Movie or Miniseries to Diane Chambers. The stunned gang remembers that waitress Diane had left the bar six years earlier promising

its owner, Sam Malone, that she would return. Sam sees Diane and sends her a congratulatory telegram. She calls to say she will be coming to Boston.

Rebecca, the bar's former manager, is distraught after rejecting a marriage proposal from plumber Dan Santry. She pretends to be Sam's wife to impress the supposedly married Diane, but after both marriages are revealed as fake, Sam and Diane talk.

Dan proposes to Rebecca again and she accepts, Cliff receives a promotion, Woody becomes a Boston city councilor and his wife, Kelly, is pregnant, and Norm gets a job with Woody's help. Now Sam announces that he and Diane are getting married. Everyone is speechless. Sam and Diane board a plane to California, but both realize it will not work. Sam returns to Cheers and smokes Cuban cigars with the regulars. He agrees with Norm that love is the most important thing in life, and Sam's real love is Cheers above all else.

Backstory. The last episode of *Cheers* earned notoriety because the cast and crew celebrated watching it even more than a lot of viewers did. To draw even more publicity to the finale of NBC's top-rated series of the last three years (it was #1 in the 1990-1991 season, #4 in 1991-1992 and #8 in 1992-1993), the network sent them to Boston's Bull & Finch Pub, which served as the setting for the bar for the sitcom. The liquor flowed on the third floor, and the group became giggly and unruly.

By the time sober Jay Leno joined the group to host a special live edition of *The Tonight Show* for the Eastern and Central time zones, their activities had gone from waving to the crowd to the unruly whooping up of Danson, Grammar and the rest of the male regulars in response to a film clip of Kirstie Alley apologizing that she could not join them. It was a smash that ended up with most participants being smashed.

Most of them had been there from the start, when the series stayed near the bottom of the ratings after it debuted on Sept. 30, 1982, despite near-unanimous critical praise. The show's central couple was a playboy ex–major league baseball player (Sam Malone) attracted to a pretentious, artistic blonde (Diane Chambers), both working at a saloon whose regular customers included hefty, gregarious Norm Peterson and know-it-all, windy Cliff Clavin, and whose chief waitress was the much-married, often pregnant and Diane-loathing Carla. Even the now-familiar warm theme song, "Where Everybody Knows Your

Name," sung by Gary Portnoy, struggled to make the lower rungs of the Hot 100 for just four weeks in the spring of 1983.

But it won the Emmy for best comedy series in 1983, and that led to more viewers. By 1985 *Cheers* was a perpetual top 10 hit, and the series' dynamics had changed with the introduction of Dr. Frasier Crane, who broke up Sam and Diane when he psychoanalyzed and then romanced her. The character was meant to last only seven episodes, but Grammer's expert comic delivery kept him on the series — as did one other factor. "Though I was clearly responsible for the success of Frasier, I credit Shelley Long for his longevity," Grammer wrote in his memoirs *So Far...* "The rumors about her are numerous and often vicious, but grossly exaggerated. I have nothing against Shelley personally; I am even in her debt. But there was a problem: Shelley didn't want Frasier in the show."

Grammer added that when Long accepted the Golden Globe for best actress in a comedy in 1985, she said in her acceptance speech that it had not been a joyful year for her working on *Cheers* specifically due to the addition of Frasier. That public statement resulted in the writers creating even more dialogue and plots for Grammer, and when Long left the series in 1987 to pursue a movie career, there was hardly a beat missed as Alley joined the cast as Rebecca Howe, the new operator of the Cheers bar. Rebecca was not interested romantically in Sam (who still worked there), but her often desperate hopes to impress her boss and marry a rich man eventually endeared her to viewers.

The other major new character was Dr. Lilith Sternin, Frasier Crane's very uptight colleague, who defrosted her exterior enough to inspire him to marry her. The relationship did not last, but she remained as a good comic foil. (She was not included in the last episode.)

With all these elements in place, *Cheers* could have easily run more than its 11 seasons, but the main participants wanted to end it while it was still popular and creatively relevant, like *M*A*S*H* (see 1). The expanded two-hour episode preempted *Seinfeld* (see 21) and *L.A. Law*, which usually followed *Cheers* on the Thursday night lineup.

The finale was amusing but could have been a little tighter, and it ended rather monotonously. It included an inside reference: When Sam adjusted a picture of Geronimo on the wall before closing up shop, it was a tribute to Nicholas Colasanto, who played Coach Ernie Pantusso on the series until his death in 1985 and had the photo hanging in his dressing room wall.

NBC devoted the entire evening of May 20, 1993, to the series. Before this episode ran, the network broadcast the hour special of highlights *Cheers Last Call: A Celebration* hosted by Bob Costas. He noted that the series' 275 episodes over 11 seasons had received 26 Emmys and 111 nominations (it would win two more Emmys out of seven additional nominations following the airing of this show, for editing and for Danson as lead actor). The victories included four for Best Comedy Series, two for Danson as best actor, one each for Long and Alley as best actress, four times for Perlman and twice for Neuwirth as best supporting actress, once for Woody Harrelson as supporting actor, twice for writing and twice for directing.

The last episode of *Cheers* ran on Aug. 19, 1993. Four weeks later, NBC unveiled a spin-off, *Frasier*, in which Grammer's character begins a new life in Seattle. But he could not shake off his old gang entirely. In three different episodes of *Frasier*, the doctor encountered his former bar buddies — once with Sam visiting, another with Woody in town, and a third with Carla, Norm and Cliff at the bar in Boston — as well as a few run-ins with his exes, Diane and Lilith. Though it was nice to see the old crew each time they appeared, it was somewhat of a jolt, especially since the comedic style on *Frasier* was more of a sophisticated farce than what *Cheers* was.

In 2006, two years after *Frasier* ended, most of the principals, even Long, reunited to accept the TV Land Legend Award. Faithful fans have hoped since that time that a full-fledged reunion might take place, but as of this writing, they have had to content themselves with *Cheers* reruns. Here's hoping when they watch this finale, they don't party as hard as the show's personnel did in Boston in 1993.

---

9 — *The Fugitive*

Aug. 29, 1967 ("The Judgment," Part Two). **Rating:** 45.9. **Share:** 72.

Aired on ABC Tuesday 10–11 P.M. Eastern and Pacific, 9–10 P.M. Central

Competition: *CBS News Hour* documentary "The Tenement" on CBS, *Pardners* (second hour of 1956 movie; repeat) on NBC

Cast: David Janssen (Dr. Richard Kimble), Barry Morse (Lt. Philip Gerard), Bill Raisch (Fred Johnson), Diane Brewster (Helen Kimble), William Conrad (Narrator). **Guests:** Richard Anderson (Leonard Taft),

J.D. Cannon (Lloyd Chandler), Jacqueline Scott (Donna Kimble Taft), Diane Baker (Jean Carlisle), Louise Latham (Betsy Chandler), Johnny Jensen (Billy Taft; character listed as Bobby Taft in end credits). **Crew:** Quinn Martin (executive producer), Wilton Schiller (producer), John Meredyth Lucas, George Eckstein (co-producers), Don Medford (director), George Eckstein, Michael Zager (writers).

Synopsis. In Part One, Lt. Gerard arrested his long sought-after quarry Richard Kimble, a doctor (wrongly accused and sentenced to death for his wife Helen's killing) who had escaped while en route to the death house. Kimble had heard that Gerard had captured Fred Johnson, a one-armed man that Kimble believes was the real killer, in Los Angeles. But Johnson got out on bail, killed his bondsman and left town, while Gerard found Kimble.

Now, Kimble convinces Gerard that Johnson has returned to his (Kimble's) hometown of Stafford, Indiana, and that he can prove Johnson's guilt within 24 hours. During this time, Richard's sister, Donna, receives a phone call from Johnson claiming that her husband, Leonard, was with Helen the night of the murder. Lloyd Chandler hears about the call and realizes it is Johnson calling to blackmail him, as Chandler had posted bail for Johnson in Los Angeles. Chandler had witnessed Johnson beating Helen but was too cowardly to stop him or testify to that fact. Johnson wants $50,000, but Chandler decides he is going to kill Johnson instead.

Kimble and Gerard search for Chandler and Johnson at an abandoned amusement park where Gerard is shot in the leg by Johnson. Kimble chases Johnson to the top of a tower where the latter confesses killing Helen and plans to kill Kimble as well. Gerard shoots and kills Johnson.

Backstory. The Fugitive provided television with the first "grand finale" episode. Some may argue that credit should be given instead to *The Buick Circus Hour*, which alternated with Milton Berle's show during the 1952-1953 season and finished at #6. That show had a continuing storyline where the female lead wanted a relationship with the male star, and it eventually ended with that happening. But that was really more of a closer for a variety series with a storyline, and next to nobody under retirement age can recall it nowadays. Others may say *The Life and Legend of Wyatt Earp* deserves the honor for showing the title character at the legendary gunfight at the O.K. Corral at the end of its six-year run (1955–1961), but that series already was finishing third in its time period opposite *The Many Loves of Dobie Gillis* on CBS and *Alfred Hitchcock Presents* on NBC when that episode ran.

So no popular scripted series had ever attempted showing viewers a concluding episode until *The Fugitive*. And it paid off mightily, with the highest ratings ever recorded for a summer TV show.

Admittedly *The Fugitive* was not as hot as it had been two seasons earlier, when it peaked at #5 in 1964-1965, but it still routinely outrated the competing *CBS News Hour* and movies on NBC. But it was still surprising that no entertainment program up to that time had high ratings like this finale.

The closing episode was planned as part of the original series concept when creator Roy Huggins put it on paper in 1960. *The Fugitive* came into his mind when he thought, "How can I do a show that has all the elements of a Western but in a modern setting?" He knew the character had to be free to roam like cowboys did, "and I decided that the only way you could get it was that it would have to be the protagonist was wanted by the law — that he had to act that way," Huggins recounted to Irv Broughton in *Producers on Producing*. "He had to be a wanderer and a man without an identity, who refused to stay in one place. That's how I wrote *The Fugitive*."

It would take three years before *The Fugitive* made its TV debut on Sept. 17, 1963. For the next four years, Dr. Richard Kimble tried to eke out a living while roaming America and at the same time trying to prove he did not kill his wife. He had seen Fred Johnson leave his house after Helen's murder, but a jury did not believe him. Kimble's protest that he was innocent elicited no sympathy from Lt. Gerard, who simply viewed Kimble as a man avoiding serving his penalty.

Toward the end of the fourth season, Janssen announced that he would no longer do the series due to its grueling hours and his hopes of becoming a movie star. Executive producer Quinn Martin decided he would follow through on Huggins' vision for a conclusion in order to reward those who made *The Fugitive* a popular and critical hit. (The series won the Emmy for outstanding drama in 1966, plus three nominations for Janssen as lead actor and one for cinematography.) Because this decision came rather late in the production schedule, Martin had to hurry to make it a reality. Co-producer George Eckstein had written nine scripts for the series, so drafting him to do the job was natural; Martin paired him with Michael Zager, who had never written for *The Fugitive*.

The result was a nicely intense, intricately plotted sendoff that teased viewers into believing that Richard's brother-in-law, Leonard, might have had a part in Helen's murder by the end of Part One (which aired a week earlier on Aug. 22 and generated its own whopping numbers, 37.2/57).

On *The Joey Bishop Show* later that night, a weary-sounding Janssen took a break from filming the movie *The Green Berets* in Georgia to thank the public for their support as shown by the high ratings for Part One (ratings obviously were not going to be available for Part Two the same night). The program scored its first victory over *The Tonight Show* thanks to interest in Janssen's appearance.

There was a hit movie adaptation of *The Fugitive* in 1994 starring Harrison Ford that was nominated for Best Picture, as well as a flop revival on CBS from 2000-2001. Only one other TV finale has rated higher that this one. For that, see *M*A*S*H* at 1.

8 — *The Day After*

Nov. 20, 1983 (*ABC Theatre* TV-movie). **Rating:** 46.0 **Share:** 62.

Aired on Sunday 8–10:25 P.M. Eastern and Pacific, 7–9:25 P.M. Central

Competition: *Alice* (special hour show), *The Jeffersons*, *Goodnight Beantown* and *Trapper John, M.D.* on CBS; *Kennedy* (first of three-part miniseries) on NBC

Cast: Jason Robards (Dr. Russell Oakes), JoBeth Williams (Nancy Bauer), Steve Guttenberg (Stephen Klein), John Cullum (Jim Dahlberg), John Lithgow (Joe Huxley), Bibi Besch (Eve Dahlberg), Lori Lethin (Denise Dahlberg), Amy Madigan (Alison Ransom), Jeff East (Bruce Gallatin), Georgann Johnson (Helen Oakes), William Allen Young (Airman McCoy), Calvin Jung (Dr. Sam Hachiya), Lin McCarthy (Dr. Austin), Dennis Lipscomb (the Rev. Walker). **Crew:** Robert A. Papazian (producer), Nicholas Meyer (director), Edward Hume (writer).

Synopsis. In Lawrence, Kansas, Dr. Russell Oakes loves his wife Helen, and farmer Jim Dahlberg and his wife Eve prepare for the wedding of their daughter Denise and Bruce Gallatin. But military buildup between the Soviets and Americans at the border of East and West Germany has servicemen including Airman McCoy realizing this could result in an all-out war. Then FEMA warns the public about a nuclear attack, and chaos ensues. People clear out all the goods from stores.

Highways are jammed. Nurse Nancy Bauer assists pregnant Alison Ransom, while college student Stephen Klein tries to hitchhike home. Soon missiles are launched, either in response to the Russians or as a first line of attack, and bombs arrive in return, vaporizing those who did not seek shelter.

The blasts level buildings and kill Helen and Bruce. Radiation fallout sickens McCoy; Denise and Stephen, who hid with the Dahlbergs in their basement; and Russell, who returns to the Kansas University hospital to help until he is too ill. At the campus science building, Joe Huxley establishes radio contact and hears the president deliver a ridiculously upbeat message of how America has not retreated in the war but everyone needs to follow government orders. Life worsens, as Bauer dies of meningitis and a man kills Jim. A dying Russell returns to Kansas City and breaks down crying over the devastation as the scene fades to black and the credits roll.

Backstory. "It is powerfully done — all $7 mil. worth. It's very effective & left me greatly depressed."

That review of *The Day After* came from President Ronald Reagan, who received an advance copy while at Camp David on Oct. 10, 1983, and wrote about it in his diaries. While he was uncertain whether the movie would sway public opinion, he did note, "My own reaction was one of our having to do all we can to have a deterrent & to see there is never a nuclear war."

Few other TV entertainment projects caused as much debate as *The Day After*. Discussion about the film began among ABC executives in the spring of 1981, with all agreeing that the depiction of a nuclear attack would raise the consciousness of viewers without making a political statement. But some knew that simply depicting that possibility would be interpreted by many as favoring nuclear disarmament. Many conservatives, including the Rev. Jerry Falwell, president of the Moral Majority, and Reed Irvine, chairman of Accuracy in Media, attacked the TV-movie before it aired as political propaganda for the Soviets.

Meanwhile, leaders of ABC Broadcast Standards and Practices wanted to avoid promoting either side and being too graphic in presenting the effects of nuclear fallout. They drafted Dr. Harold Brode, a former senior physicist with the Rand Corporation and advisor to NATO, as scientific consultant to offer advice. Brode called the first draft of the script fairly balanced, but he had concerns about the presentation of treatment effects. For the second draft, he wanted corrections regarding fallout. Even with those changes made, when Brode saw a rough cut of the film in December 1982, he felt there still were inaccuracies and overstatements and requested that his name be dropped from the credits, which it was.

After the film was completed, the ABC sales department previewed it for advertisers. Few decided to participate, and most spots were sold well below the average cost of commercial time. The sales difficulties extended to ABC's affiliates, with many local businesses (and franchises of national companies) shying away from what was judged a loaded subject. When *Variety* asked spokesmen for the Young & Rubicam and BBDO advertising agencies whether reports were true that they wrote memos to their clients advising them not to support the movie, both responded "No comment."

The network and its stations could have profited if they had accepted "advocacy ads" from both sides of the issue, but they forbade it. Even an anti-nuclear arms spot with Paul Newman for the Center for Defense Information was rejected. The project was simply viewed as a loss leader. Eventually, thanks to foreign sales, ABC made a small profit off the movie.

To alleviate concerns about children's reactions, ABC screened it in advance for a group of 8- to 12-year-olds. The responses were a lack of interest among the younger ones and concerns, but not fears, about nuclear war with the older ones, despite some psychologists and educators saying it would result in nightmares.

At the start of the movie, actor John Cullum warned parents not to let very young children watch due to potentially disturbing scenes, and to watch it together with their older offspring. Another parental discretion advisory ran at the end of the last commercial break, before the bombs detonated.

When it ended, ABC ran an epilogue that included this: "In its presentation ABC has taken no position as to how such an event may be initiated or avoided. It is hoped that the images of this film will inspire the nations of this earth, their peoples and leaders, to find the means to avert the fateful day."

After that, the network aired a live 65-minute *ABC News Viewpoint* special with host Ted Koppel discussing the program with George Schultz, Henry Kissinger, William F. Buckley, Robert S. McNamara, Carl Sagan and Elie Wiesel. Koppel and his production staff attempted to ease public

fears further by airing a series of four mock war game exercises on his *Nightline* program from Nov. 22 to 25, 1983. "The Last Game" featured Edmund Muskie playing the president facing such premises as the Soviets invading Germany and portraying his responses to it.

While *Nightline* aired those shows, its NBC competition Johnny Carson made good-natured cracks about the movie on *The Tonight Show* (Carson always had the ability to make fun of serious subjects in a non-offensive manner). For most Americans, it was just a thought-provoking piece which did come across as powerful drama. Positive calls to ABC outweighed negative ones three to one. Letters were five to one in favor of the movie. A survey by ABC Research found three-fourths of viewers rated it good to excellent. An estimated 100 million Americans saw at least part of the movie.

The movie's few advertisers reported mostly favorable reactions too, according to a *Variety* report. A spokesman for Dollar Rent-A-Car, which aired three spots, said, "The response has been great.... We have gotten very few hate calls." The representative for Commodore Computers, which ran five commercials, reported the same and added, "Some people, including several stockholders, wanted to know how we had the guts to advertise on such a program."

The Day After receiving 12 Emmy nominations, with wins for film sound editing and special visual effects (it tied with the Grammy Awards for the latter). It competed unsuccessfully for outstanding drama/comedy special, supporting actor (John Lithgow), directing, writing, photography, art direction/set direction, editing, makeup, hairstyling and film sound mixing.

To appease right-wing critics still livid at ABC for airing what they viewed as propaganda, the network aired a $40 million, 14½-hour miniseries depicting how the United States would function if taken over by Russian Communists. But *Amerika* (Feb. 15–22, 1987) was not *The Day After*; only once did it achieve the 35–40 share promised to advertisers. Most critics dismissed it.

Controversy again arose when ABC repeated *The Day After* on Jan. 23, 1989. The network informed director Nicholas Meyer that in order to fit a two-hour slot with commercials, some 23 minutes would need to be edited out while four remaining minutes would be compressed (run at a faster speed without distortion on the soundtrack). Offered first cut of the film, Meyer refused. The rerun generated unimpressive numbers of

12.8/20, which placed it third in its time slot for the first of its two hours.

On June 17, 1992, Russian President Boris Yeltsin addressed a joint session of the U.S. Congress and said, "Despite what we saw in the well-known American film *The Day After*, it can be said today, tomorrow will be a day of peace, less of fear and more of hope for the happiness of our children."

7 — The Bob Hope Christmas Special

Jan. 15, 1970 (special). **Rating:** 46.6. **Share:** 64. Aired on NBC Thursday 8:30–10 P.M. Eastern and Pacific, 7:30–9 P.M. Central

Competition: *Bewitched* and *This Is Tom Jones Show* on ABC, *The Jim Nabors Hour* (last 30 minutes) and *Escape from Fort Bravo* (first hour of two-hour movie released in 1953; repeat) on CBS

Cast: Bob Hope, Connie Stevens, Teresa Graves, Miss World Eva Rueber-Staier, The Piero Brothers, Romy Schneider, Neil Armstrong, Les Brown and His Band of Renown. **Crew:** Bob Hope (executive producer), Mort Lachman (director), Mort Lachman, Bill Larkin, Mel Tolkin, Lester White, Charles Lee, Gig Henry, Gene Moss, James Thurman (writers), Lee Hale, Jay Livingston, Ray Evans (writers of special material).

Synopsis. The cast and crew left Los Angeles to begin a 15-day global tour in December 1969. First, in Washington, D.C., Bob Hope performed for President Richard Nixon and guests at the White House. In Berlin, Hope entertained the troops with witty byplay with Romy Schneider, a former Miss Germany. There were visits to the USS *Saratoga* off Gaeta, Italy, the Incirlik Air Force Base in Turkey and other stopovers before the troupe reached Vietnam, where America was at war.

After opening in Lai Khe, Hope performed before Thailand's king and queen in Bangkok. The next day Hope went to Long Binh, the largest military installation in Vietnam, and introduced Miss World to an appreciate audience. He visited Nakhon Phanom, near Laos, then did a night show at the Royal Thai Navy airfield U Taphao. A stop at Cu Chi Vietnam 25th Division included a meeting with Cardinal Cooke, then it was on the hospital ship USS *Ranger* in the China Sea for a Christmas Eve performance.

On Christmas Day at the new base Camp Eagle in Hue, Connie Stevens sang "Wedding Bell Blues" and danced with sailors in the 101st Airborne Division. At Khorat, Teresa Graves did a comic bit with Hope. Neil Armstrong, the first man on the moon six months earlier, got a standing ovation at Da Nang. After the last stop in Taiwan, Hope read a statement supporting the soldiers before saying good night.

Backstory. From his network TV debut on Easter Sunday 1950, Bob Hope remained a TV fixture for 46 years, usually as a top-rated attraction in the 1950s, '60s and '70s. A 1961 *Variety* article revealed that most of the 80 specials he had done up to that point had won their time slots. He seemed to get more popular every year the rest of the decade, despite — or maybe because of — the fact he had been entertaining people via broadcasts since the 1930s (and been entertaining professionally since the 1920s).

In fact, Hope had the top three specials of the 1968-69 season and seven of the top 11 specials for the 1969-70 season. Nearly 20 of his specials from 1964 onward had ratings at least as high as the bottom entry in this book's top 100 listing. Topping them all was this, his sixth special filmed at Vietnam, and his 19th Christmas entertaining troops abroad, going back to his radio days in 1948.

Officially titled *Chrysler Presents the Bob Hope Christmas Special*, and subtitled *Around the World with the USO*, this show was the same sort that Hope had been doing for years. There were scenes of him amusing dignitaries interspersed with stage shows on mostly outdoor platforms at different camps. Each show started with a monologue of topical jokes Hope read off huge cue cards, with shots of cheering and laughing servicemen whose visual reactions could be out of sync with the soundtrack. Sometimes he would wield a golf club as a prop during his rapid-fire delivery. A sexy woman would come out to wolf whistles and deliver straight lines to his racy jokes (Romy Schneider: "What do you think about all this sex in the theater?" Hope: "Well, it's okay, as long as the usher doesn't catch you!"). There would be some songs, dances, maybe even a sketch, and then Hope and the company would say goodbye.

Still, there was one distinguishing feature that made this special a cut above previous ones: Hope was headlining the first evening solely devoted to entertainment at Nixon's White House, which attracted news coverage in advance of the program. The president was a little awkward introducing Bob, making a weak joke that Hope couldn't afford the taxes to pay for the event. (The comedian already was under fire for taking his overseas trips as part of the USO, a federal government program, therefore having taxpayers foot the bill for his tour.)

What stands out in retrospect is how many poorly conceived jokes managed to make the final cut. Gags about the new draft lottery and Paris peace talks generated a mixed reception at best. To the show's credit, however, they included the boos and refused to "sweeten" the reception with applause, although it appears they did so in other spots.

Besides visiting injured soldiers, Hope showed how GIs were helping needy Vietnamese children. And only a cynic who hated everything associated with the war could take issue with his parting plea to the public about returning soldiers: "They need our full support. They're giving everything. Remember, you don't take a bullet 60 percent. They deserve our backing to a man, and our prayers. It's the least we can do. Good night."

There was very little footage shown at Da Nang, which corroborates Connie Stevens' recollection in *My Greatest Day in Show Business: Screen Legends Share Their Fondest Memories*: She said that when Hope told the soldiers the president would get them home soon, they grew angry, having heard that promise many times before, and the ill will continued through the end of the show, when Bob introduced her. "I'm standing there in the wings feeling like I'm about to be assaulted," Stevens told author Ray Richmond. "Honestly, it was that bad. It seemed like a riot was imminent." After the crowd drowned out her repartee with Hope, Stevens carried on with a song she had sung in previous shows, "Silent Night." Soon the audience began to sing the hymn along with her, making it what she called "the single most moving experience of my life." A montage of her performing the tune at various bases, including Da Nang, appeared in the special.

In his memoir *Don't Shoot, It's Only Me*, Hope incorrectly recalled the Da Nang disaster as having happened in his first stop, Lai Khe. "I later found out they were really in a state of shock; they had been in a firefight that day and lost a lot of friends, and then they had been rushed in to catch my show," he wrote to explain his poor reception by the soldiers.

The special pre-empted *Ironside* and *Dragnet*. Its sponsor, Chrysler, aired its car ads only at the beginning and end, letting the bulk of the special run without commercial interruption. Even by Hope's standards, this show's ratings were so huge,

it stunned the TV industry. NBC programming head Paul Klein told *TV Guide* reporter Richard K. Doan, "It reached the Silent Majority. Hope identifies with people who support the Vietnam War." It received an Emmy nomination, for film editing for an entertainment special or feature-length program made for television.

Hope twice returned to Vietnam for Christmas specials. He made specials for NBC through 1996, including his last overseas special in Beirut in 1990, but in the last five years they were painful to watch. Hope was no longer as spry in his delivery and had to rely on major guest stars to carry the bulk of the shows.

Ol' Ski Nose passed away on July 27, 2003, at the age of 100. NBC, the network with whom he had been associated for an incredible six decades (radio and TV), declined to have an evening news special in his honor as had been done with previous TV legends Jack Benny and Lucille Ball. For a man whose theme song had been "Thanks for the Memories," the Peacock Network displayed remarkably poor recall about how much his success meant to them.

6 — Gone with the Wind

Nov. 7, 1976 (*The Big Event*, Part 1 of two parts; first released theatrically in 1939). **Rating:** 47.7. **Share:** 65.

Aired on NBC Sunday 8–11 P.M. Eastern and Pacific, 7–10 P.M. Central

Competition: *The Six Million Dollar Man* (last 60 minutes of expanded two-hour episode) and *21 Hours at Munich* (TV-movie) on ABC; *Sonny & Cher, Kojak* and *Delvecchio* on CBS

Cast: Vivien Leigh (Scarlett O'Hara), Clark Gable (Rhett Butler), Olivia de Havilland (Melanie Hamilton), Leslie Howard (Ashley Wilkes), Hattie McDaniel (Mammy), Thomas Mitchell (Gerald O'Hara), Butterfly McQueen (Prissy), Rand Brooks (Charles Hamilton), Laura Hope Crews (Sarah Jane "Aunt Pittypat" Hamilton), Cammie King (Bonnie Blue Butler), Ona Munson (Belle Watling). **Crew:** David O. Selznick (producer), Victor Fleming (director), Sidney Howard (writer).

Synopsis. Southern belle Scarlett O'Hara has many suitors but only wants Ashley Wilkes. Yet he loves Melanie Hamilton, who adores Scarlett without realizing the latter's obsession for Ashley. Smarting from this, Scarlett encounters dashing Rhett Butler, who is smitten by her vivacious nature. Ashley remains Scarlett's obsession, and when Melanie's older brother Charles proposes marriage to her, she accepts to keep up with Melanie and thus Ashley, who wed one day before Scarlett and Charles. Charles, Ashley and Rhett then serve in the Rebel Army as the Civil War breaks out.

Charles dies, and Scarlett and Melanie move to Atlanta to stay with Melanie's Aunt Pittypat and help wounded soldiers. Scarlett meets Rhett again, and the widow scandalizes Atlanta society by dancing with him before he returns to action. Ashley visits and tells Scarlett to take care of Melanie, which she does despite multiple hardships. They return home, and Scarlett eventually weds Rhett. They have a child, Bonnie Blue, which they raise in Tara, the mansion Scarlett inherited after her father Gerald's death in a riding accident.

But Scarlett still wants Ashley, who leaves when Melanie dies. That, along with Bonnie's death, prompts a discouraged Rhett to divorce her. Scarlett begs Rhett not to leave, asking him what she will do without him. "Frankly, my dear, I don't give a damn," he responds before leaving. Scarlett then realizes she can return to Tara and survive because, as she says, "Tomorrow is another day."

Backstory. Long considered one of the greatest films of all time, *Gone with the Wind* was one of the few major American studio sound movies made before 1948 that was not released to local TV stations in the 1950s. Everyone desired it, but MGM, its distributor, refused to allow a showing, feeling (rightly) that it could earn much more by theatrically re-releasing the motion picture every seven years or so. This additional cash made it the all-time #1 box office champion (that record fell in the 1970s as blockbusters like *Star Wars* surpassed it, but when adjusted for inflation, *Gone with the Wind* still tops the list). CBS wanted it as early as 1956, but MGM felt $1 million for one showing was not sufficient, so CBS settled for *The Wizard of Oz* (see 52) instead.

Then on May 21, 1974, NBC announced that it paid $5 million to run the film once, as well as spent $500,000 on each of eight other films from MGM. The studio had offered the same deal to CBS and ABC, but both passed, feeling the price was too high. It was the biggest TV payment for a theatrical movie to that point, passing the $3.2 million set by *The Poseidon Adventure* (see 31), only to be surpassed two months later by NBC paying double that amount for *The Godfather* (see 27). *Gone with the Wind* did set a record for the longest wait between the release of a sound movie

in theaters and its network TV debut (nearly 37 years).

Atlanta native Margaret Mitchell wrote the novel in 1936, and the buzz before publication was so great that independent movie producer David O. Selznick paid the unprecedented sum of $50,000 for the film rights before it became a smash bestseller. Clark Gable, the top star at the time, was everyone's pick to play Rhett, so to secure him, Selznick agreed to give Gable's studio, MGM, half the rights for the movie. But it was Selznick's production company, so he was allowed to pick his cast, therefore overruling MGM's choice of Joan Crawford as Scarlett, among other choices.

The public told Selznick they preferred a newcomer to play Scarlett, but a nationwide search found no one right for the part. With screen tests, Selznick narrowed the contenders down to Jean Arthur (whose test was horrible), Paulette Goddard, Joan Bennett, and British import Vivien Leigh, who impressed Selznick by having the right look for Scarlett. He picked Leigh, whose fiery, full-bodied portrait remains one of the greatest performances on film.

Initial director George Cukor coordinated much of the casting and sets before Selznick replaced him with Victor Fleming, feeling that Cukor was too slow for the shoot. Still, Leigh and Olivia de Havilland consulted with Cukor at nights and on weekends about how to deliver their lines.

Filming started on Dec. 10, 1938, then ran mainly from Jan. 26, 1939, through June 27, 1939. When it premiered in Atlanta on Dec. 15, 1939, there was praise all around, and a few months later, the film received 13 Oscar nominations. It won for Best Picture, Actress (Leigh), Supporting Actress (Hattie McDaniel, beating de Havilland), Writing, Directing, Editing, Cinematography and Art Direction, plus two special awards.

The stature of *Gone with the Wind* grew following this triumph, with Selznick's main regret being that Mitchell would not consent to allow a sequel to be made (she also never wrote another novel). It did spawn tributes in other areas of pop culture. For example, the movie's magnificent melody by Oscar nominee Max Steiner, "Tara's Theme," provided the music for "My Own True Love," a top 40 hit for Jimmy Clanton in 1959 and the Duprees in 1962. A musical version appeared in London in 1973, but it closed on the way to Broadway.

When NBC announced their upcoming broadcast, ABC tried to counterprogram with a special edition of *The Six Million Dollar Man* that introduced Vincent Van Patten as "The Bionic Boy," but it was for naught. The second part ran on Monday, Nov. 8, 1976, nearly equaling Sunday's numbers with a 47.4/64. With the average minute for a commercial costing $240,000 and NBC running the movie for five hours total, the network made a cool $8.42 million in ad sales. For a network running in third place at the time, this was a huge triumph.

Some observers wondered why NBC did not repeat it. Alvin Rush, executive vice-president of NBC-TV, told *Variety* it did not happen because of his conversations with MGM. "They used my own pitch against me, when I had told them a TV show would attract a whole new generation to *Gone with the Wind.* They said they agreed with me and planned to reissue it theatrically again."

However, MGM had second thoughts and held back on the reissue when CBS offered them the biggest TV deal ever: $35 million for 20 runs of the picture. On its initial rerun on Sunday, Feb. 11, 1979, the first part faced off against the TV-movie *Elvis* on ABC and the network TV debut of 1975's *One Flew Over the Cuckoo's Nest* on NBC. The three programs split the audience fairly evenly, with *Gone with the Wind* earning a 24.3/36, but many complained about how the networks were putting their best shows against each other and forcing them to make a tough choice. The second part, running on Monday, Feb. 12, 1979, fared better with a strong 28.8/40. CBS then reran the movie in two parts in 1980, 1981, 1983 and 1984 before bringing it back in 1987, again in two parts.

Then Ted Turner bought MGM, and with his purchase came the rights to *Gone with the Wind,* his favorite movie (not surprising for a native Atlantan). He ran the film frequently on his TBS and TNT cable channels for two years before putting it up for sale to local TV stations in 1990.

The next year, a hit book sequel came out, written by Alexandra Ripley. *Scarlett* became a CBS miniseries in 1994, with Joanne Whalley as the title character and Timothy Dalton as Rhett. Critically disdained, it nonetheless drew high ratings when it ran on Nov. 13 (21.4/32), Nov. 15 (17.1/25), Nov. 16 (17.8/28) and Nov. 17 (17.7/27). It also received one Emmy, for art direction.

But only the original remains in most people's minds. Even today, many will argue it is the greatest film of all time. I take no position except to say that *Gone with the Wind* remains the highest-rated theatrical movie ever shown on American television, and that's one achievement that is unlikely ever to be broken.

5 — XVII Winter Olympics

Feb. 23, 1994 (11th day of competition). **Rating:** 48.5. **Share:** 64.

Aired on CBS Wednesday 8–11 P.M. Eastern and Pacific, 7–10 P.M. Central

Competition: *Thea, The Critic, Home Improvement, Grace Under Fire* and *Secrets Revealed* (special) on ABC; *Beverly Hills 90210* and *Melrose Place* on Fox; *Unsolved Mysteries, Now* and *Law & Order* (repeat) on NBC

Cast: Greg Gumbel (host), Verne Lundquist (play-by-play announcer), Scott Hamilton, Tracy Wilson (commentators).

Synopsis. The featured event was women's figure skating, with highlights edited from earlier in the day at Lillehammer, Norway. America was represented by Nancy Kerrigan and Tonya Harding. The latter was a controversial inclusion, as suspicion surrounded Harding following an attack on Kerrigan a month earlier. But Harding had sued to retain her position on the team, and with no definitive evidence proving her guilt, she was allowed to attend.

Harding skated first in the technical program and finished tenth among 27 competitors, while Kerrigan finished at the top. Next in the free skate category, Harding came out late, stopped less than a minute into her routine and went to the judges to protest that her bootlace had broken. She told them she must replace it in the name of fair competition. They allowed her to make the change in the two-minute warning period. Adding to the surreal tone, Harding skated to the theme from *Jurassic Park,* the hit movie about dinosaurs coming back to life in the present day. Her numbers for the routine were strong enough to bump her up to eighth place.

Kerrigan outdid Harding by nailing a triple lutz in her routine. She received a standing ovation from the crowd. But Oksana Baiul from the Ukraine performed just as well, winning the gold medal. Kerrigan won the silver. Harding left the Olympics with no medal at all.

Backstory. There was little to indicate that the 1994 Winter Olympics would be a blockbuster program in America at first. The sporting event always attracted a considerable amount of attention in the United States, ever since it first received extended coverage in 1960 (on CBS with Walter Cronkite as host), but there was nothing particularly notable in advance to attract more than the typical amount of viewers.

That all changed on Jan. 6, 1994, when beefy Shane Stant clubbed Nancy Kerrigan above her knee with a collapsible metal baton after she finished practicing in Detroit for the Olympic trials competition. Kerrigan had earned a bronze medal for figure skating at the 1992 Winter Olympics and was likely to do better this time.

Kerrigan recovered from the injury, which turned out to be only a bruise, while police arrested two people associated with the skater's main competitor, Tonya Harding, for the crime. Jeff Gillooly, Harding's ex-husband, and Shawn Eckhardt, Harding's bodyguard, faced charges of plotting the ambush that eventually resulted in both men going to jail, along with Stant, whom Gillooly had hired to do the job.

Harding originally professed that she had no connection to the crime, then admitted that she knew about the plans but did not organize them. In the wake of these revelations, the U.S. Figure Skating Association voted to include a recovered Kerrigan as a representative even though she finished behind Harding in the trials. They were not able to force out Harding (who threatened a lawsuit), so both women competed for America, and that is where the drama began.

Soon Tonya Harding and Nancy Kerrigan were household names even in households that had no idea what a triple lutz was, much less how big a deal it was to nail one. A lot of the interest had to do with the disparity between the women.

With her poise, toothy grin and dark hair, Kerrigan resembled America's favorite former ice skating queen Peggy Fleming. Her to-the-manor-born heritage contrasted sharply with that of Harding, a scrappy blonde who was the product of her mother's fifth marriage. As comedian Garry Shandling aptly quipped, Kerrigan looked like the girls in high school who turned him down for a date, while Harding looked like the ones who beat him up.

While Kerrigan and Harding carefully avoided each other up to and during the Olympics, the media had a field day building up a rivalry — or better yet, a hoped-for catfight. Naturally, CBS exploited the situation for all it was worth in its on-air promos to heighten the drama. NBC ran *Shattered Glory*, a sensationalized hour-long summary of the duo's skating standoff, three days before their skating programs. However, audiences did not gravitate to the show, as it finished behind its CBS competition *60 Minutes* (see 89). NBC later tried for better ratings with a TV-movie called *Tonya and Nancy: The Inside Story* (April 30, 1994), but it did not impress viewers either.

There was some bitterly cold weather in most of America the night the women competed, which encouraged people to stay at home and watch TV. The result was a big ratings gold medal for CBS; it won the night having more viewers than ABC, NBC and Fox shows that night not only combined, but also doubled. This was huge. Bill Croasdaile, president of Western International national broadcast division, viewed the appeal of the show this way in *Variety*: "With the tabloid assault of the Bobbitts, the Buttafuocos and the Menendezes, Americans were ready for something pure, for a hero. And they got that with the Olympics and Nancy Kerrigan. Just look at the numbers."

In fact, the Kerrigan-Harding faceoff was the peak of a week (Feb. 21–27, 1994) that provided CBS with its highest average ratings ever, 30.5/45. The slightly less popular Winter Olympics coverage before and after that week still ended up with impressive overall numbers of 27.8/42, with ratings up 45 percent from what CBS had averaged during the 1992 Winter Olympics.

Those Olympic ratings were so stellar that CBS reaped $5 million in advertisement sales from it, while it cost ad revenue in the range of $12 million to $14 million for NBC, $8 million to $10 million for ABC, and $3 million for Fox.

To escape his notoriety, Gillooly decided to change his surname to Stone. That prompted a protest from actor Paul Petersen, who played Jeff Stone on *The Donna Reed Show* from 1958 to 1966 and argued that his character's good name should not be besmirched and associated with Gillooly.

Meanwhile, Harding pled guilty on March 16, 1994, to conspiring with Gillooly and Eckhardt to impede investigation of the assault. Fined $160,000 and put on probation for three years, she was banned for life from competition by the U.S. Figure Skating Association.

Rather than redeem her image, she appears to have accepted being known as a bad girl. In the fall of 1994, Gillooly released a sex video that he and Harding supposedly taped on their honeymoon. Harding beat up Bill Clinton's sexual harassment accuser Paula Jones in the ring on a *Celebrity Boxing* special in 2002, which led to two years of professional fighting jobs. In her autobiography, *The Tonya Tapes*, she maintained she was against the attack on Kerrigan but was forced by Gillooly to accept it.

The true winner for the whole situation was CBS. Beside the ratings, it won eight Emmys for its Olympic coverage.

4 — Super Bowl XVI

Jan. 24, 1982 (San Francisco 49ers vs. Cincinnati Bengals). **Rating:** 49.1. **Share:** 73.

Aired on CBS Sunday 4:15–7:45 P.M. Eastern, 3:15–6:45 P.M. Central, 2:15–5:45 P.M. Mountain, and 1:15–4:45 P.M. Pacific

Competition: *The Making of Superman* (documentary) on ABC, *The Sound of Music* (repeat of 1965 movie; first hour only) on NBC; both aired against the last 45 minutes of the game only in the Eastern and Central time zones

Cast: Pat Summerall (play-by-play announcer), John Madden (color commentator). **Crew:** Charles H. Milton III (senior producer), Terry O'Neil (producer), Sandy Grossman (director).

Synopsis. The Silverdome at Pontiac, Michigan, hosted one of the most exciting Super Bowls ever, one whose outcome came down to the final seconds of play. The 49ers started out strong and had a 20–0 lead over the Bengals by halftime. San Francisco quarterback Joe Montana ran in the first score, a one-yard touchdown, in the first quarter and threw to fullback Earl Cooper for another TD followed by two field goals in the second quarter.

But in the third quarter, Cincinnati came out blazing and scored a touchdown on a drive following the opening kick. The defense held San Francisco's offense much of the quarter, yet the Bengals could not score despite strong drives during the quarter. In the fourth period Cincinnati finally got another touchdown, only to see the 49ers respond with two field goals to make it 26–14. The Bengals managed to score another touchdown to close the gap to five points. With 20 seconds left in the game, they tried an onside kick to recover the ball and scored a winning touchdown, but the 49ers controlled it and ran out the clock. The 49ers won 26–21, making it the franchise's first Super Bowl championship, and Montana was named MVP.

At the end of the game, President Ronald Reagan, who starred in the movie *Knute Rockne All-American*, referred to it when he calls 49ers coach Bill Walsh to congratulate him and said, "And you might want tell Joe Montana and the fellows that they really did win one for the Gipper."

Backstory. It's overhyped, overextended and often overdone, but for the majority of Americans since the 1970s, there is no bigger annual TV event than the Super Bowl. In a recent tally of the 100 highest-rated shows of all time since 1960, 38 of the professional football championship games have made the list, far more than its nearest competitor, 13 for *The Beverly Hillbillies* (see 12). There was perhaps no bigger indication of how powerful a draw it was than when it was decided in 1985 to postpone Ronald Reagan's inauguration for a second term in office as president 24 hours because that year's Super Bowl fell on the same day (Jan. 20), and his supporters did not want him to be overshadowed.

That is the case with virtually everything else during Super Bowl Sunday. In fact, that can now apply pretty much to the two weeks leading up to the big event, once the AFC and NFC conferences winners are picked. They are a flurry of covering every minuscule activity related to the game, and competing players and coaches have to grin and bear some of the most ridiculous questions from the media.

It was not always this way. The first game (Jan. 15, 1967) occurred as a result of merger talks between the National Football League and the upstart American Football League, with the latter being absorbed by the bigger organization. By 1970 they would be one league divided into conferences, but both parties agreed to have an annual end-of-season game effective three years before that occurred. Lamar Hunt, owner of the Kansas City Chiefs franchise, came up with the title after seeing his children play with a toy called a Super Ball, and it stuck, although the official title through 1969 was the World Championship Game.

There were 30,000 unsold seats in Los Angeles Memorial Coliseum as the NFL's Green Bay Packers demolished the AFL's Kansas City Chiefs 35–10 in the opening game. But it was a far different story on television. Airing on two networks (CBS had carried NFL games and NBC AFL ones, so this was felt to be a fair compromise on the inaugural effort), the event swamped ABC and everything else airing on TV, with CBS getting a 23.0/44 for its coverage and NBC a 17.8/34. Surveys had shown that football was overtaking baseball as America's favorite spectator sport on television, but these results really shocked the industry. (Incidentally, both networks erased their videotapes of the game; one incomplete copy of the CBS version was found in January 2011.)

The next year (Jan. 14, 1968) proved the bowl's ratings were no fluke: It earned a 36.8 rating for

CBS and a whopping 68 share, ratings unheard of for a Sunday afternoon show of any kind, and far better than the average ratings for the #1 series on TV at the time, *The Andy Griffith Show* (see 79). The rating dipped a little on NBC for Super Bowl III, but the network probably did not mind a 36.0 with a 70 share of the audience. The next two editions were even stronger: a 39.4 rating and 69 share for CBS on Jan. 11, 1970, and a 39.9 rating and 75 share for NBC on Jan. 17, 1971.

Emboldened by the results, and seeing how well football was doing on ABC Monday nights starting in 1970, CBS decided to move the start time later in the afternoon for Super Bowl VI on Jan. 16, 1972, so it could air partly in the nighttime in the East. The result was a 44.2 rating, making it the fifth-highest rated TV program up to that time. Since then, the Super Bowl has been the highest-rated TV show every year except for seven times—1976, 1977, 1980, 1983, 1984, 1993 and 1994—when it was in second place or among the top five for the year.

The 1981 Super Bowl was the lowest-rated contest in five years, although its rating of 44.4 was nothing to belittle. Advertisers paid a then-record high cost of $345,000 for 30-second commercial spots during the 1982 game, so CBS easily cleared $10 million in profits after expenses.

CBS invested $1.4 million to cover the game, including 100 microphones, 23 cameras and 14 videotape machines. "I don't think we're at the stage of overkill yet," producer Terry O'Neil told Tony Schwartz in *The New York Times*.

O'Neil was proud to unveil for Super Bowl XVI the "CBS Chalkboard," a monitor that would allow John Madden to diagram plays with white lines on top of a camera's still picture. That device became better known as the Telestrator and stayed part of most sports coverage on television thereafter.

It was not gadgetry that attracted audiences to this Super Bowl, but rather Mother Nature: More than three-fourths of North America was covered with snow on game day, the highest amount ever recorded. That meant that following the traditional pre-game coverage (*Super Bowl Today* started at 2:30 P.M. Eastern with Brent Musberger, Irv Cross, Phyllis George and Jimmy the Greek), conditions were prime for people to watch in droves, and they did.

Nielsen said the San Francisco market alone had a 53.2 rating and a mindboggling 91 share of the audience. Other top markets had big numbers too, for example 41.4/63 in New York City, 40.7/66 in Chicago and 47.6/64 in Philadelphia.

Even in Los Angeles, where there was no snow, the audience was very impressive (44.2/78). The post-game show with the presenting of the trophy to the 49ers and comments from the coach and players ran a half-hour and received a 39.6/56.

At the sports Emmys, Super Bowl XVI was nominated as best live sports special but lost the NCAA basketball championship final on CBS. Other nominations included Pat Summerall as sports personality-host, cinematography (for program titles), associate directors, and technical directors, electronic camerapersons and senior video operators. It did win Emmys for Madden as sports personality-analyst, theme music, graphics in its opening title sequences and technical/engineering supervisors. And the introduction of the CBS Chalkboard even merited a Special Classification for Individual Achievement notice (but not an award) for O'Neil.

Since its peak in 1982, the Super Bowl has drawn huge audiences while the rest of network TV shows have lost them, making it the top venue for advertisers. If the trend continues — and there is every reason to believe it will — within 15 years, half of the 100 highest-rated TV shows of all time in America will be the Super Bowl. A super achievement indeed.

---

3 — *Roots*

Jan. 30, 1977 (Part 8 of eight-part miniseries). **Rating: 51.1. Share: 71.**

Aired on ABC Sunday 9–11 P.M. Eastern and Pacific, 8–10 P.M. Central

Competition: *Switch* and *Delvecchio* on CBS; *McMillan* (last half-hour of 90-minute episode) and *Lanigan's Rabbi* (series debut) on NBC

Cast: LeVar Burton (Kunta Kinte as a young man), John Amos (Kunta Kinte as an adult), Ed Asner (Capt. Thomas Davies), Louis Gossett, Jr. (Fiddler), Robert Reed (Dr. William Reynolds), Madge Sinclair (Bell), Leslie Uggams (Kizzy), Chuck Connors (Tom Moore), Ben Vereen (Chicken George), Olivia Cole (Mathilda), Lloyd Bridges (Evan Brent), Georg Stanford Brown (Tom Harvey), Lynne Moody (Irene Harvey), Brad Davis (Ol' George Johnson). **Crew:** David L. Wolper (executive producer), Stan Margulies (producer), David Greene, Marvin Chomsky (directors), Ernest Kinoy, William Blinn, James Lee, M. Charles Cohen (writers).

Synopsis. Kunta Kinte, born in 1750, is transported from Africa to America in a slave ship commanded by Capt. Davies. Sold to the Reynolds family's plantation in Spotsylvania County, Virginia, he is renamed Toby. Fiddler, a fellow slave, teaches him how to survive. Kunta's foot is hacked off when he tries to escape. He and his wife Bell raise a daughter named Kizzy. Kunta teaches Kizzy his family's history before she is sold to chicken farmer Tom Moore, who rapes her. Their son, Chicken George, marries Mathilda. Kizzy briefly romances driver Sam Bennett, who takes her to the grave of Kunta, and she cries as she vows she will teach her children about him and Africa.

Chicken George and Mathilda have a son, Tom Harvey, who marries Irene. After the end of the Civil War in 1865, Ku Klux Klan members terrorize them and burn their property. Mr. Harvey, owner of their plantation, has to sell it when he cannot afford to keep them on as sharecroppers. New owner Evan Brent tells them they owe him debts on their goods they must pay off first, except for Ol' George Johnson, a Caucasian who is elevated to overseer. Ol' George saves Tom from a lashing by the KKK members, including Brent. Eventually they overthrow Brent and leave the land for a new life in Tennessee. Chicken George and Tom pay a tribute to Kunta Kinte there. Alex Haley then summarizes the rest of his family's story.

Backstory. "Tonight, we present a landmark in television entertainment — *Roots*, the true story Alex Haley uncovered in his 12-year search across the seven generations of his ancestry." That voiceover came at the start of a phenomenal ratings hit, a miniseries that still has each of its eight parts ranked among the top 100 TV shows of all time. This show definitely had a major impact on the medium.

In 1963, after having retired from the U.S. Coast Guard, Haley began researching the genealogy of his family back to Africa. His grandmother had told him about Kunta Kinte when he was a boy in Tennessee. Actress Ruby Dee told producer David L. Wolper about the project in 1969 and updated him on it three years later. The producer was hooked, as he always wanted to tell a story about several generations of a family. But Columbia Pictures held the movie rights, so Wolper dropped the idea. Then a serendipitous meeting with Haley's secretary at a restaurant led him to discover that Columbia had dropped its option.

Wolper approached ABC executive Brandon Stoddard by having Haley explain his book in person. "Alex was an incredible storyteller," Stoddard said in the *Roots* DVD. "He started to tell this story, and the story was really about how he had spent maybe ten years discovering his own roots, and the struggle that it was to go all the way back

finally to the tiny little village in Africa where he came from." The pitch sold almost instantly.

While the book was being written, Wolper negotiated with Barry Diller, head of ABC's TV-movie division, to run it as a miniseries, using a *Reader's Digest* excerpt as part of his pitch. He succeeded, and ABC bought *Roots* in August 1974 even before it was published. (Haley didn't finish the book until after the script was completed.)

Screenwriter William Blinn talked with Haley often while writing the script. His original outline had Haley searching in the present for information about his ancestry, but that didn't work as well as just starting the chronology from Kunta Kinte onward. He made some characters composites from the book. Blinn was one of four Caucasian writers for the miniseries. Wolper said that Haley specifically said he did not want any black writers because he wanted his own perspective about his life and being black to come through, and not theirs.

Most black actors approached did appear in the film. Prior commitments prevented appearances by James Earl Jones (first cast as Chicken George) and Billy Dee Williams. Sidney Poitier had a dispute with ABC and thus did not appear either.

More than 150 actors auditioned to play the part of Kunta Kinte, including LeVar Burton, an 18-year-old sophomore at the University of Southern California. Burton had never been filmed before when he auditioned on March 24, 1976, but he wowed the crew, so they hired him.

When Fred Silverman moved from head of programming from CBS to ABC in 1975, he approved increasing *Roots* from six to 12 hours. Filming began in April 1976 in Savannah, Georgia, and then later moved to Southern California. It lasted six months. The production's biggest problem came when 80 percent of the extras in the slave ship sequence refused to show up the next day, finding it emotionally taxing. "We were all walking around with these wounds that were so unresolved, so unhealed, so raw," Burton said in the DVD. "And in many instances, those wounds had been covered with scabs, and *Roots* had the effect of ripping those scabs off, exposing the wound all over again."

ABC censor Alfred Schneider spent two hours with Wolper and Stoddard reviewing the number of lashes Kunta Kinte received. He allowed bare-breasted African women, but mainly in long shots and only at the opening. The project went over budget $1.386 million. Meanwhile, some of the ABC sales staff grumbled about trying to sell a show where the blacks were the good guys and the whites were the villains.

"The night before it aired, I was one scared puppy," Stoddard said. The night after its debut, at 5 A.M., Los Angeles–based Stoddard received a phone call from his New York research department telling him the show had the highest rating he had ever heard in his life. The following installments gave the network staff even more reason to smile.

Roots ended with an average rating of 44.9 and an incredible 66 share. It was estimated that 130 million Americans viewed at least part of the miniseries. Many bars suffered a slump in business unless they had a sign saying they were showing the series that night. All the top 15 shows that week were on ABC, with *Roots* being the top seven, and all 21 shows that ABC aired in prime time finished in the top 26. No show had less than a 31 share, and ABC won all but six half-hours in prime time.

Roots won more than 50 awards. It earned 37 Emmy nominations in 14 categories, competing against itself with multiple nominees in ten categories. Its nine wins were for outstanding limited series, lead actor for single performance (Louis Gossett, Jr., beating John Amos, Burton and Ben Vereen in the first Emmy category ever swept by nominees from the same show), supporting actor for single performance (Ed Asner, over Moses Gunn, Robert Reed, Ralph Waite and the only non–*Roots* competitor, Charles Durning for *Captains and the Kings*), supporting actress for single performance (Olivia Cole over *Roots* co-stars Sandy Duncan and Cicely Tyson, among others), directing (David Greene for Part 1), writing (Ernest Kinoy and Blinn for Part 2), film editing, film sound editing and music composition. The latter win was shared by Quincy Jones and Gerald Fried for Part 1. Jones also cracked the *Billboard* pop singles chart with his "*Roots* Medley" in 1977.

Genealogy studies exploded as a result of *Roots*, as did the use of African names among black children. Warner Brothers sold the miniseries to 32 countries, and the book was translated into 12 languages. Its repeats in September 1978 got a very strong average of 25.4/42. That same year, a court ruled against Margaret Walker Alexander's claim that *Roots* improperly appropriated part of *Jubilee*, her novel based on her great grandmother's life. A sequel appeared in 1979 (see 99 —*Roots: The Next Generations*).

In 2002 there was a documentary celebrating the 25th anniversary of *Roots*. ABC rejected a celebration of its biggest hit of all time, even though it was fully sponsored. It aired on NBC instead.

In 2007 the Emmy awards held an onstage reunion of the surviving cast, and they received an ovation. They deserved it. They participated in a story about great history that created its own place in it.

2 — *Dallas*

Nov. 21, 1980 ("Who Done It?"). **Rating:** 53.3. **Share:** 80.

Aired on CBS Friday 10–11 P.M. Eastern and Pacific, 9–10 P.M. Central

Competition: *Convoy* (last hour of two-hour 1976 theatrical movie) on ABC; *NBC Magazine with David Brinkley* on NBC

Cast: Barbara Bel Geddes (Miss Ellie Ewing), Jim Davis (Jock Ewing), Patrick Duffy (Bobby Ewing), Linda Gray (Sue Ellen Ewing), Larry Hagman (J.R. Ewing), Steve Kanaly (Ray Krebbs), Ken Kercheval (Cliff Barnes), Victoria Principal (Pamela Barnes Ewing), Charlene Tilton (Lucy Ewing). **Guests:** Mary Crosby (Kristin Shepard), Susan Howard (Donna Culver), Leigh McCloskey (Mitch Cooper). **Crew:** David Jacobs (creator), Philip Capice (executive producer), Leonard Katzman (producer-director), Loraine Despres (writer).

Synopsis. Charged with shooting her husband J.R. Ewing, Sue Ellen honestly does not know if she did it because she was drinking. The incriminating facts are that the gun was found in her closet and has her fingerprints. J.R.'s brother Bobby wants to bail out Sue Ellen over the objections of his mother, Miss Ellie, and father, Jock. J.R.'s business rival, Cliff Barnes, who is the brother of Bobby's wife Pamela, offers Sue Ellen support, as does Sue Ellen's sister, Kristin Shepard.

Under hypnosis, Sue Ellen recalls that she carried a gun and went to find J.R. at Kristin's apartment. He was not there, but Sue Ellen vowed she would locate and kill J.R., because she was not willing to return to a sanitarium and lose access to her son. She had additional drinks, then could not recall more details before she woke up in the airport parking lot. She realizes through her testimony that she did not have the gun when she awoke, but it somehow ended in her closet.

Deducing the truth, Sue Ellen returns to the Ewings' Southfork Ranch and confronts Kristin with J.R. watching. Kristin shot J.R. while Sue Ellen was passed out, then hid the gun in the closet while Sue Ellen showered the next morning. J.R. plans to call the police, but Kristin tells him she is pregnant with his child, and the scandal of his mistress giving birth in jail could ruin him. "I'll handle Kristin my own way," he snarls at her.

Backstory. The biggest question for TV couch potatoes during the summer of 1980 was "Who shot J.R.?" after *Dallas'* scheming lead character was wounded in his office during the season finale on March 21, 1980. The producers set up the plot to a point where almost everybody on the show had a motive.

The cliffhanger was big in many countries besides America. When Larry Hagman visited Great Britain that summer, bookmakers there were placing their odds on who was the culprit. There was even a novelty record called "Who Shot J.R.?" by Gary Burbank with Band McNally (get it?) that grazed the pop charts in July 1980. The episode sparked a frenzy that had never been created previously on such a massive level by a soap opera, and it inspired a wave of continuing melodramas in the nighttime in its wake. But none have been as popular as this one.

Oddly, it was what would become the spin-off of *Dallas, Knots Landing,* that producers Lee Rich and David Jacobs first attempted to sell to CBS. Network officials said they really wanted instead a series like the sprawling 1956 movie *Giant.* "We've got it!" Rich told the head honchos, even though he and Jacobs really had no idea for such a show. But they put their heads together to create a storyline fast. "We came with *Dallas.* We said, 'That's great. There's oil down there, we can do that,'" Rich told in an Archive of American Television interview.

Starting on April 2, 1978, CBS tested the show out. Originally Bobby Ewing and his wife Pamela were to be the prime characters in a Romeo-and-Juliet conflict between the Ewings and the Barneses, but fate intervened when casting Bobby's older brother.

"We offered the J.R. role to Robert Forster, and he turned it down," Rich said. Then Rich recalled a flop sitcom he had done in 1971, *The Good Life* with Hagman, and how he got along well with the star, so he proposed him for it. Hagman was so delicious in enacting his dirty deeds that the producers switched directions and began building stories around him instead.

Series personnel found a real ranch as well as locations in Dallas where they shot footage, but they duplicated the front of the house and its pool on a soundstage. Even with the beautiful settings and overheated melodrama, the series did not become a top 10 hit until the 1979-1980 series, when it finished at #6 and settled into a Friday night time slot. Meanwhile Jacobs, who created the early scripts before he left the series to do *Knots*

Landing (1979–1993), left as producer and Leonard Katzman assumed the post.

By this season, J.R. had an uneasy relationship with Bobby, who lacked the ethics in business deals his older brother appeared to have forgotten; Cliff Barnes, Pamela's brother, who was convinced that J.R. played a part in the downfall of his father; and Sue Ellen, who as indicated by the summary endured J.R. cheating on her with her sister, Kristin, even after giving birth to their son. All were prime suspects when J.R. heard a noise while working at his office, went to investigate and ended up wounded in the season finale.

Adding to the suspense over the summer of 1980 was the actors' strike that prevented the show from returning on schedule in September, and reports that Hagman wanted so much more money to do the series that the producers were considering replacing him with Robert Culp by claiming that J.R. had undergone an ambulance fire while being transported to the hospital that resulted in plastic surgery.

The strike finally ended and Hagman returned. To heighten interest about the denouement, there were multiple possible conclusions shot. "We never told anybody which ending we were going to use," Rich said. "We hid the script, so nobody could see that either." The only ones who knew who shot J.R. before the episode aired were Rich and Katzman.

CBS reran the season closing episode from 9–10 P.M. Eastern and Pacific on Friday, Nov. 7, 1980 (31.8/51), followed by the season opener (38.2/61). Two days later, a Sunday special called *Dallas—Part 2* got a 40.0/59 and was the #1 show of the week. Five days after that (Friday, Nov. 14), *Dallas* was #1 again for the week for that episode with a 35.7/56.

On that same day, *The New York Post* ran a full-page spread on the odds Las Vegas put on 14 suspects for next week's episode. That same week, *People* magazine polled 35,625 readers, some as far away as Japan and Saudi Arabia, about who they thought was guilty. Dusty Farlow, Sue Ellen's ex-flame, won with 21 percent, followed by Kristin with 14 percent, Vaughn Leland (an old business crony of J.R.'s) at 13 percent, Sue Ellen at 8 percent and Miss Ellie at 7 percent. Some supposedly comical guesses included the Ayatollah Khomeini, President Jimmy Carter and Fred Silverman (considering how far NBC was in third place behind CBS and ABC at this time under his leadership, I can see that as a legitimate possibility). A total of 83.6 million Americans watched the show. CBS charged $250,000 per 30-second commercial, $100,000 more than usual, and it made $3 million from ad sales alone. With all that anticipation, this episode is a letdown. It is obvious that Sue Ellen could not have done it, and the revelation that Kristin was the killer is rather ho-hum.

Dallas had enough momentum from this and subsequent episodes to finish the 1980-1981 season at #1 with a 34.5 average, the highest seasonal average for a series since *Bonanza* (see 20) ended the 1964-1965 season with a 36.3. Its numbers declined thereafter but it still made #1 in the 1981-1982 and 1983-1984 seasons before falling out of the top 10 in 1987. Finally, with ratings dropping, the show ended on May 3, 1991. It ended with four Emmy wins out of 21 nominations, for Barbara Bel Geddes as lead actress in 1980, for music composition in 1983 and 1984, and for costume design in 1985.

And what happened to Kristin? After being sent out of town with a monthly income from J.R. supporting her, she returned in 1981 only to be found drowned in the Southfork pool by Bobby. He thought J.R. had killed her, but her death was accidental. Kristin's final storyline turned out to be as anticlimactic as this episode, although hardcore *Dallas* fans (and there remain plenty as of this writing) might argue otherwise.

1 — *M*A*S*H*

Feb. 28, 1983 ("Goodbye, Farewell and Amen"). **Rating:** 60.2. **Share:** 77.

Aired on CBS Tuesday 8:30–11 P.M. Eastern and Pacific, 7:30–10 P.M. Central

Competition: *That's Incredible!* (last half-hour) and *American Gigolo* (network TV debut of 1980 movie) on ABC; *The Night The Bridge Fell Down* (last two and a half-hours of three-hour TV movie originally scheduled for 1980) on NBC

Cast: Alan Alda (Capt. Benjamin Franklin "Hawkeye" Pierce), Mike Farrell (Capt. B.J. Hunnicut), Harry Morgan (Col. Sherman Potter), David Ogden Stiers (Maj. Charles Emerson Winchester III), Loretta Swit (Maj. Margaret "Hot Lips" Houlihan), William Christopher (Father Francis Mulcahy), Jamie Farr (Cpl. Maxwell Klinger). **Guests:** Allan Arbus (Dr. Sidney Freeman), Rosalind Chao (Soon-Lee Klinger), G.W. Bailey (Sgt. Luther Rizzo), John Shearin (Chopper Pilot), Kellye Nakahara (Nurse Kellye), Jeff Maxwell (Igor), Lang Yun (Woman on the Bus). **Crew:** Burt Metcalfe (executive producer, co-writer), Thad Mumford, Dan Wilcox (producers, co-writers), Alan Alda (director, co-writer), John Rappaport, Elias Davis, David Pollock, Karen Hull (writers).

Synopsis. During the Korean War, Capt. Hawkeye Pierce (stationed in Korea) had a mental break-down after an incident on a bus where a woman smothered her baby to death to keep it from being heard during an ambush by the Chinese. The rest of the 4077th is celebrating the upcoming end of the Korean War, although a stuck tank makes the Army hospital a bombing target. One explosion leaves Father Mulcahy temporarily deaf.

Hawkeye regains his sanity and returns to camp. He is upset to learn that his pal B.J. has already left for home, yet he selflessly drives the tank into the trash dump and saves the 4077th from further bombing. An encroaching fire forces the camp to bug out to another location, where B.J. rejoins them as flights back to America are booked up. When everyone returns to the compound to treat the final batch of incoming wounded, they see the fire gutted it except for their operating room.

Col. Potter says goodbye to his beloved horse, Corp. Klinger marries girlfriend Soon-Lee, and Maj. Winchester teaches some Chinese prisoners how to play classical music (when the prisoners are taken in custody, they are killed, to the major's great sorrow). The company members tell each other what they plan to do after the war (Hawkeye's returning to Crabapple Cove, Maine, Maj. Houlihan will work in a hospital), then leave one by one. B.J. says goodbye to Hawkeye with stones spelling out the words as Hawkeye's chopper departs.

Backstory. Who would have thought that a series that finished third in its time slot during its inaugural season would end up with the all-time highest-rated episode? When *M*A*S*H* debuted on CBS on Sept. 17, 1972, it was swamped by its competition, *Disney* on NBC and *The F.B.I.* on ABC. Yet it had an excellent critical reception and several Emmy nominations (eventually more than 100 of them), so CBS moved it to a much better time period the next season, following *All in the Family* (see 25). From that point onward, even though it would have four more time slot changes and several cast defections as well, *M*A*S*H* was a top 15 hit for its remaining ten seasons.

The show was based on the 1970 Oscar nominee for Best Picture (which debuted on CBS on Sept. 13, 1974, with strong but not stellar numbers of 20.5/36). M*A*S*H stood for Mobile Army Surgical Hospital, a unit designed to treat injured combatants in the Korean War. Capt. Hawkeye Pierce was a womanizer adamantly opposed to many military processes, but his skills as a surgeon were appreciated in the setting. He, Maj. Margaret Houlihan and Father Mulcahy were the only characters seen in the first and last shows.

What made *M*A*S*H* stand out was its ability

to weave comic and dramatic moments together in equally fascinating and unexpected storylines, drawing out the humanity of those involved in an inhumane event. It treated its audience much more intelligently than most other series on the air, whether humorous or serious.

"The cast and crew behaved like they were producing the best show on television," director Alan Rafkin wrote in his memoirs. "This attitude translated not into arrogance, but dedication. Everybody knew they were doing something special, and they wouldn't settle for anything less each week.... There was a quality about the show that was rare."

Finally, at the end of the tenth season in the spring of 1982, the whole cast met and agreed that the following year would be their last one on the air. "We wanted to end the show while we were still on top," Mike Farrell wrote in his autobiography. "And we wanted to wrap it up with an end-of-the-war episode that would give us a chance to say goodbye and thank you to each other, to the characters and to the audience."

But executives at CBS and Fox were aghast at losing one of their chief moneymakers, not to mention Fox fearing that such a closer would damage the rerun ratings of *M*A*S*H* in syndication the way many believed the finale for *The Fugitive* (see 9) hurt its popularity thereafter. A compromise between all parties was reached wherein the series would produce only 15 new episodes in order to work on a special two-hour movie ending, but the latter would not be included as part of the syndication rerun package (Fox added it to the mix in 1993).

"First it was to be written by two writers, Elias Davis and David Pollock, who were very much the story editors on the show," Thad Mumford recalled to Tom Stempel in *Storytellers to the Nation*. "Then we all got pissed off because we thought this was going to be very historic. What ended up, I think, hurting the piece [was that] they bowed to our requests and our concerns made us all part of it."

Indeed, while this finale has some warm moments, it unfortunately spent too much time on the drama at the expense of laughs and fun viewers had come to appreciate. It's not a disastrous closer by any means, but it just feels over-the-top when it should have been more intimate.

Before filming concluded on the episode, a fire hit the series' compound on location in Malibu Canyon on Oct. 11, 1982, so the inferno was included as part of the storyline. The damage seen onscreen really happened.

When the finale aired, *TV Guide* took the unprecedented step of devoting half the magazine to it, including Alan Alda's picks for his favorite episodes, an appreciation by Alistair Cooke, and an article on current and former cast members by series writer Burt Prelutsky. *Variety* produced its first-time farewell tribute section for a TV series and noted that a few weeks before the movie ran, CBS affiliates convinced the network to move the show's starting time from 8 to 8:30 P.M. so that it would lead directly into their late night news shows rather than the special episode of *Alice* originally slated for 10:30–11 P.M.

That Monday evening, the nighttime syndicated series *PM Magazine* and *Entertainment Tonight* ran special tributes to the show. The episode of *Alice* which preceded it won its time slot with solid if not spectacular numbers of 30.7/41.

"The night the series ended, all of us who had worked together on the show went to the studio and watched the last episode projected on a big screen," Alda said in his autobiography. "The last reel ended for us just as the rest of the country began to see the program on their television screens." As cast and crew headed to a restaurant to celebrate, Alda noted that the streets were totally empty of people. Indeed, homes and bars across America held parties to commemorate the ending.

"It was sensational — much more of an event than we ever anticipated," an unnamed CBS vice-president told *TV Guide*. The network sold 35 30-second commercials for $450,000 on average, grossing CBS $15 million in ad sales from this episode alone. (The finale received pretty low numbers of 10.8/18 when CBS repeated it on Sept. 18, 1984.)

On March 9, 1988, the cast reunited for the fifth annual Los Angeles Television Festival at the Museum of Broadcasting (now the Paley Center for Media) in New York City. On May 17, 2002, Fox aired the *M*A*S*H: 30th Anniversary Reunion* special.

An estimated 106 million viewers watched this show. That number would not be surpassed until when Super Bowl XLIV just nudged it out with 106.48 million viewers on average on Feb. 7, 2010. But there were more people available to watch that show in 2010 than in 1983. Percentage-wise, more Americans saw the *M*A*S*H* finale more than any other sponsored show. I doubt the circumstances will ever be right in today's multimedia world for it to happen again.

Appendix A: Chronology

1960
Nov. 23 — *Wagon Train* (#48)
Dec. 8 — *Peter Pan* (#93)

1961
Jan. 1 — *Candid Camera* (#66)
Jan. 28 — *Gunsmoke* (#24)
May 16 — The 13th Annual Emmy Awards (#98)
Sept. 9 — Miss America Pageant (#19)

1962
Oct. 1 — *The Lucy Show* (#62)

1963
Jan. 21 — *Ben Casey* (#88)
Feb. 19 — *The Red Skelton Hour* (#68)
Feb. 24 — *Carol & Company* (#33)

1964
Jan. 1 — The Rose Bowl (#67)
Jan. 1 — *The Dick Van Dyke Show* (#59)
Jan. 8 — *The Beverly Hillbillies* (#12)
Jan. 26 — *The Wizard of Oz* (#52)
Feb. 9 — *The Ed Sullivan Show* (#11)
March 8 — *Bonanza* (#20)

1965
Jan. 29 — *Gomer Pyle, U.S.M.C.* (#55)
Feb. 22 — *Cinderella* (#18)
March 14 — Danny Thomas Special: *Wonderful World of Burlesque* (#32)

1966
Sept. 25 — *The Bridge on the River Kwai* (#38)
Oct. 12 — *Friends and Nabors* (#87)

1967
Feb. 21 — *The Andy Griffith Special* (#54)
Aug. 29 — *The Fugitive* (#9)

1968
Jan. 26 — *The Birds* (#35)
Jan. 29 — *The Andy Griffith Show* (#79)
Sept. 23 — *Mayberry, R.F.D.* (#50)

1969
March 24 — *Rowan and Martin's Laugh-In* (#53)
Dec. 7 — *A Charlie Brown Christmas* (#61)

1970
Jan. 15 — Bob Hope Christmas Special (#7)
Jan. 15 — *The Dean Martin Show* (#77)
Feb. 22 — *Born Free* (#73)
April 7 — Academy Awards (#13)
Nov. 29 — *John Wayne: Swing Out Sweet Land* (#39)

1971
Jan. 5 — *Marcus Welby, M.D.* (#40)
Feb. 14 — *Ben-Hur* (#44)
Nov. 4 — *The Flip Wilson Show* (#94)
Nov. 30 — *Brian's Song* (#92)
Dec. 14 — Andy Williams Christmas Show (#95)

1972
Jan. 1 — The Cotton Bowl (#81)
Jan. 8 — *All in the Family* (#25)
Jan. 11 — *The Night Stalker* (#84)
Sept. 4 — Summer Olympics (#80)
Oct. 1 — *Love Story* (#17)
Nov. 12 — *True Grit* (#34)
Nov. 19 — *Patton* (#36)
Dec. 10 — Christmas with the Bing Crosbys (#70)

1973
Feb. 18 — *The Ten Commandments* (#83)
April 4 — *Elvis: Aloha from Hawaii* (#75)
Sept. 14 — *Planet of the Apes* (#57)
Sept. 20 — *Bonnie and Clyde* (#78)
Nov. 11 — *Airport* (#16)

1974
Feb. 7 — *The Waltons* (#69)
Feb. 20 — *A Case of Rape* (#86)
Oct. 27 — *The Poseidon Adventure* (#31)
Oct. 28 — *Rhoda* (#58)
Nov. 18 — *The Godfather* (#27)
Dec. 27 — *Sanford and Son* (#72)

1976

Jan. 18 — *Jeremiah Johnson* (#42)
Feb. 29 — *The Sound of Music* (#76)
April 2 — *Helter Skelter* (#41)
Sept. 21— *Happy Days* (#64)
Nov. 7 — *Gone with the Wind* (Part 1) (#6)

1977

Jan. 16 — *Little Ladies of the Night* (#47)
Jan. 30— *Roots* (#3)
Feb. 6 — *How the West Was Won* (#82)
Sept. 25 — *The Longest Yard* (#85)

1978

Jan. 3 — *Fish* (#96)
April 19 — *Holocaust* (#60)
Sept. 15 — Ali-Spinks Fight (#43)

1979

Jan. 14 — *Dallas Cowboys Cheerleaders* (#91)
Jan. 16 — *Laverne & Shirley* (#56)
Feb. 4 — *Rocky* (#45)
Feb. 20— *Roots: The Next Generation* (#99)
Feb. 21— *Eight Is Enough* (#97)
March 13 — *Three's Company* (#37)
March 13 — *The Ropers* (#49)
Nov. 4 — *Jaws* (#30)

1980

Jan. 20— *60 Minutes* (#89)
Sept. 17 — *Shogun* (#46)
Oct. 21— World Series Game 6 (#26)
Nov. 21— *Dallas* (#2)

1982

Jan. 2 — AFC Division Championship Game (#74)
Jan. 10— NFC Championship Game (#15)
Jan. 24 — Super Bowl XVI (#4)

1983

Feb. 13 — *The Winds of War* (#23)
Feb. 28 — *M*A*S*H* (#1)
March 29 — *The Thorn Birds* (#14)
Nov. 20— *The Day After* (#8)

1984

Oct. 8 — *The Burning Bed* (#51)
Nov. 19 — *Fatal Vision* (#100)

1986

Feb. 27 — *You Again?* (#63)
April 13 — *Return to Mayberry* (#90)

1987

Jan. 22 — *The Cosby Show* (#22)
Jan. 22 — *Family Ties* (#29)

1993

Feb. 10— Michael Jackson Talks to ... Oprah (#28)
May 20— *Cheers* (#10)

1994

Feb. 23 — XVII Winter Olympics (#5)

1998

May 14 — *Seinfeld* (#21)

Appendix B: Top-Rated Shows Prior to 1960

Most sources cite these three shows as the biggest ratings draws of the 1950s.

1. *I Love Lucy*

Jan. 19, 1953 ("Lucy Goes to the Hospital"). **Rating:** 71.7.
Aired on CBS Monday 9–9:30 P.M. Eastern and Pacific, 8–8:30 P.M. Central
Cast: Lucille Ball (Lucy Ricardo), Desi Arnaz (Ricky Ricardo), Vivian Vance (Ethel Mertz), William Frawley (Fred Mertz). **Guests:** Charles Lane, Peggy Rea, Barbara Pepper. **Crew:** Desi Arnaz (executive producer), Jess Oppenheimer (producer), William Asher (director), Jess Oppenheimer, Madelyn Pugh, Bob Carroll Jr. (writers).

Synopsis
Lucy Ricardo experiences labor pains and has her husband Ricky and apartment friends the Mertzes take her to the hospital where she gives birth to Little Ricky.

The Story Behind the Hit
I Love Lucy was the most popular series of the 1950s (it was in the top three all seven seasons it ran, with five of them at #1). It reached its peak with this episode, which coincided with Lucille Ball's own real-life delivery of Desi Arnaz Jr.

Anything more I would have to say about this show would be redundant, except this little interesting little-known nugget shared with me by Shu Shostak, Ball's film archivist: As the series' 35th anniversary loomed in 1986, he and Tom Watson (Ball's business affairs manager) came up with the idea of a reunion show in which Little Ricky gets married. It would have made references to old episodes and featured players from the originals, such as Mary Wickes.

When they proposed it to CBS, management instead wanted a retrospective show where stars like Robin Williams talked about the series. The whole thing was dropped when Ball announced she would returning to series television on ABC in the fall of 1986 (the lousy *Life with Lucy* sitcom). What a missed opportunity.

Even so, what Viacom said to promote the series in 1976 remains just as true today: "To a world of television viewers, it will always be the greatest show on earth."

2. *The Ed Sullivan Show*

Sept. 9, 1956 (Elvis Presley as guest). Rating: 82.6.
Aired on CBS Sunday 8–9 P.M. Eastern and Pacific, 7–8 P.M. Central
This was Presley's first appearance on the show. Charles Laughton was guest host. Presley returned two more times through 1957, with Sullivan introducing him. For more details on this, see entries 11 and 75.

3. *Cinderella*

March 31, 1957 (special). Rating: 60.0.
Aired on CBS Sunday 8–9:30 P.M. Eastern and Pacific, 7–8:30 P.M. Central
For more details on this, see entry 18.

Appendix C:
Top 100 Facts and Figures

Breakdown by Network

ABC — 35
CBS — 34
NBC — 31

Breakdown by Days of the Week Aired

Sunday — 34
Monday — 14
Tuesday — 16
Wednesday — 12
Thursday — 12
Friday — 6
Saturday — 6

Breakdown by Month Aired

January — 28
February — 21
March — 6
April — 5
May — 3
June — 0
July — 0
August — 1
September — 11
October — 7
November — 13
December — 5

Breakdown by Genre

Sitcoms — 22 (includes expanded episodes)
Theatrical Movies — 20
Specials (Entertainment) — 16
TV Movies — 10
Specials (Sports) — 9
Miniseries — 7 (including *How the West Was Won*)
Variety Series — 6 (including *Candid Camera*)
Drama Series — 6
Westerns — 3
News-Informational — 1 (*60 Minutes*)

Series Debuts

The Ropers
Mayberry R.F.D.
The Lucy Show
You Again?

Series Finales

*M*A*S*H*
The Fugitive
Cheers
Seinfeld

Number One Series for a Season That Failed to Make the Top 100 (1960–1993 only)

Dynasty (1984–1985)
Roseanne (1989–1990)

Bibliography

General Works

The following books include information that was used in three or more entries in the top 100 list.

Block, Alex Ben, and Lucy Autrey Wilson, editors. *George Lucas's Blockbusting*. New York: HarperCollins, 2010.

Brooks, Tim, and Earle Marsh. *The Complete Directory to Prime Time Network and Cable TV Shows 1946–Present*, 9th ed. New York: Ballantine, 2007.

Broughton, Irv. *Producers on Producing*. Jefferson, NC: McFarland, 1986.

Dowdy, Andrew. *Movies Are Better Than Ever*. New York: William Morrow, 1973.

Heston, Charlton. *In the Arena: An Autobiography*. New York: Simon & Schuster, 1995.

Hyatt, Wesley. *Emmy Award Winning Nighttime Television Shows, 1948–2004*. Jefferson, NC: McFarland, 2006.

_____. *The Encyclopedia of Daytime Television*. New York: Billboard, 1997.

Leonard, Sheldon. *And the Show Goes On*. New York: Limelight, 1994.

Lucas, Eddie. *Close-Ups: Conversations with Our TV Favorites*. Albany, GA: Bear Manor Media, 2007.

Marill, Alvin H. *Movies Made for Television: The Telefeature and the Miniseries 1964–1984*. New York: New York Zoetrope, 1984.

Marshall, Garry, with Lori Marshall. *Wake Me When It's Funny*. Holbrook, MA: Adams, 1995.

McNeil, Alex. *Total Television*, 4th ed. New York: Penguin, 1996.

Segrave, Kerry. *Movies at Home: How Hollywood Came to Television*. Jefferson, NC: McFarland, 1999.

Steinberg, Cobbett. *TV Facts*. New York: Facts on File, 1980.

Stempel, Tom. *Storytellers to the Nation*. Syracuse, NY: Syracuse University Press, 1996.

Stevens, George, Jr. *Conversations with the Great Moviemakers of Hollywood's Golden Age*. New York: Random House, 2006.

Terrace, Vincent. *Encyclopedia of Television Series, Pilots and Specials, 1937–1973*. New York, NY: Zoetrope, 1986.

Whitburn, Joel. *Top Pop Albums 1955–2001*. Menomonee Falls, WI: Record Research, 2001.

_____. *Top Pop Singles 1955–2002*. Menomonee Falls, WI: Record Research, 2003.

Websites

The Internet Movie Database
TV By the Numbers
TV.com
Wikipedia

Works on Specific Shows (Alphabetical)

The Academy Awards

Kanter, Hal. *So Far, So Funny*. Jefferson, NC: McFarland, 1999.

Wiley, Mason, and Damon Bona. *Inside Oscar, 10th Anniversary Ed*. New York: Ballantine, 1996.

Airport

Hayes, Helen, with Katherine Hatch. *My Life in Three Acts*. New York: Harcourt Brace Jovanovich, 1990.

Stapleton, Maureen. *A Hell of a Life*. New York: Simon & Schuster, 1995.

Ali-Spinks Fight

Cosell, Howard, with Peter Bonventre. *I Never Played the Game*. New York: William Morrow, 1985.

"Muhammad Ali KOs Nielsens," *Los Angeles Times*, Oct. 5, 1977, Part IV, p. 16.

Putnam, Pat. "Once More to the Top," *Sports Illustrated*, Sept. 25, 1978, pp. 16–19.

Simms, Gregg. "Can 'Old Man' Ali Accomplish the Impossible?" *Ebony*, September 1978, pp. 112–20.

All in the Family

Emery, Robert J. *The Directors Take Two*. New York: TV Books, 2000.

Rich, Lee. *Warm Up the Snake: A Hollywood Memoir*. Ann Arbor, MI: University of Michigan Press, 2006.

Strouse, Charles. *Put on a Happy Face: A Broadway Memoir*. New York: Sterling Publishing, 2008.

The Andy Griffith Show

Kelly, Richard. *The Andy Griffith Show*. Winston-Salem, NC: John F. Blair, 1981.

The Andy Griffith Special

Hawn, Goldie, with Wendy Holden. *A Lotus Grows in the Wind*. New York: G.P. Putnam & Sons, 2005.

Andy Williams Christmas Show

Osmond, Marie, with Marcia Wilkie. *Might As Well Laugh About It*. New York: Penguin, 2009.

Williams, Andy. *Moon River and Me: A Memoir*. New York: Viking, 2009.

Ben Casey

Doan, Richard K. "The Doan Report: New Tune for ABC; 'Strauss Family' In for Julie Andrews," *TV Guide*, Feb. 17–23, 1973, p. A-1.

Krampner, Jon. *Female Brando: The Legend of Kim Stanley*. New York: Back Stage Books, 2006.

Ben-Hur

Ben-Hur DVD documentaries "*Ben-Hur*: The Making of an Epic" (1993) and "*Ben-Hur*: The Epic That Changed Cinema" (2005) plus commentary, all included in 2005 MGM release.

"Metro's *Ben-Hur* to be CBS Spec," *Variety*, Sept. 2, 1970, p. 45.

The Birds

Aulier, Dan. *Hitchcock's Notebooks*. New York: Avon, 1999.

"Letters to the Editor," *TV Guide*, Jan. 27–Feb. 2, 1968, p. A-2.

McGilligan, Patrick, ed. *Backstory 3: Interviews with Screenwriters of the 60s*. Los Angeles: University of California Press, 1997.

The Bob Hope Christmas Special

Doan, Richard K. "The Doan Report," *TV Guide*, Feb. 7–13, 1970, p. A-1.

Hope, Bob, with Melville Shavelson. *Don't Shoot, It's Only Me*. New York: Putnam's, 1990.

Richmond, Ray. *My Greatest Day in Show Business: Screen Legends Share Their Fondest Memories*. Dallas, TX: Taylor Publishing, 1999.

Rosen, George. *Variety*, April 26, 1961, p. 178.

Bonanza

Dann, Mike, as told to Paul Berger. *As I Saw It: The Inside Story of the Golden Years of Television*. El Prado, NM: Levine Mesa Press, 2009.

"260 *Ponderosa* Segs on Market," *Variety*, March 22, 1972, p. 55.

Bonnie and Clyde

Caron, Leslie. *Thank Heaven: A Memoir*. New York: Viking Adult, 2009.

Dunaway, Faye, with Betsy Sharkey. *Looking for Gatsby*. New York: Simon & Schuster, 1995.

Friedman, Lester D.,ed. *Arthur Penn's* Bonnie and Clyde. New York: Cambridge University Press, 2000.

McGilligan, Patrick, ed. *Backstory 4: Interviews with Screenwriters of the 1970s and 1980s*. Los Angeles: University of California Press, 2006.

Strouse, Charles. *Put on a Happy Face: A Broadway Memoir*. New York: Sterling, 2008.

Wilder, Gene. *Kiss Me Like a Stranger: My Search for Love and Art*. New York: St. Martin's Press, 2005.

Born Free

"*Born Free*," *Look*, April 19, 1966, pp. 106–09.

Dann, Mike, as told to Paul Berger. *As I Saw It: The Inside Story of the Golden Years of Television*. El Prado, NM: Levine Mesa Press, 2009.

Brian's Song

Brian's Song DVD commentary with James Caan and Billy Dee Williams and featurette "Gale Sayers First and Goal," 2000.

The Bridge on the River Kwai

Guinness, Alec. *Blessings in Disguise*. New York: Alfred A. Knopf, 1986.

Organ, Steven, ed. *David Lean Interviews*. Jackson, MS: University Press of Mississippi, 2009.

The Burning Bed

Ahern, Louise Knott. "*The Burning Bed*: A Turning Point in Fight Against Domestic Violence," *The Lansing State Journal*, Sept. 27, 2009, www.lansingstatejournal.com

Crist, Judith. "This Week's Movies," *TV Guide*, Oct. 6–12, 1984, p. A-10.

Diliberto, Gioia. "A Violent Death, A Haunted Life," *People*, Oct. 8, 1984, pp. 100–06.

Hall, Jane. "Farrah Talks About Her Role of a Lifetime," *People*, Oct. 8, 1984, pp. 109–10.

Candid Camera

Funt, Bill. Podcast interview with Stu Shostak, Stu's Show website (www.stushow.com), June 24, 2009.

Oldenburg, Ann. "Smile! You're on Many Candid Cameras," *USA Today* website, July 21, 2004.

Stahl, Bob. "Godfrey's Back!" *TV Guide*, Oct. 8–14, 1960, pp. 17–19.

Carol & Company

Efron, Edith. "The Girl in the Rubber Mask," *TV Guide*, Feb. 23–March 1, 1963, pp. 6–9.

Harding, Henry. "For the Record," *TV Guide*, March 9–15, 1963, p. A-3.

Martin, Pete. "Backstage with Carol Burnett," *The Saturday Evening Post*, March 10, 1962, pp. 36–38.

A Case of Rape

"NBC to Start Filming *Rape* in October," *The Los Angeles Times*, Sept. 22, 1973, Part II, p. 5.

A Charlie Brown Christmas

Inge, M. Thomas, ed. *Charles M. Schulz: Conversations*. Jackson, MS: University of Mississippi Press, 2000.

Melendez, Lee. A Charlie Brown Christmas: *The Making of a Tradition*. New York: HarperCollins, 2000.

Cheers

Grammer, Kelsey. *So Far ...* New York: Penguin, 1995.

Cinderella

"CBS *Cinderella* Remake Hot Again," *Variety*, July 17, 1963, p. 23.

Rodgers, Richard. *Musical Stages: An Autobiography*. New York: Random House, 1975.

The Cosby Show

Klein, Todd. "Bill Cosby: Prime Time's Favorite Father," *The Saturday Evening Post*, April 1986, pp. 42–45 and 110.

"No *Cos* For Concern: Presales of Viacom Hit $500-Mil Gross from Stations in Off-Net Syndie," *Variety*, Jan. 6, 1988, p. 80.

Vamos, Mark N. "Cosby Could Stuff $500 Million More Into Viacom's Pocket," *Business Week*, Nov. 10, 1986, pp. 42–43.

The Cotton Bowl

Nelson, Lindsey. *Hello Everybody, I'm Lindsey Nelson.* New York: William Morrow, 1985.

Wallace, William N. "Quick, Bouncy Lion Defense Cracks Wishbone," *The New York Times*, Jan. 2, 1972, Section V, p. 4.

White, Gordon S., Jr. "Lions Rout Texas on 2nd-Half Surge," *The New York Times*, Jan. 2, 1972, Section V, pp. 1, 4.

Dallas

"Odds Hype Over 'J.R.' Assailant Gives *Dallas* Rating Record Shot," *Variety*, Nov. 19, 1980, p. 37.

Dallas Cowboys Cheerleaders

Bedell, Sally. "TV Update: Are TV Newsmen Pressured to Plug Network Projects?" *TV Guide*, Jan. 27–Feb. 2, 1979, p. A-4.

Newman, Bruce. "Gimme an 'S,' Gimme An 'E,' Gimme..." *Sports Illustrated*, May 22, 1978, pp. 18–19.

Danny Thomas Special: Wonderful World of Burlesque

"Morality, Not Legality," *Variety*, Dec. 16, 1964, p. 27.

The Day After

Brinkley, Douglas, ed. *The Reagan Diaries.* New York: HarperCollins, 2007.

"*Day After* Reaction Mixed from Advertising & Viewers; CBS Runs Tape, ABC Fumes," *Variety*, Nov. 23, 1983, pp. 90 and 104.

Goldman, Kevin. "*The Day After* Fallout: ABC Affils Eat Ad Time," *Variety*, Nov. 16, 1983, pp. 30 and 52.

_____. "Mock Wargame to Air on ABC After Nuke Pic," *Variety*, Nov. 9, 1983, pp. 45 and 70.

The Dean Martin Show

Darren, Brad. "Dean Martin's Passion for Young, Young Beauty," *Photoplay*, March 1970, pp. 57–59, 95, 96.

Fallaci, Oriana. "Dean Martin Talks About His Drinking, Frank Sinatra, Women, Bobby Kennedy," *Look*, Dec. 26, 1967, pp. 78–88.

Hale, Lee, with Richard D. Neely. *Backstage at the Dean Martin Show.* Dallas, TX: Taylor Publishing, 2000.

The Dick Van Dyke Show

Hill, Tom, ed. *Nick at Nite's Classic TV Companion.* New York: Fireside, 1996.

The Ed Sullivan Show

McCall, Mitzi, and Charlie Brill. Podcast interview with Stu Shostak, Stu's Show website (www.stushow.com), Aug. 5, 2009.

Eight Is Enough

Van Patten, Dick, and Robert Baer. *Eighty Is Not Enough.* Beverly Hills, CA: Phoenix, 2009.

Elvis: Aloha from Hawaii

Torgensen, Ellen. "NBC Wishes Itself Happy Birthday," *TV Guide*, Nov. 11–20, 1976, pp. 6–8.

Family Ties

Gittleson, Natalie. "*Family Ties*: The Day-Care Center a TV Show Built," *McCalls*, August 1987, pp. 61–64.

Goldberg, Gary David. *Sit, Ubu, Sit.* New York: Harmony, 2008.

Fatal Vision

"Convicted Dr. Objects to *Vision*," *Variety*, Nov. 28, 1984, p. 47.

Rein, Richard K. "A Stepdaughter's Murder Began Paul Kassab's 9-Year Crusade to See His Son-in-Law on Trial," *People*, Aug. 6, 1979, pp. 89–91.

Zoglin, Richard. "Long Voyage," *Time*, Nov. 19, 1984, p. 112.

Fish

Bridges, Todd, with Sarah Tomlinson. *Killing Willis.* New York: Simon & Schuster, 2010.

Shimokawa, Gary. Podcast interview with Stu Shostak, Stu's Show website (www.stushow.com), July 27, 2007.

The Flip Wilson Show

Fry, William A., and Melanie Allen. *Life Studies of Comedy Writers: Creating Humor.* New Brunswick, NJ: Transaction Publishers, 1998.

Jahr, Cliff. "Hellzafloppin: Is This the End of Jerry Lewis?" *New York*, Feb. 7, 1977.

Friends and Nabors

Fox, William Price, Jr. "That Jim Nabors Assignment," *TV Guide*, Oct. 8–14, 1966, pp. 20–24.

The Fugitive

Robertson, Ed. The Fugitive *Recaptured.* Los Angeles: Pomegranate Press, 1993.

The Godfather

"*Godfather* in Nov.," *Variety*, July 21, 1974, p. 35.

"*Godfather* Picketed," *Variety*, Nov. 20, 1974, p. 31.

"*Godfather* Sold Out," *Variety*, Nov. 6, 1974, p. 39.

Jones, Jenny M. *The Annotated* Godfather*: The Complete Screenplay.* New York: Black Dog & Leventhal, 2007.

Gomer Pyle, U.S.M.C.

Schell, Ronnie. Podcast interview with Stu Shostak, Stu's Show website (www.stushow.com), Aug. 8, 2007.

Gone with the Wind

Behlmer, Rudy. *Memo from David O. Selznick.* New York: Modern Library, 2000.

Michie, Larry. "A Bunch of TV Records Are *Gone with the Wind*," *Variety*, Nov. 17, 1976, pp. 42, 54.

Molt, Cynthia Marylee. Gone with the Wind *on Film:*

A Complete Reference. Jefferson, NC: McFarland, 1990.

"NBC Shaking Up Sports," *Variety*, April 20, 1977, p. 100.

"Record Prices on *GWTW*, *Zhivago* & NBC's Got 'Em," *Variety*, May 22, 1974.

Gunsmoke

Arness, James, with James E. Wise Jr. *James Arness: An Autobiography*. Jefferson, NC: McFarland, 2001.

Gunsmoke: The Directors Collection DVD commentary by Dennis Weaver, 2006.

Helter Skelter

"Affils Dump, Bump Manson Family Pic; CBS O&O Delays," *Variety*, March 31, 1976, p. 95.

Dempsey, John. "Viacom Into Court Over *Helter Skelter* and *Sybil*," *Variety*, Dec. 19, 1979, p. 45.

"Lady of the Chainsaw: An Interview with Marilyn Burns," The Terror Trap Website (www.terrortrap.com).

Lamkin, Elaine. "*The Devil's Rejects*: Star Steve Railsback," Bloody Disgusting Website (www.bloody-disgusting.com), July 2005.

"Sponsors Fled *Helter Skelter*, But CBS Won Ratings Gamble," *Variety*, April 21, 1976, p. 73.

Holocaust

"Austria Reacts Mostly Favorable to *Holocaust*; 13% Negative," *Variety*, March 21, 1979, pp. 64 and 74.

"Bombs Are Prelude to Germany's Airing of *Holocaust* Mini," *Variety*, Jan. 24, 1979, p. 51.

"Dailies Order 16-Page ADL Wrap on Nazis, Timed to *Holocaust*," *Variety*, April 12, 1978, p. 84.

Dempsey, John. "Problems and Potential for NBC's *Holocaust*," *Variety*, April 5, 1978, pp. 47 and 70.

"French *Holocaust* Controversy: Mag Raises Coin to Air Show," *Variety*, Nov. 22, 1978, p. 89.

"French TV Begins *Holocaust* Amid Touches (???) of Controversy," *Variety*, Feb. 14, 1979, pp. 65 and 88.

Green, Gerald. "In Defense of *Holocaust*," *The New York Times*, April 23, 1978, Section II, p. 1 and 30.

"The *Holocaust* Controversy Continues," *The New York Times*, April 30, 1978, Section II, pp. 29 and 30.

"A *Holocaust* of Emotions," *Variety*, April 5, 1978, p. 47.

"*Holocaust* Study Aids and Spinoffs," *The New York Times*, April 14, 1978, Section III, p. 26.

Lazarus, Charles. "Issue in Israel: Should *Holocaust* Be Aired?" *Variety*, May 3, 1978, pp. 54 and 73.

Shepard, Richard F. "Ethnic Leaders React to the Impact of *Holocaust*," *The New York Times*, April 16, 1978, p. 60.

Wiesel, Elie. "Trivializing the Holocaust: Semi-Fact and Semi-Fiction," *The New York Times*, April 16, 1978, Section III, pp. 1 and 29.

"Wiesel Answers Green," *The New York Times*, April 30, 1978, Section II, p. 30.

How the West Was Won

Arness, James, with James E. Wise Jr. *James Arness: An Autobiography*. Jefferson, NC: McFarland, 2001.

"*Family, How West Was Won* Resurrected by LBS for Syndie," *Variety*, Dec. 8, 1982, p. 82.

Jaws

Emery, Robert J. *The Directors Take Three*. New York: Allworth Press, 2003.

Gottlieb, Carl. *The Jaws Log: 25th Anniversary Edition*. New York: Newmarket Press, 2001.

Jaws DVD commentary, *The Making of Jaws*, 2000.

McGilligan, Patrick, ed. *Backstory 4: Interviews with Screenwriters of the 1970s and 1980s*. Los Angeles: University of California Press, 2006.

Jeremiah Johnson

Emery, Robert J. *The Directors Take One*. New York: TV Books, 1999.

Froug, William. *The Screenwriter Looks at the Screenwriter*. Hollywood, CA: Silman-James Press, 1991.

McGilligan, Patrick, ed. *Backstory 4: Interviews with Screenwriters of the 1970s and 1980s*. Los Angeles: University of California Press, 2006.

John Wayne: Swing Out Sweet Land

Finnegan, Joseph. "America — A Wayne's Eye View," *TV Guide*, Nov. 28–Dec. 4, 1970, pp. 20–23.

Gould, Jack. "TV: Wayne's Cavalcade of History," *The New York Times*, Nov. 30, 1970, p. 83.

Laverne & Shirley

Rafkin, Alan. *Cue the Bunny on the Rainbow*. Syracuse, NY: Syracuse University Press, 1998.

Little Ladies of the Night

"ABC Plans to Skyjack NBC: *Little Ladies* May Air in Sweeps," *Variety*, Sept. 3, 1976, p. 54.

Crist, Judith. "This Week's Movies," *TV Guide*, Jan. 15–21, 1977, p. A-10.

Morgan, Ted. "*Little Ladies of the Night*," *New York Times Magazine*, Nov. 16, 1975, pp. 39–50.

Spelling, Aaron, with Jefferson Graham. *Aaron Spelling: A Prime Time Life*. New York: St. Martin's, 1996.

The Longest Yard

The Longest Yard DVD commentaries, 2005.

Reynolds, Burt. *My Life*. New York: Hyperion, 1994.

Love Story

Emery, Robert J. *The Directors Take Two*. New York: TV Books, 2000.

Evans, Robert. *The Kid Stays in the Picture*. New York: Hyperion, 1994.

Love Story DVD commentary, 2000.

The Lucy Show

Fidelman, Geoffrey Mark. *The Lucy Book*. Los Angeles: Renaissance Books, 1999.

Loving Lucy Panel Show 1998 DVD, 1998, courtesy of Stu Shostak.

Stu Shostak interview, Aug. 6, 2010.

Marcus Welby, M.D.

"ABC Takes *Welby* Dosage," *Variety*, Aug. 29, 1984, p. 65.

Smith, Cecil. "Tuesday Escapes the ABC Shuffle," *Los Angeles Times*, Jan. 19, 1971, Part IV, p. 12.

Tinker, Grant, and Bud Rukeyser. *Tinker in Television: From General Sarnoff to General Electric*. New York: Simon & Schuster, 1999.

M*A*S*H

Alda, Alan. *Never Have Your Dog Stuffed and Other Things I've Learned*. New York: Random House, 2005.
"CBS 'M*A*S*H' Cast, Crew Reunion," *Variety*, Feb. 17, 1988, p. 159.
Farrell, Mike. *Just Call Me Mike: A Journey to Actor and Activist*. New York: RDV Books, 2007.

Mayberry R.F.D.

Fernandes, David, and Dale Robinson. *A Guide to Television's* Mayberry R.F.D. Jefferson, NC: McFarland, 1999.

Michael Jackson Talks to ... Oprah

Benson, Jim. "ABC's Newscast on Michael a Thriller," *Variety*, Feb. 15, 1993, p. 20.
"Michael Jackson Gives First Live Interview to Oprah Winfrey," *Jet*, Feb. 8, 1993, pp. 62–63.

Miss America Pageant

Deford, Frank. *There She Is*. New York: Viking, 1971.

NFC Championship Game

Anderson, Dave. "A 49er Play from Day 1," *The New York Times*, Jan. 11, 1982, Section C, page 7.

The Night Stalker

Dawidziak, Mark. *Night Stalking: A 20th Anniversary Kolchak Companion*. East Meadow, NY: Image, 1991.
The Night Stalker DVD interview with Dan Curtis, 2004.

Patton

Brown, Les. "As Movies Go, So Goes ABC," *Variety*, Oct. 4, 1972, pp. 33 and 68.
_____. "TV Going on 'Bold' Standard," *Variety*, Dec. 6, 1972, pp. 1 and 71.
Patton DVD documentaries "The Making of *Patton*" (1997) and "*Patton*," (2000), both included in 2006 20th Century–Fox release.

Peter Pan

Lawrence, Greg. *Dance with Demons: The Life of Jerome Robbins*. New York: G.P. Putnam & Sons, 2001.
McGovern, Dennis, and Deborah Grace Winer. *Sing Out, Louise! 150 Stars of the Musical Theatre Remember 50 Years on Broadway*. New York: Schirmer, 1993.
"What Makes Mary Fly?" *TV Guide*, Dec. 3–9, 1960, pp. A-1, A-2.

Planet of the Apes

Behind the Planet of the Apes documentary, 1998.

The Poseidon Adventure

"ABC Wins *Poseidon* for $3,200,000," *Variety*, Nov. 14, 1973, p. 31.
Borgnine, Ernest. Archive of American Television Interview, on YouTube, Part 3 of 3, Sept. 16, 2009.
Borgnine, Ernest. *Ernie: The Autobiography*. New York: Kensington Publishing, 2008.

McGilligan, Patrick, editor. *Backstory 3: Interviews with Screenwriters of the 60s*. Los Angeles: University of California Press, 1997.
"*Poseidon* Sinks Dems in N.Y.," *Variety*, Aug. 13, 1980, p. 51.

The Red Skelton Hour

Hyatt, Wesley. *A Critical History of Television's* The Red Skelton Show, *1951–1971*. Jefferson, NC: McFarland, 2004.
"*Red Skelton Show* Goes Syndie, Group W Offers 130 Half-Hours," *Variety*, Nov. 10, 1982, p. 82.
"Skelton Waves Red Flag in CBS' Eye; Exec Defends Axe," *Variety*, Feb. 5, 1975, p. 45.
"3 Dropped Stars Pitched to ABC," *Variety*, March 17, 1971, p. 39.

Return to Mayberry

Hall, Jane. "Going Home to Mayberry," *People*, April 14, 1986, pp. 90–97.
Zoglin, Richard (reported by Jane Hall). "Back to the Time Warp," *Time*, March 3, 1986, p. 84.

Rhoda

Tinker, Grant, and Bud Rukeyser. *Tinker in Television: From General Sarnoff to General Electric*. New York: Simon & Schuster, 1999.

Rocky

"CBS Does a *Heidi*," *Variety*, Feb. 7, 1979, p. 71.
Emery, Robert J. *The Directors Take Two*. New York: TV Books, 2000.
Meredith, Burgess. *So Far, So Good: A Memoir*. New York: Little, Brown, 1994.

Roots

"ABC's Long Long Novels-for-TV," *Variety*, Jan. 22, 1975.
Knight, Bob. "*Roots* Remakes TV World in 8 Nights," *Variety*, Feb. 2, 1977, pp. 51 and 70.
Roots DVD featurettes "*Roots*: One Year Later" and "Crossing Over: How *Roots* Captivated an Entire Nation," 2007.
Wolper, David L. *Producer*. New York: Scribner's, 2003.

Roots: The Next Generation

"Protests at *Roots* Stations," *The Washington Post*, Feb. 21, 1979, p. B-8.
Roots: The Next Generations—The Legacy Continues. DVD feature, 2003.
"*Roots II* Leads ABC Ratings Sweep," *Los Angeles Times*, Feb. 28, 1979, Part IV, p. 7.
"Sequel to *Roots* at Tripled Budget," *Variety*, April 12, 1978, p. 66.
Wolper, David L. *Producer*. New York: Scribner's, 2003.

The Ropers

Mann, Chris. *Come and Knock on Our Door*. New York: St. Martin's, 1998.

The Rose Bowl

Kopay, David, and Perry Deane Young. *The David Kopay*

Story. Revised edition. New York: Donald I. Fine, 1988.

Michelson, Herb, and Dave Newhouse. *Rose Bowl Football Since 1902*. New York: Stein and Day, 1977.

Nelson, Lindsey. *Hello Everybody, I'm Lindsey Nelson*. New York: William Morrow, 1985.

White, Betty. *Here We Go Again: My Life in Television*. New York: Scribner's, 1995.

Rowan and Martin's Laugh-In

A Friendship: The Letters of Dan Rowan and John D. MacDonald 1967–1974. New York: Alfred A. Knopf, 1986.

Hawn, Goldie, with Wendy Holden. *A Lotus Grows in the Wind*. New York: G.P. Putnam & Sons, 2005.

Sanford and Son

Rich, Lee. *Warm Up the Snake: A Hollywood Memoir*. Ann Arbor, MI: University of Michigan Press, 2006.

XVII Winter Olympics

Miller, Stuart, "CBS Spruces Up Record Collection," *Variety*, Feb. 28–March 6, 1994, pp. 54.

Miller, Stuart, "New 'Tom' Emerges from Olympic Dust," *Variety*, Feb. 28–March 6, 1994, pp. 40.

Robins, J. Max. "Tough Sledding for Losers," *Variety*, Feb. 28–March 6, 1994, pp. 53 and 56.

Shogun

Chamberlain, Richard. *Shattered Love*. New York: HarperCollins, 2003.

"Son of *Shogun*," *Variety*, Sept. 24, 1980, p. 98.

60 Minutes

Einstein, Daniel. *Special Edition: A Guide to Network Television Documentary Series and Special News Reports, 1980–1989*. Lanham, MD: Scarecrow, 1997.

The Sound of Music

Brady, John. *The Craft of the Screenwriter*. New York: Simon & Schuster, 1981.

Hirsch, Julia Antopol. The Sound of Music: *The Making of America's Favorite Movie*. Chicago, IL: Contemporary Books, 1993.

Rodgers, Richard. *Musical Stages: An Autobiography*. New York: Random House, 1975.

"*Sound of Music* for TV," *Variety*, Dec. 18, 1974, p. 45.

Summer Olympics

Arledge, Roone. *Roone: A Memoir*. New York: HarperCollins, 2003.

Super Bowl XVI

Beermann, Frank. "S.F. Fans CBS Super Ratings Fire," *Variety*, Jan. 27, 1982, p. 46.

Schwartz, Tony. "Television's High-Ante Extravaganza," *The New York Times*, Jan. 24, 1982, Section V, p. 7.

"Super Bowl Ratings," *Variety*, Feb. 17, 1988, p. 46.

The Ten Commandments

Hayne, Donald, ed. *The Autobiography of Cecil B. DeMille*. Englewood Cliffs, NJ: Prentice Hall, 1959.

The Ten Commandments DVD commentary by Katherine Orrison, 2006.

The 13th Annual Emmy Awards

Gelman, Morrie, and Gene Accas. *The Best in Television: 50 Years of Emmy*. Santa Monica, CA: General Publishing Group, 1998.

Harding, Henry. "For the Record," *TV Guide*, June 2, 1961, p. A-1.

The Thorn Birds

Chamberlain, Richard. *Shattered Love*. New York: HarperCollins, 2003.

"*The Thorn Birds*: Old Friends ... New Stories" documentary on *The Thorn Birds* DVD, 2003.

Wolper, David L. *Producer*. New York: Scribner's, 2003.

Three's Company

Mann, Chris. *Come and Knock on Our Door*. New York: St. Martin's, 1998.

True Grit

True Grit DVD commentaries, 2007.

Wagon Train

Whitney, Douglas. "How Wagon Master Bond Bushwhacked Movie Master John Ford," *TV Guide*, Nov. 19–25, 1960, pp. 5–7.

The Winds of War

Gelman, Marnie. "ABC Facing Maxi Woes From Mini Wars," *Variety*, Nov. 25, 1987, pp. 89, 115.

Winds of War DVD documentary "Making *The Winds of War*," 1983.

"*Winds of War* Mini for ABC," *Variety*, Nov. 19, 1980, p. 40.

The Wizard of Oz

Burke, Billie, with Cameron Shipp. *With a Feather on My Nose*. New York: Appleton-Century Crafts, 1949.

Harmetz, Aljean. *The Making of* The Wizard of Oz. New York: Alfred A. Knopf, 1977.

World Series Game 6

Garagiola, Joe. *It's Anybody's Ballgame*. Chicago: Contemporary, 1988.

Luciano, Ron, and David Fisher. *Strike Two*. New York: Bantam, 1984.

Smith, Curt. *Voices of the Game, Updated Edition*. New York: Simon & Schuster, 1992.

You Again?

Leahy, Michael. "'The Approval ... Maybe it Means Too Much to Me,'" *TV Guide*, June 28–July 4, 1986, pp. 16–21.

Index

References are to entry numbers.